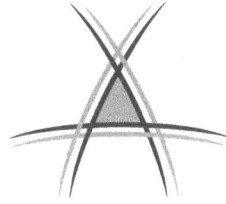

ASCENT®
CENTER FOR TECHNICAL KNOWLEDGE

CATIA V5-6R2018
Introduction for Managers and Reviewers

Learning Guide
1st Edition

ASCENT - Center for Technical Knowledge®
CATIA V5-6R2018
Introduction for Managers and Reviewers
1st Edition

Prepared and produced by:

ASCENT Center for Technical Knowledge
630 Peter Jefferson Parkway, Suite 175
Charlottesville, VA 22911

866-527-2368
www.ASCENTed.com

Lead Contributor: Scott Hendren

ASCENT - Center for Technical Knowledge is a division of Rand Worldwide, Inc., providing custom developed knowledge products and services for leading engineering software applications. ASCENT is focused on specializing in the creation of education programs that incorporate the best of classroom learning and technology-based training offerings.

We welcome any comments you may have regarding this guide, or any of our products. To contact us please email: feedback@ASCENTed.com.

Contents

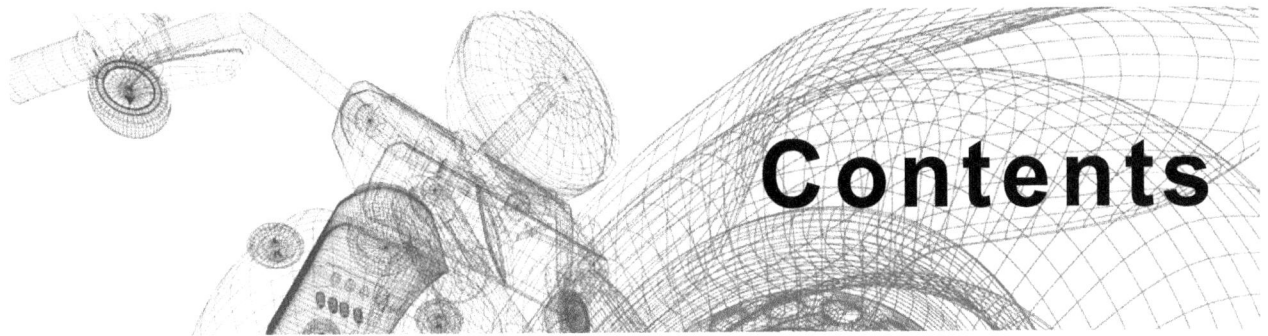

© 2019, ASCENT - Center for Technical Knowledge®

Preface

The *CATIA: Introduction for Managers and Reviewers* guide introduces you to the interface and analysis capabilities of CATIA V5. This guide, with numerous practice exercises, focuses on the concepts of measurement, analysis, image capture, and drawing creation.

Topics Covered

- Overview of Parametric Design Process
- Customization of CATIA V5 Environment
- Feature Management Using the Hide/Show, Activate/Deactivate Functions
- Obtaining Part Information
- Assembly Design Workbench and assembly creation techniques
- Performing measurements and clash analyses
- Creating and viewing cross sections
- Creating and managing annotations
- Image raptures
- Working with cache
- Creating scenes
- Drawing view creation
- Creating and Constraining Sketch Geometry
- Adding Material with Pad and Shaft Features
- Removing Material with Pocket and Groove Features

Note on Software Setup

This guide assumes a standard installation of the software using the default preferences during installation. Lectures and practices use the standard software templates and default options for the Content Libraries.

Lead Contributor: Scott Hendren

Scott Hendren has been a trainer and curriculum developer in the PLM industry for over 20 years, with experience on multiple CAD systems, including Pro/ENGINEER, Creo Parametric, and CATIA. Trained in Instructional Design, Scott uses his skills to develop instructor-led and web-based training products.

Scott has held training and development positions with several high profile PLM companies, and has been with the ASCENT team since 2013.

Scott holds a Bachelor of Mechanical Engineering Degree as well as a Bachelor of Science in Mathematics from Dalhousie University, Nova Scotia, Canada.

Scott Hendren has been the Lead Contributor for *CATIA: Introduction for Managers and Reviewers* since 2013.

In this Guide

The following images highlight some of the features that can be found in this guide.

Practice Files

To download the practice files for this student guide, use the following steps.

1. Type the URL shown below into the address bar of your Internet browser. The URL must be typed **exactly as shown**. If you are using an ASCENT ebook, you can click on the link to download the file.

2. Press <Enter> to download the ZIP file that contains the Practice Files.

3. Once the download is complete, unzip the file to a local folder. The unzipped file contains an .EXE file.

4. Double-click on the .EXE file and follow the instructions to automatically install the Practice Files on the C:\ drive of your computer.

   Do not change the location in which the Practice Files folder is installed. Doing so can cause errors when completing the practices in this student guide.

http://www.ASCENTed.com/getfile?id=xxxxxxxx

Link to the practice files

Practice Files

The Practice Files page tells you how to download and install the practice files that are provided with this guide.

Chapter 1

Getting Started

In this chapter you learn how to start the AutoCAD® software, become familiar with the basic layout of the AutoCAD screen, how to access commands, use your pointing device, and understand the AutoCAD Cartesian workspace. You also learn how to open an existing drawing, view a drawing by zooming and panning, and save your work in the AutoCAD software.

Learning Objectives in this Chapter

- Launch the AutoCAD software and complete a basic initial setup of the drawing environment.
- Identify the basic layout and features of AutoCAD interface including the Ribbon, Drawing Window, and Application Menu.
- Locate commands and launch them using the Ribbon, shortcut menus, Application Menu, and Quick Access Toolbar.
- Locate points in the AutoCAD Cartesian workspace.
- Open and close existing drawings and navigate to file locations.
- Move around a drawing using the mouse, the Zoom and Pan commands, and the Navigation Bar.
- Save drawings in various formats and set the automatic save options using the Save commands.

Learning Objectives for the chapter

Chapters

Each chapter begins with a brief introduction and a list of the chapter's Learning Objectives.

Side notes

Side notes are hints or additional information for the current topic.

Instructional Content

Each chapter is split into a series of sections of instructional content on specific topics. These lectures include the descriptions, step-by-step procedures, figures, hints, and information you need to achieve the chapter's Learning Objectives.

Practice Objectives

Practices

Practices enable you to use the software to perform a hands-on review of a topic.

Some practices require you to use prepared practice files, which can be downloaded from the link found on the Practice Files page.

Practice Files

To download the practice files for this guide, use the following steps:

1. Type the URL shown below into the address bar of your Internet browser. The URL must be typed **exactly as shown**. If you are using an ASCENT ebook, you can click on the link to download the file.

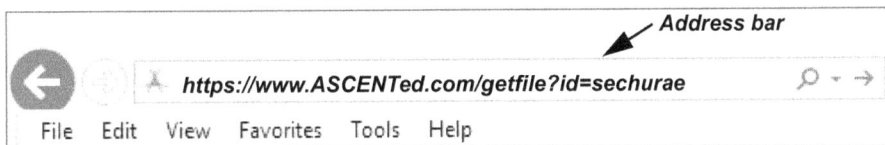

Address bar

https://www.ASCENTed.com/getfile?id=sechurae

File   Edit   View   Favorites   Tools   Help

2. Press <Enter> to download the .ZIP file that contains the practice files.

3. Once the download is complete, unzip the file to a local folder. The unzipped file contains an .EXE file.

4. Double-click on the .EXE file and follow the instructions to automatically install the practice files on the C:\ drive of your computer.

   Do not change the location in which the practice files folder is installed. Doing so can cause errors when completing the practices.

   The default practice files folder location is:
   C:\Introduction for Managers and Reviewers Practice Files

https://www.ASCENTed.com/getfile?id=sechurae

Stay Informed!

Interested in receiving information about upcoming promotional offers, educational events, invitations to complimentary webcasts, and discounts? If so, please visit:

www.ASCENTed.com/updates/

Help us improve our product by completing the following survey:

www.ASCENTed.com/feedback

You can also contact us at: *feedback@ASCENTed.com*

Overview

This chapter provides an overview of solid modeling, where you will use features and parameters to build a model. The relationships created with these features and parameters can be used to establish the design intent on the model. You will learn how CATIA maintains associativity between the model, assemblies, and drawings. You will become familiar with the CATIA user interface and will learn how to customize it, making it more efficient to work with.

Learning Objectives in this Chapter

- Understand the basics of solid modeling.
- Understand feature-based modeling.
- Understand the parametric and associative nature of CATIA.
- Understand how and why you capture a model's design intent during modeling.
- Become familiar with the CATIA user interface.
- Learn how to work with a model by opening it, customizing the display settings, and selecting entities.
- Learn how to access the online help system.

1.1 Fundamentals

Solid Modeling

CATIA is used to create three-dimensional (3D) solid models. The software *understands* that the model is *filled* with material. With a solid model, you can perform the following:

- Obtain the mass properties of a part.

- Determine if components in an assembly interfere with one another.

- Create cross-sections of an assembly or display part cross-sections in a drawing. Instead of manually *drawing* the views on the drawing, you can reference the part model to generate views and show the dimensions from the 3D geometry, as shown in Figure 1–1.

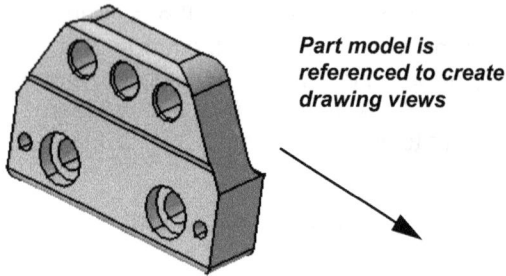

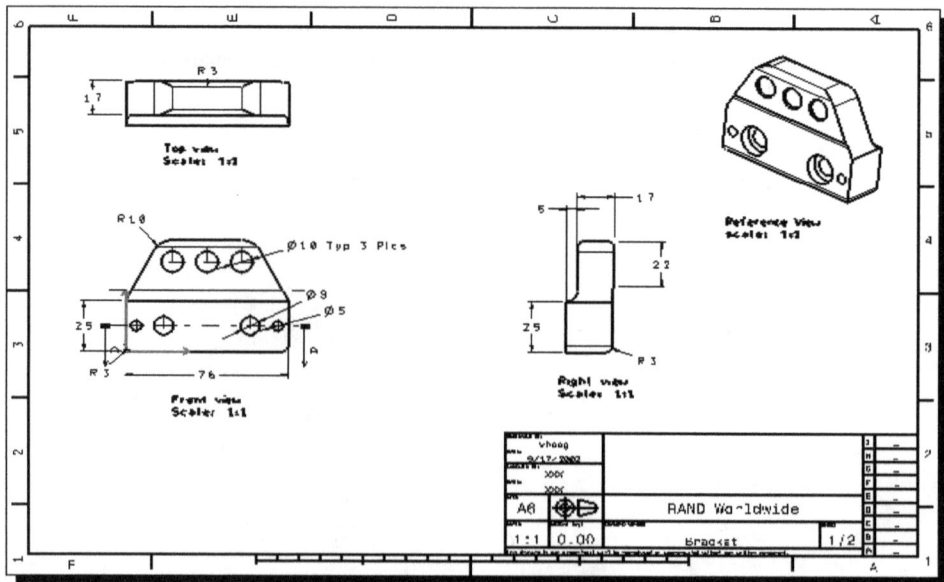

Part model is referenced to create drawing views

Figure 1–1

This process also applies to assemblies, as shown in Figure 1–2. You can locate existing part and assembly models relative to one another.

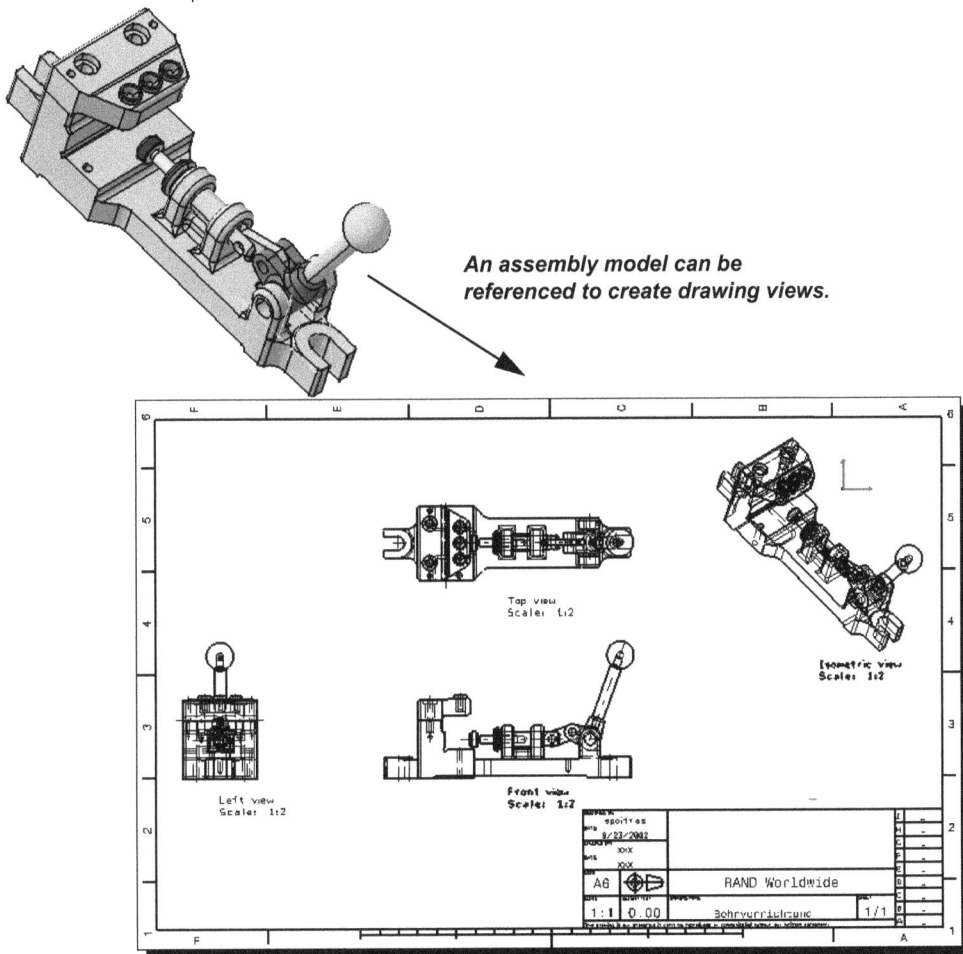

An assembly model can be referenced to create drawing views.

Figure 1–2

Feature-Based

The solid model evolves by creating features, one by one, until the geometry is complete. The part model (shown in Figure 1–3) is constructed by consecutively creating the following features:

1. Create a sketch.
2. Create a Pad feature.
3. Draft several walls of the part using a Draft feature.
4. Remove sharp edges of the geometry by creating a Fillet feature.
5. Create a Shell feature to hollow out the part.

6. Create another Pad feature to act as a cylindrical boss.
7. Center a Hole feature on the cylindrical Pad.
8. Duplicate the boss and hole to create the second boss, as shown in Figure 1–3.

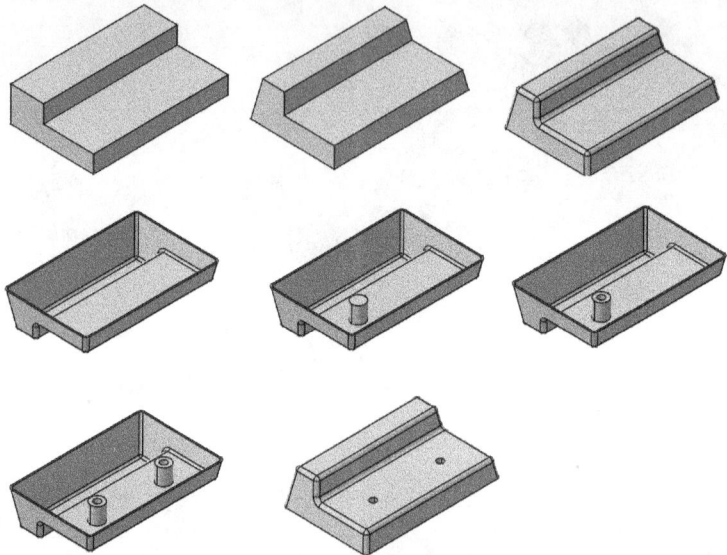

Figure 1–3

You can organize features based on the design intent by initially defining the overall size, major geometric shapes, and then later the finishing details.

Parametric

Features created in CATIA are parametric. All of the dimensional constraints used to define a feature's shape are considered *parameters*, and are accessible at any time. Double-click on a feature to display its dimensional constraints and change any of those values to alter the geometry. The dimensional value that positions the Pocket feature (shown in Figure 1–4) has changed. The position of the feature updates to reflect the design change.

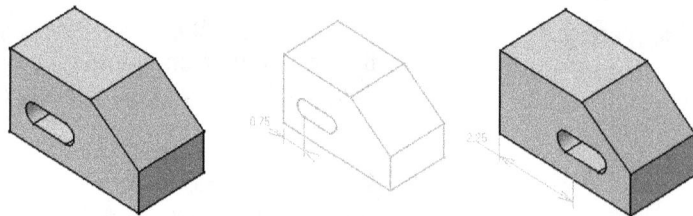

Figure 1–4

Associative

Drawings are created by referencing a model. When the model is changed, any drawings of that model are automatically updated the next time they are opened. Similarly, changing a part model automatically reflects in the assembly. Also, changes made in the assembly update in all other modes in CATIA, as shown in Figure 1–5.

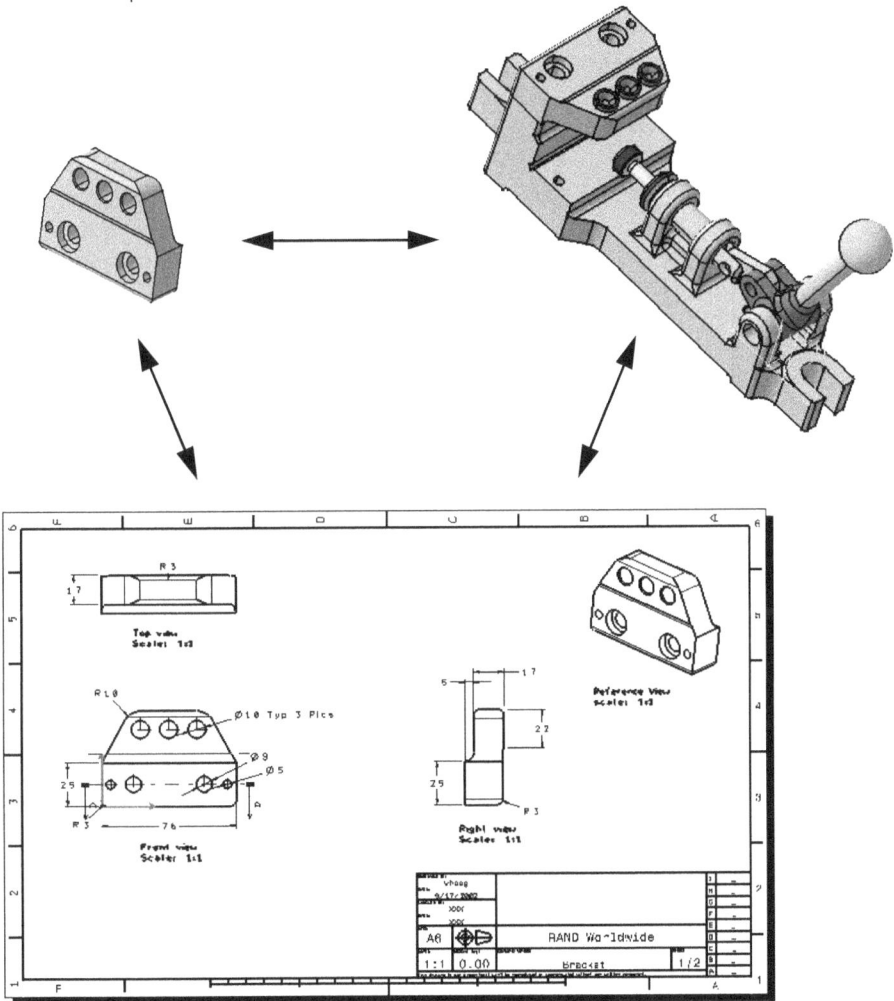

Figure 1–5

Associativity creates a dependency between models. The part models referenced by an assembly and/or drawing must be retrievable to work with the assembly and/or drawing.

1.2 Design Intent

The key to building parametric, feature-based, solid models is to ensure that they have a flexible and predictable behavior. This process is known as capturing *design intent*.

Method 1

One method of capturing design intent is to determine the feature's dimensioning scheme. Figure 1–6 shows an example of a part with a hole. When the Pad feature increases in length, the design intent of the hole determines how it behaves. If the hole is dimensioned to the end of the Pad, the hole moves to remain a distance of 3.00 from that end. If the hole is dimensioned to the face, it remains a distance of 6.00 from that face.

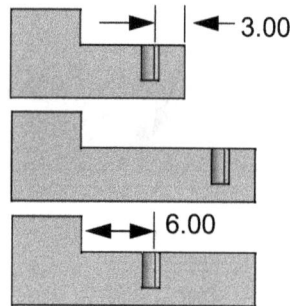

Figure 1–6

Method 2

A second method of capturing design intent is to select an option to limit your feature. A part with a hole is shown in Figure 1–7.

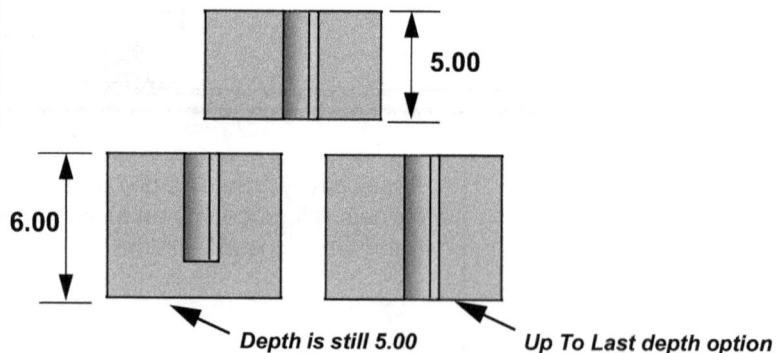

Depth is still 5.00   *Up To Last depth option*

Figure 1–7

The design intent is for the hole to pass through the entire model. When the Pad changes from 5.00 to 6.00, the resulting geometry displays differently depending on how the hole is limited. If the hole was created with a depth of 5.00, it no longer passes though the entire part. It must be changed to maintain the design intent. A better solution is to limit the hole using the **Up To Last** option and ensure that it always passes through the part, regardless of the height of the Pad feature.

Method 3

A third method of capturing design intent is to create symmetrical geometry. The design intent for the part (shown in Figure 1–8) is to have the Pocket remain at the center of the part.

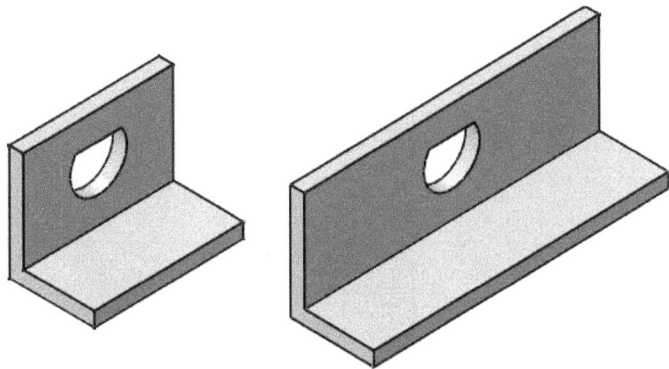

Figure 1–8

Constraining the Pocket from either end of the Pad feature does not capture the design intent. Constructing the Pad and Pocket relative to a center datum reference is preferable.

1.3 User Interface

Screen Layout

When you open a model in CATIA, the screen displays as shown in Figure 1–9. The major areas of the interface that are labeled are discussed in the following topics.

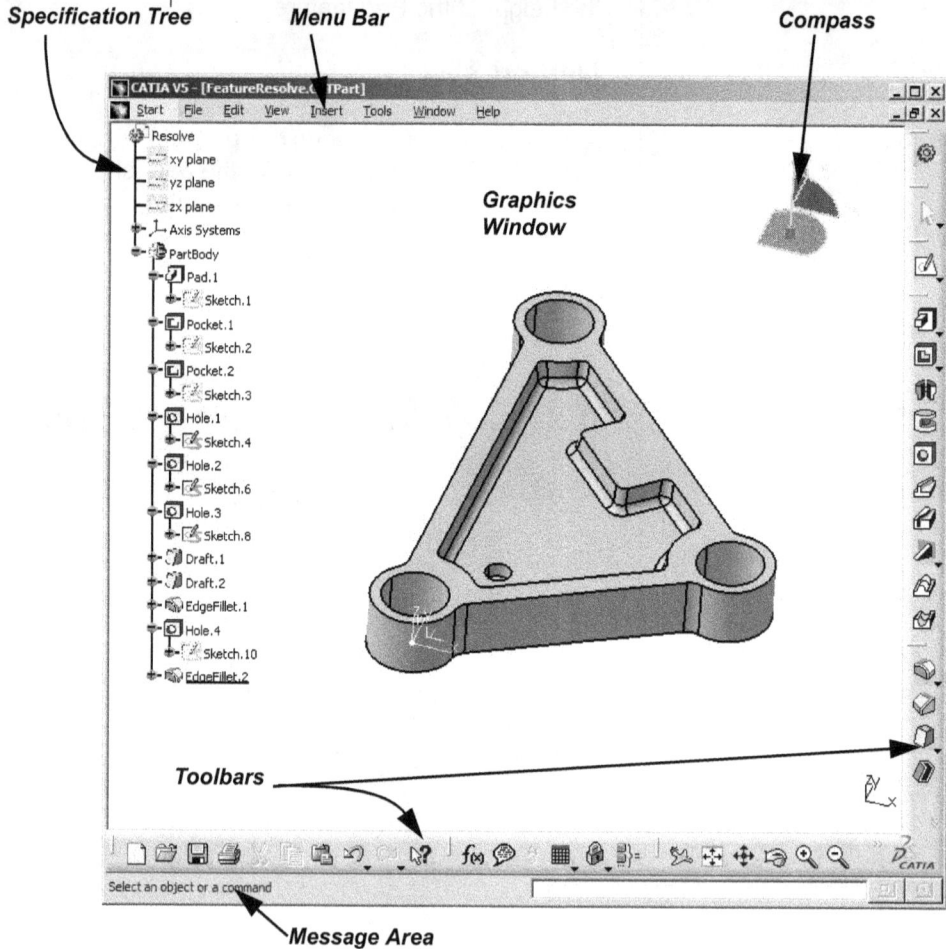

Figure 1–9

Toolbars and Menus

The primary way of interacting with the software is to select icons in the toolbars or commands in the menu bar. You can customize the interface by arranging the location of the toolbars and selecting the icons to display.

Message Area

In many cases, the software displays a single line prompt in the *Message* area, intended to help you perform a certain task. The following are the four messages that correspond to creating the keyhole sketch shown in Figure 1–10.

1. Define the center of the large radius.
2. Define the center of the small radius.
3. Select a point on the key hole profile to define the small radius.
4. Select a point on the key hole profile to define the large radius.

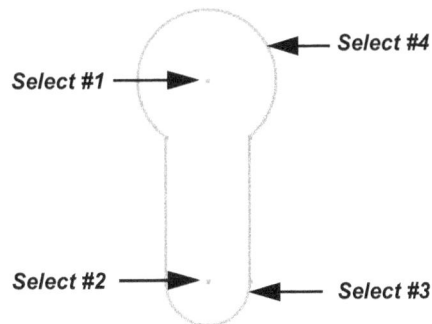

Figure 1–10

Specification Tree

The specification tree is available when working with parts, assemblies, and drawings. It displays a variety of information about the model and displays the features of the part in the order in which they were created, as shown in Figure 1–11. This provides quick access to parameters, functions, materials, and commonly used measurements.

The specification tree can be quickly toggled on and off by pressing <F3>.

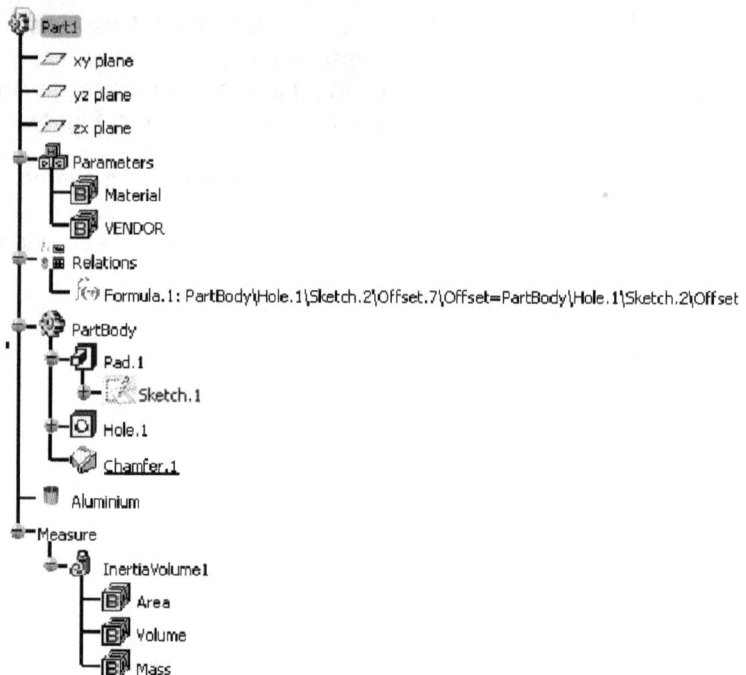

Figure 1–11

Compass

The compass is available for part and assembly models. It displays in the upper right corner of the model window and can perform various functions, as shown in Figure 1–12. The compass is used to:

- Freely rotate the model in all three directions.

- Rotate the model in a plane.

- Pan along one direction.

- Pan in a plane.

- View down an axis direction by selecting the X, Y, or Z letter. Selecting again flips the view in the opposite direction.

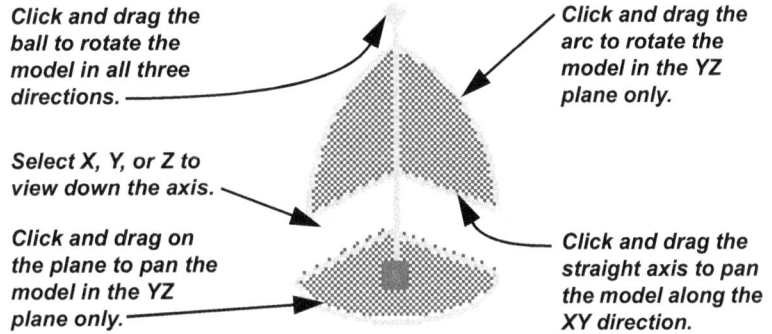

Click and drag the ball to rotate the model in all three directions.

Click and drag the arc to rotate the model in the YZ plane only.

Select X, Y, or Z to view down the axis.

Click and drag on the plane to pan the model in the YZ plane only.

Click and drag the straight axis to pan the model along the XY direction.

Figure 1–12

Workbenches

A workbench is a set of tools used to complete certain tasks. The workbenches used in this course are described as follows:

Icon	Workbench
	Sketcher
	Part Design
	Drafting
	Assembly Design

Other workbenches can be used for Analysis, Manufacturing, Digital Mock Up, and other advanced tasks. The active workbench is indicated by an icon in the toolbar, usually in the upper right corner of the screen, as shown in Figure 1–13.

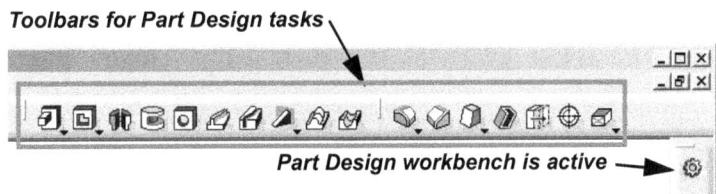

Toolbars for Part Design tasks

Part Design workbench is active

Figure 1–13

1.4 Working with Models

Opening a Model

Models can be opened by clicking ⬜ (Open) and selecting the model from a location on your computer. The file formats you will be working with are listed as follows:

Each time you save an object, it overwrites the file with the new information.

Object	File Extension	Example
Part	.CATPart	**bracket.CATPart**
Drawing	.CATDrawing	**N12345.CATDrawing**
Assembly	.CATProduct	**AXLE.CATProduct**

Rendering a Model

Although you are working with a solid model, you can change how the geometry displays. These options can be accessed through the View Mode toolbar, as shown in Figure 1–14.

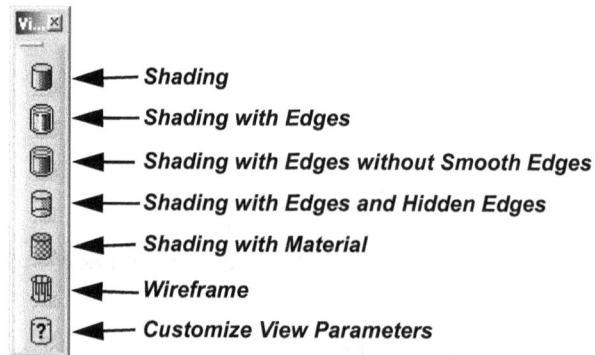

Shading
Shading with Edges
Shading with Edges without Smooth Edges
Shading with Edges and Hidden Edges
Shading with Material
Wireframe
Customize View Parameters

Figure 1–14

To make all icons visible, drag the handle of the flyout menu to the toolbar.

This toolbar is an example of a modal menu. The icon changes to indicate your current View Mode. Each icon contains a flyout menu that expands when you click the down arrow.

Figure 1–15 shows an example of each icon listed in the View Mode toolbar. The **Customized View** option enables you to configure the display to suit your preferences, such as with hidden edges shown, with the material shown, or with faceted faces.

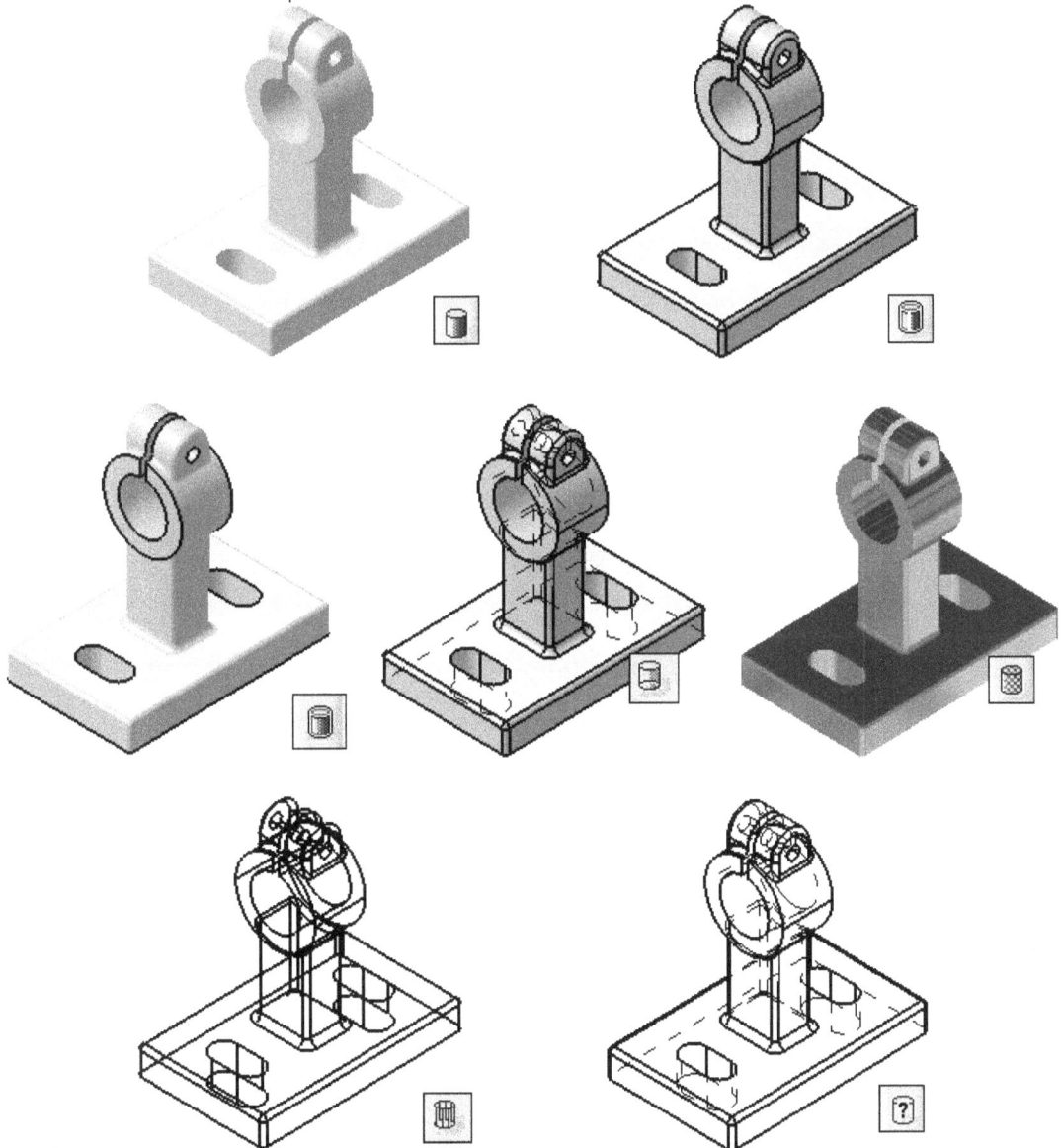

Figure 1–15

Model Navigation

To thoroughly inspect your models, you must learn how to reorient the model, zoom in and out, and pan. There are several methods to navigate a model.

- The Quick Views toolbar contains predefined model orientations enabling you to view the model from commonly used orientations. Figure 1–16 shows the available Quick Views.

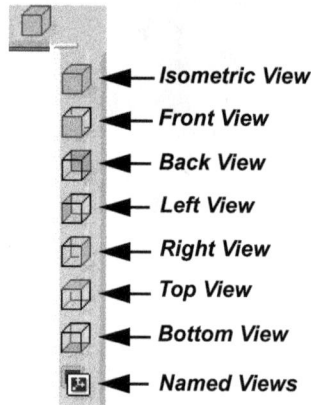

*This toolbar is another example of a modal menu, where the icon changes each time you click a different **Quick View** icon.*

← Isometric View
← Front View
← Back View
← Left View
← Right View
← Top View
← Bottom View
← Named Views

Figure 1–16

To dynamically navigate the model, you can use specific toolbar icons, menu commands, or mouse shortcuts. The navigation functions are listed as follows:

Icon	Function	Mouse	Menu
	Pan	Hold Middle	**View>Pan**
	Rotate	Hold Middle + Hold Right or Hold Middle + Hold Left	**View>Rotate**
	Zoom	Hold Middle + Click Right or Hold Middle + Click Left	**View>Zoom In Out**
N/A	**Zoom Area**	N/A	**View>Zoom Area**
	Fit All In	N/A	**View>Fit All In**

⊞	**Create Multi-view**	N/A	**N/A**
N/A	**Re-center on Geometry**	Click Middle on required geometry	**N/A**

Use the **Re-center on Geometry** function to rotate the model around a specific location on the model or geometry. Click the middle mouse button on the required geometry or model location to re-center the model. Then, use the **Rotate** function to spin the model around the centered geometry.

Preselect Navigator

The **Preselect Navigator** tool enables you to select geometric entities that are hidden or difficult to select on a model. The software lists all entities that exist beneath the current cursor position and enables you to scroll through this list to select the required entity.

How To: Use the Preselect Navigator

1. Position the cursor over the geometry that you want to select.
2. Press the <Up Arrow> or <Down Arrow>. The software lists all entities that are beneath the current cursor position, as shown in Figure 1–17. A display window opens, indicating the currently highlighted entity.

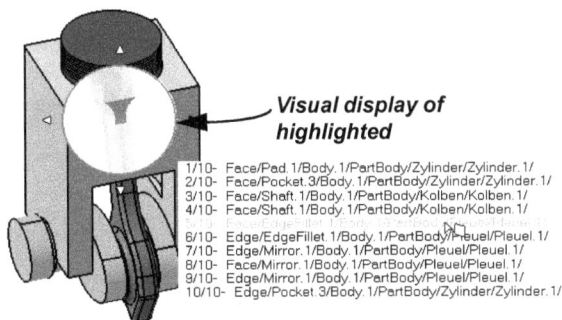

Visual display of highlighted

1/10- Face/Pad.1/Body.1/PartBody/Zylinder/Zylinder.1/
2/10- Face/Pocket.3/Body.1/PartBody/Zylinder/Zylinder.1/
3/10- Face/Shaft.1/Body.1/PartBody/Kolben/Kolben.1/
4/10- Face/Shaft.1/Body.1/PartBody/Kolben/Kolben.1/
5/10- Face/EdgeFillet.1/Body.1/PartBody/Pleuel/Pleuel.1/
6/10- Edge/EdgeFillet.1/Body.1/PartBody/Pleuel/Pleuel.1/
7/10- Edge/Mirror.1/Body.1/PartBody/Pleuel/Pleuel.1/
8/10- Face/Mirror.1/Body.1/PartBody/Pleuel/Pleuel.1/
9/10- Edge/Mirror.1/Body.1/PartBody/Pleuel/Pleuel.1/
10/10- Edge/Pocket.3/Body.1/PartBody/Zylinder/Zylinder.1/

Figure 1–17

3. To scroll through the list, continue pressing the <Up Arrow> or <Down Arrow>. Press the <Left Arrow> and <Right Arrow> to navigate the possible selections for the active component only. You can also navigate the list using the cursor.
4. To select an entity for further operation, select it from the list using the cursor or press <Enter>.

An alternative method is as follows:

1. Position the cursor over the geometry that you want to select.
2. Press and hold <Alt> and then select the model. The software lists all of the entities that are beneath the selection point.
3. Right-click to navigate through the possible selections, or move the cursor to make the appropriate selection, as shown in Figure 1–18.

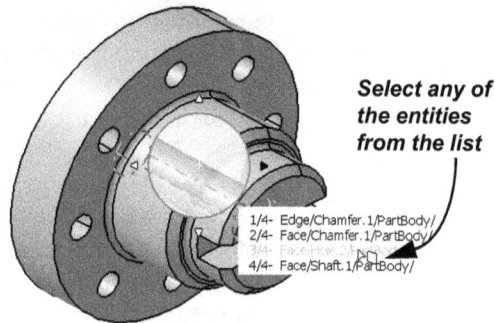

Select any of the entities from the list

1/4- Edge/Chamfer.1/PartBody/
2/4- Face/Chamfer.1/PartBody/
3/4- Face/Hole.1/PartBody/
4/4- Face/Shaft.1/PartBody/

Figure 1–18

This option is controlled through the **Preselect in geometry view** option (**Tools>Options>General>Display>***Navigation* tab).

User-Defined Views

To create a user-defined view, orient the model to the required orientation and select **View>Named Views.** The Named Views dialog box opens, as shown in Figure 1–19.

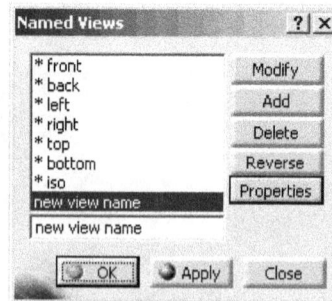

Figure 1–19

- Click **Add**. The name defaults to **Camera 1**. Enter the required name and click **Apply**.

1.5 Online Documentation

Online documentation is very useful and easily accessible. To learn about any function, press <F1> when working with that function. Your Internet browser opens the page where the topic is described, as shown in Figure 1–20.

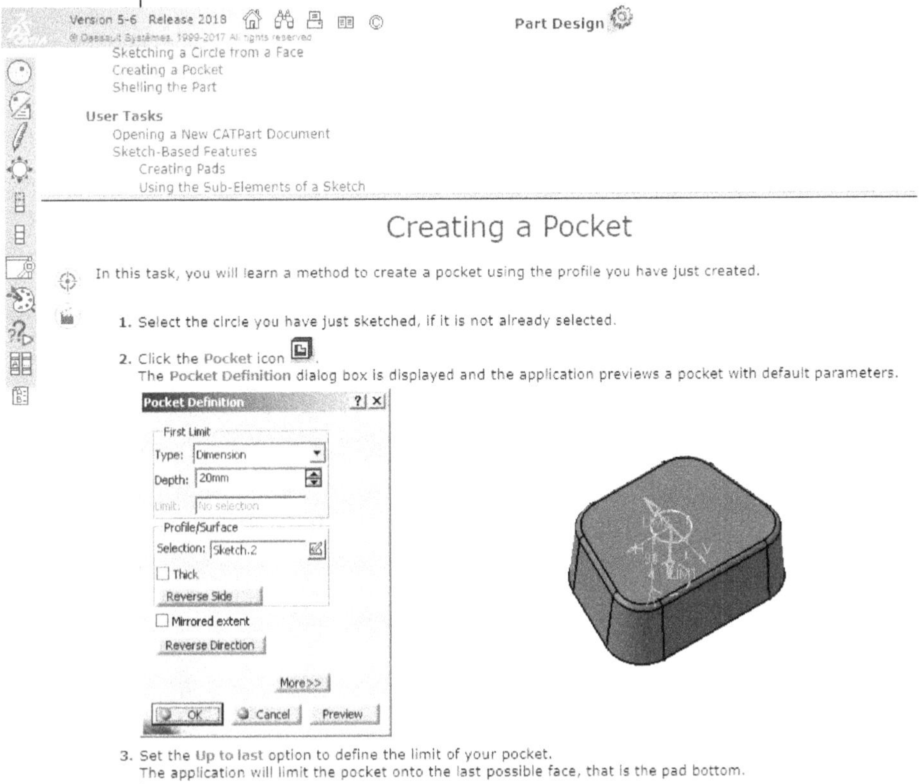

Version 5-6 Release 2018   Part Design
© Dassault Systèmes, 1999-2017 All rights reserved

Sketching a Circle from a Face
Creating a Pocket
Shelling the Part

User Tasks
   Opening a New CATPart Document
   Sketch-Based Features
     Creating Pads
     Using the Sub-Elements of a Sketch

Creating a Pocket

In this task, you will learn a method to create a pocket using the profile you have just created.

1. Select the circle you have just sketched, if it is not already selected.

2. Click the Pocket icon .
The Pocket Definition dialog box is displayed and the application previews a pocket with default parameters.

Pocket Definition

First Limit
Type: Dimension
Depth: 20mm
Limit: No selection

Profile/Surface
Selection: Sketch.2
☐ Thick
Reverse Side
☐ Mirrored extent
Reverse Direction

More>>

OK   Cancel   Preview

3. Set the Up to last option to define the limit of your pocket.
The application will limit the pocket onto the last possible face, that is the pad bottom.

Figure 1–20

Online documentation usually includes structured practices that you can follow to gain hands-on experience with a particular function. At the top of the practice, the name of the component used in the practice displays as a blue hyperlink.

Practice 1a

Viewing a Part

Practice Objectives

- Open a part model and view it from different orientations.
- Change the display settings for the model.
- Investigate associativity between parts, drawings and assemblies.

In this practice, you will open an existing model and work with various visualization tools. You will also change the geometry of a model by editing parameters and deleting features, and note how these changes update in drawings and assemblies.

Task 1 - Open a part and change the display of the model.

1. Click ⬜ (Open) in the toolbar to open a part.

2. In the File Selection dialog box, select **Flange_Lock.CATPart** and click **Open**.

3. Change the display to **Shading** by selecting the **Shading** icon in the flyout menu, as shown in Figure 1–21.

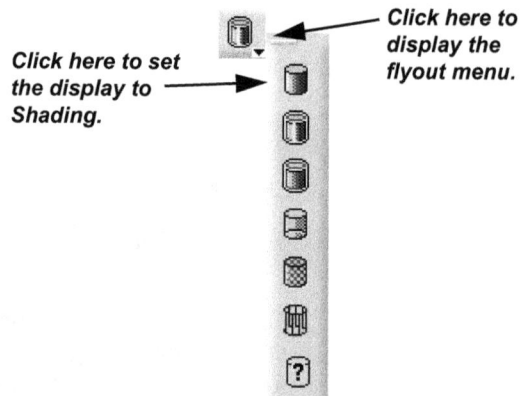

Click here to set the display to Shading.

Click here to display the flyout menu.

Figure 1–21

4. Repeat Step 1 to set the display to  (Shading with Edges), (Shading with Material), and (Shading With Edges and Hidden Edges).

5. Set the display to (Custom View Parameters).

*To change these settings at a later time, select **View>Render Style>Customize View**.*

6. Set the options, as shown in Figure 1–22. Click **OK**. The model displays as shown in Figure 1–23.

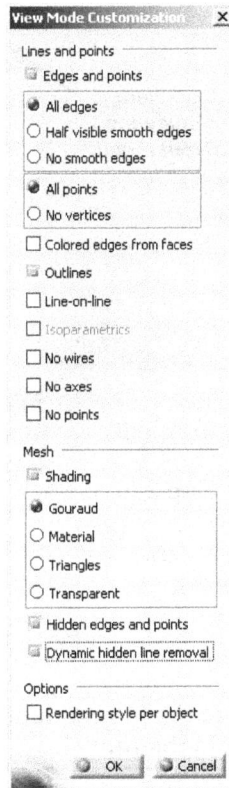

Figure 1–22   **Figure 1–23**

Task 2 - Use the Quick Views toolbar to change the model orientation.

1. Click ⬚ (Shading with Edges) to set the display to **Shading With Edges**.

2. Change the display to **Front** by clicking ⬚ (Front View) in the flyout menu, as shown in Figure 1–24.

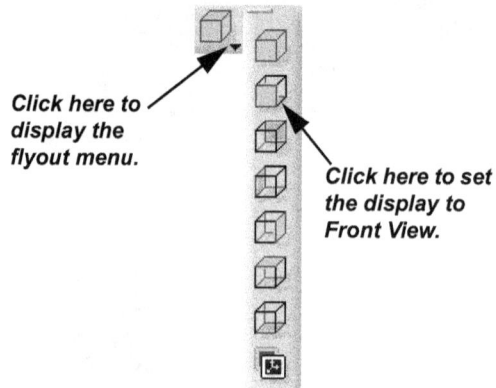

Click here to display the flyout menu.

Click here to set the display to Front View.

Figure 1–24

3. Repeat Step 2 for the ⬚ (Back View), ⬚ (Right View), ⬚ (Left View), ⬚ (Top View), and ⬚ (Bottom View) quick views.

4. Return to the Isometric quick view.

Task 3 - Use the toolbar icons and menus to zoom, pan, and spin the model.

1. Click ⬚ (Zoom In) several times to zoom in.

2. Click ⬚ (Fit All In) to fit the model in the window.

In some cases, the zoom area box does not display on the screen, although the functionality works correctly.

3. Click ⊖ (Zoom Out) several times to zoom out.

4. In the menu bar, select **View>Zoom Area**. Use the left mouse button to draw a box around the area you want to zoom in to, as shown in Figure 1–25.

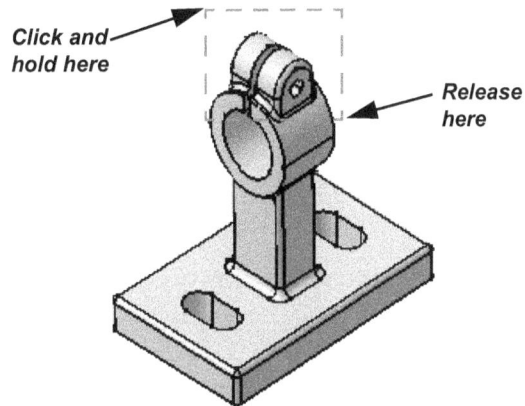

Click and hold here

Release here

Figure 1–25

5. Click ✛ (Pan) to pan the model. The icon turns orange to indicate that it is active.

6. Place the cursor near the bottom of the graphics window, hold the left mouse button, and drag the cursor to the top of the screen. You have panned down on the model.

7. ✛ (Pan) is no longer orange. This means you must click the icon each time you want to pan.

You learn additional ways of panning and zooming later in the practice.

8. Click ✛ (Fit All In) to fit the model in the window.

9. Click ↻ (Rotate) to rotate the model. Hold the left mouse button and move the cursor to rotate the model. The **Rotate** icon behaves in the same manner as the **Pan** icon, where you must click the icon each time you want to rotate the model.

Task 4 - Use the compass to dynamically rotate and pan the model.

1. Click ⬛ (Isometric View) to return to the Isometric quick view.

2. Click and drag the ball on top of the compass to rotate the model, as shown in Figure 1–26.

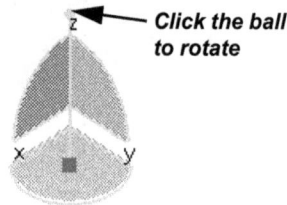

Click the ball to rotate

Figure 1–26

3. Return to the Isometric quick view.

4. Click and drag the curved edge of the XY plane to rotate the model about the Z-axis only, as shown in Figure 1–27.

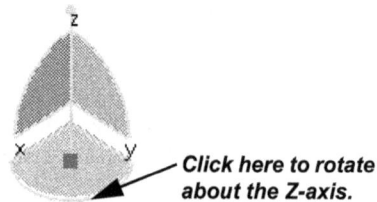

Click here to rotate about the Z-axis.

Figure 1–27

5. Repeat Step 4 for the other two curved edges.

6. Return to the Isometric quick view.

7. Click and drag the X-, Y-, and Z-axes of the compass to translate the model along that direction, as shown in Figure 1–28.

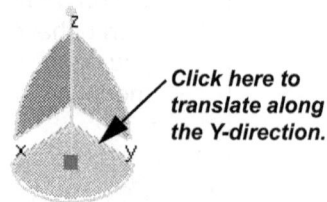

Click here to translate along the Y-direction.

Figure 1–28

Task 5 - Use the mouse to dynamically rotate, pan, and zoom the model.

Click *(Fit All In) to center your model in the graphics window.*

Try repeating these mouse shortcuts when possible.

1. Return to the Isometric quick view and fit the entire model in the window.

2. Hold the middle mouse button and move the cursor to pan the model.

3. Hold the middle mouse button and then left-click (or right-click) once. Move the cursor up and down to zoom in and out.

4. Press and hold the middle mouse button and then press and hold the left mouse button (or right mouse button), and move the cursor to rotate the model.

Task 6 - Use the specification tree to review the model geometry.

1. In the specification tree, select **Multipad.1** (you might need to expand PartBody by clicking the **+** symbol). The feature highlights in orange in the tree and on the model, as shown in Figure 1–29.

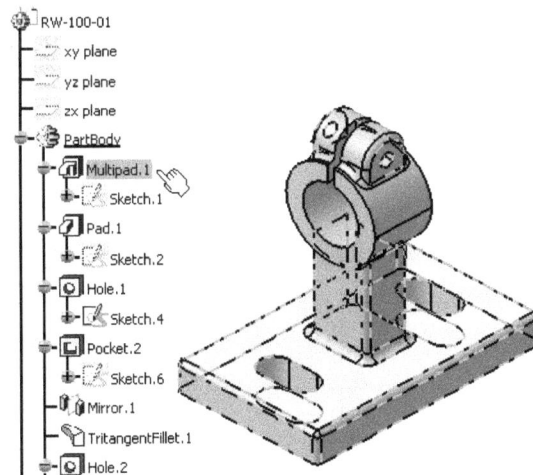

Figure 1–29

2. Repeat Step 1 for each feature under the PartBody branch (i.e., Pad.1, Hole.1, Pocket.2, Mirror.1, etc.). The selected feature is highlighted on the model and in the specification tree.

If you accidentally change the focus to the specification tree, you must understand how to activate the model.

3. Select the coordinate system in the lower right corner of the screen, as shown in Figure 1–30. The model turns gray, indicating that it is inactive. Select it again to make it active.

Figure 1–30

You can also change the focus to the specification tree by selecting any of the tree branches.

4. Press <F3> several times to hide and display the specification tree.

Task 7 - Change the size of several features.

1. Place the cursor over the large fillet at the base of the neck to highlight it, as shown in Figure 1–31. Double-click on it to display the radius dimension.

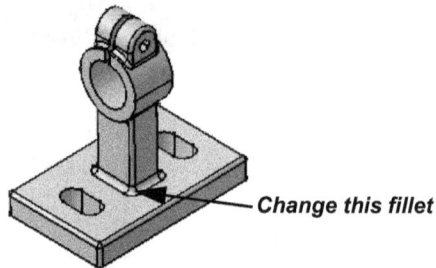

Change this fillet

Figure 1–31

2. In the Edge Fillet Definition dialog box, change *Radius* to **6.00mm (0.236 in)**, as shown in Figure 1–32. Click **OK**.

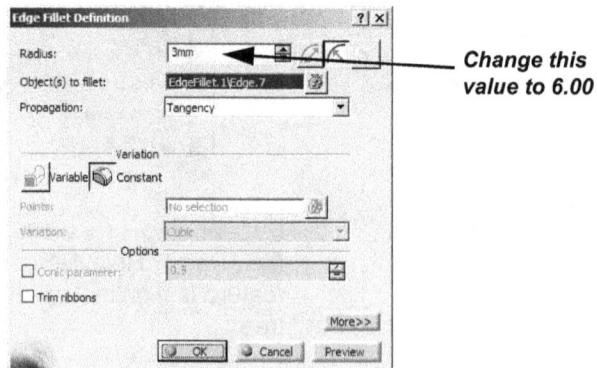

Change this value to 6.00

Figure 1–32

3. In the specification tree, double-click on ⊙ Hole.1 .

4. In the Hole Definition dialog box, change the *Diameter* to **13.00mm (0.512 in)**, and click **OK**. The updated model is shown in Figure 1–33.

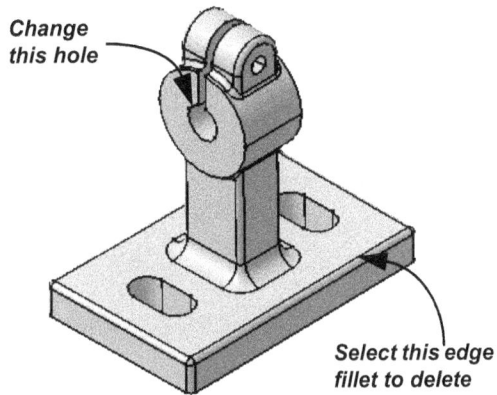

Figure 1–33

Task 8 - Delete features.

1. Select the edge fillet shown in Figure 1–33.

2. Right-click and select **Delete**.

3. Delete **Sketch.6** from the specification tree, as shown in Figure 1–34.

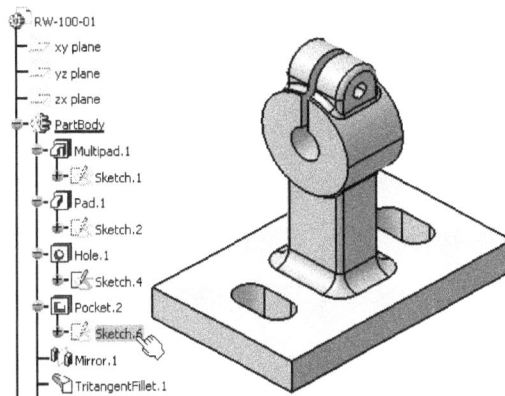

Figure 1–34

4. The Delete dialog box opens, as shown in Figure 1–35. It prompts you that the sketch is a parent feature and when deleted, its children are also deleted.

Figure 1–35

5. Click **OK**. The model displays as shown in Figure 1–36.

6. Click 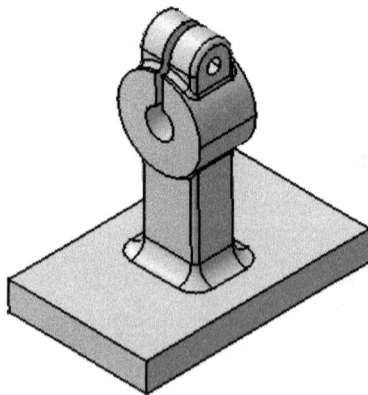 (Undo) to undo the deleting operations. The model displays as shown in Figure 1–37.

Figure 1–36   **Figure 1–37**

Task 9 - Cause a feature to fail.

1. In the specification tree, double-click on ⬡EdgeFillet.5 .

2. Modify the radius of the fillet to **30.00mm (1.181 in)** and click **OK**.

   The radius of the fillet is too large and causes the **EdgeFillet.5** feature to fail. An Update Diagnosis dialog box opens, as shown in Figure 1–38.

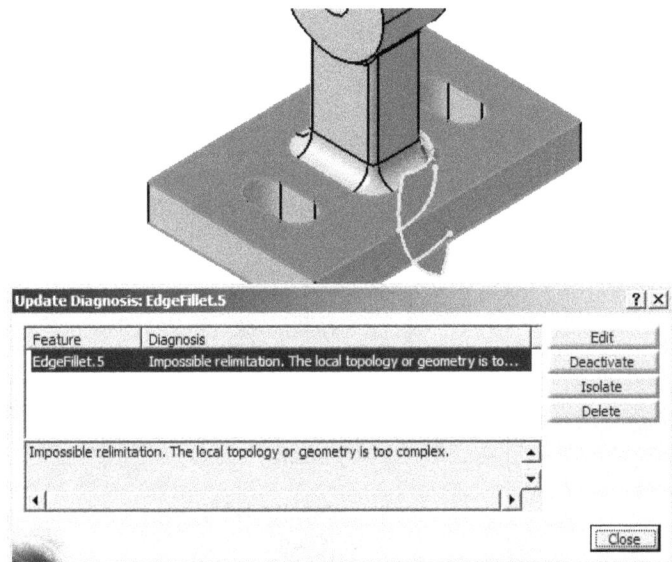

Figure 1–38

3. Undo the changes made to the Fillet feature and resolve the failure by clicking ↩ (Undo).

Task 10 - Open a drawing of the part to verify it has been updated.

1. In the toolbar, click ⬚ (Open) to open the drawing.

2. In the File Selection dialog box, select **Flange_Lock.CATDrawing**.

3. Click **Open**.

4. The specification tree for the drawing displays ⊚ (Update current sheet), as shown in Figure 1–39. This indicates that the drawing is not up-to-date.

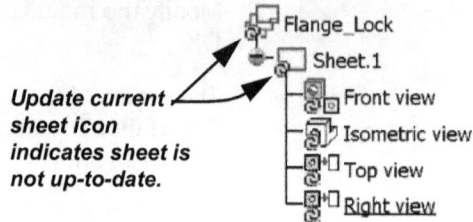

Update current sheet icon indicates sheet is not up-to-date.

Figure 1–39

5. Click ⊚ (Update current sheet) to update the views. The updated drawing is shown in Figure 1–40. Note that if set to inches, it will display with different dimensions.

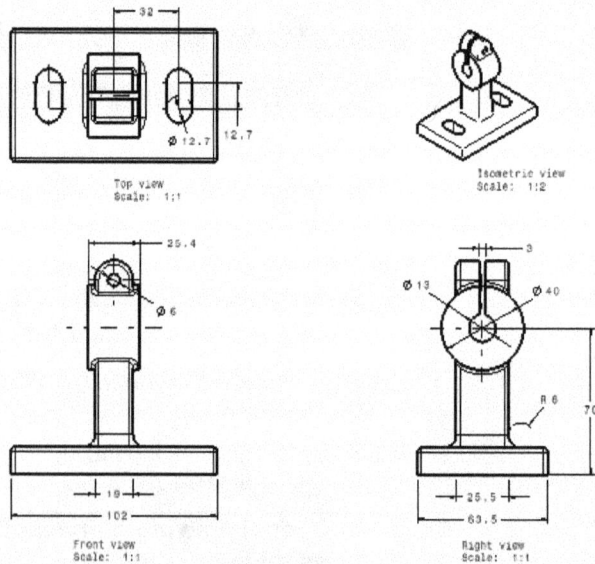

Figure 1–40

6. Select **Window>Tile Vertically** to display the model and drawing windows side-by-side.

7. Select **Window>Cascade** to arrange the windows with the window titles displaying.

Task 11 - Close the models to clear the screen.

1. With the drawing active, click ⊡ (Save) to save the drawing. A message displays, informing you that saving the modified drawing does not save the modified part, as shown in Figure 1–41.

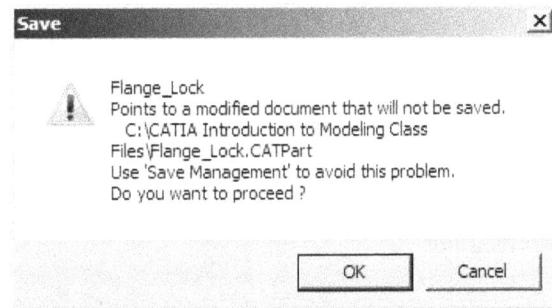

Figure 1–41

2. Click **OK**.

3. Select **File>Close** to close the drawing window. The Close dialog box opens as shown in Figure 1–42. The software is warning you that the model is going to be closed without saving.

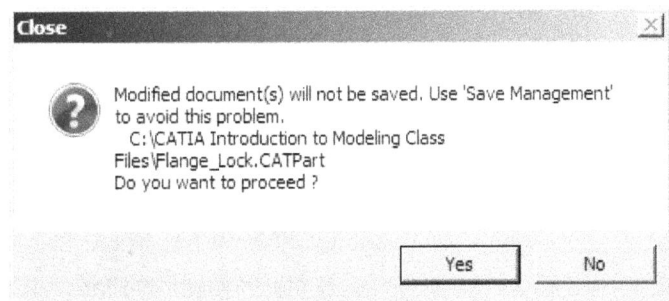

Figure 1–42

4. Click **Yes** to close the drawing without saving the changes to the model.

Task 12 - Open the assembly model Flange_Lock.CATProduct.

1. Click [Open icon] (Open) in the toolbar to open the assembly.

2. Select **Flange_Lock.CATProduct** in the File Selection dialog box.

3. Click **Open**. The assembly opens as shown in Figure 1–43. The assembly contains **Flange_Lock.CATPart** as one of its components.

You might have to collapse the constraints entry in the specification tree by selecting the - symbol.

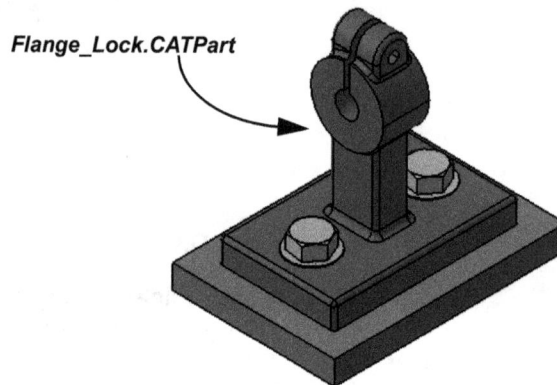

Flange_Lock.CATPart

Figure 1–43

4. Select **Window>Flange_Lock.CATPart** to activate the part model.

5. In the specification tree, double-click on [icon] Hole.1 .

6. In the Hole Definition dialog box, change the *Diameter* to **25.0 (0.984 in)** and click **OK**.

7. Select **Window>Flange_Lock.CATProduct** to activate the assembly model. The change in the diameter of **Hole.1** has updated in the assembly model, as shown in Figure 1–44.

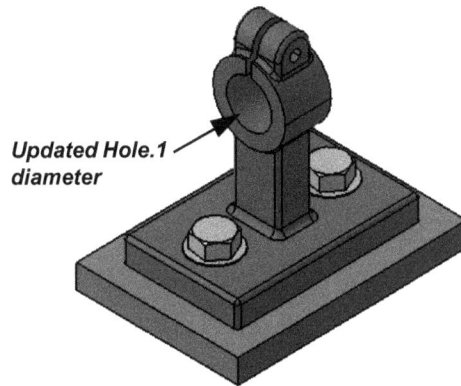

Updated Hole.1 diameter

Figure 1–44

8. With the assembly active, click ⊡ (Save) to save the model.

9. With the assembly active, select **File>Close**.

Design Considerations

By closing the assembly, the software detects that the modified component **Flange_Lock.CATPart**, must also be saved, as shown in the dialog box in Figure 1–45. It is recommended that you check modified assembly components to ensure that no changes are lost. Using **Save Management** ensures that all modified documents are saved.

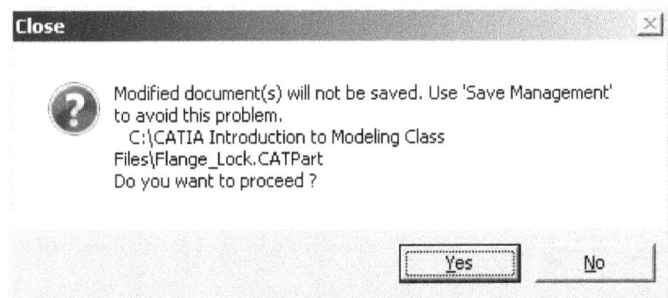

Figure 1–45

10. Click **Yes** to close the assembly file.

11. Save **Flange_Lock.CATPart** and close the window.

Feature Management

CATIA provides several tools to simplify the display of your model. Three of these tools are Search, Hide/Show, and Activate/Deactivate. Using these tools will increase your overall efficiency. You can also use Selection Sets to quickly select groups of features at the same time.

Learning Objectives in this Chapter

- Use Search in complex models to find specific objects.
- Show and hide features to simplify the display and make working with complex models more efficient.
- Understand how hidden features display in the specification tree.
- Learn how to Activate and Deactivate objects.
- Learn how to group features using selection sets.

2.1 Search for Features

In complex models with a large number of features, locating specific features in the model might become difficult. The **Search** tool enables you to locate and select the feature in the specification tree using a variety of search parameters.

- Select **Edit>Search** to perform a search. The Search dialog box opens and it displays the results of a sample search for a feature with a name containing the string **Rib,** as shown in Figure 2–1.

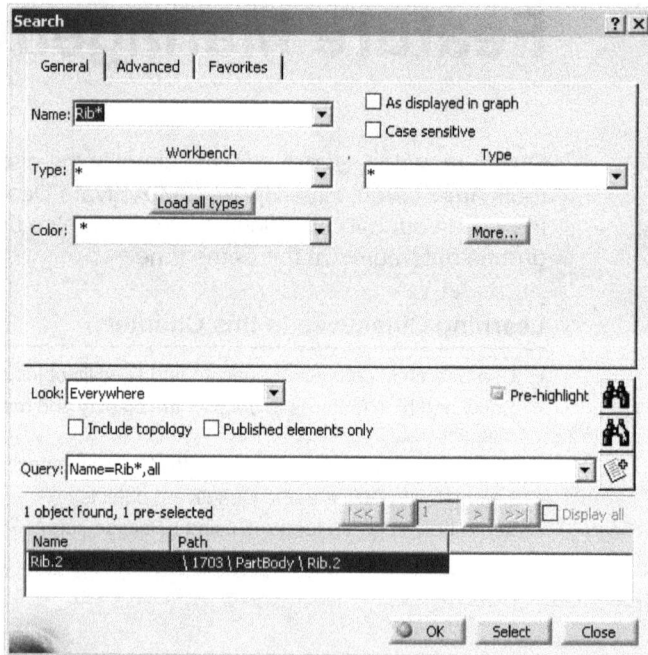

Figure 2–1

When you select the found objects, the features are highlighted in the main window and specification tree. The feature can be selected for use in the current operation by clicking **Select**.

- The *Advanced* tab provides options to define more search parameters.

- The *Favorites* tab provides access to search results that have been stored using (Add to favorites).

2.2 Hide and Show

CATIA contains two default display spaces - invisible and visible. You have been working in visible space. As you create additional features and your models become more complex, the display area of the screen becomes cluttered. To simplify the display, the **Hide** and **Show** commands can be used to move features between the two spaces.

A model with all elements visible is shown in Figure 2–2.

Sketches are normally hidden after they are referenced by a feature. They are shown here for illustration purposes.

The display shows many elements that no longer need to be shown.

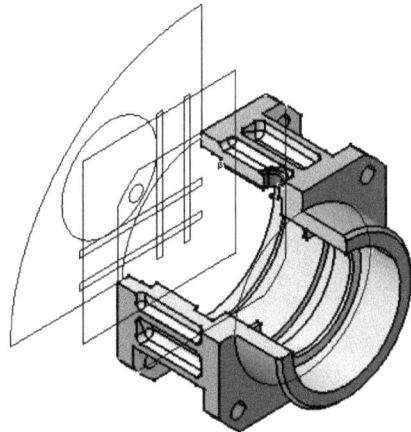

Figure 2–2

The model shown includes all of the sketches, lines, and reference planes. Individual features can be moved from the visible space to the invisible space by using one of the following methods:

- Click (Hide/Show) in the View toolbar and select the feature(s) to hide/show. You can also use this method in reverse.

- Select the feature in the display area or in the specification tree, right-click, and select **Hide/Show**. When a feature is switched to the invisible space, it no longer displays. However, the features still exist.

To select all features of a particular type, use the **Hide** or **Show** commands in the **Tools** menu, as shown in Figure 2–3.

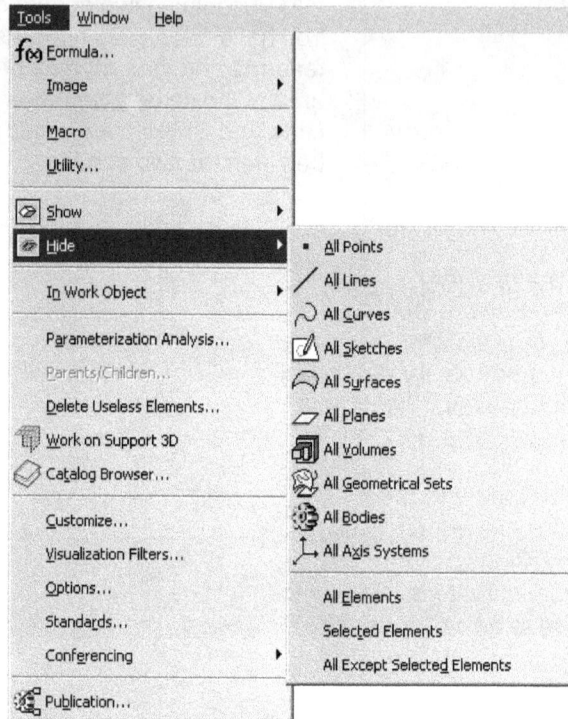

Figure 2–3

As a result, the display area is much less cluttered. Figure 2–4 shows the same model as the one shown in Figure 2–2, except that all sketches, planes, points, and axis systems are hidden from visible space.

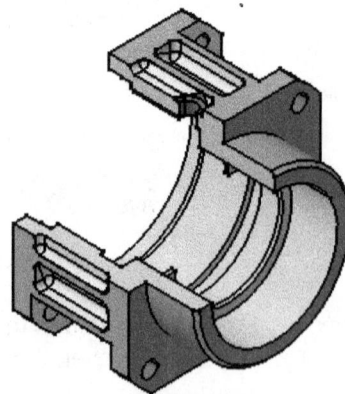

Figure 2–4

Indication of Hidden Features

The specification tree displays hidden features as faded or grayed icons, as shown in Figure 2–5.

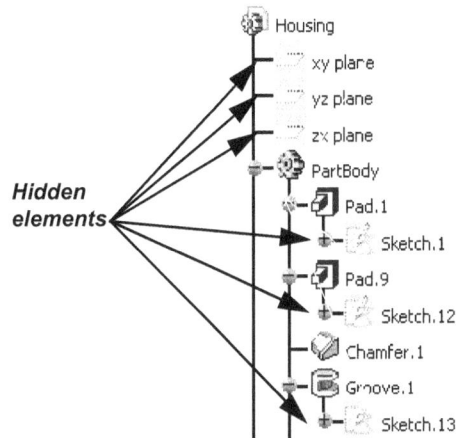

Hidden elements

- Housing
  - xy plane
  - yz plane
  - zx plane
  - PartBody
    - Pad.1
      - Sketch.1
    - Pad.9
      - Sketch.12
    - Chamfer.1
    - Groove.1
      - Sketch.13

Figure 2–5

- To swap between the visible working space and invisible working space, click ✏ (Swap visible space) in the View toolbar. Hidden features are shown in a separate working space (i.e., invisible). Click the icon again to return to the visible working space.

- To make individual features visible after they have been hidden, select them in the specification tree, right-click and select **Hide/Show**.

Tips and Techniques

Use the **Hide** and **Show** commands carefully. Although no real harm can be done to your model, the **Hide** and **Show** commands can produce unexpected results if you select inactive features, or select the wrong types of features.

- A feature in the specification tree that affects the mass properties of the model cannot be hidden without hiding all solid features. To control the display of solid features independently, the feature must be deactivated.

2.3 Activate and Deactivate

If features are deactivated, the update sequence time decreases.

When features are added to the model, the software updates them with any changes made. When a change occurs that forces subsequent features to change drastically, the update can fail. To deactivate a feature and help solve an update failure, select the feature, right-click and select the feature object name (e.g., **Hole.1 object**), and then select **Deactivate**, as shown in Figure 2–6.

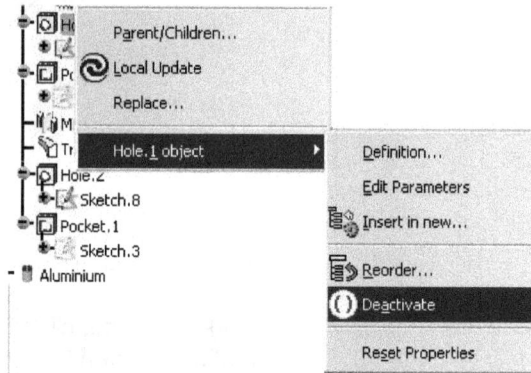

Figure 2–6

The **Deactivate** option temporarily removes the feature from the update sequence. This enables you to keep the feature as currently defined, without deleting it. The feature icon displays with a deactivation symbol in the specification tree, as shown for the **Hole.1** object in Figure 2–7.

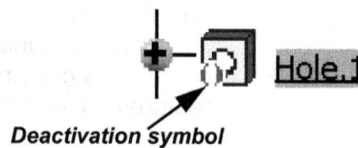

Deactivation symbol

Figure 2–7

You can modify any previous features to help solve an update failure. Once solved, the feature can be returned to the update sequence by selecting it in the specification tree, right-clicking on the feature object name, and selecting **Activate**.

Features should only be deactivated temporarily. If they are not required, they should be deleted from the model.

You can use the **Deactivate** option to:

- Reduce the chance of unwanted parent/child relationships.

- Make models run faster.

- De-feature the model for Finite Element Analysis purposes.

- Try alternative designs for a feature.

To avoid accidentally referencing a Fillet feature when creating additional features, deactivate the Fillet feature on your model, as shown in Figure 2–8. Deactivating fillets is one way to help CATIA run faster for modeling design and Finite Element Analysis.

- You can also deactivate specific features and create alternative types. This option enables you to keep fillets for use at a later time without having to recreate them.

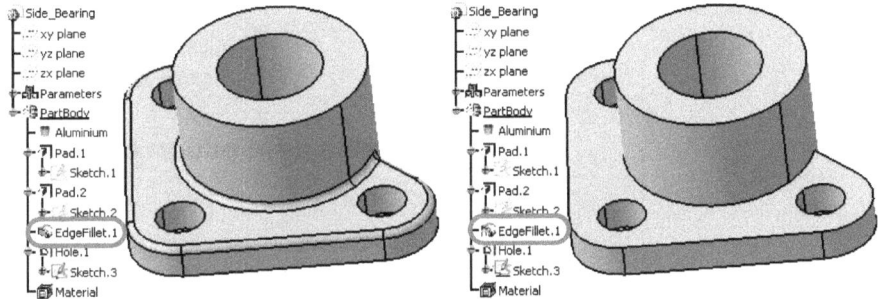

Figure 2–8

Once the design is finalized, it is recommended that you delete all unused features, rather than keep them deactivated in the model. If not deleted, these features can unnecessarily increase file size and cause confusion to someone else using this file at a later time.

Parent/Child Considerations

If a parent feature is selected for deactivation, its children must also be deactivated. Children features that are impacted by deactivating the parent are highlighted in the specification tree and the model. Figure 2–9 shows the **Hole.1** feature selected for deactivation and the Deactivate dialog box. The Draft feature is the child feature and is consequently deactivated.

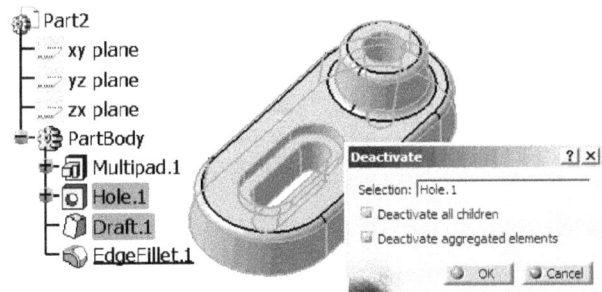

Figure 2–9

2.4 Creating Selection Sets

Selection sets enable you to define groups of features that can be quickly selected at the same time. This function is ideal for groups of features that are selected often. For example, you can quickly deactivate and activate fillet, chamfer, and other dress-up features by adding them to a selection set.

- The Selection Sets toolbar is shown in Figure 2–10.

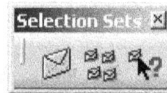

Figure 2–10

How To: Create a Selection Set

1. Click (Selection sets edition) to create a selection box. The Selection Sets Edition dialog box opens, as shown in Figure 2–11.

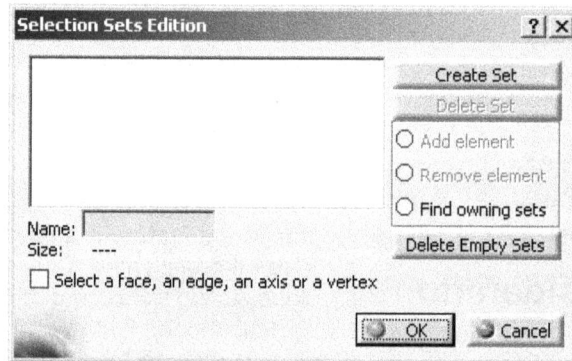

Figure 2–11

2. Click **Create Set** and enter a name for the set in the *Name* field.
3. With the new set highlighted, select the **Add element** option. Select features in the specification tree to add to the set. The **Select a face, an edge, an axis or a vertex** option, enables you to select geometry from the model.
4. Click **OK** to complete the creation of the set.

5. Click ⬛ (Selection sets) to select a feature. The Selection Sets Selection dialog box opens, as shown in Figure 2–12.

Figure 2–12

6. Select the set from the list and click **Select**. Close the dialog box to complete the selection.

Practice 2a | # Feature Management

Practice Objectives

- Simplify the model display using the Hide/Show commands.
- Activate and deactivate features.
- Create and use selection sets.

In this practice, you will use feature management techniques to modify a part. You will use the **Hide/Show**, **Activate/Deactivate** and **Selection Set** commands. In addition, you will learn the properties of these commands and how they affect the model display.

Features are selected for visual clarity.

Task 1 - Hide reference geometry and sketch features.

1. Click . Select **BlockMgt.CATPart** and click **Open**. Note that the reference elements and feature sketches are also displayed.

2. View the invisible space by clicking ![icon](Swap visible space). The background changes to the invisible space color. Some measurements are hidden in the model. Therefore, they display in the invisible space.

3. Return to the visible space by clicking ![icon](Swap visible space).

4. Using <Ctrl>, select the three default reference plane features.

5. Right-click over any of the selected features in the display area and select **Hide/Show**.

6. The planes are removed from visible space and added to invisible space. Click ![icon](Swap visible space) to switch to invisible space. The three planes display as shown in Figure 2–13.

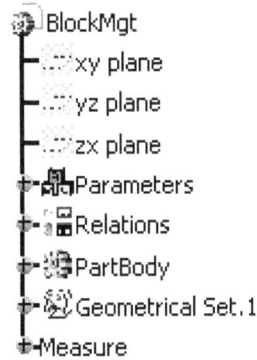

Figure 2–13

7. Click ![Swap visible space icon] (Swap visible space) to switch back to visible space.

8. By default, sketches that are used to create other features, such as pads, grooves, pockets, etc., are automatically hidden from display. Currently, they are all set to display. Select **Tools>Hide>All Sketches** to remove all sketches from visible space. The model updates, as shown in Figure 2–14.

Note that all hidden feature icons are grayed in the specification tree.

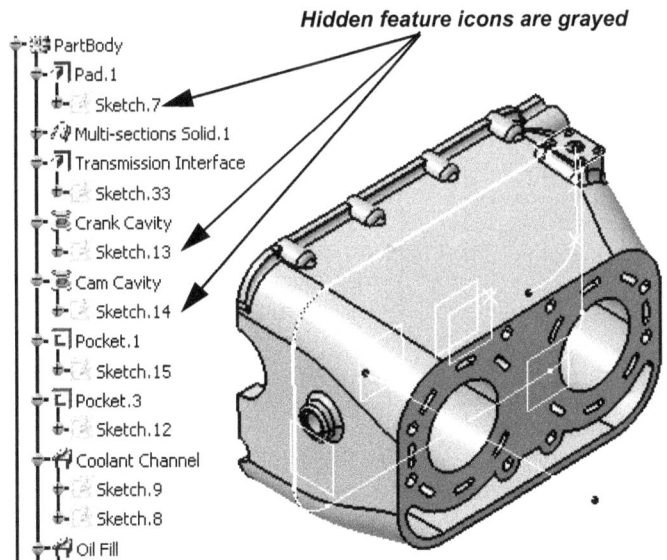

Figure 2–14

9. Reference geometry features are still set to display in visible space. Right-click on **Geometrical Set.1** and select **Geometrical Set.1 object>Hide Components**.

10. Click [icon] (Swap visible space) to switch to invisible space.

11. Switch back to visible space.

Task 2 - Attempt to hide a Hole feature.

1. Select the **Hole.5** feature in the specification tree, right-click and select **Hide/Show**. If you are unable to locate the feature in the specification tree, you can select any other solid feature to hide.

   Note that the contents of the PartBody switch to invisible space. Solid features cannot be hidden or shown independently from the rest of the PartBody solid features.

2. Select the **Hole.5** feature in the specification tree again, right-click and select **Hide/Show** to return PartBody to visible space.

Task 3 - Deactivate the Hole feature.

Design Considerations

As shown in Task 2, individual solid geometry features cannot be hidden independently. However, you can deactivate the individual solid features independently.

1. Right-click on the **Hole.5** feature in the specification tree and select **Hole.5 object>Deactivate**.

2. Click **OK** in the Deactivate dialog box, as shown in Figure 2–15.

*Select the **Deactivate aggregated elements** option to deactivate all geometry grouped below the main element node being deactivated.*

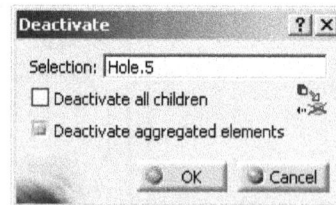

Figure 2–15

The Hole feature is deactivated and removed from visible space, as shown in Figure 2–16.

Deactivation symbol displays on feature icon

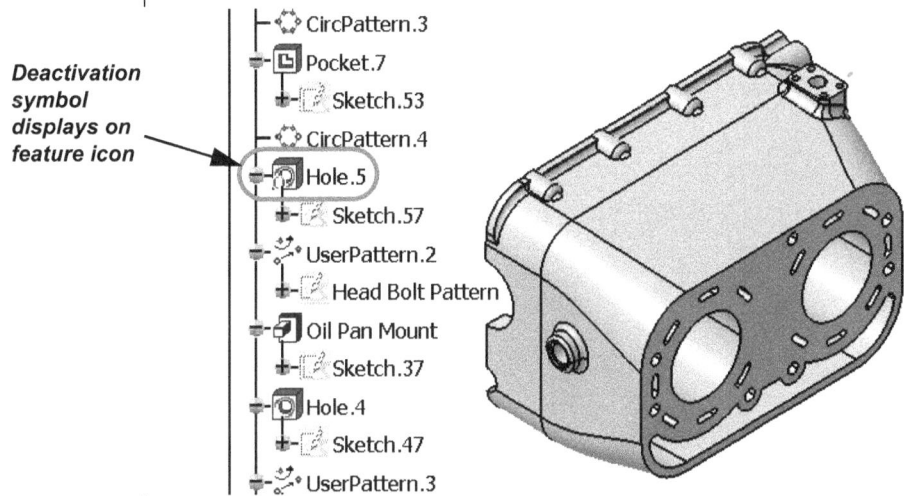

Figure 2–16

Design Considerations

The feature is not switched to invisible space because it is deactivated and therefore no longer updates with the rest of the model. In this case, deactivation is useful in illustrating the manufacturing process of the model for a marketing presentation. The last step is to drill the hole in the part. To obtain a graphic of the model without the hole, it is recommended to deactivate the feature, generate the graphic, and then re-activate the feature, rather than deleting the feature.

3. In the specification tree, select the deactivated **Hole.5** feature. Right-click, and select **Hole.5 object>Activate**.

4. Click **OK** then click in the background to clear the selection. The model returns to the active state.

Task 4 - Deactivate the Fillet features.

---

1. Click [✉] (Selection sets edition). You might need to display the Selection Sets toolbar to access the icon (check the top toolbar). The Selection Sets Edition dialog box opens.

2. Click **Create Set**.

3. Enter **FilletSet** in the *Name* field. Select the **Add element** option as shown in Figure 2–17.

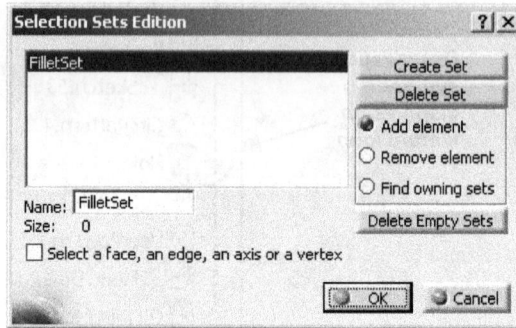

Figure 2–17

Design Considerations

The Windows shortcut keys for Find (<Ctrl>+ <F>) also opens the Search dialog box.

You must perform a search operation to locate the Fillet features to add to the selection set. Searching is the most efficient way to locate and select all of the Fillet features in the model.

4. Select **Edit>Search**. The Search dialog box opens.

5. In the workbench **Type** menu, select **Part Design** and select **Type>Fillet**. The Search dialog box opens as shown in Figure 2–18.

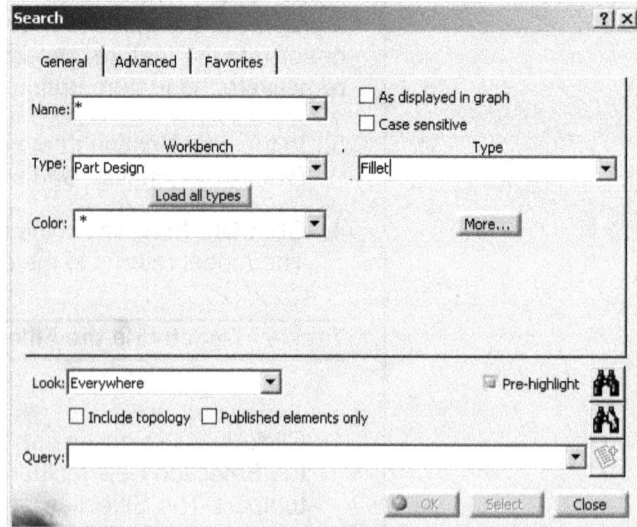

Figure 2–18

6. Click ▦ (Search) to start the search. The results of the search is shown in Figure 2–19.

7. In the Search dialog box, click **OK** to add the Fillet features to the selection set. The Fillet feature is highlighted in the model and the specification tree. In the Selection Sets Edition dialog box, *Size* updates to **10**, as shown in Figure 2–20.

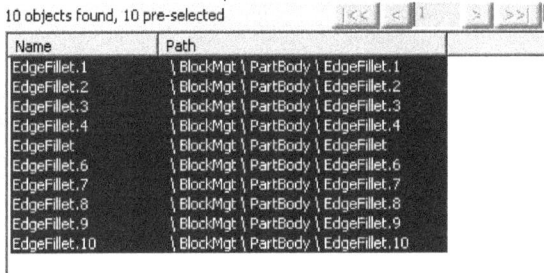

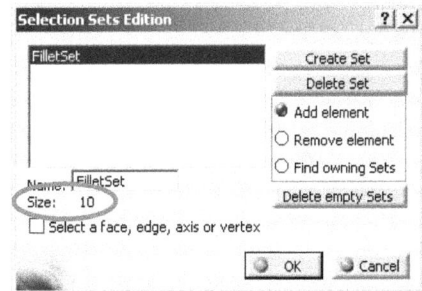

Figure 2–19   **Figure 2–20**

8. Click **OK** to close the Selection Sets Edition dialog box. The Fillet features should still be selected.

9. In the menu bar, select **Edit>Selected objects>Deactivate**. The Fillet features are deactivated from the model, as shown in Figure 2–21.

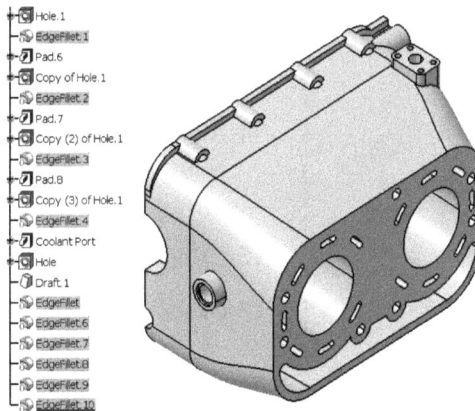

Figure 2–21

10. Clear the Fillet features by clicking in the background.

You can also click

(Selection sets) to open the Selection Sets Selection dialog box.

11. Click 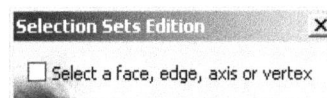 (Find Owning Selection Sets). The Selection Sets Edition dialog box opens as shown in Figure 2–22.

Figure 2–22

12. In the specification tree, select any of the Fillet features. The Selection Sets Selection dialog box opens as shown in Figure 2–23.

Figure 2–23

Design Considerations

When many unnamed or ambiguous selection sets (e.g., groups of fillets) exist and are difficult to distinguish, use **Find Owning Selection Sets** to locate the required set. Selection sets are accessed through the **Selection Sets** icon. Therefore, remember to name your selection sets meaningfully.

13. In the list, select **FilletSet** and click **Select**. Close the Selection Sets Selection dialog box to complete the selection. The Fillet features are highlighted in the specification tree.

14. Right-click on a Fillet feature in the specification tree and select **Selected objects>Activate**.

15. Click ![Save icon] (Save).

16. Close the file.

Task 5 - Clean up the display of other models.

---

1. Open three models worked on previously.

2. Practice modifying the display of the models by hiding/showing features. Use the different methods described here.

3. Save the parts and close the windows.

Part Information

CATIA provides you with several tools that can be used to obtain information about a part's measurements and inertia. You can also use the feature investigation tools to determine how the model was constructed.

Learning Objectives in this Chapter

- Use measure entities.
- Update measurements that result from a model modification.
- Learn how to measure between items.
- Understand Standard, Chain, and Fan modes.
- Apply material to a model.
- Measure 2D and 3D inertia.
- Position a section plane to visualize a 3D section of the model.

3.1 Measuring Items

The **Measure Item** tool is a one-click measurement tool that enables you to select one of the following items in the specification tree or on screen to measure:

*   Point

*   Edge (straight or curved)

*   Surface (flat or curved)

*   PartBody

Click ▨ (Measure Item) in the Measure toolbar to open the Measure Item dialog box, as shown in Figure 3–1. The measurements results depend on what you select and what result settings are in place. The results for a curved surface are shown in Figure 3–2.

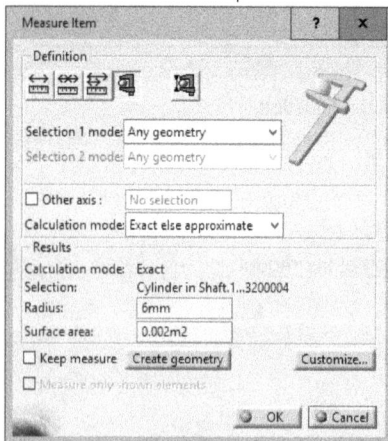

Figure 3–1

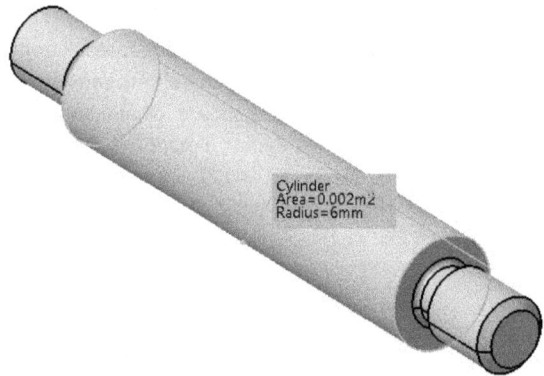

Figure 3–2

You can use the *Selection 1 mode* and *Selection 2 mode* drop-down lists to set the entities to measure.

Note that to measure the thickness, you can either select **Thickness** from the selection mode drop-down list or click

▨ (Measures the Thickness).

The measure item results can be customized for the selected item by clicking **Customize**. The Measure Item Customization dialog box opens as shown in Figure 3–3.

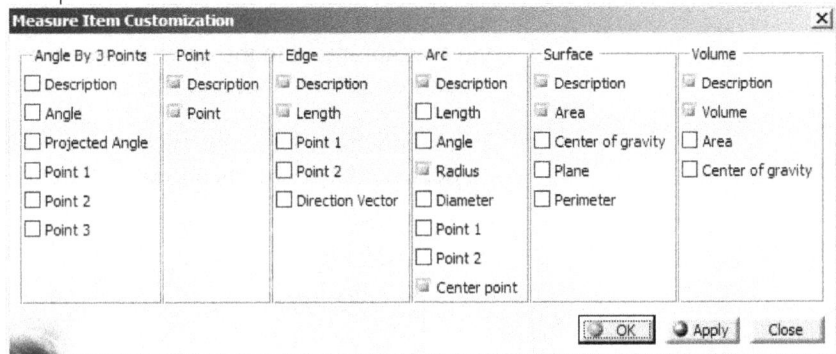

Figure 3–3

Once an item is measured, you can save the measurement with the model data by selecting the **Keep Measure** option in the Measure Item dialog box, as shown in Figure 3–4.

Select to save measurement with model data.

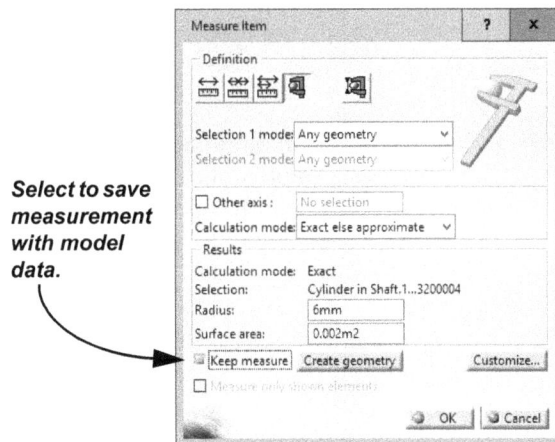

Figure 3–4

The measurement is then added to the specification tree, as shown in Figure 3–5.

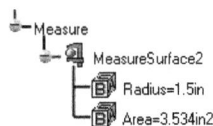

Figure 3–5

3.2 Updating Measurements

If modifications are made in the model that result in a change to a measured value (e.g., geometry change), ⊚ displays next to the measurement in the specification tree, indicating that the measured value is not updated.

To update the value, right-click on the measurement name and select **Local update**, as shown in Figure 3–6.

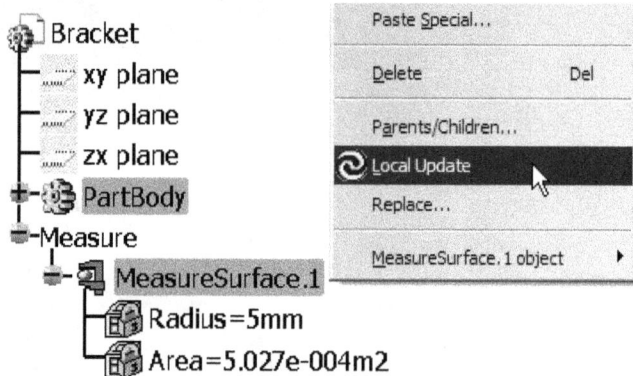

Figure 3–6

To automate the update of these measurements, enable the automatic update options under **Tools>Options>General> Parameters and Measure>**_Measure Tools_ tab, as shown in Figure 3–7.

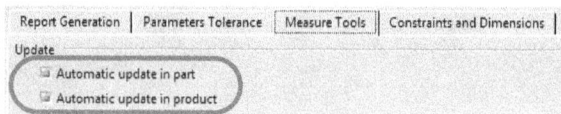

Figure 3–7

3.3 Measuring Between Items

Click (Standard) in the Measure toolbar to open the Measure Between dialog box, as shown in Figure 3–8.

Measure Between Modes

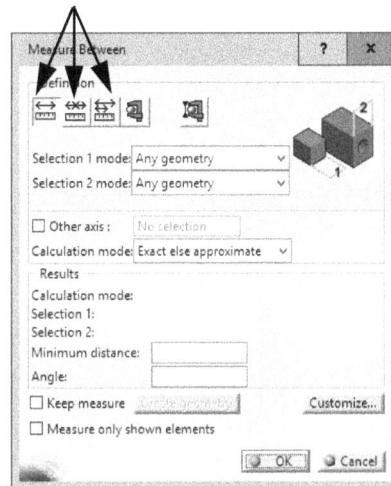

Figure 3–8

The three modes of Measure Between tools available are described as follows:

- Standard

- Chain

- Fan

Standard Mode Measure Between

The **Standard Mode Measure Between** tool is the default Measure Between mode. It is a two-click measurement tool that enables you to measure between two selected items of the same or mixed types. You can select from the specification tree or on the screen. The different selectable item types for the **Measure Between** tool are shown in Figure 3–9.

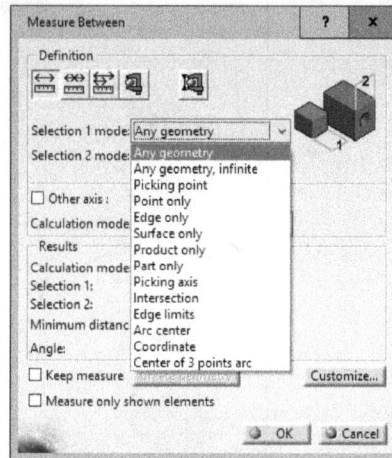

Figure 3–9

- Using **Any geometry**, the software enables you to measure between geometry of any type. If this causes difficulty in selecting a specific type of element, select a more applicable element in the menu.

- **Any geometry, infinite** extends the selected plane, curve, or line infinitely to obtain an accurate minimum distance.

- **Standard Mode Measure Between** is a two-click tool that can be used to take measurements, such as the distance between items or angle between items.

An example of a measurement between two selected surfaces is shown in Figure 3–10. The results can be saved and customized using the same method as the **Measure Item** tool.

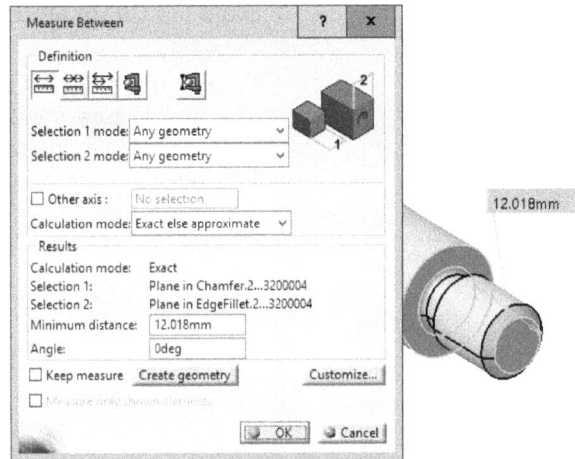

Figure 3–10

When selecting hole and arc centers, you can display an axis by moving the cursor over the approximate center of the hole and arc, as shown in Figure 3–11.

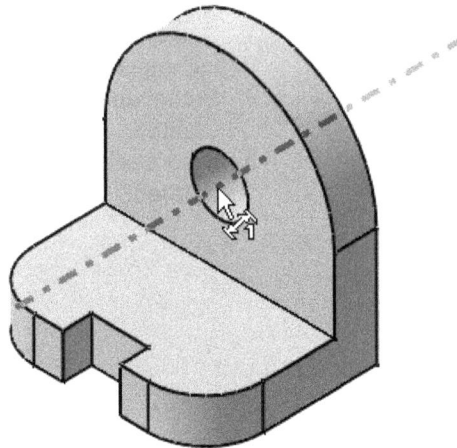

Figure 3–11

Chain Mode Measure Between

The **Chain Mode Measure Between** tool enables you to quickly gather multiple measurements between pairs of selected items in a chain.

To activate the **Chain Mode Measure Between** tool, click

⬚ (Chain) in the Measure Between dialog box. Figure 3–12 shows three measurements that can be created using four item selections in Chain mode rather than six item selections in Standard mode.

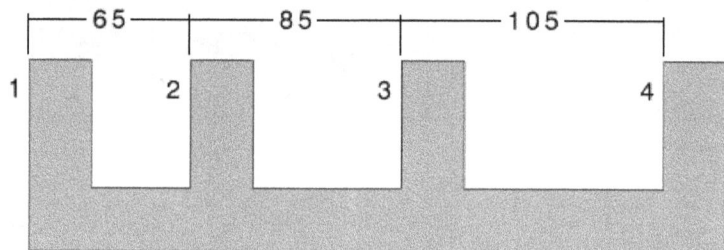

Figure 3–12

How To: Create Measurements using Chain mode

Figure 3–12 shows an example of measurements using chain mode:

1. Select **edge 1** and **edge 2**. The measurement distance of 65 inches is created.
2. Select **edge 3**. The measurement distance of 85 inches is created.
3. Select **edge 4**. The measurement distance of 105 inches is created.

After the first measurement is created, the software creates measurements between any newly selected items and the last selected item. The results can be saved and customized using the same method as the **Measure Item** *tool.*

Fan Mode Measure Between

The **Fan Mode Measure Between** tool enables you to quickly gather multiple measurements between one base item and any number of other items. To activate the **Fan Mode Measure Between** tool, click [Fan icon] (Fan) in the Measure Between dialog box.

The three measurements shown in Figure 3–13 can be created using four item selections in Fan mode rather than six item selections in Standard mode.

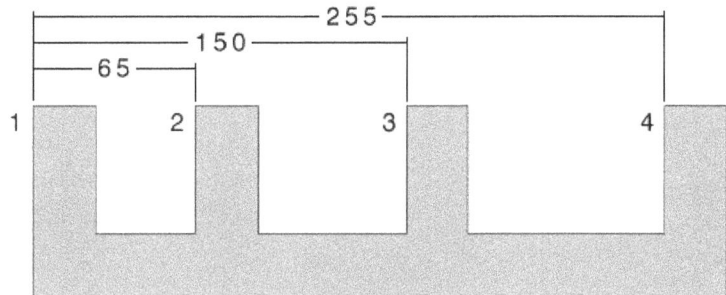

Figure 3–13

*After the first measurement is created, the software creates measurements between any newly selected items and the first selected item (base item). The results can be saved and customized using the same method as the **Measure Item** tool.*

How To: Create Measurements using Fan mode

Figure 3–13 shows an example of measurements using Fan mode:

1. Select **edge 1** and **edge 2**. The measurement distance of 65 inches is created.
2. Select **edge 3**. The measurement distance of 150 inches is created.
3. Select **edge 4**. The measurement distance of 255 inches is created.

Measuring with Reference Elements

In situations where the part geometry is complex, such as models created using surfacing techniques, it is difficult to find planar references to measure between. In this case, reference elements can be constructed to generate an exact measurement reference.

- Consider the simplified example shown in Figure 3–14. In this case, a measure between operation referencing the top and bottom faces can report the minimum and maximum distances. The software is free to select the location on the curved surface from which the measurement is made.

- To measure the distance between an exact location on the top surface, a reference point can be created to define the location, as shown in Figure 3–15.

- To further define the type of measurement, a reference plane can be created. This restricts the measurement direction to be normal to the plane, as shown in Figure 3–16.

Another option is to use ***Customize> Components****. This reports the X, Y, and Z components of a measurement, enabling you to extract the required direction.*

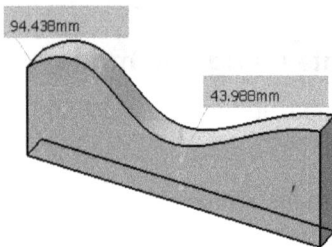

94.438mm

43.988mm

Figure 3–14

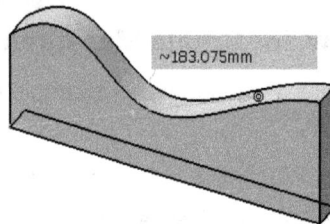

~183.075mm

Figure 3–15

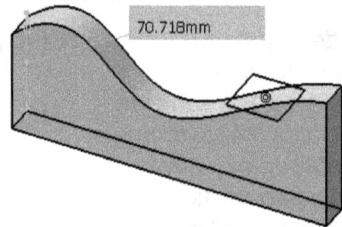

70.718mm

Figure 3–16

3.4 Measuring Inertia

Before measuring the inertia of the model, it is recommended that you first define the model's material properties.

Apply a Material

When you apply a material to a model, the properties of the model (such as density and Young's modulus) are defined. This ensures that accurate inertia values are computed for the model.

How To: Apply a Material

1. Click ⬜ (Apply Material) to define the material for the model. The Library dialog box opens as shown in Figure 3–17.

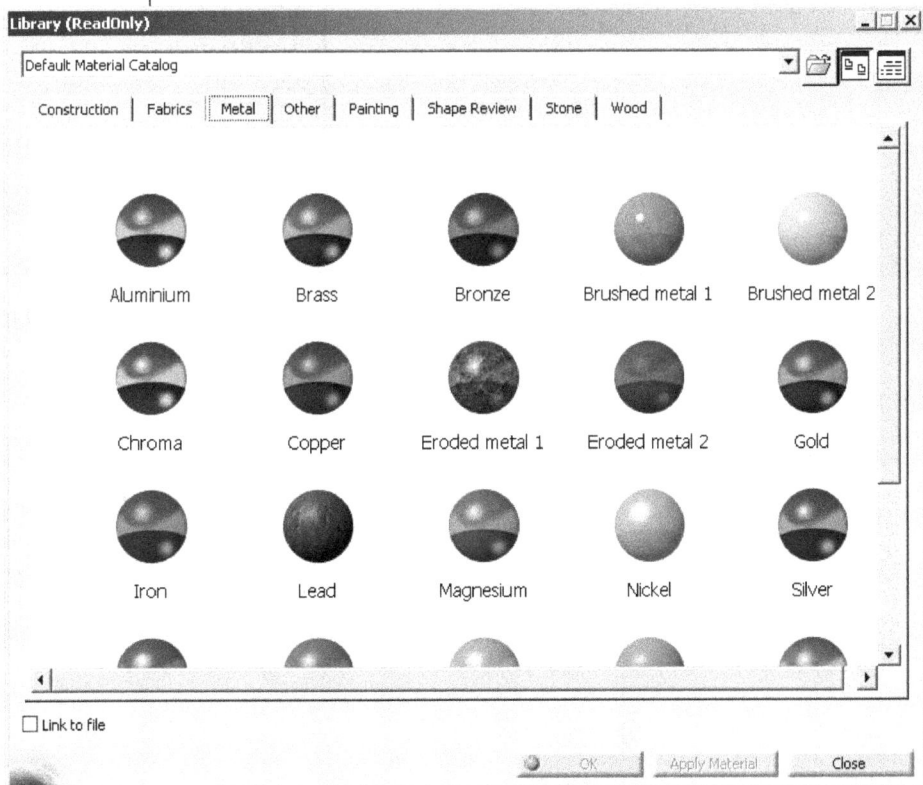

Figure 3–17

2. Double-click on a graphic representing the required material in the dialog box to view the material properties.
3. Select a material from the dialog box and drag it onto the part body or part number. The material is listed in the specification tree, as shown in Figure 3–18. All properties for the selected material are defined for the model to which the material is applied. The properties are also used in the inertia calculations.

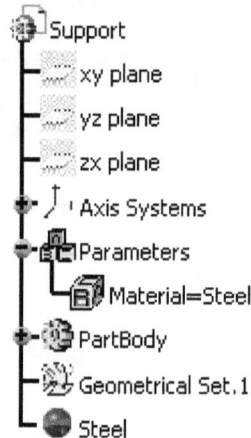

By placing the material into a part body, you can measure the inertia of each body. By placing the material into the part number, you apply one material to the entire part. To measure its inertia, you must select the part number in the specification tree.

Figure 3–18

Viewing the Material

The model can also be viewed in a custom View mode with the material rendering applied.

Click (Shading with Material) or select **View>Render Style>Customize View** to apply the material rendering to a model. The View Mode Customization dialog box opens as shown in Figure 3–19. Verify that the **Material** option is selected.

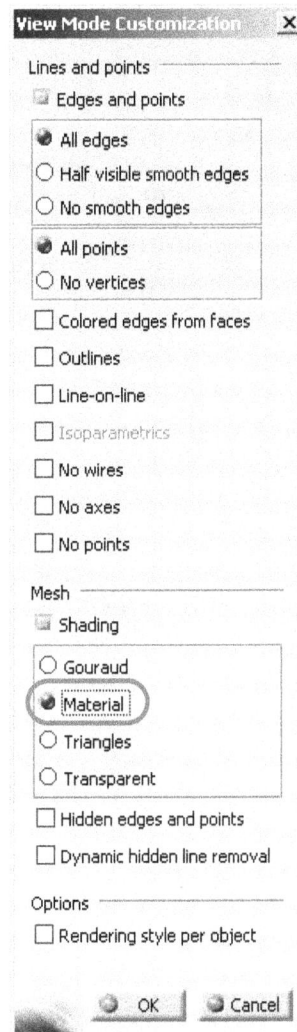

Figure 3–19

Measure Inertia 3D

The inertia of an object is defined as the property by which it retains its present velocity (speed and direction) so long as it is not acted upon by an external force. An equivalent definition of inertia is the resistance of an object to a change in its motion.

To compute the model inertia using the model's current material properties, select a model to create measurements for and click

![icon] (Measure Inertia) in the toolbar. With ![icon] (Measure Inertia 3D) selected, you can select 3D entities (such as features or bodies) in the specification tree and measure their inertia. The results display in the Measure Inertia dialog box, as shown in Figure 3–20.

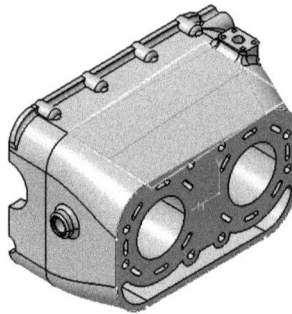

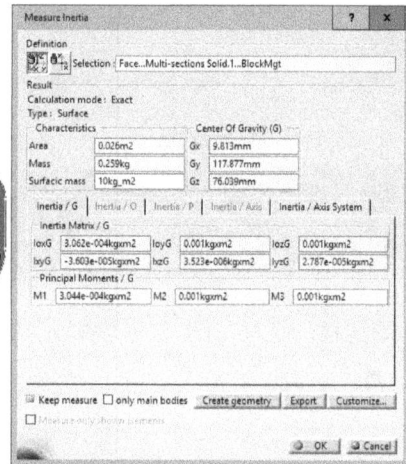

Figure 3–20

The dialog box reports the following information:

*   Characteristics, such as volume, area, mass, and density.

*   The center of gravity relative to the origin of the part.

*   Inertia data of the part.

The inertia data of the part can be measured with respect to a variety of elements by selecting one of the following tabs.

Tab	Meaning
Inertia / G	Measure inertia with respect to the center of gravity of the model.
Inertia / O	Measure inertia with respect to the origin of the model.
Inertia / P	Measure inertia with respect to a selected point.
Inertia / Axis	Measure inertia with respect to a selected axis.
Inertia / Axis System	Measure inertia with respect to a selected axis system.

The *Inertia / G* tab is activated by default. To activate the other four tabs, click **Customize** to open the Measure Inertia Customization dialog box shown in Figure 3–21.

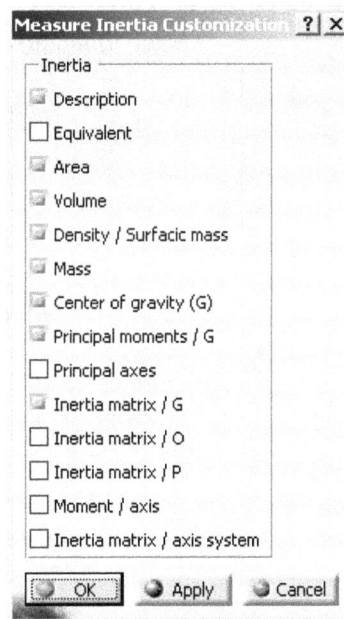

Figure 3–21

Each tab displays a variety of inertia data that is relevant to the measurement reference. For example, the following parameters are reported for an Inertia / G calculation.

Parameter	Meaning
Iox	Area moment of inertia about the X-axis.
Ioy	Area moment of inertia about the Y-axis.
Ioz	Area moment of inertia about the Z-axis.
Ixy	Mass moment of inertia on the XY plane.
Ixz	Mass moment of inertia on the XZ plane.
Iyz	Mass moment of inertia on the YZ plane.

The **Measure Inertia** tool also enables you to create a point and/or an axis system at the center of gravity in the part. To create geometry, click **Create geometry** in the Measure Inertia dialog box. The Creation of Geometry dialog box opens as shown in Figure 3–22.

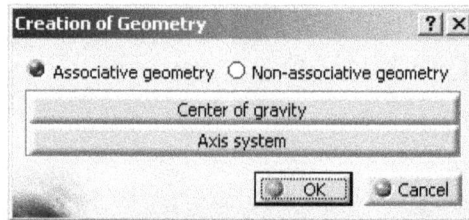

Figure 3–22

The results of the ***Measure Inertia*** *tool can be saved and customized using the same method as the* ***Measure Item*** *tool.*

Figure 3–23 shows an example of an axis system and a point at the center of gravity that has been created using the **Create geometry** tool.

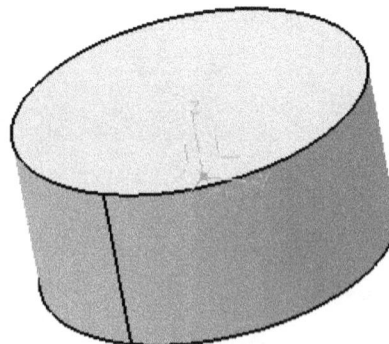

Figure 3–23

Measure Inertia 2D

Measuring the inertia of a section or surface is useful for rapidly determining the structural properties of complex shapes. With

![icon] (Measure Inertia 2D) selected, you can select solid faces from the model and measure their two-dimensional inertia properties. This tool is identical to its 3D counterpart, except that certain calculations that do not apply to two-dimensional surfaces (mass, density, volume, etc.) are not present, as shown in Figure 3–24.

Only the Inertia / G tab is available when measuring in 2D.

*Note that **Create geometry** is not available when measuring inertia in 2D.*

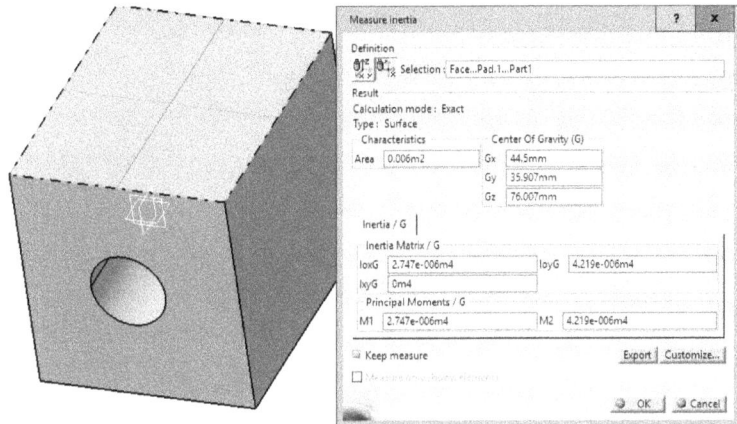

Figure 3–24

3.5 Dynamic Sectioning

The Dynamic Sectioning enables you to position a section plane to visualize a 3D section view of a part, as shown in Figure 3–25. The section plan can be dynamically adjusted.

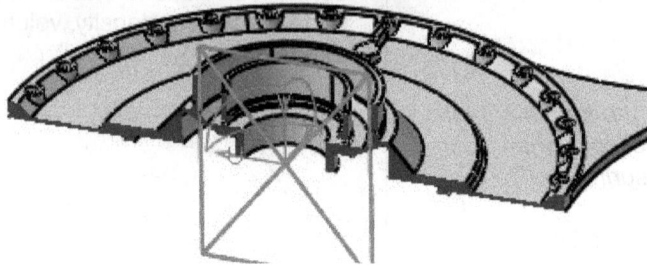

Figure 3–25

To use the Dynamic Sectioning tool, click [icon] (Dynamic Sectioning) from the Dynamic Sectioning toolbar. A red section plane is automatically displayed on the model.

The location of the section plane can dynamically be modified. To adjust the position, select an edge, surface, plane, or curve in the model. If you are selecting a reference in the model, a purple section plane locater icon displays, as shown in Figure 3–26.

Section plane locater

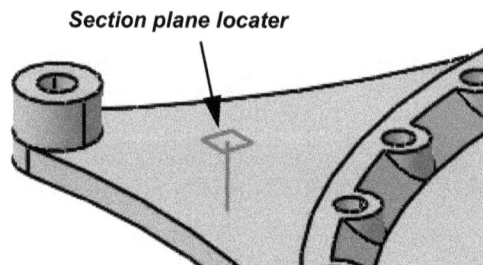

Figure 3–26

To translate the section plane along about the selected reference, hover the cursor over the red section plane, as shown in Figure 3–27. When the green arrow displays, click and drag the plane to the required location. The model is dynamically cut about the section plane as you click and drag.

To rotate the section plane, hover the cursor over one of the red arcs on the section plane compass. Click the arc, and drag the section plane to the required location, as shown in Figure 3–28.

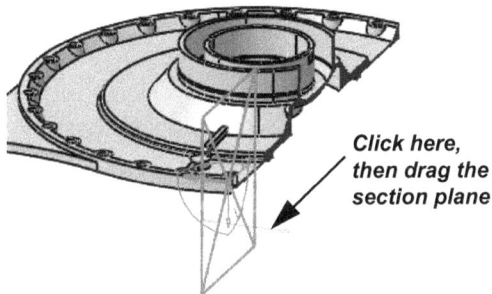

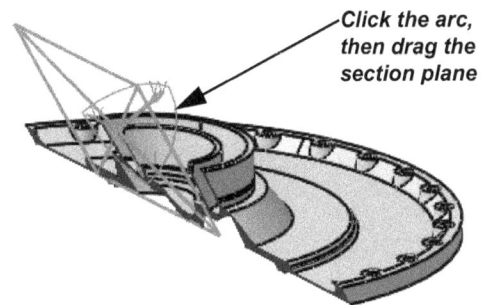

Click the arc, then drag the section plane

Click here, then drag the section plane

Figure 3–27　　　　　　　　**Figure 3–28**

The section plane can be adjusted repeatedly. When done using the Dynamic Sectioning tool, deactivate by clicking the **Dynamic Sectioning** icon.

3.6 Feature Investigation

CATIA provides several tools to investigate a model. The investigation tools can be used to determine how a model is constructed. These tools are useful if:

- A model is created by someone else.

- It has been a long time since you worked on the part.

- The model is complex and you need to modify the feature structure.

Scanning the Model

Scanning the model enables you to review the construction history of a model, one feature at a time. This is helpful when working with models that are created by other users. The **Scan** tool enables you to review and replay the design, giving you an idea of the model creator's design intent and modeling techniques.

To use the **Scan** tool, select **Edit>Scan or Define In Work Object**. The Scan dialog box opens, as shown in Figure 3–29. Use the control icons to play, step forward, rewind, or stop the model at the current feature creation location.

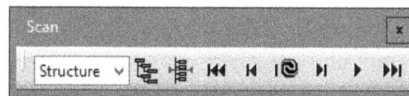

Figure 3–29

By default, the **Structure** option is selected in the Scan dialog box. With this setting, the software replays the features of the active body based on the feature order displayed in the specification tree. Features in other bodies or geometrical sets are not replayed.

If the **Update** option is selected, the software replays the features in the model in the order in which they are updated, as shown in Figure 3–30.

Figure 3–30

Figure 3–31 shows an example of a part that was created by first adding a reference plane that was used as a support for **Sketch.1**. The scan order, based on the **Structure** or **Update** option, is shown in Figure 3–31.

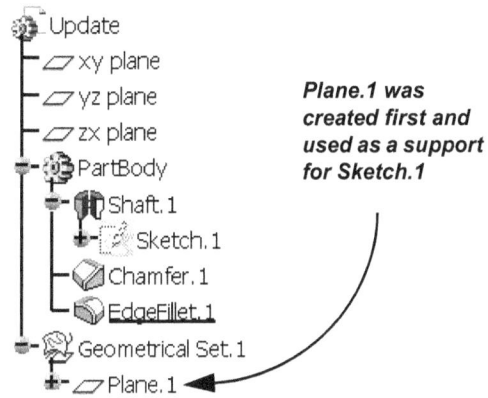

Plane.1 was created first and used as a support for Sketch.1

Figure 3–31

	Structure	Update
1	Shaft	Plane.1
2	Chamfer	Sketch.1
3	EdgeFillet.1	Shaft.1
4	**End**	Chamfer.1
5		EdgeFillet.1
6		**End**

Practice 3a

Take Measurements

Practice Objectives

- Review the feature creation history.
- Assign a material to the part.
- Determine the mass, volume, and surface area of the part.

In this practice, you will use the **Scan** tool to view the model's creation history. You will also assign a material to the part, take measurements of the part, and analyze some of its properties, such as mass and volume.

Task 1 - Open a part and scan the model.

Design Considerations

Scanning the model is another way of reviewing its creation history. This is often a helpful tool if you did not create the model, but need to update it. The **Scan** tool enables you to review the creation process and grasp the original designer's design intent.

1. Open **Support_Info.CATPart**. Note the feature order in the specification tree to review how the model is created.

2. Select **Edit>Scan or Define In Work Object** to activate the **Scan** tool.

3. Click [◄◄] to reset the model to the first feature created. The model displays as shown in Figure 3–32. A Pad is the first feature created for the model.

4. Click [▶I] and note the addition of a second Pad feature.

5. Click [▶] to automatically play the addition of the remaining features, as shown in Figure 3–33.

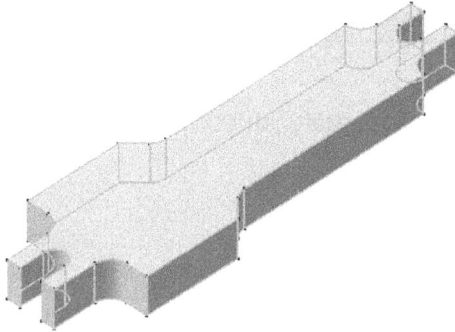

Figure 3–32

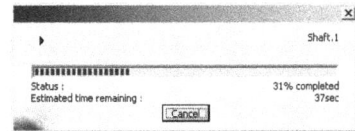

Figure 3–33

6. Close the **Scan** tool.

Task 2 - Review some of the parent/child relations in the model.

---

1. Expand PartBody in the specification tree to display the features under **PartBody**.

2. A design change requires that the Shaft support of **Pad.6** be modified. Before making modifications, it is recommended to review which child features rely on **Pad.6** as a parent. Select the **Pad.6** feature in the specification tree, right-click and select **Parents/Children**. The Parents and Children dialog box opens, as shown in Figure 3–34.

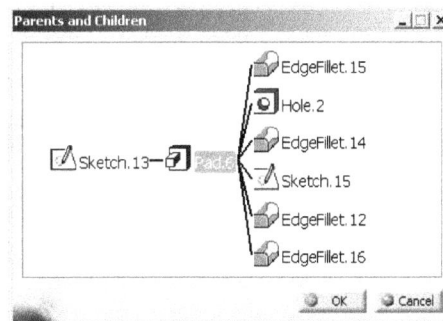

Figure 3–34

All items listed on the right side of **Pad.6** are child features that reference **Pad.6**. Modifications to **Pad.6** might result in modifications or failures with the child features. The parent feature (**Sketch.13**) is listed on the left side of **Pad.6**.

3. Double-click on various items in the dialog box to see further levels of the parent/child relations.

Task 3 - Assign iron as the model material before you calculate inertia.

1. Click (Apply Material) to open the material library.

2. Select the *Metal* tab.

3. Drag ᵢᵣₒₙ (Iron) onto the model and click **OK** in the Library dialog box.

4. Double-click on the Iron feature listed in the specification tree, as shown in Figure 3–35.

Figure 3–35

5. The Iron Properties dialog box populates with the feature properties. Review the properties and note the density value. Close the dialog box.

Task 4 - Display the model with iron material.

1. Click (Shading with Material). The model is rendered with the material applied to it, as shown in Figure 3–36.

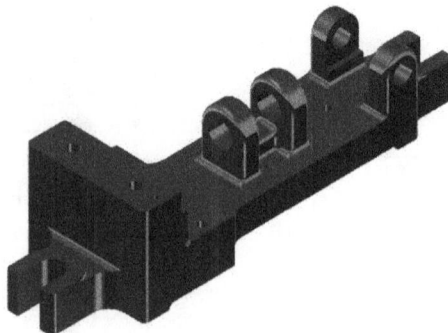

Figure 3–36

Task 5 - View inertia results using the iron material properties.

1. Select the part body in the specification tree and click

   ![icon] (Measure Inertia) to measure the model inertia. The resulting data displays in the Measure Inertia dialog box, as shown in Figure 3–37.

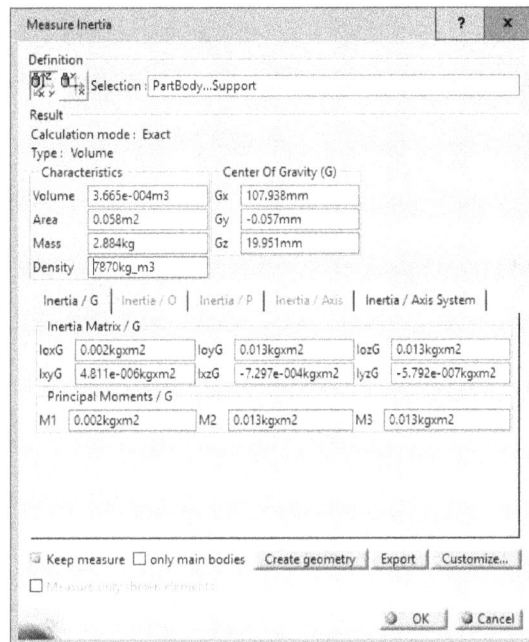

Figure 3–37

Note that the density value displayed is that of iron, shown in the Properties dialog box from Task 4. Note the surface area value. This might be important if the part is powder-coated or plated. Also note the volume value. This might be important in calculating the material cost of molded or cast parts.

2. Review the other measurements that are calculated. Close the dialog box.

3. Change the View mode back to ![icon] (Shading with Edges), as required.

Task 6 - Measure inertia with respect to an axis system.

1. Expand the specification tree right-click on **Axis System.1** and select **Hide/Show**.

2. Select the PartBody in the specification tree and click

   ![icon] (Measure Inertia) to measure the model inertia.

3. Click **Customize** and select the **Inertia matrix / axis system** option, as shown in Figure 3–38.

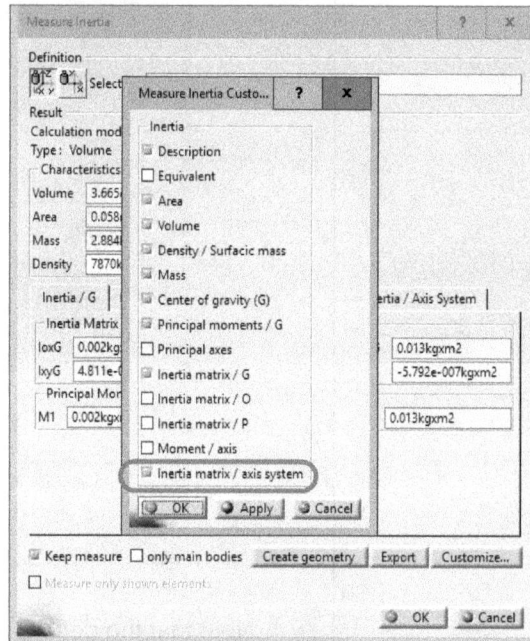

Figure 3–38

4. Click **OK** and select the *Inertia / Axis System* tab.

5. Select the **Select Axis System** option and select **Axis System.1** as the axis system, as shown in Figure 3–39.

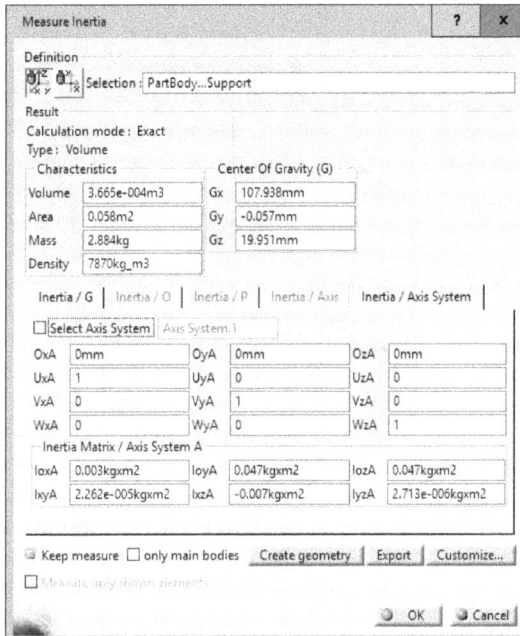

Figure 3–39

6. Note how the values of the Inertia Matrix are different than the values measured in the *Inertia / G* tab

7. Close the dialog box.

Task 7 - Measure inertia in 2D.

1. Click (Measure Inertia) to measure the model inertia.

2. Click (Measure Inertia 2D).

3. Select the surface shown in Figure 3–40. The Measure Inertia dialog box opens as shown in Figure 3–41.

Select this face

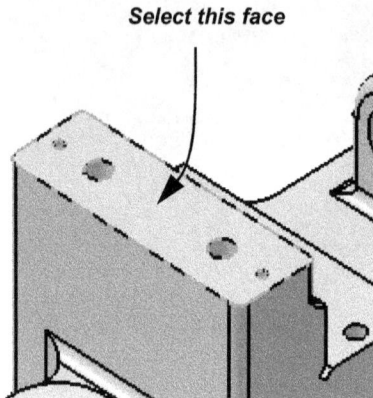

Figure 3–40

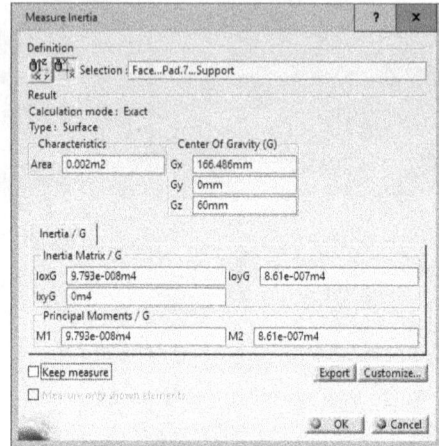

Figure 3–41

4. Note that some information that is present when measuring 3D inertia is not available when measuring 2D inertia. This includes information such as the volume, density, and the different inertia tabs (*Inertia / O*, *Inertia / P*, etc.).

5. Close the dialog box.

Task 8 - Take a series of one-click measurements.

1. Click ▣ (Measure Item) to make some one-click measurements.

2. Select the cylindrical surface shown in Figure 3–42. Note that both the area and radius display.

*If the units for the area calculation are incorrect, select **Tools>Options> Parameters and Measure**, select the Units tab and set the Area units to square meter.*

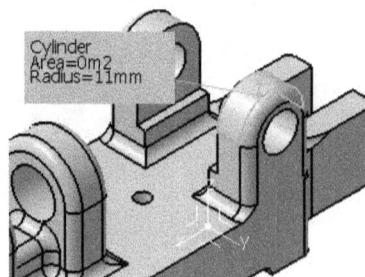

Figure 3–42

Design Considerations

Note that you obtain an area of 0m^2. This is because the area of the cylindrical surface is relatively small. You can determine the correct area by changing the number of decimal places displayed for measurement.

3. Select **Tools>Options>Parameters and Measure>**_Units_ tab.

4. Select **Area** in the _Units_ field.

5. Change the value in the _Decimal places for read/write numbers_ field to **7**, as shown in Figure 3–43.

Decimal places cannot be set globally. You must set the number of decimal places for each type of unit individually.

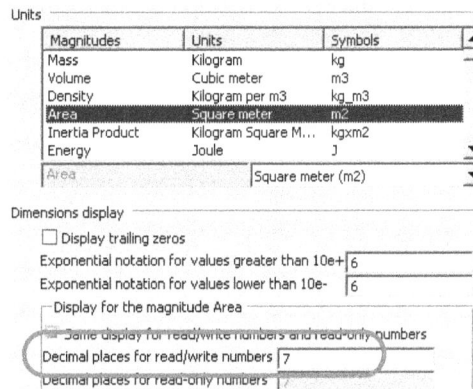

Magnitudes	Units	Symbols
Mass	Kilogram	kg
Volume	Cubic meter	m3
Density	Kilogram per m3	kg_m3
Area	Square meter	m2
Inertia Product	Kilogram Square M...	kgxm2
Energy	Joule	J

Area — Square meter (m2)

Dimensions display

☐ Display trailing zeros
Exponential notation for values greater than 10e+ 6
Exponential notation for values lower than 10e- 6

Display for the magnitude Area

Same display for read/write numbers and read-only numbers
Decimal places for read/write numbers 7
Decimal places for read-only numbers 7

Figure 3–43

6. Click **OK** to close the Options dialog box.

7. Repeat the measurement of the cylindrical surface. The results display as shown in Figure 3–44.

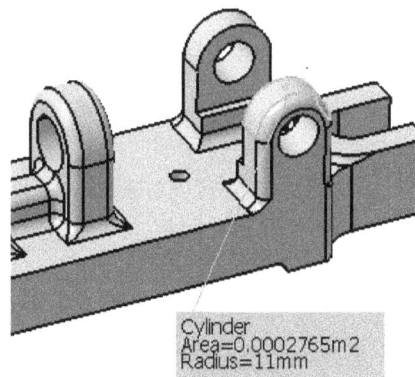

Cylinder
Area=0.0002765m2
Radius=11mm

Figure 3–44

8. Take additional one-click measure item measurements for different items in the model, including flat surfaces, the part body, and a vertex.

9. Close the Measure Item dialog box.

Task 9 - Take a series of measure between measurements.

1. Click ⟷ (Measure Between) to take some measure between measurements.

2. Activate the Standard Measure Between mode by clicking ⟷ (Standard) in the Measure Between dialog box.

3. Select the flat face and hole axis to measure between, as shown in Figure 3–45.

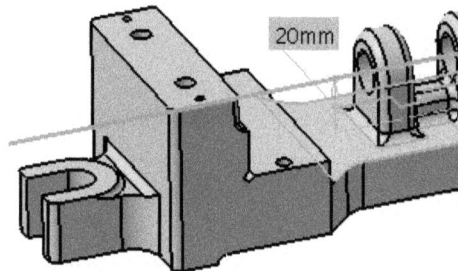

Figure 3–45

4. Note that the Angle dimension is calculated in the dialog box but not on the model. This dimension is not required.

5. Click **Customize** to customize the results.

6. Clear the **Angle** option in the *Panel* column in the Measure Between Customization dialog box.

7. Click **Apply** and **OK**.

8. Repeat Step 3 for a different flat face and hole axis. Note that only the distance is measured and displayed in both the dialog box and on the model.

9. Practice making additional measurements using Standard mode.

10. Set the named view to top by clicking ⬛ (Top).

11. Activate the **Chain Mode Measure Between** tool by clicking ⬛ (Chain) in the Measure Between dialog box.

12. Enable the **Keep Measure** option.

13. Select **Edge 1** and **Hole 1**, as shown in Figure 3–46.

14. Once the measurement displays, continue to select **Hole 2**, followed by **Hole 3**, **Hole 4**, and finally **Edge 2**. The measurements display in order, as shown in Figure 3–47.

Edge 1   Hole 1   Hole 2   Hole 3   Hole 4   Edge 2

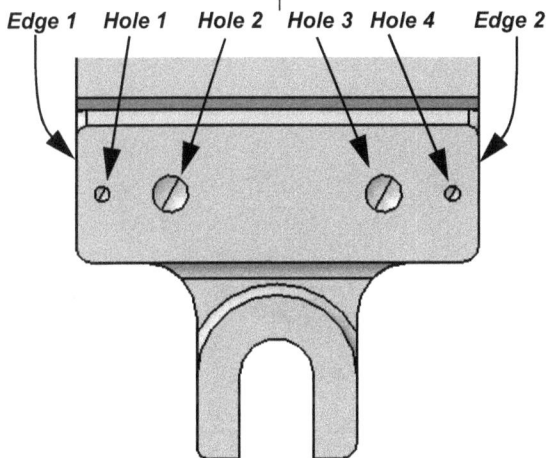

Figure 3–46

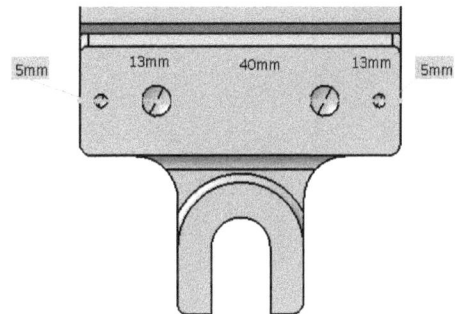

Figure 3–47

*To show all measurements at once, select the **Keep Measure** option in the Measure Between dialog box to save measurements with model data.*

15. Hide the parameters you have just created.

16. Activate the Fan Mode Measure Between tool by clicking ⬛ (Fan) in the Measure Between dialog box.

17. Repeat steps 12 to 13 and compare the results with the results in Figure 3–47.

18. Hide the parameters you have just created.

19. Click ⬛ (Save).

20. Select **File>Close**.

Practice 3b

Measuring with Reference Geometry

Practice Objective

• Create reference geometry to perform measure operations.

In this practice, you will develop packaging for the game controller as shown in Figure 3–48. To create a box for the part, you will first determine the maximum width, height, and length of the model. To do this, you will develop reference geometry, such as points and planes, to assist in your measurements.

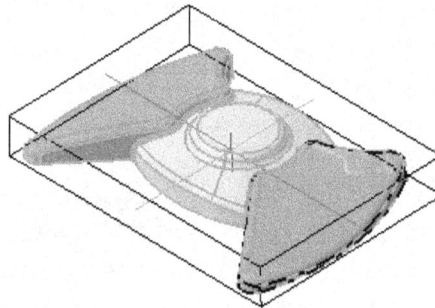

Figure 3–48

Task 1 - Open GameController.CATPart and take a measurement.

1. Open **GameController.CATPart**.

2. Click (Standard) and measure between the two arc edges on the bottom of the model, to obtain the overall height of the model, as shown in Figure 3–49.

   The software reports the distance between the centers of the two arcs, as shown in Figure 3–50. To obtain the overall height of the part, 153.355mm (6.038 in), additional reference geometry must be developed.

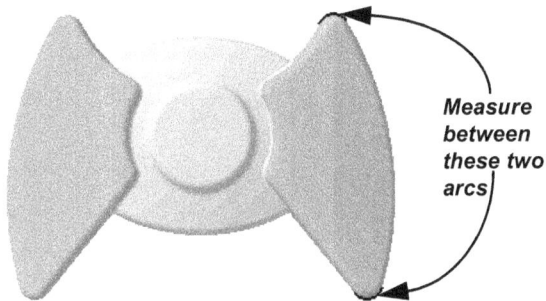

Figure 3–49

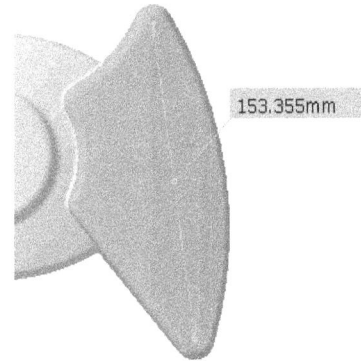

153.355mm

Figure 3–50

3. Cancel the measurement.

Task 2 - Create reference geometry.

In this task, you will build reference points that mark the extremities of the two arc edges previously measured. The **Tangent on curve** option is used in this case, as it forces the software to locate the outermost point of the selected curve when viewed from the selected plane.

1. Create a reference point using the following parameters:

   - *Point Type:* Tangent on curve
   - *Curve:* Select the arc edge shown in Figure 3–51.
   - *Direction:* ZX plane

   The resulting point displays as shown in Figure 3–52.

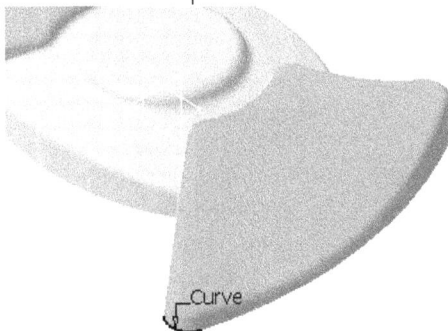

Curve

Figure 3–51

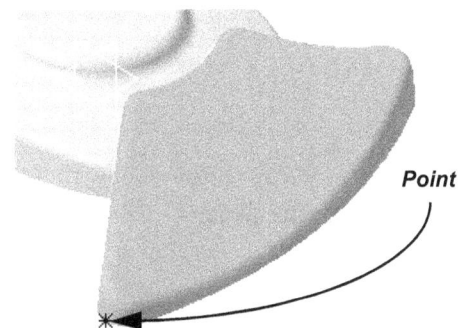

Point

Figure 3–52

2. Repeat this process to create a point on the top arc edge. The point displays as shown in Figure 3–53.

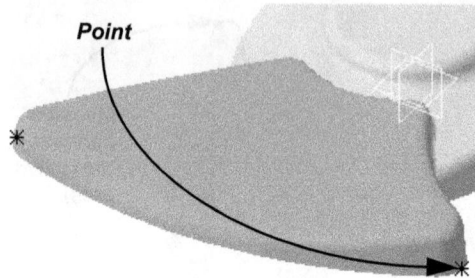

Point

Figure 3–53

Task 3 - Take a measurement between points.

---

1. Repeat the Measure Between operation, selecting the two points created. The resulting measurement, 173.194 mm (6.819 in), displays as shown in Figure 3–54.

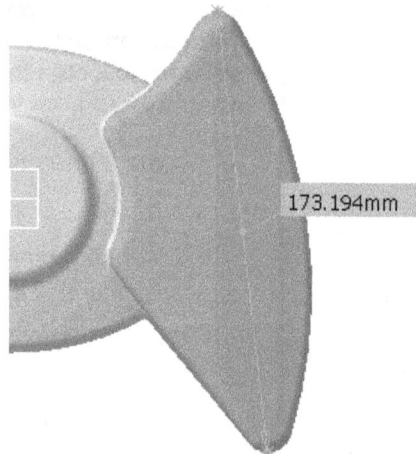

173.194mm

Figure 3–54

Design Considerations

The measurement still does not show the true height of the model. Since it cannot be guaranteed that the two points are vertically aligned, you can use the **Measure Between** tool to obtain the components of the measured distance.

2. Click **Customize** and enable the **Components** option in both the *3D* and the *Panel* columns. The dialog box updates to display the X, Y, and Z components of the measurement. The true height of the model is approximately 171.96mm (6.770 in).

Task 4 - Use reference planes to display distance in one direction.

In this task, you will build reference planes through the point elements. Measuring between two reference planes ensures that the measured distance is in the exact required direction. This also enables you to keep only the required component(s) of a measurement and display it on the model.

1. Create a reference plane using the following options:

    • *Plane type:* **Parallel through point**
    • *Reference:* **YZ plane**
    • *Point:* **Point.1**

    The completed reference plane displays as shown in Figure 3–55.

2. Create a second reference plane that is parallel to the YZ plane and through Point.2. The model displays as shown in Figure 3–56.

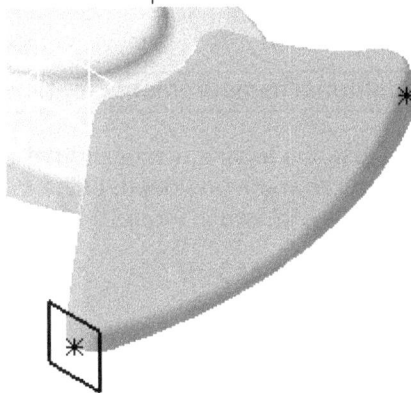

Figure 3–55

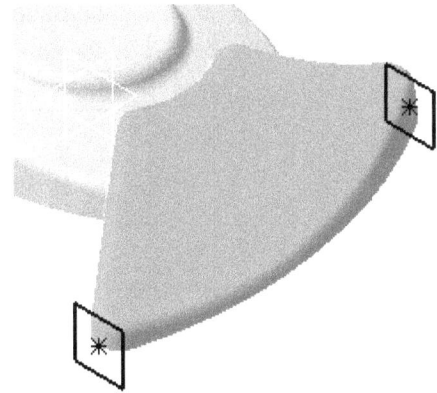

Figure 3–56

3. Measure between the two reference planes just created. Ensure that the **Keep Measure** option is enabled. The model displays the dimension 171.961mm (6.770 in), as shown in Figure 3–57.

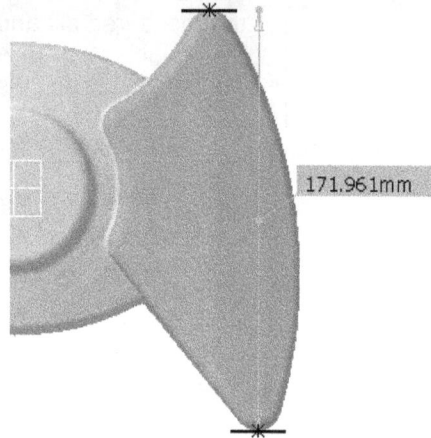

171.961mm

Figure 3–57

4. Save the model and close the file.

Task 5 - Take additional measurements (optional).

1. If time permits, use the techniques described in this practice to determine the true width and depth of the model. The measured values are shown in Figure 3–58.

- *Width:* **241.62mm (9.513 in)**
- *Depth:* **30.28mm (1.192 in)**

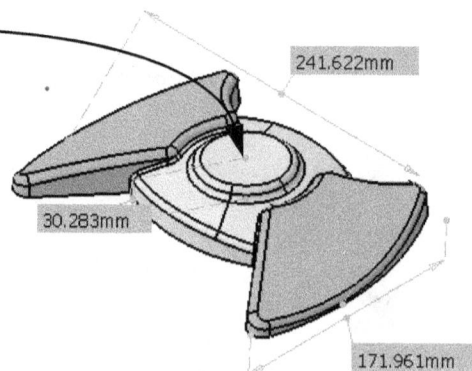

Assume that the highest point on the model is at the center.

241.622mm

30.283mm

171.961mm

Figure 3–58

2. Save the model and close the file.

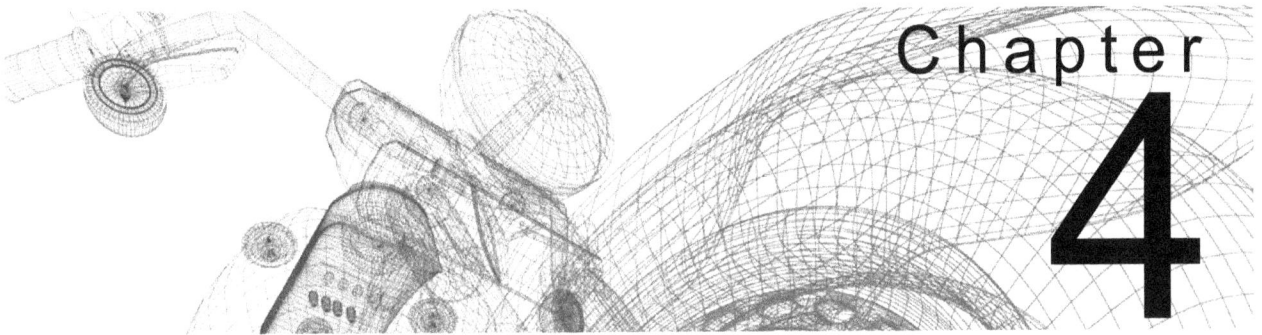

Assembly Design

This chapter covers how to activate the Assembly workbench and access assembly-specific toolbars. This chapter also guides you through the process of creating an assembly and describes the available assembly constraints.

Learning Objectives in this Chapter

- Learn about the Assembly Workbench interface.
- Create an assembly and add components to it.
- Understand product properties and assembly product structure.
- Use the compass to move components.
- Automatically snap objects to the compass.
- Understand the various constraints available for parametrically locating components.
- Understand what PDM systems are and their benefits.

4.1 Assembly Workbench

*The terms **Product** and **Assembly** can be used interchangeably.*

In the Part workbench, features are created in the model to build the final part. In the Assembly workbench, components can be added to a product file to create an assembly. To activate the Assembly workbench, use one of the following methods:

- Select **Start>Mechanical Design>Assembly Design**.

- Click (Assembly Design) in the Workbench toolbar.

- Select **File>New>Product**.

A CATIA V5 assembly file is identified with the .CATProduct file extension. Assembly-specific toolbars become available once the Product workbench is enabled.

Commonly Used Toolbars

The Assembly Workbench contains various toolbars. These are described as follows:

- The Product Structure toolbar controls how new components are added to the assembly. This toolbar is shown in Figure 4–1.

- The Constraints toolbar controls the relative position of components in the assembly. This toolbar is shown in Figure 4–2.

Figure 4–1

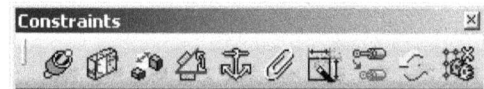

Figure 4–2

- The **Update All** option in the Update toolbar updates the position of components as assembly constraints are applied or if constraints have been modified. The options is shown in Figure 4–3.

- The Measure toolbar enables you to perform various analyses within the assembly. This toolbar is shown in Figure 4–4.

Figure 4–3

Figure 4–4

4.2 Create an Assembly

How To: Create a New Assembly

1. Create a new product file by activating the Assembly Design workbench.
2. Modify any product properties (i.e., defining part numbers).
3. Add components to the assembly using the Product Structure Tools.
4. Position components using the compass and/or using parametric constraints.
5. Add assembly features to the model or modify parts within the context of the assembly.
6. Analyze and extract any critical information from the assembly.
7. Prepare the assembly for drawing creation.
8. Create the drawing showing the assembly.

Product Properties

When a new product file is created, the software assigns a default filename and part number. The filename takes the form of Product#, where # is the number of new Product in session.

The filename is also the default part number. To change the part number, select **Edit>Properties**. The Properties dialog box opens as shown in Figure 4–5.

You can also change the part number using the shortcut menu.

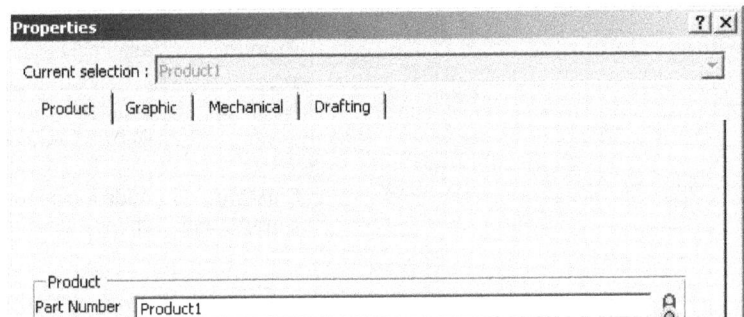

Figure 4–5

Adding Components

A component is an object that is added to an assembly. The following components can be added to a *.CATProduct assembly.

- *.CATPart

- *.CATProduct

- *.model (V4)

- *.iges

Components can be added to the assembly in the following ways:

- Select the assembly in the specification tree and use the shortcut menu.

- Use the icons in the Product Structure Tools toolbar.

- Use the **Insert** menu in the menu bar.

The following icons are found in the Product Structure toolbar.

Icon	Option	Description
	New Component	Creates a new component that has no file associated with it.
	New Product	Creates a new subassembly in the top-level assembly with its own CATProduct file.
	New Part	Creates a new part in the top-level assembly with its own CATPart file.
	Existing Component	Adds a component to the assembly whose file already exists at the operating system level.

- When using the **Existing Component** option, multiple objects can be added to the assembly at the same time by pressing <Ctrl> or <Shift> while selecting objects.

Product Structure

The product structure of an assembly consists of the top level assembly (.CATProduct), components (.CATParts), and subassemblies (.CATProducts) as shown in Figure 4–6.

- The active level in the product structure is highlighted in blue in the specification tree. When performing actions on a top level or subassembly (such as Inserting Components), the active level of the product structure is affected by the actions performed.

- To activate a subassembly, double-click on the subassembly from the specification tree.

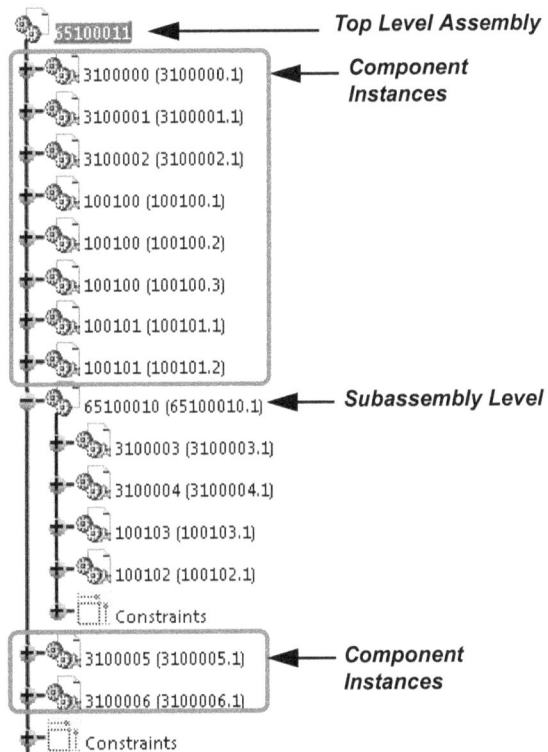

Figure 4–6

- Once components are added to the assembly, they display in the specification tree. The part number and the instance name in parenthesis is listed, as shown in Figure 4–7.

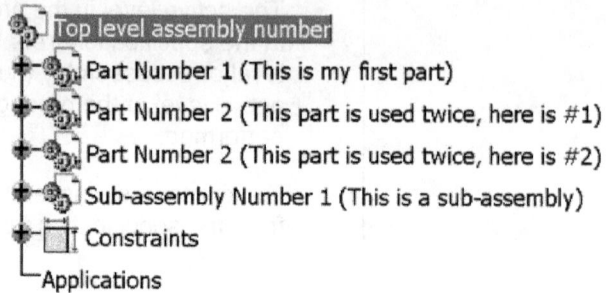

Figure 4–7

- In this example, Part Number 2 is used twice in the assembly. The instance name in parenthesis is the unique identifier for each time the part number is used in the assembly.

- Both the part number and the instance name can be modified by right-clicking and selecting **Properties**.

- If you need to investigate the CATPart specification tree, expand the specification tree for the component.

4.3 Use the Compass

Once existing components are added to the assembly, the components display in a default position and orientation. The compass is used to move components in the main window.

General Steps

Use the following general steps to move selected components with the compass:

1. Activate a component to move.
2. Move the component.
3. Complete the movement.

Step 1 - Activate a component to move.

Hover the cursor over the red dot in the compass until the cursor changes to a move symbol, as shown in Figure 4–8. Once the move symbol displays, press the left mouse button to move the compass.

Once the move symbol displays, press the left mouse button to move the compass.

Figure 4–8

Drag the compass to the component to be moved. The compass will snap and reorient to geometry belonging to the component, as shown in Figure 4–9. Once the orientation is correct, release the left mouse button to place the compass.

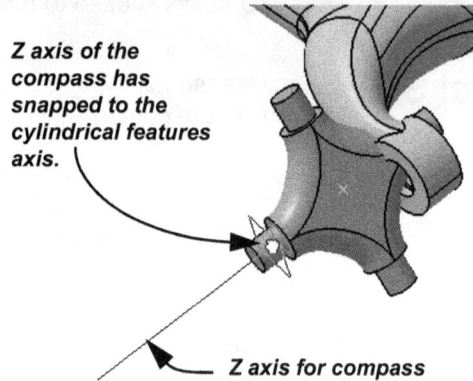

Z axis of the compass has snapped to the cylindrical features axis.

Z axis for compass

Figure 4–9

Once the compass has snapped to a component, the compass turns green. If the compass does not turn green, verify that the active model in the specification tree is an assembly. Then, select the component from the model or specification tree to activate movement of the selected component. You can activate any component for movement; it does not need to be the component the compass is snapped to.

You can also activate multiple components by selecting them while pressing <Ctrl>.

Automatic Snap

You can automatically snap the compass to a selected object by right-clicking and selecting **Snap Automatically to Selected Object**, as shown in Figure 4–10.

Ensure that this option is toggled off once you have finished moving components.

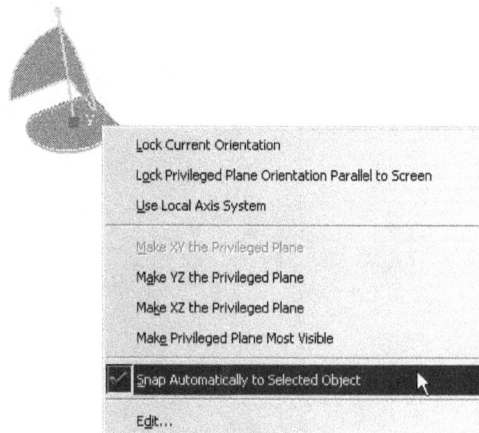

Lock Current Orientation
Lock Privileged Plane Orientation Parallel to Screen
Use Local Axis System

Make XY the Privileged Plane
Make YZ the Privileged Plane
Make XZ the Privileged Plane
Make Privileged Plane Most Visible

Snap Automatically to Selected Object

Edit...

Figure 4–10

Once the option is activated, select from the model or component you want to move. The compass automatically snaps to the selected component, as shown in Figure 4–11.

The software automatically selects the orientation of the compass based on the origin of the selected component.

Compass snaps to selected component automatically and turns green

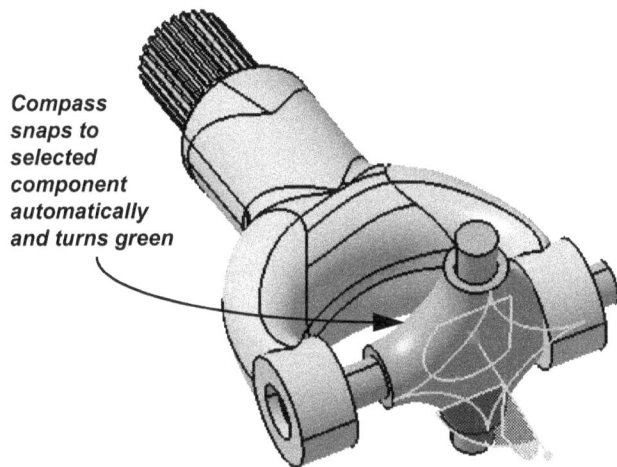

Figure 4–11

Step 2 - Move the component.

Once the compass is activated on the component, only compass movements control the selected component(s). To move components while accounting for the placement constraints, hold <Shift> while pressing the left mouse button. Note that more than one component might move, depending on how the constraints are defined.

*It is recommended to restore any changed values to 0 once you have completed the **Move** operation. This ensures that further operations do not snap to the previous increment values.*

More precise movements of a component can be achieved by right-clicking on the compass and selecting **Edit**. The Parameters for Compass Manipulation dialog box, shown in Figure 4–12, enables you to enter exact translation or rotational increment values for precise movements.

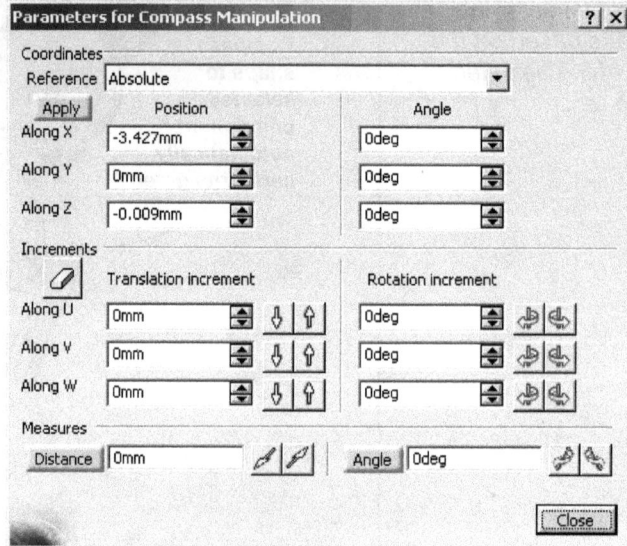

Figure 4–12

Step 3 - Complete the movement.

Once the component has been moved to the correct location, complete the movement by selecting another component to move or clicking anywhere on the screen to deactivate the compass control. The compass returns to its default color and controls the entire assembly. To return the compass to its default position, select **View>Reset Compass**, or drag the compass off the model and move it anywhere in the background of the screen.

4.4 Constraints

Constraints are specified to locate components parametrically with respect to existing components. Any references made to other components when constraining creates parent/child relationships. The available constraints are described as follows:

Icon	Name	Description
	Coincidence	Aligns axes, planes, or points.
	Contact	Mates two planar surfaces. Can also force curved surfaces to touch. Note that reference planes cannot be used as a contact surface.
	Offset	Specifies an offset distance between two planar elements.
	Angle	Permits a typed in value between planar selections. Parallel and perpendicular can also be specified.
	Fix	Fastens a component in the assembly space. It has no other constraints to components.
	Fix Together	*Welds* components together.
	Quick Constraint	Enables the software to automatically select which constraint to use based on your selection. This constraint can be changed later.

Coincidence

Once additional components are added to the assembly, how they are constrained is dependent on their geometry. Coincidence can be used to align axes and planes. Figure 4–13 shows a T-brace positioned over the mounting block by using the coincidence constraint and selecting the axis of the holes. The T-brace can be further constrained by using the coincidence constraint and selecting planar surfaces, as shown in Figure 4–14.

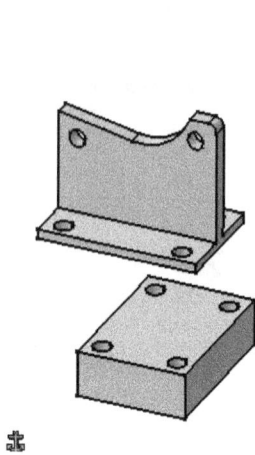
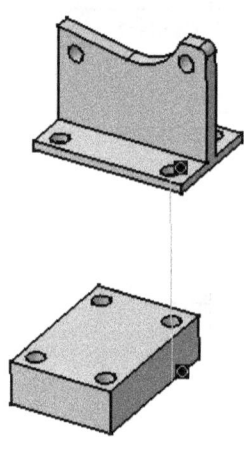
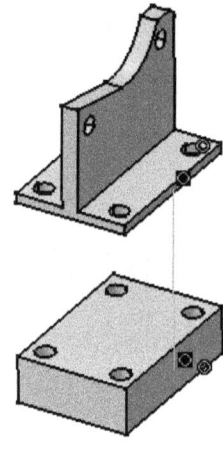

Figure 4–13   **Figure 4–14**

When specifying the coincidence constraint with planar surfaces, you can change the orientation of the surfaces, as shown in Figure 4–15.

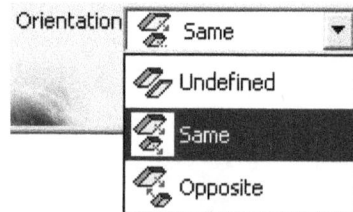

Figure 4–15

Contact

Contact mates two surfaces. Figure 4–16 shows a T-brace fully constrained after mating the top surface of the mounting block with the underside surface of the T-brace.

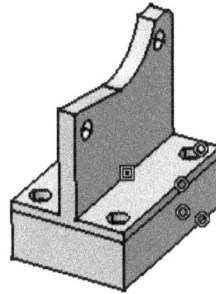

Figure 4–16

Offset

Offset behaves like contact or align with planar surfaces, without the selections being coplanar. The selections are parallel with a specified offset distance. Figure 4–17 shows a bolt offset from the T-brace to permit space for future washer placement. Similar to coincidence, the direction of orientation can be specified.

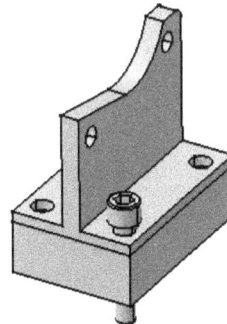

Figure 4–17

Angle

Figure 4–18 shows an example of a finger that is assembled with a coincidence constraint. Note the intersecting geometry.

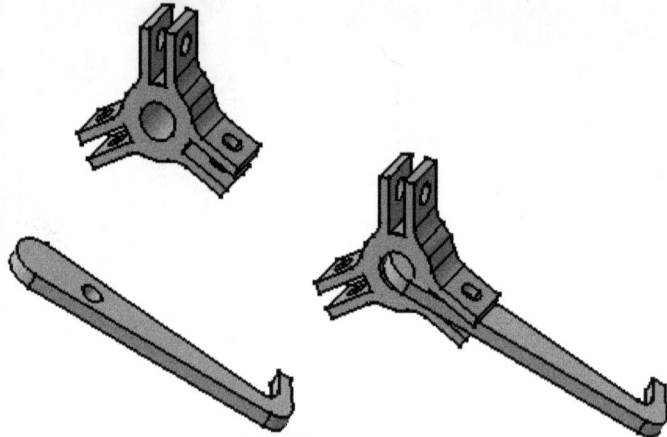

Figure 4–18

The angle constraint is used to show the correct orientation of components. Figure 4–19 shows an example where interference exists. The finger component is under-constrained; therefore, a parallel or angle constraint must be added. The parallel and angle options are shown in Figure 4–19.

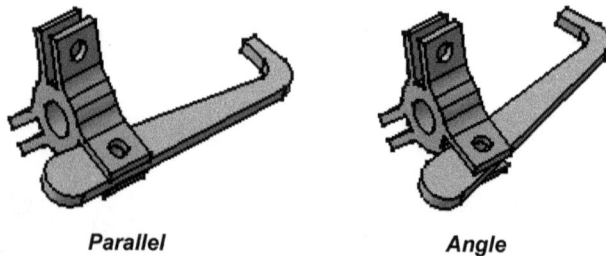

Parallel   *Angle*

Figure 4–19

Fix Component

In CATIA, the base component is usually constrained to be fixed. This essentially creates a zero position of reference. Once constrained to be fixed, the *Constraints* area displays in the specification tree, as shown in Figure 4–20, and 🔧 displays.

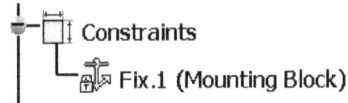

Figure 4–20

Fix Together

Fix together is normally used to fix any remaining degrees of freedom from an under-constrained component. The components behave as a single body in space.

When moving components assembled with a fix together constraint, press <Shift> while using the compass. This forces CATIA to obey the assembly constraints during the move. If a component is moved without pressing <Shift>, the fix together constraint updates based on the new locations.

Quick Constraint

Quick constraint enables the software to decide which constraint to use on a component. If planar surfaces are selected, CATIA might select a coincidence, offset, or contact constraint. If the required constraint is not selected, you can click 🔄 (Change Constraint) in the toolbar and select the correct constraint in the Possible Constraints dialog box, as shown in Figure 4–21.

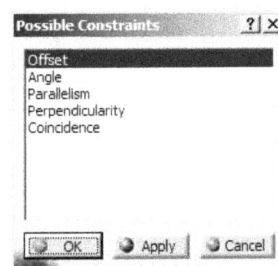

Figure 4–21

Assembly Considerations

When modeling parts, consider what feature form best captures the design intent of the base feature. When working with assemblies, consider which component is best suited for use as the base component.

Additionally, consider the active level of the product structure. If the top level of the structure is active (highlighted in blue), then the constraint you are creating will be grouped with the top level assembly constraints.

If you want to create a constraint specific to the components in a subassembly, double-click on the subassembly level in the specification tree to activate it. When you create the constraint, it is grouped with the subassembly constraints. The product structure, top level assembly constraints, and subassembly constraints are shown in Figure 4–22.

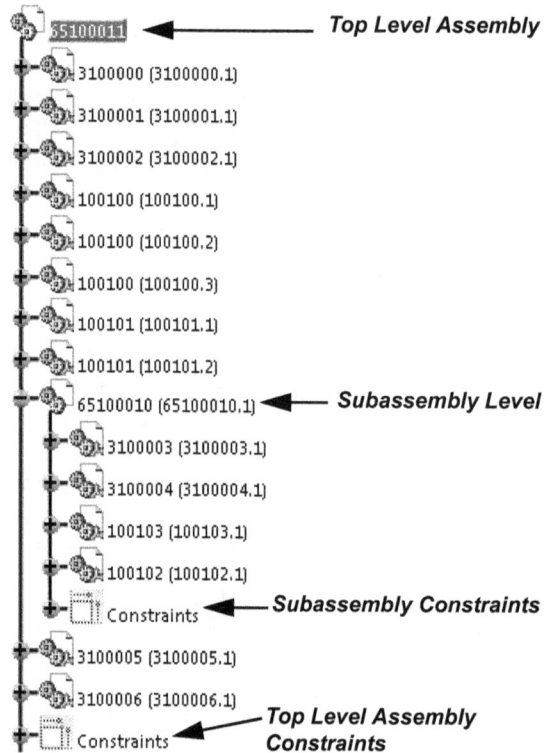

Figure 4–22

4.5 Product Data Management

What is PDM?

Product Data Management (PDM) is a type of software that organizes and manages files in a database. Files in a PDM system are related to the development of a product. While most of these files are engineering-related, it is not limited to managing engineering data.

Types of files that a PDM system can organize depend on the specific PDM software being used. Some examples include:

- Parts
- Assemblies
- Drawings
- Metadata
- Spreadsheets
- Word processing documents

These files are stored on a server commonly referred to as the vault. From here, you open files and save them back to the server. The PDM system keeps track and controls all file operations. Multiple users can view the file at the same time, but only one person can work on it.

Common capabilities of a PDM system include:

- Track revisions of a document.
- Advanced tools to search documents in the database.
- Viewing file information.
- Managing change orders.
- Managing bill of materials.
- Permissions control over files.

Some of the benefits of implementing a PDM system include:

- Vital data is kept organized.
- You can work with the most up-to-date information and concurrent engineering is promoted.
- Productivity is increased through a controlled design collaboration environment where the modification and status of a file is communicated by the PDM system.

PDM Considerations

Some PDM systems manage assemblies and their related data differently. It is important to understand the capabilities of the PDM system because this might impact the way that you build your assemblies. Your company might have corporate standards for assemblies and their use in a PDM system.

Some PDM systems might delete the constraints that have been created to define the relative position of components when the assembly is checked in. In this case, the company might enforce a design standard that in-place modeling techniques are required.

- In-place modeling positions components relative to a central axis system so that no constraints are required.

- It is recommended that you speak to your CAD administrator regarding the presence of a PDM system. Additionally, you should be aware of any company standards or assembly design procedures that need to be followed to maximize the benefits of the PDM system. This could affect how you use the Assembly Design workbench.

Practice 4a

Creating Assemblies I

Learning Objectives

- Change product properties.
- Move components with the compass.
- Apply assembly constraints.

In this practice, you will create a new ball mount assembly, as shown in Figure 4–23. You will use constraints to assemble the four components of the assembly. The ball mount assembly that you create is a subassembly of a larger assembly.

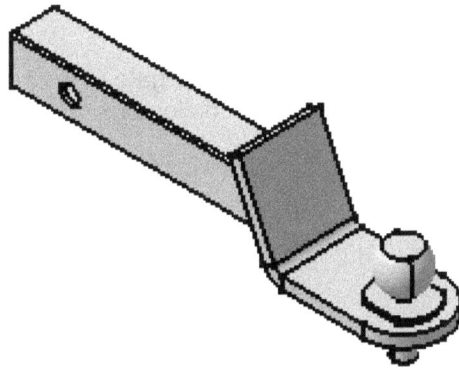

Figure 4–23

Task 1 - Assign properties for the product.

You should be in the Assembly Design workbench. This workbench is indicated by [icon] *in the Workbench toolbar.*

1. Select **File>New** and select the **Product** option in the *Type* area.

2. Save the file as **Ball_Mount**. Verify that it is saved in the *Hitch* folder.

3. Select **Product1** in the specification tree. Note that the default part number is applied. Right-click and select **Properties**.

4. Select the *Product* tab. Change the *part number* to **65000010**.

5. Click **OK** to confirm the change.

Task 2 - Assemble the first component and fix it.

1. Right-click on the top level assembly (**65000010**) in the specification tree and select **Components>Existing Component**, as shown in Figure 4–24.

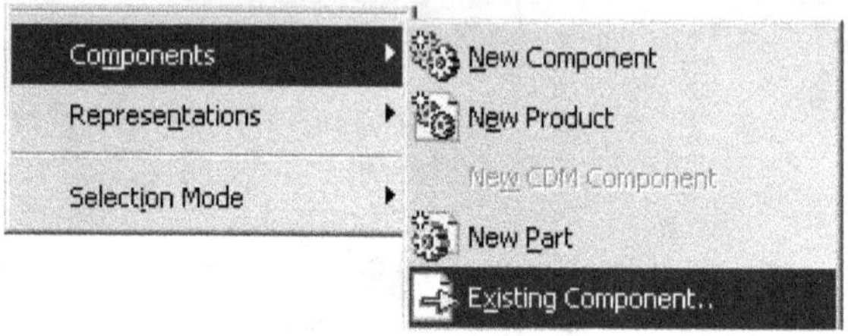

Figure 4–24

2. Navigate to the *Hitch* folder and select the **Slide** part in the dialog box, as shown in Figure 4–25.

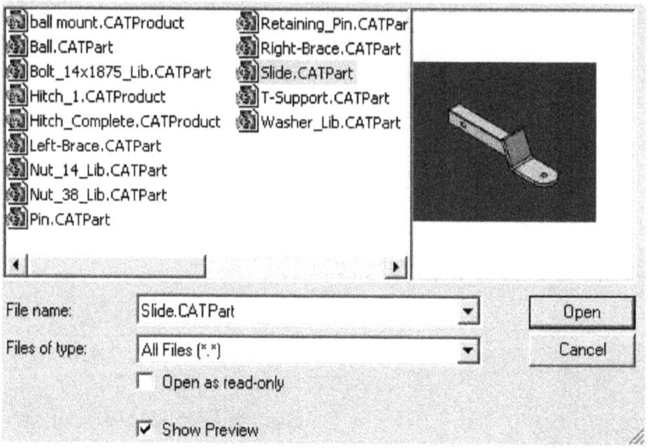

Figure 4–25

3. Click **Open**. The **Slide** part is brought into the assembly.

4. The Slide is the base component that is referenced by subsequent components. The component should be fixed.

   Click  (Fix Component) in the Constraints toolbar.

5. Select the part from the display area. This component is now fixed. Note the *Constraints* area in the specification tree, as shown in Figure 4–26.

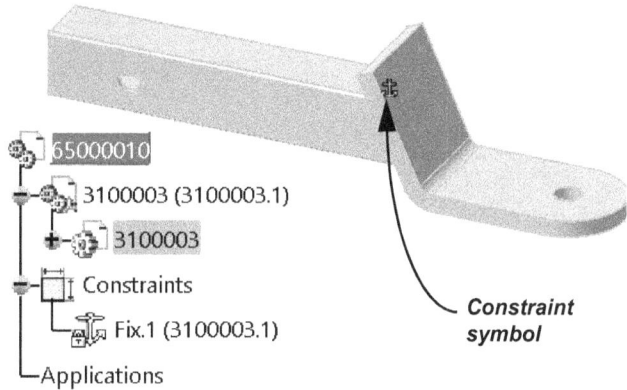

Figure 4–26

Task 3 - Add the second component in a free position.

1. Bring another component into the assembly by selecting **65000010** in the specification tree. Right-click and select **Components>Existing Component**.

2. Select **Ball** as the component to assemble and click **Open**. Note that the part is placed in the default position and intersects the Slide component.

3. To view the **Ball** geometry, the part needs to be moved away from the fixed assembly. Drag the compass onto the Ball part. Once positioned, the compass color changes to green.

4. Use the compass to position the **Ball** in a similar position to the one shown in Figure 4–27. In this position, you can more easily apply assembly constraints.

*To reset the compass, select **View>Reset Compass**.*

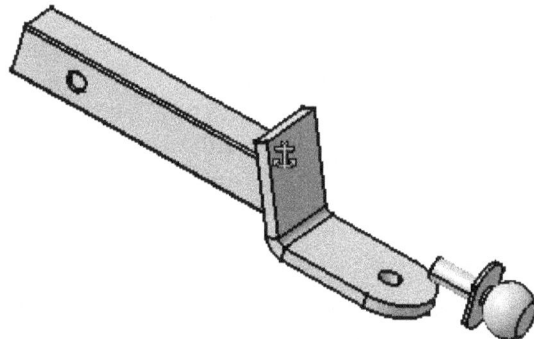

Figure 4–27

Task 4 - Constrain the Ball part.

1. Create a coincidence constraint by clicking

    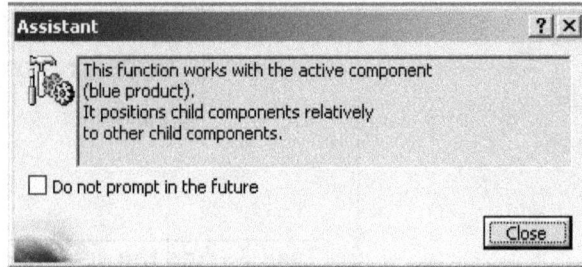 (Coincidence Constraint).

2. If the dialog box shown in Figure 4–28 opens, select the **Do not prompt in the future** option and close the window.

Figure 4–28

3. Select the axis of the **Ball** stem by selecting the cylindrical surface, as shown in Figure 4–29. You might need to zoom into the part.

4. Select the axis on the **Slide** by selecting the inner cylindrical surface of the hole, as shown in Figure 4–30.

Figure 4–29

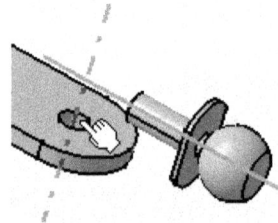

Figure 4–30

5. The **Ball** is now partially constrained. Show the position of

    Ball by clicking (Update All). The assembly updates the position of all components. The assembly displays similar to that shown in Figure 4–31.

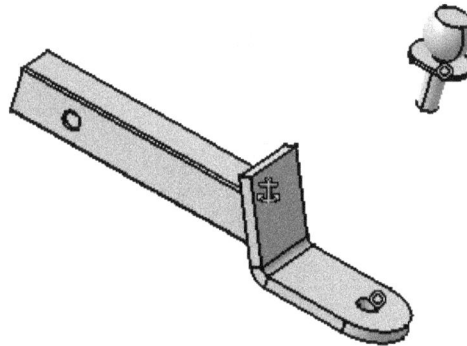

Figure 4–31

Design Considerations

The **Ball** is only constrained along its axis. Therefore, it can still be translated and rotated on its axis.

6. To position the **Ball** along the coincident axis, use a contact constraint. Click ⬜ (Contact Constraint).

7. Select the mating surface of the **Slide**, as shown in Figure 4–32.

8. Select the underside surface of the **Ball**, as shown in Figure 4–33.

9. Update the position of the components. The assembly displays as shown in Figure 4–34.

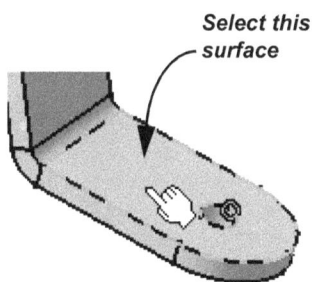

Select this surface

Figure 4–32

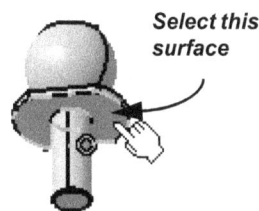

Select this surface

Figure 4–33

Figure 4–34

10. The **Ball** can still rotate about the coincident axis. Add an angle constraint to fully constrain the ball by clicking ⬜ (Angle Constraint).

11. Select the two surfaces shown in Figure 4–35.

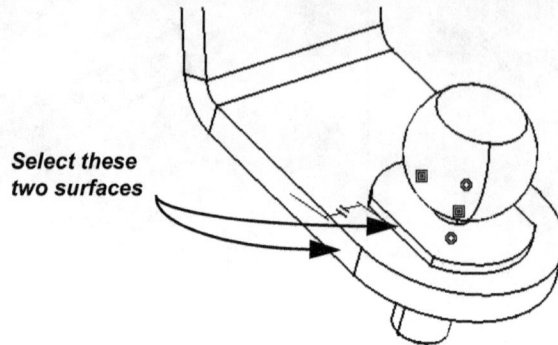

Select these two surfaces

Figure 4–35

12. Select the following options when the Constraint Properties dialog box opens, as shown in Figure 4–36:

   - Select **Parallelism**.
   - *Orientation:* **Same**

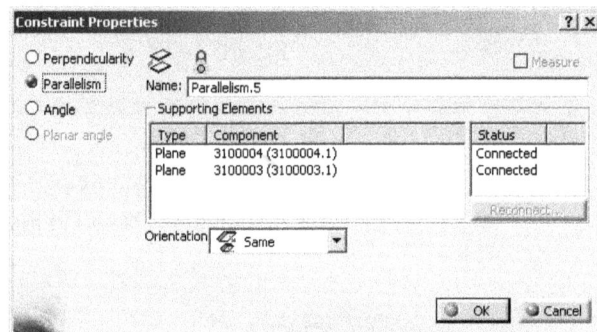

Figure 4–36

13. Click **OK**. The **Ball** component is now fully constrained and displays as shown in Figure 4–37.

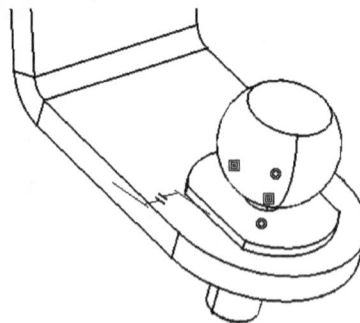

Figure 4–37

Task 5 - Hide the constraints.

1. Note that the constraint symbols display. To remove these symbols from the display, right-click on constraints in the specification tree and select **Hide/Show**.

Task 6 - Assemble the washer.

1. Insert **Washer_Lib into 65000010** by right-clicking on **65000010** and selecting **Components>Existing Component**.

2. Part number 100103 displays in the specification tree, but the washer is not visible. Position the cursor over the red square of the compass so that the cursor turns to four arrows, as shown in Figure 4–38.

Figure 4–38

3. Right-click and select **Snap Automatically to Selected Object**.

4. Select **100103** in the specification tree. The compass snaps to the washer component. Drag the washer using the compass to the position shown in Figure 4–39. Then, drag the compass off the washer.

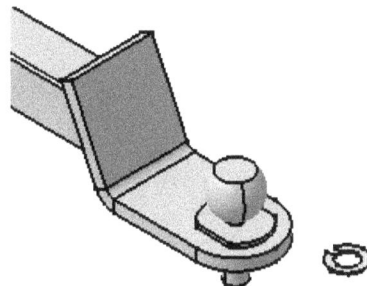

Figure 4–39

5. Create a coincidence constraint by clicking

    ![icon] (Coincidence Constraint).

6. Select the axis of the washer and the axis of the ball (zoom in to select the washer axis).

7. Create a contact constraint by clicking ![icon] (Contact Constraint).

8. Select the surface of the washer and the underside surface of the slide, as shown in Figure 4–40.

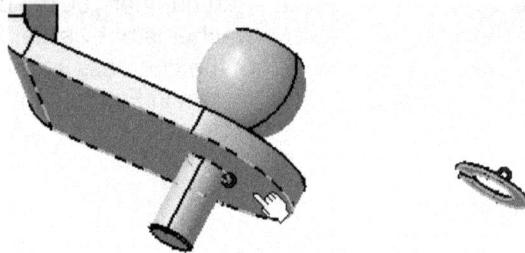

Figure 4–40

9. To update the position of the components, expand the *Constraints* area of the specification tree.

10. Select the two newly created constraints, right-click and select **Update**.

11. The washer still has a degree of freedom to rotate about the coincident axis. Click ![icon] (Fix Together) and select both the washer and the ball parts to fix them together.

12. Click **OK**.

13. Update the assembly, if required.

14. Toggle the visibility setting of the constraints so that all constraints are hidden.

Task 7 - Add the nut component.

1. Insert the **Nut_38_Lib** component into the assembly.

2. The nut is not displayed. Drag the compass onto the Slide part.

3. Select **100102** in the specification tree. Using the compass, drag the nut to the position shown in Figure 4–41.

4. Create a coincident constraint by clicking ![icon] (Coincidence Constraint). Select the axis of the nut and the axis of the ball, as shown in Figure 4–42.

5. Create a contact constraint by clicking ![icon] (Contact Constraint). Select the surface of the nut and the surface of the washer, as shown in Figure 4–43.

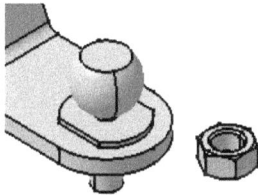

Figure 4–41

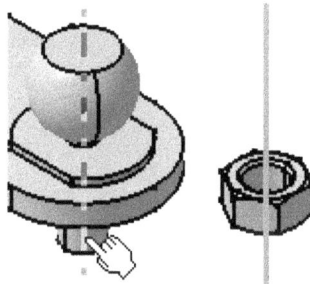

Figure 4–42

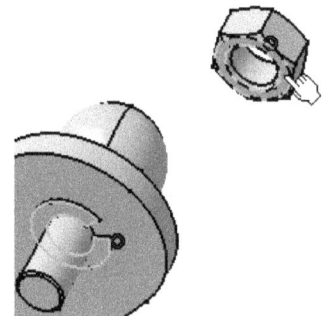

Figure 4–43

6. Update the assembly.

7. Create a ![icon] (Fix Together) constraint between the nut and the washer.

8. Save the file and close the assembly.

Practice 4b | Creating Assemblies II

Practice Objectives

- Apply constraints.
- Insert a subassembly.

In this practice, you will create the assembly shown in Figure 4–44. This assembly will consist of various parts and the subassembly that you created in a previous practice.

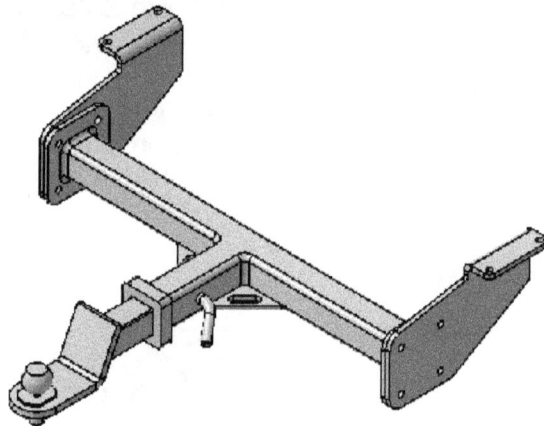

Figure 4–44

Task 1 - Assign product properties.

1. Select **File>New** and select the **Product** option in the *Type* area.

2. Save the file as **Hitch** in the *Hitch* folder.

3. Select **Product1** in the specification tree. The default part number is applied. Right-click and select **Properties**.

4. Select the *Product* tab and change the *part number* to **65000011**.

5. Click **OK** to confirm the change.

Task 2 - Assemble the first component and fix it.

1. Right-click on the top level assembly (**65000011**) in the specification tree and select **Components>Existing Component**.

2. Select the part called **T-Support** in the *Hitch* folder and click **Open**.

3. The **T-Support** is the base component that is referenced by subsequent components. The component needs to be fixed.

   Click ⚓ (Fix Component) in the toolbar.

4. Select the part in the display area. This component is now fixed. Note the *Constraints* area in the specification tree.

Task 3 - Assemble the braces.

1. Insert the **Left-Brace** component into **65000011** using the same method as in Task 2.

2. Create a 🖉 (Coincidence) constraint between the axes, as shown in Figure 4–45.

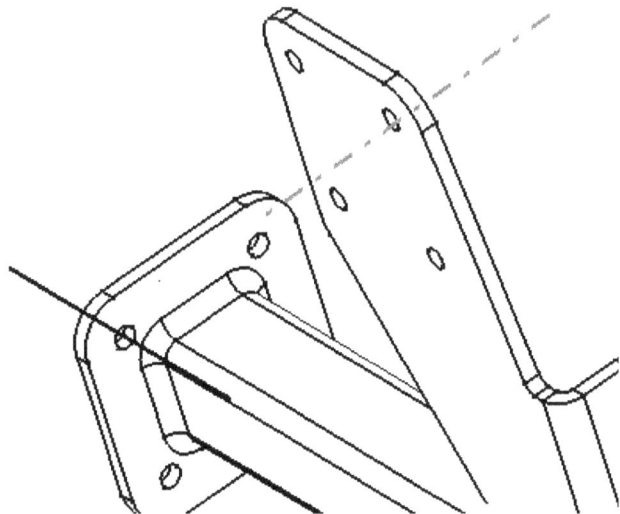

Figure 4–45

3. Create a ⬚ (Contact) constraint between the surfaces shown in Figure 4–46. Update the assembly.

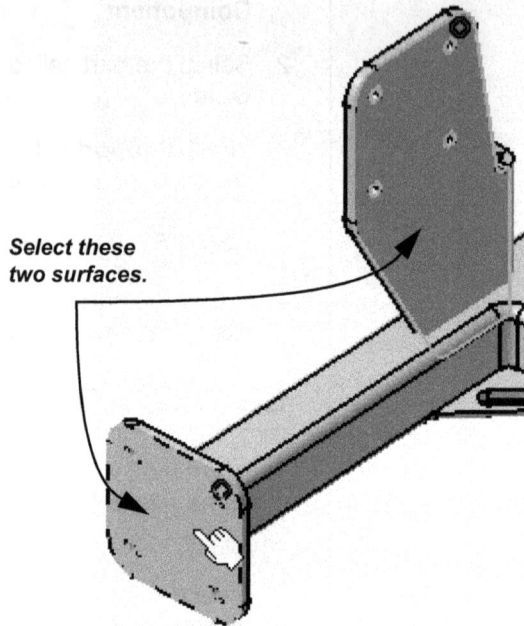

Select these two surfaces.

Figure 4–46

4. Using 📐 (Angle Constraint), apply a parallelism constraint between the surfaces shown in Figure 4–47. Update the assembly.

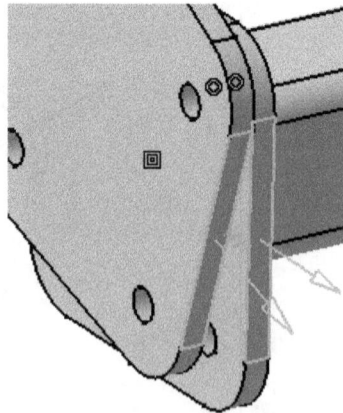

Figure 4–47

5. Assemble the **Right-Brace** using the same steps described in this task. The assembly displays as shown in Figure 4–48.

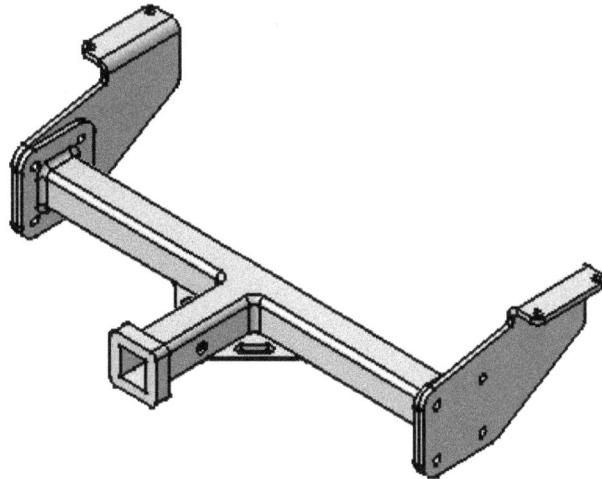

Figure 4–48

Task 4 - Assemble the Ball_Mount subassembly.

1. Insert the **Ball_Mount_Complete** assembly into **65000011** by right-clicking and selecting **Components>Existing Component**.

2. Place the compass on the **T-Support** and drag the **Ball_Mount** assembly away from the model, as shown in Figure 4–49.

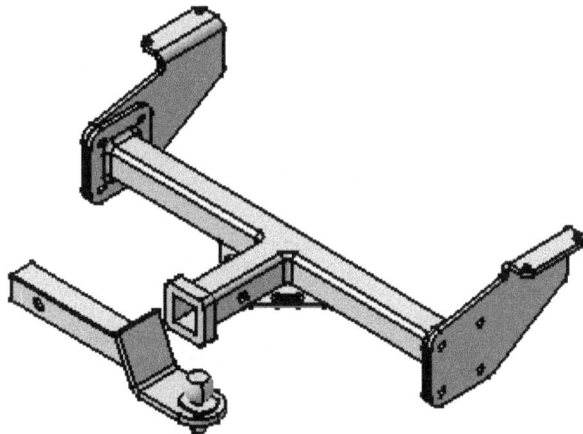

Figure 4–49

3. Create a (Coincidence) constraint between the axes shown in Figure 4–50.

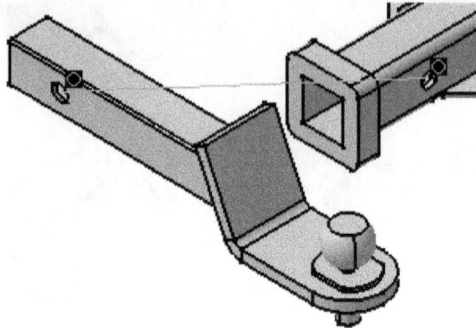

Figure 4–50

4. The **Ball_Mount** is now partially constrained. Use the (Offset) constraint to position along the axis by offsetting two surfaces.

5. Select the surface on the Slide and on the **T-Support,** as shown in Figure 4–51. The Constraint Definition dialog box opens.

Select these two surfaces.

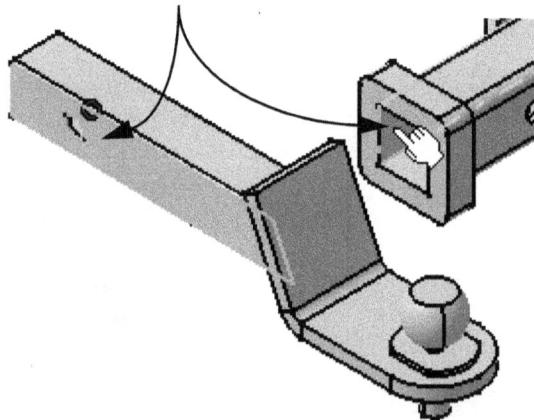

Figure 4–51

6. Select **Opposite** for the orientation and enter an *offset value* of **0.4 (0.016 in)**.

7. Click **OK** when finished.

8. Using ![icon](Angle Constraint), apply a parallelism constraint between the surfaces shown in Figure 4–52.

Select these two surfaces.

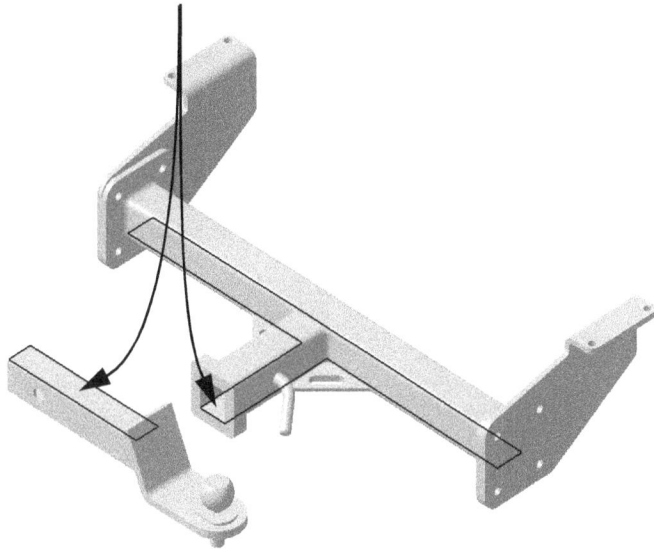

Figure 4–52

9. Update the assembly. The model displays as shown in Figure 4–53.

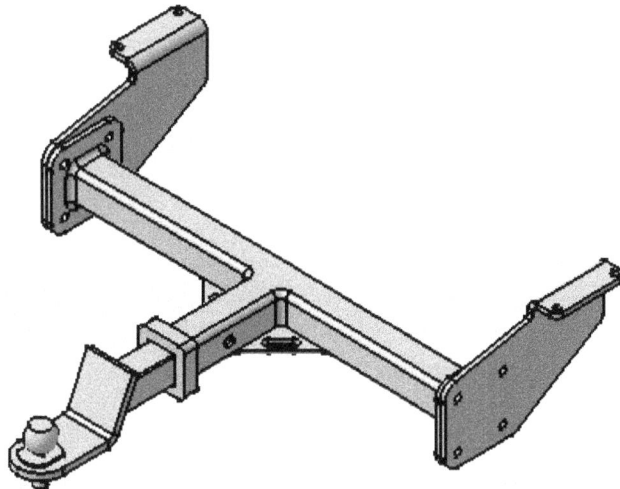

Figure 4–53

Task 5 - Assemble the pin.

1. Insert **Pin** into **65000011** by right-clicking and selecting **Components>Existing Component**.

2. Place the compass on the **T-Support**, and drag part **3100005** away from the model.

3. Create a coincidence constraint between the hole of the **T-Support** and the axis of the **Pin**, as shown in Figure 4–54.

4. Create an offset constraint and select the face of the **Pin** shown in Figure 4–55.

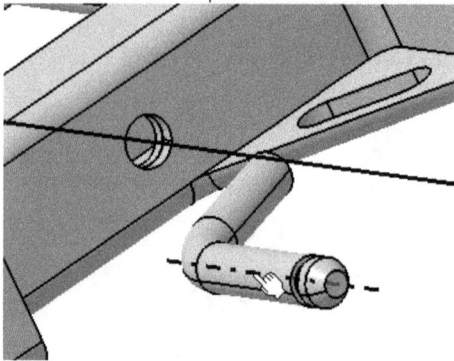

Figure 4–54

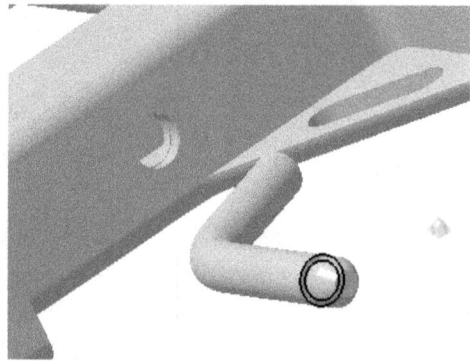

Figure 4–55

5. Select the face of **T-Support** shown in Figure 4–56. Set the following:

   • *Orientation*: **Same**
   • *Offset value*: **0**

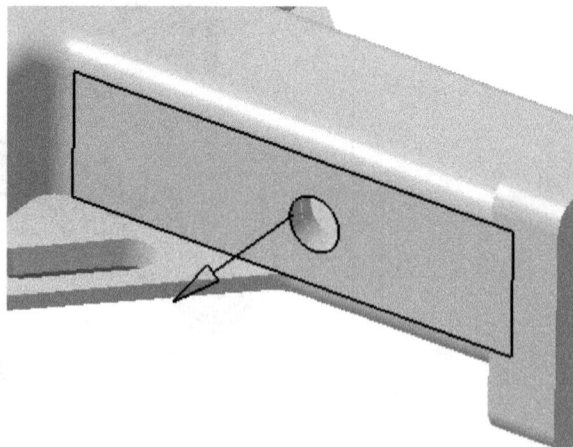

Figure 4–56

6. Update the assembly. The model displays as shown in Figure 4–57.

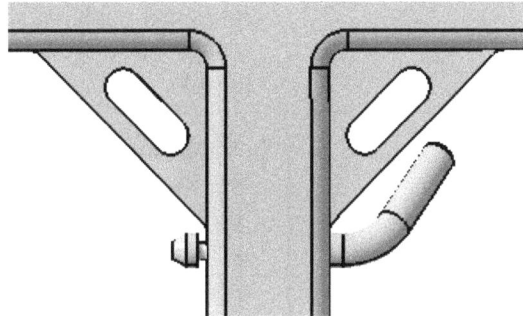

Figure 4–57

Task 1 - Assemble the Retaining_Pin.

In this task, you will position the **Retaining_Pin** model in the assembly and then constrain its location by fixing it to the Pin model.

1. Insert **Retaining_Pin** into **65000011** by right-clicking and selecting **Components>Existing Component**.

2. Using the compass, reposition **Retaining_Pin** to a location near the slotted end of Pin, as shown in Figure 4–58.

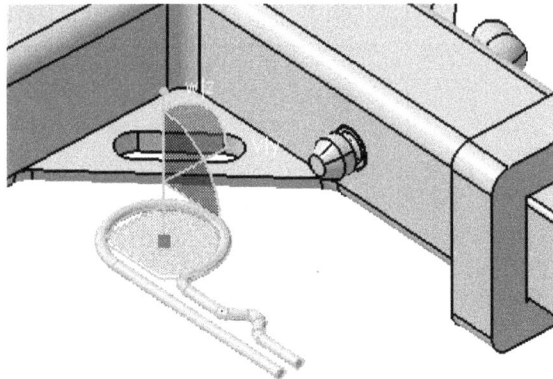

Figure 4–58

Design Considerations

Note the curved geometry of the **Retaining_Pin**. Few references can be selected from the model to position it relative to the **T-Support** and **Pin**. For this reason, reference elements have been added to the model that will assist during constraint creation.

3. Show the RefGeom geometrical set under **Retaining_Pin** (**3100006**) and **Pin** (**3100005**) in the specification tree. The **Retaining_Pin** model contains two reference planes and a reference point, as shown in Figure 4–59. The **Pin** model contains a reference plane located at the center of the groove.

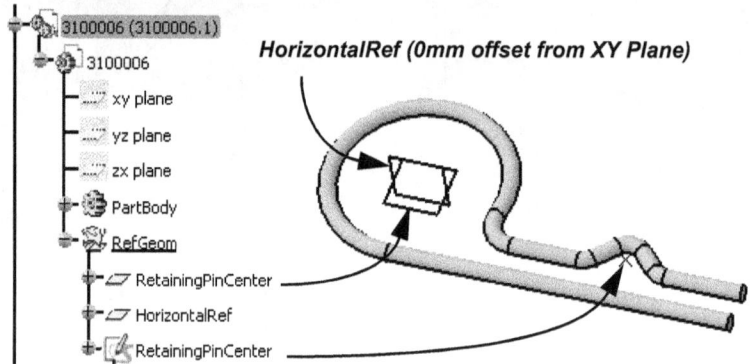

HorizontalRef (0mm offset from XY Plane)

Figure 4–59

4. Create the constraints using Figure 4–60 as a guide.

No.	Constraint	Reference 1	Reference 2
1	Coincident	Axis of Pin	RetainingPinCenter (sketched point) of Retaining Pin
2	Offset (0mm)	GrooveCenter (plane) of Pin	RetainingPinCenter (plane) of Retaining Pin
3	Parallelism	Face of T-Support	HorizontalRef (plane) of Retaining Pin

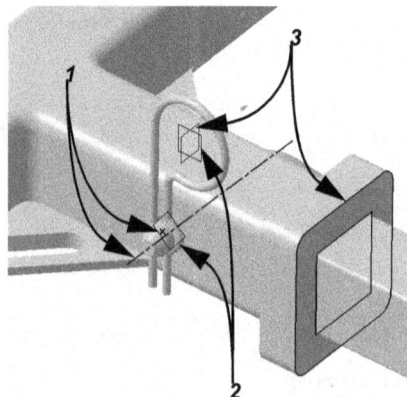

Figure 4–60

5. Update the assembly and hide **RefGeom** from **Retaining_Pin**. The completed model displays as shown in Figure 4–61.

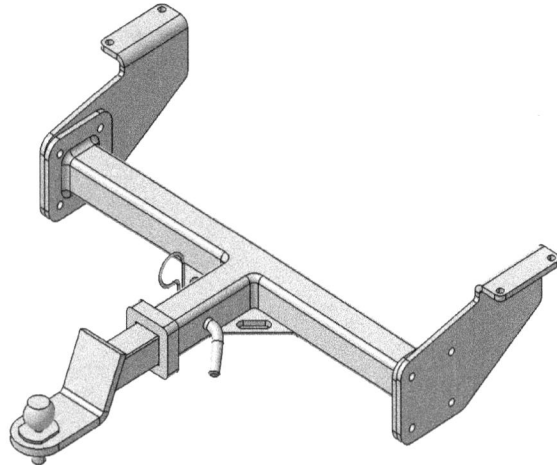

Figure 4–61

6. Save the file and close the assembly.

Practice 4c

Creating Assemblies III

Practice Objectives

- Create a new product.
- Apply constraints.

In this practice, you will create the assembly shown in Figure 4–62.

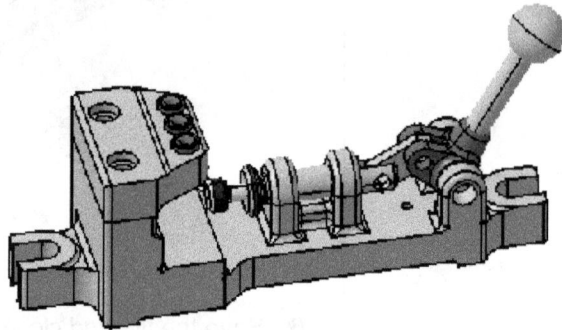

Figure 4–62

Task 1 - Create a new product file and assign properties.

1. Select **File>New** and select the **Product** option in the *Type* area.

2. Change the *part number* to **65200000**.

3. Save the file as **Bore-Device** in the *Bore_Fixture* folder.

4. Ensure that the units are set to millimeters.

Task 2 - Create the product structure.

1. Insert all ten parts contained in the *Bore_Fixture* folder into this assembly.

   Do not select **Bore-Device-Assembled.CATProduct**.

Use <Ctrl> to select multiple files at once.

2. Place the compass onto the parts and drag the components so they can be easily seen, as shown in Figure 4–63.

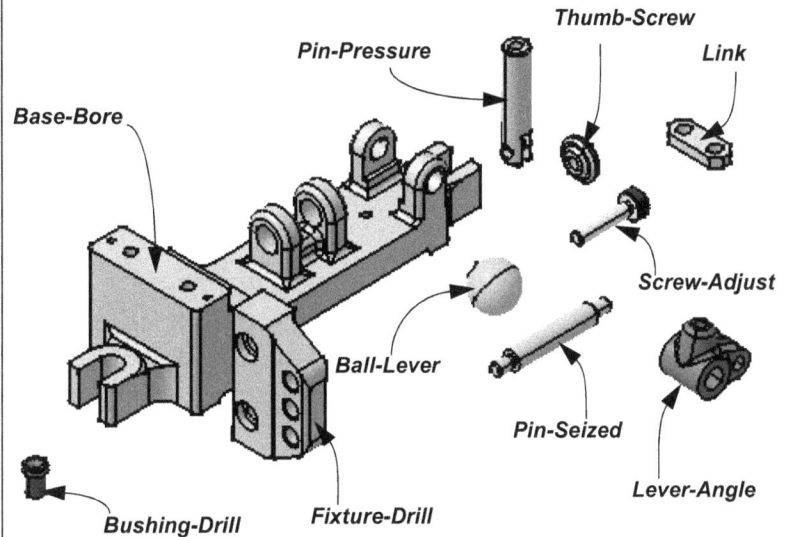

Figure 4–63

3. Create two new instances of the drill bushing (**3200003**) in the assembly.

4. Move the copies of the bushing so they can be easily seen in the display.

Task 3 - Assemble the components.

---

1. Fix the **Base-Bore** part (**3200000**).

2. Assemble the **Drill Fixture** (**3200001**) to the base shown in Figure 4–64. Use the coincidence, contact, and angle constraints.

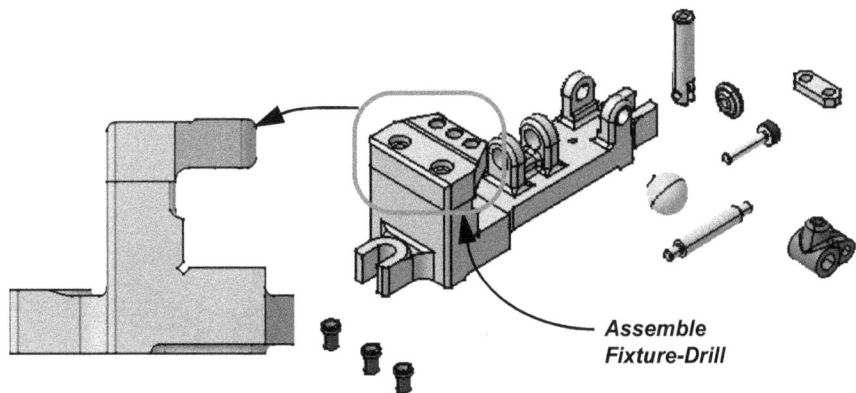

Figure 4–64

3. Assemble the three drill bushings into the drill fixture.

4. Assemble the **Ball-Lever 3200005**, **Pin-Seized 3200004**, and **Lever-Angle 3200002**, as shown in Figure 4–65.

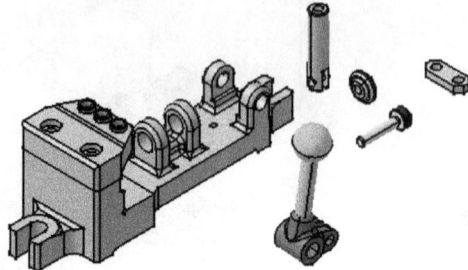

Figure 4–65

5. Assemble **Lever-Angle-3200002**, **Link-3200007**, and **Pin-Pressure 3200006,** as shown in Figure 4–66.

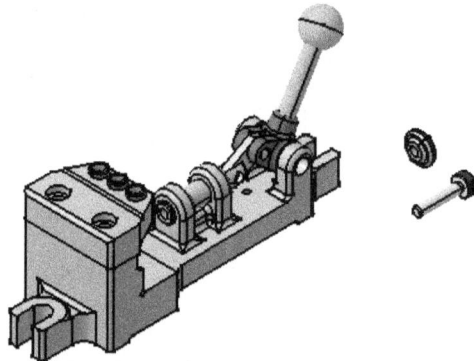

Figure 4–66

6. Assemble the remaining components, as shown in Figure 4–67.

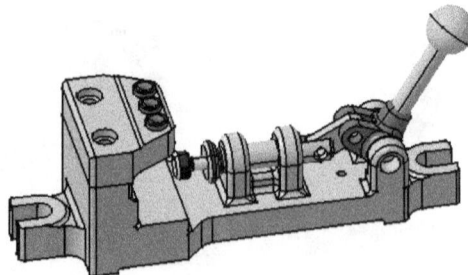

Figure 4–67

7. Save the file and close the assembly.

Practice 4d | (Optional) Motor Assembly

Practice Objective

- Create an assembly without instructions.

1. Insert the **Cylinder_Block**, **Crankshaft**, **Connecting_Rod**, and **Piston** part models. If you have not completed these parts, you can access completed models in the *Completed* folder.

2. Create a new assembly called **Motor**. Assemble the components to create the assembly shown in Figure 4–68.

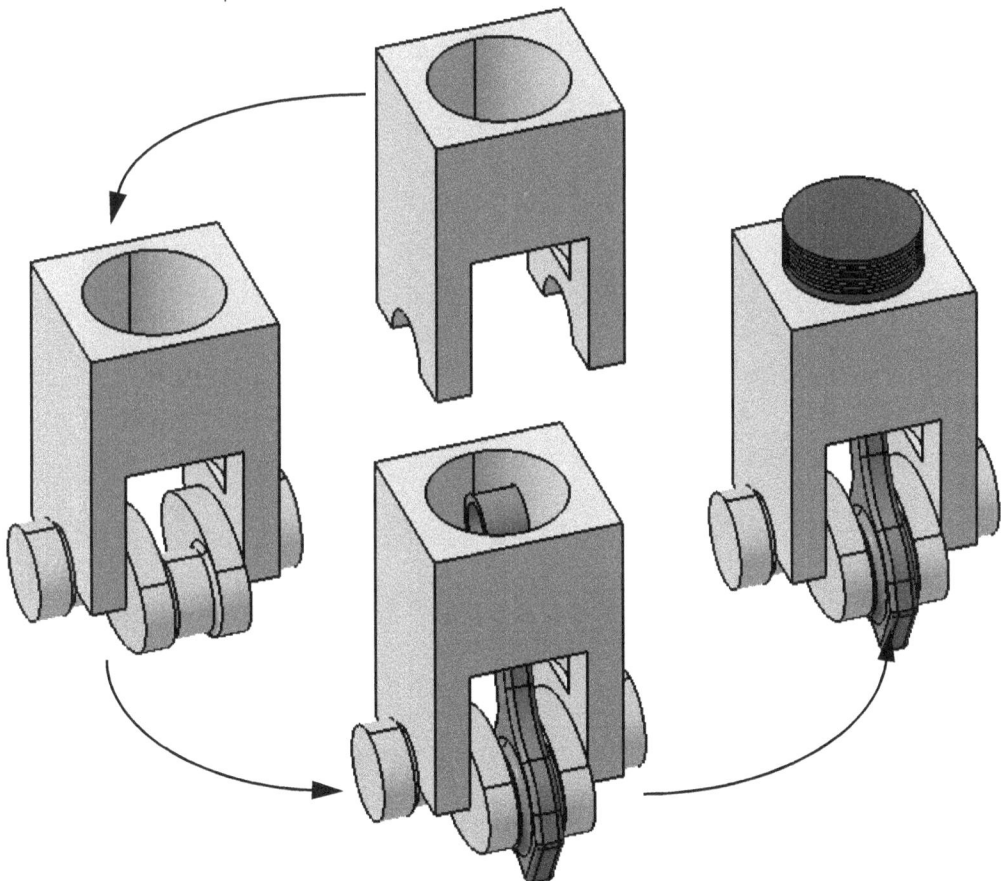

Figure 4–68

Assembly Information

This chapter covers the techniques that you can use to obtain information about an assembly. The Measure toolbar enables you to take measurements of the assembly in the same way that you take measurements of parts. The Clash and Clearance Analysis tool enables you to determine whether any interference is present in the assembly. Additionally, the bill of materials enables you to generate a list of the components that are used in the assembly.

Learning Objectives in this Chapter

- Use the measurement toolbar options for assembly components.
- Apply materials to components.
- Determine whether interference exists in an assembly.
- Create a Bill of Material report.

5.1 Measurements

CATIA provides tools to extract important information from your assembly model. The Measurements toolbar enables you to perform the following functions:

- Measure the distance between items on different parts.

- Measure the distance between items on a single part.

- Measure the mass properties of the assembly.

These functions can be accessed using the **Analyze** menu in the menu bar or the Measure toolbar, as shown in Figure 5–1.

Figure 5–1

Component Materials

Materials can be applied to the components of an assembly in the Part Design or Assembly Design workbench. Using the Assembly Design workbench, this can be accomplished by selecting the specific component(s) in the specification tree before applying the material. When finished, the system considers each component's material property when performing measure inertia calculations.

- If the entire assembly is to be manufactured from the same material, it is faster to apply this material to the assembly and not to the components. This is done by selecting the assembly from the tree when applying the material.

5.2 Clash and Clearance

When creating an assembly, the software permits interference between components. The clash functionality must be used to determine whether interference exists. A clash analysis also calculates the degree of interference.

*This analysis can also be run from the **Analyze** menu.*

To run a clash analysis, click (Clash) in the Space Analysis toolbar. In the Check Clash dialog box, select **Contact + Clash** from the Type drop-down list. The scope of products to include in the calculation must then be selected from the drop-down list below the Type drop-down list. To see the results of this analysis, click **Apply**. The results display as shown in Figure 5–2. If any conflicts occur, you can select and preview the result.

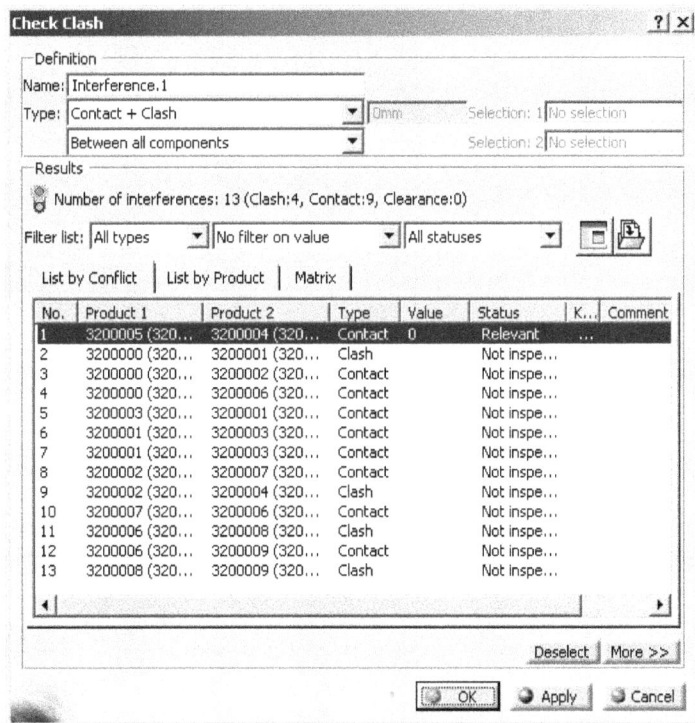

Note that the dialog boxes in this chapter may vary slightly depending on the license you have.

Figure 5–2

To check the minimum amount of clearance between components, select **Clearance + Contact + Clash** in the Type drop-down list. Set the scope of components to include in the analysis and click **Apply**. The results display as shown in Figure 5–3.

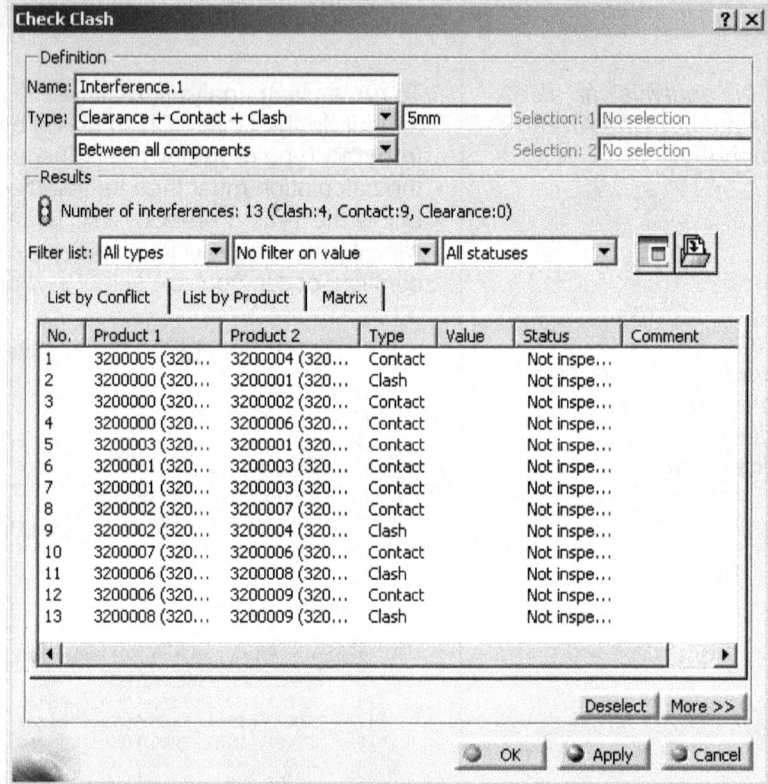

No.	Product 1	Product 2	Type	Value	Status	Comment
1	3200005 (320...	3200004 (320...	Contact		Not inspe...	
2	3200000 (320...	3200001 (320...	Clash		Not inspe...	
3	3200000 (320...	3200002 (320...	Contact		Not inspe...	
4	3200000 (320...	3200006 (320...	Contact		Not inspe...	
5	3200003 (320...	3200001 (320...	Contact		Not inspe...	
6	3200001 (320...	3200003 (320...	Contact		Not inspe...	
7	3200001 (320...	3200003 (320...	Contact		Not inspe...	
8	3200002 (320...	3200007 (320...	Contact		Not inspe...	
9	3200002 (320...	3200004 (320...	Clash		Not inspe...	
10	3200007 (320...	3200006 (320...	Contact		Not inspe...	
11	3200006 (320...	3200008 (320...	Clash		Not inspe...	
12	3200006 (320...	3200009 (320...	Contact		Not inspe...	
13	3200008 (320...	3200009 (320...	Clash		Not inspe...	

Figure 5–3

The results of both analyses are stored under Applications in the specification tree, as shown in Figure 5–4.

The interference analysis is only added to the specification tree if an SPA (DMU Space Analysis) license is obtained.

Figure 5–4

5.3 Creating Bill of Material Report

The Bill of Material (BOM) report is used to examine which components are used in the assembly and the numbers of each component present in the assembly.

How To: Create a Bill of Material Report

1. Activate the assembly by double-clicking on its name in the specification tree.
2. Select **Analyze>Bill of Material...**, as shown in Figure 5–5.

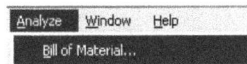

Figure 5–5

3. A Bill of Material report is generated. Two tabs of information display. The *Bill Of Material* tab shows the BOM, as shown in Figure 5–6. The report shows the top level BOM for the assembly and the BOM for each subassembly. The *Recapitulation* area shows all individual parts that are required to construct the top level assembly.

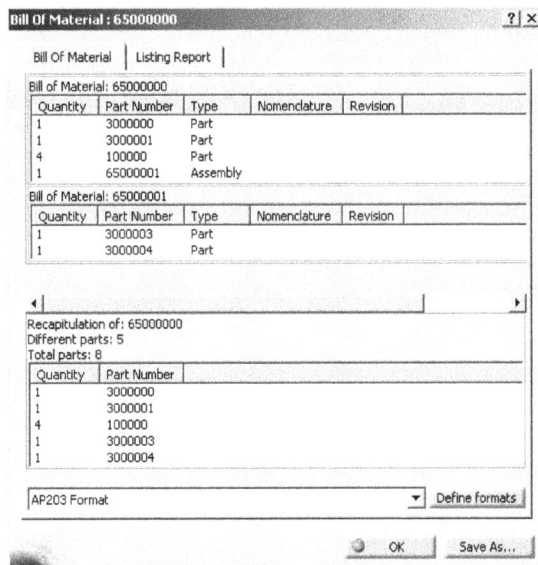

Figure 5–6

The *Listing Report* tab provides additional information about the components. The instance name and product description are added as additional displayed properties, as shown in Figure 5–7.

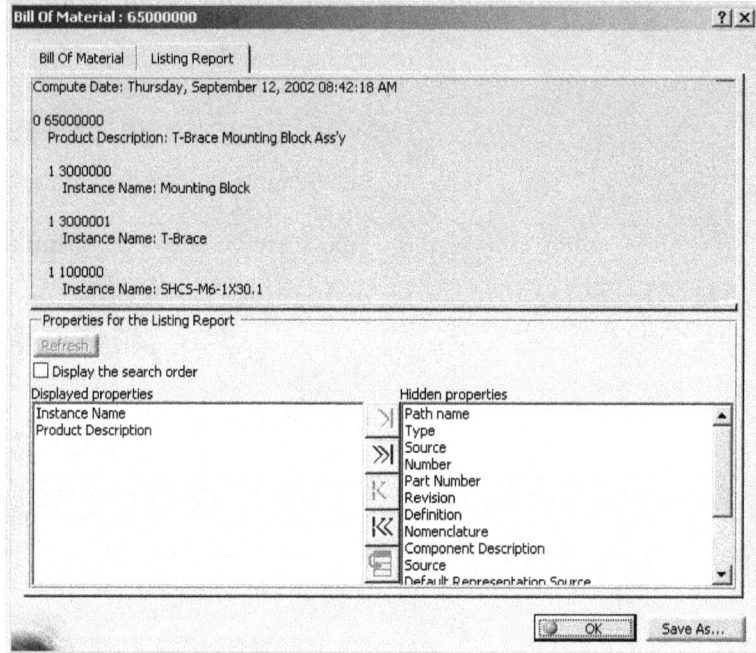

Figure 5–7

The BOM report can be exported out of CATIA by clicking **Save As**. The file can be stored as a text, HTML, or Excel file. However, the listing report can only be exported as a text file.

Practice 5a

Assembly Information

Practice Objectives

- Extract measurements from the assembly.
- Create a BOM.
- Calculate interference.

Task 1 - Open the Hitch assembly.

1. Select **File>Open** and select the **Hitch_Complete** assembly from the *Hitch* folder.

*If you completed Practice 21a, you can continue working with **Hitch.CATProduct** instead.*

2. Fit the model to the display area and activate the isometric view. The assembly displays as shown in Figure 5–8.

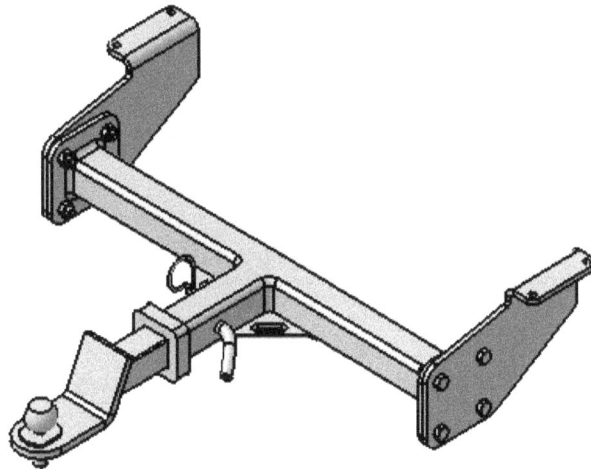

Figure 5–8

3. Ensure that the top level assembly is the active object.

4. Select **Analyze>Bill of Material**. The Bill Of Material dialog box opens, as shown in Figure 5–9.

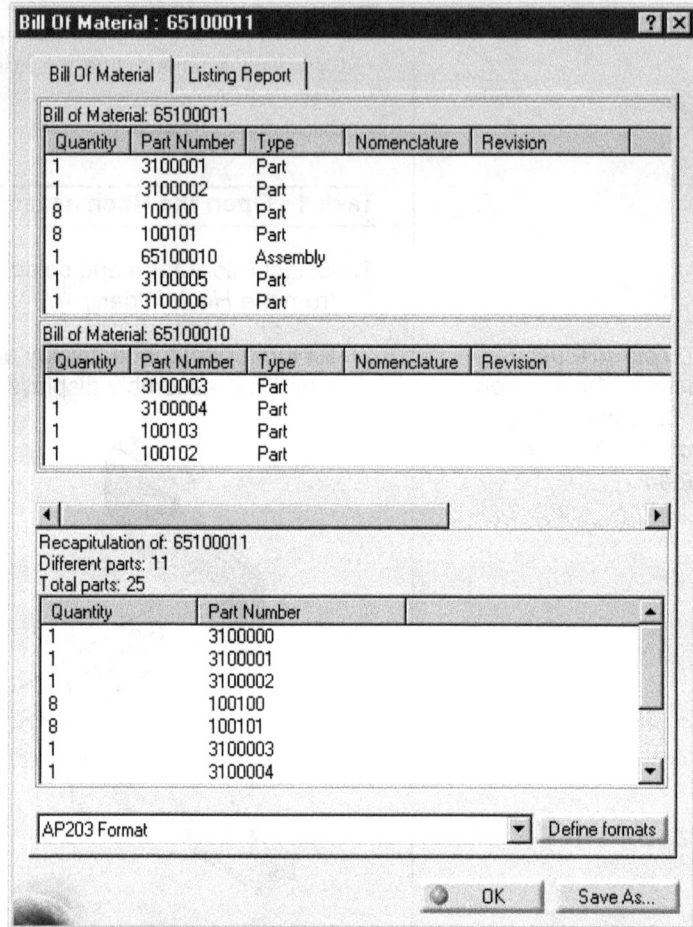

Figure 5–9

Note the structure of the report. Since a subassembly (**65100010**) is in the top level, its bill of materials is also reported.

5. Click **Save As**.

6. Save the BOM as a text file called **hitch-tla**.

7. Repeat the previous step for an Excel spreadsheet and for an HTML document.

8. Click **OK** when finished with the report.

9. Use Windows Explorer to browse to the *Hitch* folder, as shown in Figure 5–10.

ball mount.CATProduct	32 KB	CATIA Product
Ball.CATPart	121 KB	CATIA Part
Bolt_14x1875_Lib.CATPart	79 KB	CATIA Part
Hitch_1.CATProduct	34 KB	CATIA Product
Hitch_Complete.CATProduct	96 KB	CATIA Product
hitch-tla.html	3 KB	HTML Document
hitch-tla.txt	4 KB	Text Document
hitch-tla.xls	3 KB	Microsoft Excel Worksheet
Left-Brace.CATPart	281 KB	CATIA Part
Nut_14_Lib.CATPart	86 KB	CATIA Part
Nut_38_Lib.CATPart	87 KB	CATIA Part
Pin.CATPart	106 KB	CATIA Part
Retaining_Pin.CATPart	97 KB	CATIA Part
Right-Brace.CATPart	283 KB	CATIA Part
Slide.CATPart	323 KB	CATIA Part
T-Support.CATPart	597 KB	CATIA Part
Washer_Lib.CATPart	61 KB	CATIA Part

Figure 5–10

10. Open the saved BOM files to view the format of the three BOM files.

Task 2 - Check for interference.

---

1. Select **Analyze>Clash** in the menu bar. The Check Clash dialog box opens.

2. Set the following, as shown in Figure 5–11:

   - *Type:* **Contact + Clash**
   - *Type (second drop-down):* **Between all components**

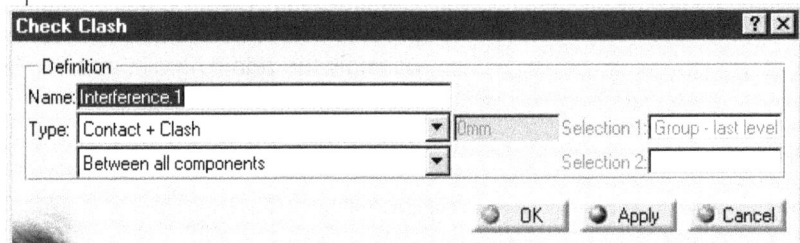

Figure 5–11

3. Click **Apply**. The results of the clash check are shown in Figure 5–12.

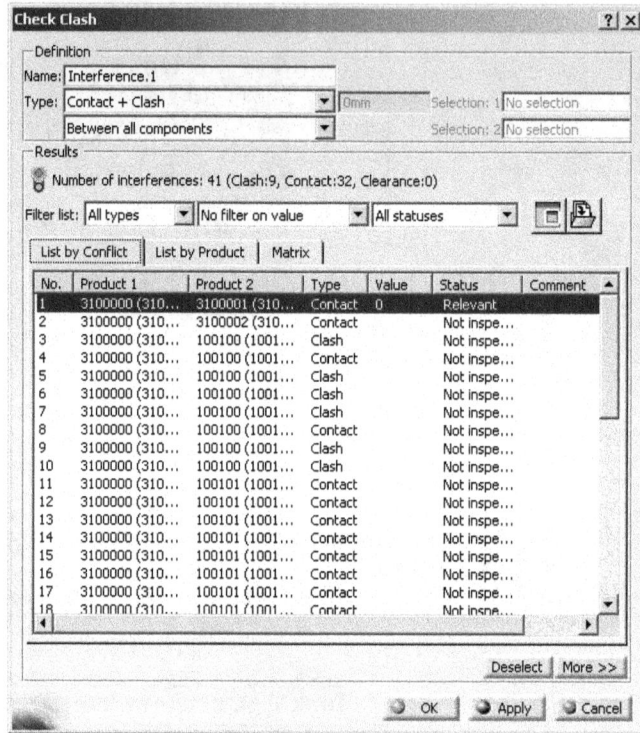

Figure 5–12

4. Note the detected clash conditions listed in the *Type* column.

5. Select the first row where clash is indicated. A preview window displays that shows the place of clash on the model. The clash is between the **T-Support** and the **Bolt**.

6. Continue to review the other clashes in the model. There is problem with the placement of some of the bolts, and possibly the retaining pin, and the **Ball_Mount** assembly.

7. Click **OK** to close the window.

Task 3 - Investigate the cause of the clash with measurements.

1. Click (Measure Item) to investigate.

2. Select the edge of the support as shown in Figure 5–13. Its value is **89.2mm (3.512 in)**.

3. Select the edge shown in Figure 5–14. Its value is also **89.2mm (3.512 in).** These dimensions are used for the increment of the hole pattern.

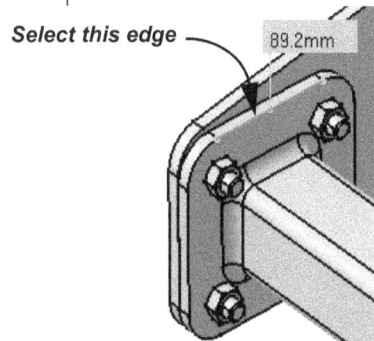
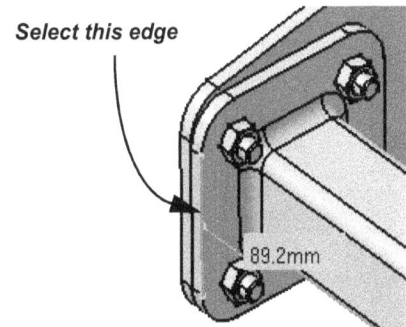

Figure 5–13   **Figure 5–14**

You might have to close the Measure Item dialog box to verify the dimensional increment of RectPattern.

4. Verify that the dimensional increment of **RectPattern.1** and **RectPattern.2** for part **3100000** is 89.2mm (3.512 in) in both directions.

5. Click (Measure Between) in the Measure dialog box.

6. Measure between the spacing of the holes in the brace, as shown in Figure 5–15.

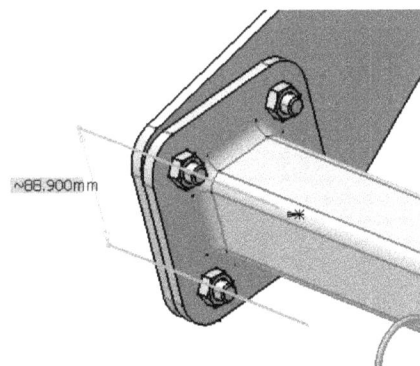

Figure 5–15

7. Note that the hole spacing for this pattern is **88.9 (3.5 in)** and not 89.2 (3.512 in), which is the dimension used by the pattern.

8. Modify the spacing of **RectPattern.1** in both the **3100001** and **3100002** parts to **89.2 (3.512 in)**.

9. Update the assembly. Ensure that the top-level assembly is active by double-clicking on **65100011** in the specification tree.

10. Check for clash again. There should not be any clash involving the bolts.

11. Click (Measure Inertia) and investigate the mass properties.

12. Save the assembly and close the window.

Annotations

Once analysis information has been captured, it can be communicated to designers or manufacturers using model annotations. These annotations enable you to display critical information about the part or assembly directly on the 3D geometry.

Learning Objectives in this Chapter

- Review the annotation tools.
- Understand the annotation process.
- Learn how to manage annotations.

6.1 Annotation Tools

This section provides an overview of the different annotation tools available in the Assembly Design workbench. The annotation tools are located in the Annotations toolbar shown in Figure 6–1.

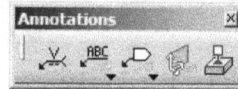

Figure 6–1

The following describes the Annotations toolbar icons.

Option	Icon	Description
Weld Feature		Creates welding symbol in the annotation view plane.
Text flyout		
Text with Leader		Creates text with a leader to geometry in the annotation view plane.
Text		Creates text in the annotation view plane.
Text Parallel To Screen		Creates text referencing geometry or an annotation plane that is always parallel to the screen.
Flag Note flyout		
Flag Note with Leader		Creates a flag note with a leader to geometry in the annotation view plane.
Flag Note		Creates a flag note in the annotation view plane.
View Creation		Defines an annotation view plane.
3D-Annotation-Query Switch On/Switch Off		When active, selecting an annotation also highlights all associated geometry.

6.2 Annotation Process

General Steps

Use the following general steps to add annotations to a model:

1. Define the annotation planes.
2. Create texts.
3. Create flag notes.
4. Create welding symbols.

Step 1 - Define the annotation planes.

Annotation planes/views are used to locate and control the orientation of 3D annotations that are created on the model. Each annotation is associated with the view that was active during its creation. If a view has not been created, one is automatically added when the first annotation is created.

The top face of the part shown in Figure 6–2 has been defined as an annotation plane.

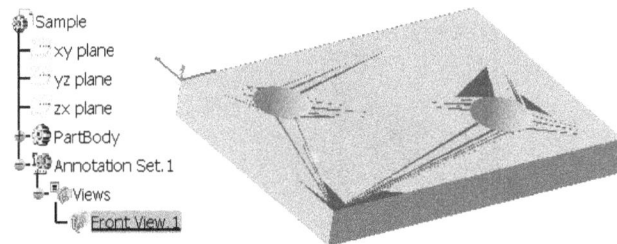

Figure 6–2

Define View

How To: Define a View Plane

1. Click ⬛ (View From Reference).
2. Select a planar reference, such as face, surface, reference plane, or axis system.
3. Select the view type:

- ⬛ - Projection View/Annotation Plane

- ⬛ - Section View

- ⬛ - Section Cut

Projection View

This icon creates an annotation plane by selecting a planar face, surface, or reference plane on the model. When used to add a drawing view, the projection view orients the model so that the annotation plane is parallel to the screen. A projection view is identified by a blue reference axis. An example is shown in Figure 6–3.

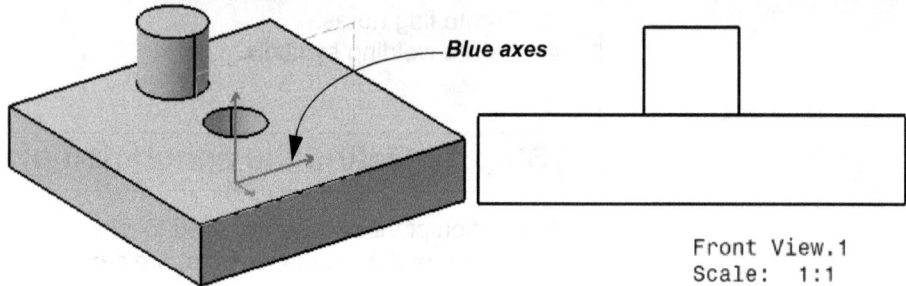

Blue axes

```
Front View.1
Scale:   1:1
```

Figure 6–3

Section View

A section view annotation plane defines both a viewing orientation and a cutting plane. When the view is extracted to the Drafting workbench, a section view is automatically generated. A section view is identified by a green reference axis. An example is shown in Figure 6–4.

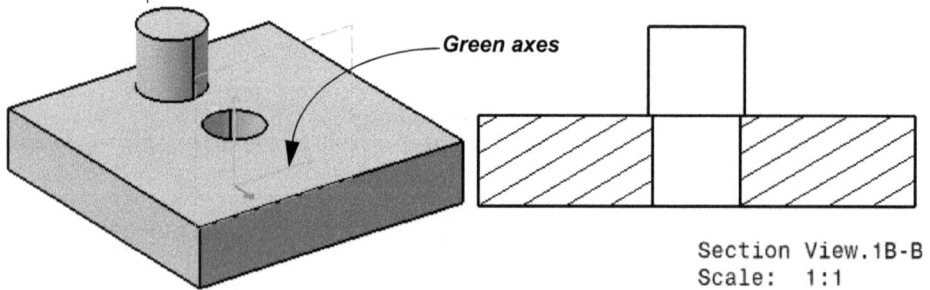

Green axes

```
Section View.1B-B
Scale:   1:1
```

Figure 6–4

Section Cut

A section cut view annotation plane defines both a viewing orientation and a cutting plane. When the view is extracted to the Drafting workbench, a section cut view is automatically generated. The section cut only displays the geometry that lies on the cutting plane. All background geometry is not displayed. A section cut is identified by a yellow reference axis. An example is shown in Figure 6–5.

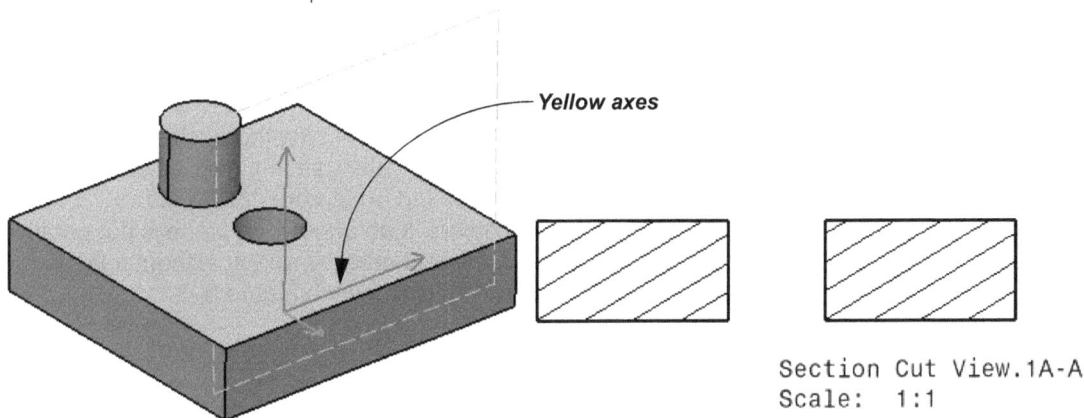

Yellow axes

Section Cut View.1A-A
Scale: 1:1

Figure 6–5

Active View

The active view plane is identified by a red border on the model. In the specification tree, the active view is displayed with a red plane and it is underlined, as shown in Figure 6–6. If no view planes exist, one is automatically created that accommodates the annotation being defined.

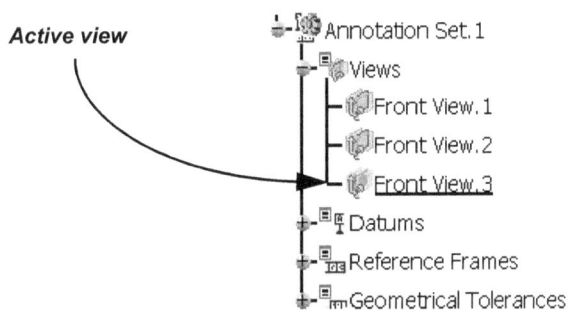

Active view

Figure 6–6

To activate a view plane, right-click on the view in the specification tree and select **Display View**. You can also activate the view by double-clicking the view frame on the model.

Step 2 - Create texts.

You can create three kinds of text annotations:

- Text with Leader

- Text

- Text Parallel to Screen

You have the option to add text with or without a leader. The text in either case is defined on an annotation plane; as a result, the orientation of the text is based on the orientation of the annotation plane you select. If an annotation plane is not parallel to the screen, then all the text created with or without a leader is not parallel to the screen, as shown in Figure 6–7.

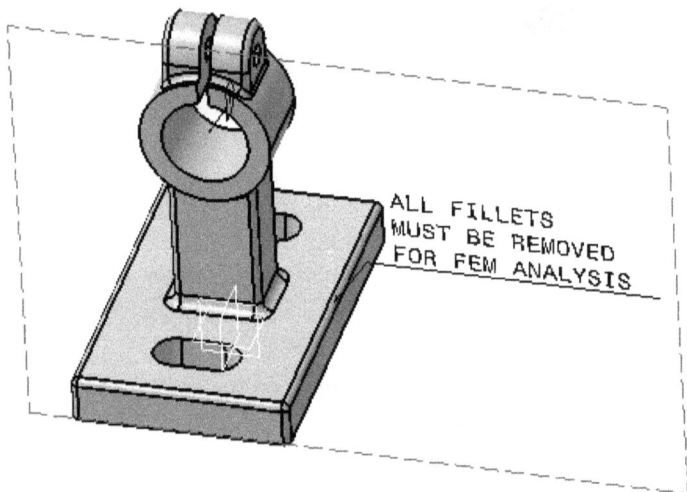

Figure 6–7

If you want some text to remain parallel to the screen, regardless of the orientation of the annotation plane, use (Text Parallel to Screen).

General Steps

To add multiple lines of text press <Shift>+ <Enter>.

How To: Create any of the three types of 3D text:

1. Activate an annotation plane:
   - Double-click on the required annotation plane in the specification tree or directly from the model to activate it. The orientation of the selected annotation plane defines the orientation of the text.
2. Select the required 3D text icon.
3. Select a geometric element in the model. The selected element is used as a reference for the location of the text. If the Text tool is being used, you can also select a location on the background of CATIA.
4. Enter the required text in the Text Editor shown in Figure 6–8.

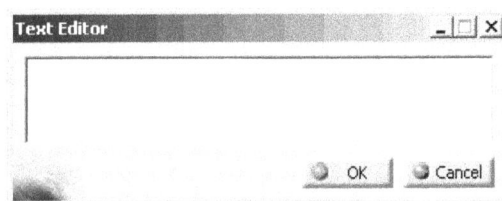

Figure 6–8

5. Click **OK** to complete the creation of the text. The text feature displays under the **Notes** node in the specification tree, as shown in Figure 6–9.

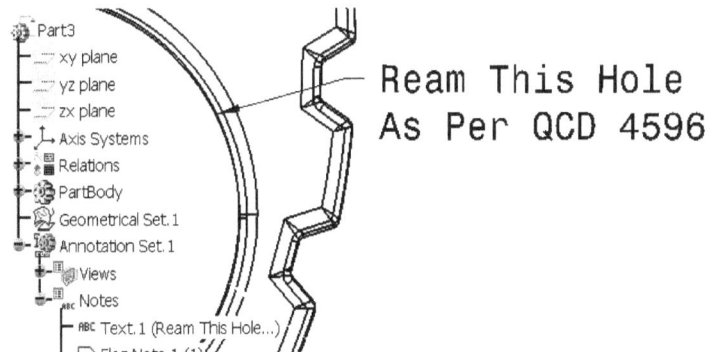

Figure 6–9

Editing Text

Formatting for all texts is applied using the Properties dialog box, as shown in Figure 6–10.

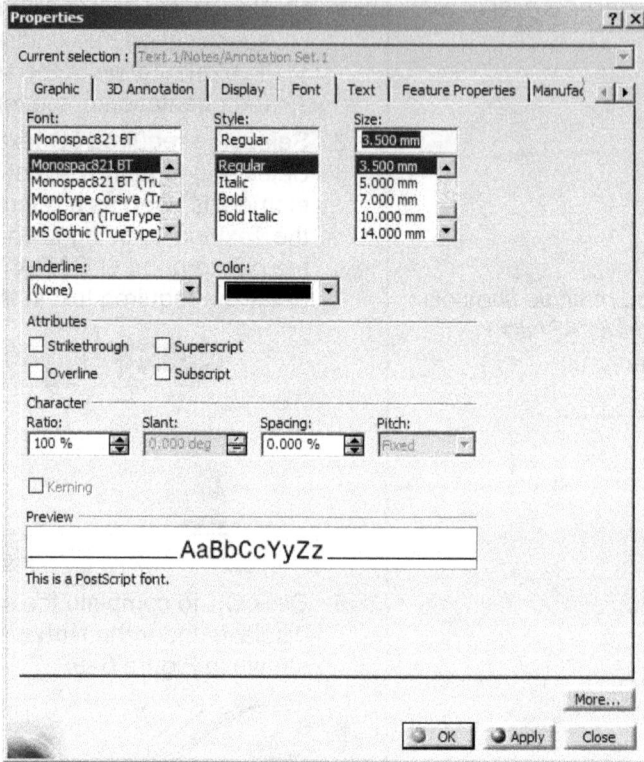

Figure 6–10

Handling Text Features

Select the text and move it using the handles shown in Figure 6–11.

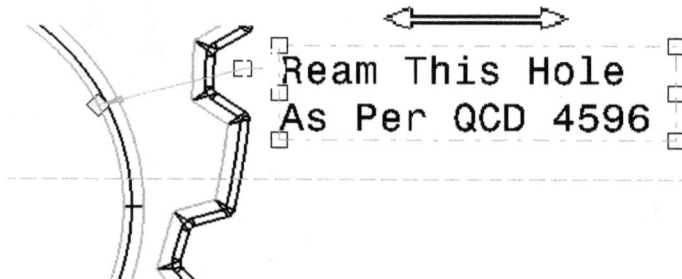

Figure 6–11

Select the yellow diamond and right-click to access the text leader handling options, as shown in Figure 6–12.

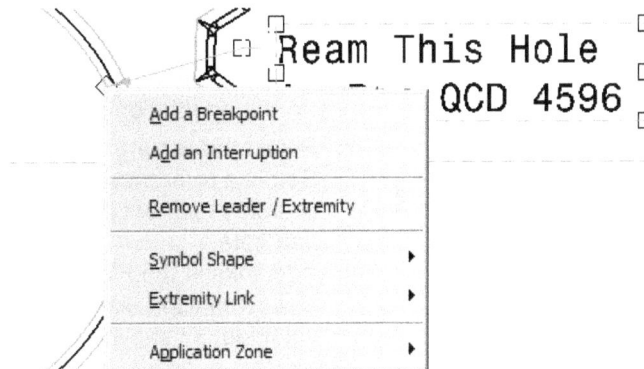

Figure 6–12

Step 3 - Create flag notes.

Flag notes enable you to add a list of files or web links to the document. You can quickly open a related spreadsheet, presentation, or web site from the CATIA document from a flag note. An example is shown in Figure 6–13.

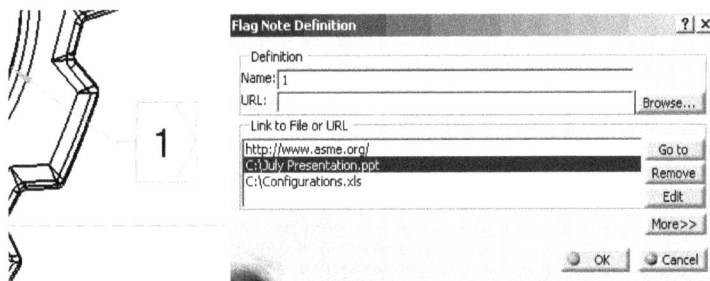

Figure 6–13

You have the option of adding flag notes with or without a leader. The flag note in either case is defined on an annotation plane similar to 3D text.

You can create two kinds of flag notes:

- Flag Note with Leader

- Flag Note

General Steps

How To: Create Flag Notes

1. Activate an annotation plane.
   - Double-click on the required annotation plane in the specification tree or directly from the model to activate it. The orientation of the selected annotation plane defines the orientation of the flag note.
2. Select the required flag note icon.
3. Select a reference geometric element in the model. The selected element is used as a reference for the location of the flag note.
4. Add links in the Flag Note Definition dialog box. The Flag Note Definition dialog box opens after a reference element is selected, as shown in Figure 6–14.

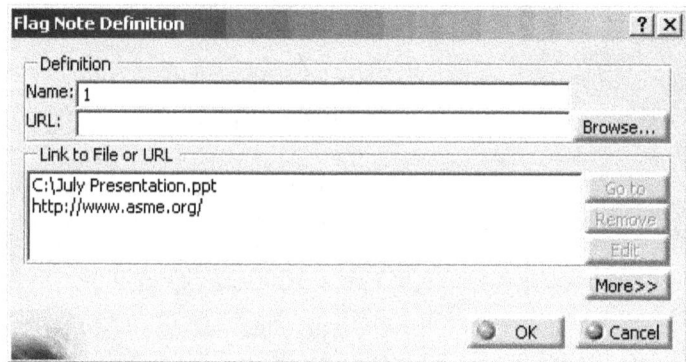

Figure 6–14

   - Enter a URL in the URL field and press the <Tab> key to add it to the Link to File or URL list. Click **Browse** and browse to the file to link from in the File Selection dialog box. Clicking **Open** adds the file path to the Link to File or URL list.

5. Click **OK** to complete the creation of the flag note. The flag note feature displays under the **Notes** node in the specification tree, as shown in Figure 6–15.

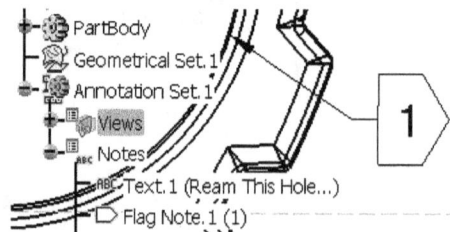

Figure 6–15

Handling Flag Note Features

Select the flag note and move it using the handles shown in Figure 6–16.

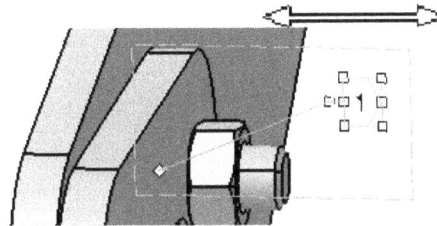

Figure 6–16

Step 4 - Create welding symbols.

Welding symbols enable you to communicate welding specification information in a CATIA model. An example is shown in Figure 6–17.

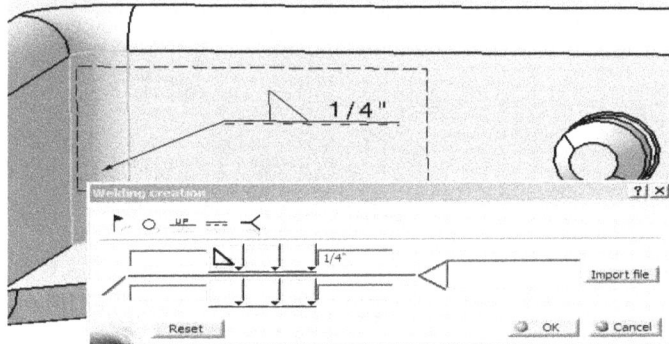

Figure 6–17

General Steps

How To: Create Welding Symbols

1. Activate an annotation plane.
   - Double-click on the required annotation plane in the specification tree or directly from the model to activate it. The orientation of the selected annotation plane defines the orientation of the welding symbol.

2. Click (Weld Feature).
3. Select a reference geometric element in the model. The selected element is used as a reference for the location of the welding symbol.

---

4. Enter information in the Welding Creation dialog box. The Welding Creation dialog box opens after a reference element is selected, as shown in Figure 6–18.

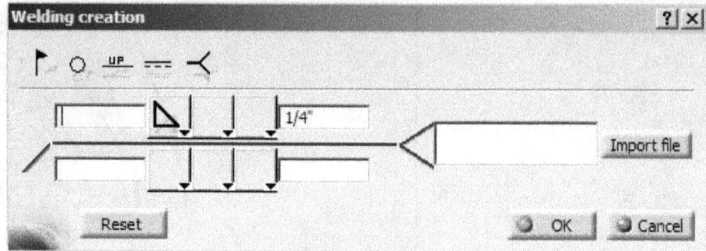

Figure 6–18

• Enter the welding specification as required.

5. Click **OK** to complete the creation of the flag note. The flag note feature displays under the **Notes** node in the specification tree, as shown in Figure 6–19.

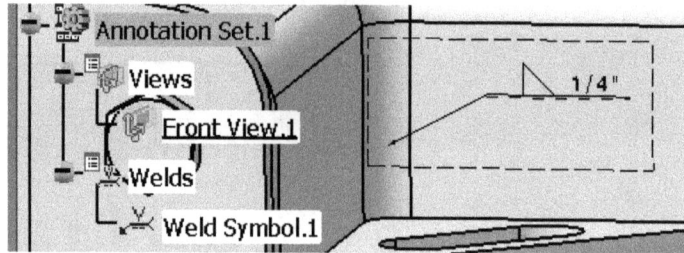

Figure 6–19

Handling Weld Features

Select the weld feature and move it using the handles shown in Figure 6–20.

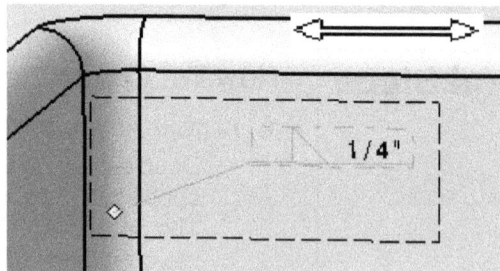

Figure 6–20

6.3 Managing Annotations

Annotation Switch On/Off

Since 3D annotations add visual complexity to the model, they can be toggled on and off to simplify the display. If you receive a model that has no annotations displayed, you must toggle on the annotation set. To toggle the annotations on and off, right-click on the annotation set and select **Annotation Set Switch On/Switch Off**. This is useful when viewing an annotated model in an assembly.

When an annotation set has been toggled off, the name of the annotation set displays in the specification tree, as shown in Figure 6–21. However, the branch cannot be expanded and no annotations display on the model.

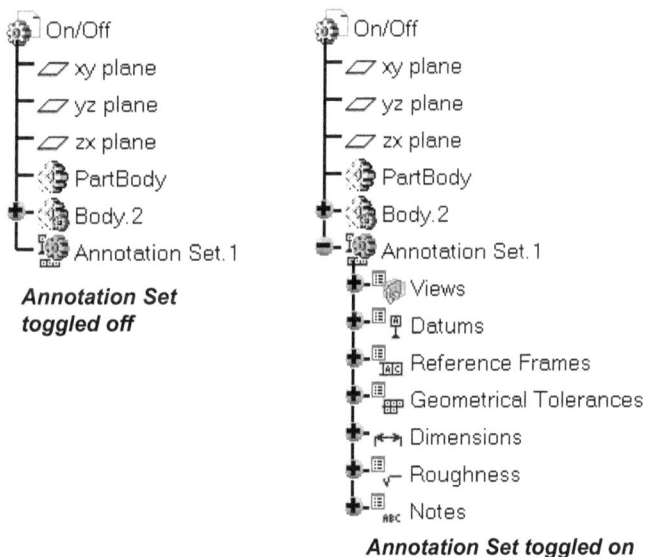

Annotation Set toggled off

Annotation Set toggled on

Figure 6–21

3D Annotation Query

The 3D Annotation Query tool ( ) is used to identify the connection between a selected annotation and the rest of the model by highlighting elements on the model and in the specification tree when enabled. For example, the system highlights the weld reference location if the weld feature is selected, as shown in Figure 6–22.

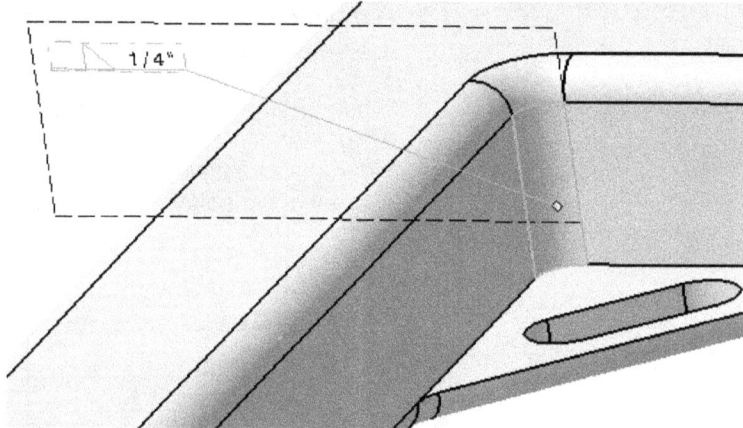

1 / 4 "

Figure 6–22

The 3D Annotation Query tool is toggled on and off by selecting it in the Annotations toolbar, as shown in Figure 6–23.

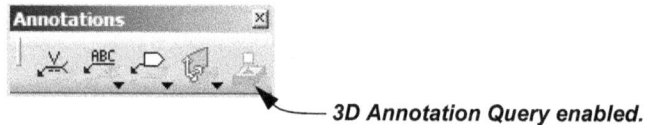

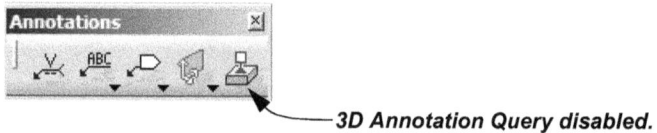

3D Annotation Query enabled.

3D Annotation Query disabled.

Figure 6–23

Practice 6a

Create and Manage Annotations

Practice Objectives

- Create an annotated view.
- Create text annotations.
- Manage annotated views.

In this practice, you will create annotation view to indicate problems on a bore assembly.

Task 1 - Open the assembly.

The files for this practice can be found in the BoreDevice directory.

1. Open **SectionBoreDevice.CATProduct**.

2. Verify that the Assembly Design workbench is active.

Task 2 - Set up an Annotated View.

Before the Annotated view can be accessed, you must ensure that the model is oriented correctly. Once in the view, the model cannot be rotated.

1. In the Annotations toolbar, click ![icon] (View From Reference). The icon should turn orange.

2. Select the Plane, as shown in Figure 6–24.

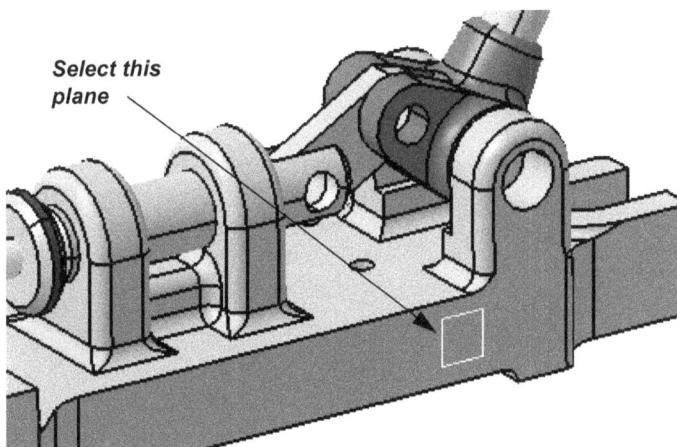

Select this plane

Figure 6–24

3. The View Creation dialog box opens, as shown in Figure 6–25. Name the new view as **Interference comments**.

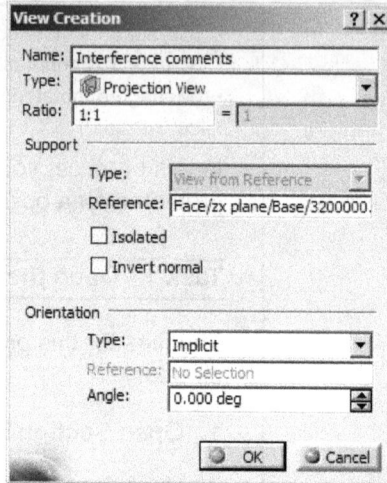

Figure 6–25

4. Leave all other parameters in the box at default values and click **OK**. The new view displays in the specification tree, as shown in Figure 6–26.

Figure 6–26

5. Click [icon] (3D-Annotation-Query Switch On/Switch Off) to activate it.

6. Select the **Interference comments** view in the tree. The model should display, as shown in Figure 6–27. The cut displays how the annotation view plane is located in the CATIA model.

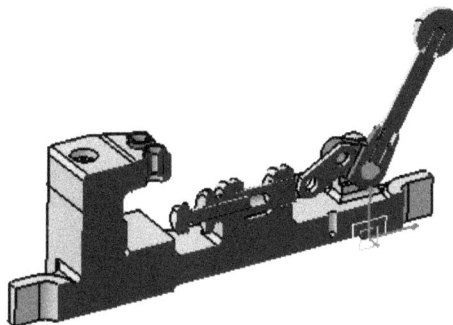

Figure 6–27

Task 3 - Create an annotation.

This annotation notes the interference detected between the ball and the lever.

1. Click ⬚ (Right View) in the View toolbar. Zoom in on the area around the ball, approximately as shown in Figure 6–28.

Figure 6–28

2. Select the **Interference comments** view in the tree to see the existing interference between the ball and the lever parts, as shown in Figure 6–29. Click anywhere in the background to return to normal view.

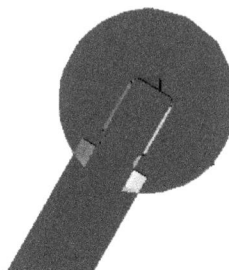

Figure 6–29

---

3. Click ![ABC] (Text with Leader) and click on the location at the junction between the ball and the lever, approximately as shown in Figure 6–30.

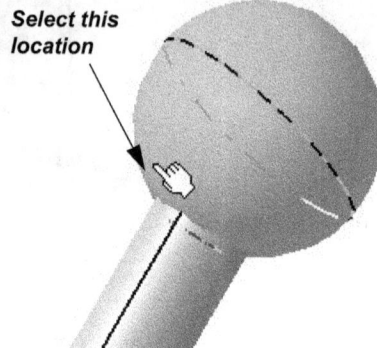

Select this location

Figure 6–30

4. In the Text Editor, enter **Interference between ball and lever**, as shown in Figure 6–31.

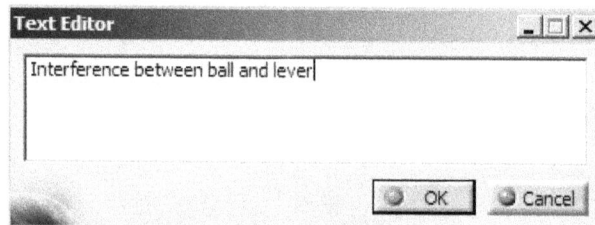

Text Editor

Interference between ball and lever

OK   Cancel

Figure 6–31

5. Click **OK**. The Text displays in the tree and in the model, approximately as shown in Figure 6–32.

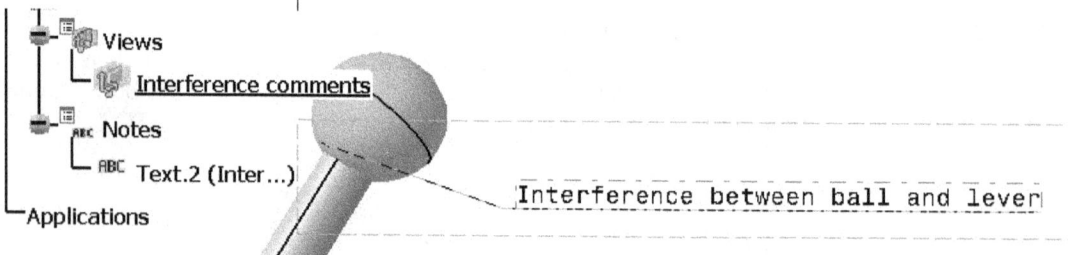

Views
Interference comments
Notes
Text.2 (Inter...)
Applications

Interference between ball and lever

Figure 6–32

6. Right-click on the text and select Properties in the menu.

7. In the Properties box that opens, select *Font* tab and select the following parameters, as shown in Figure 6–33:

- *Style:* **Bold**
- *Size:* **2.5mm**

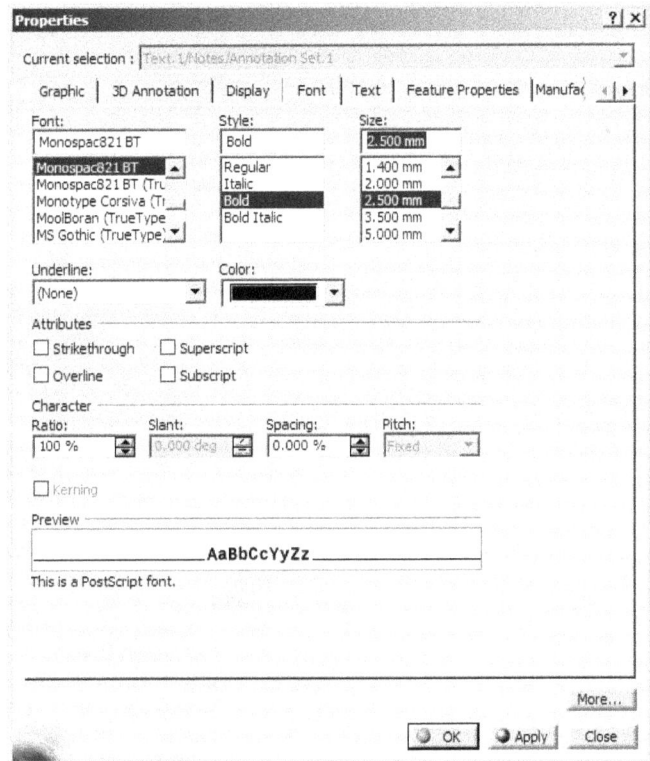

Figure 6–33

8. Click **OK** to complete.

9. Click on the text and, while holding the left mouse button, drag the text to the location shown in Figure 6–34.

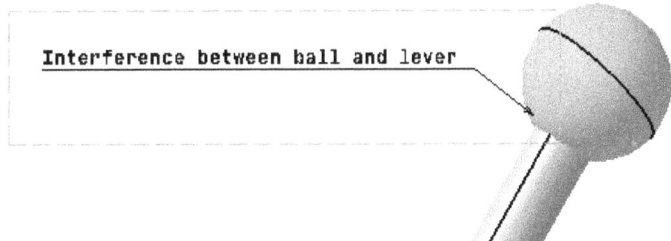

Figure 6–34

Task 4 - Add another annotation.

This annotation notes the interference detected between the lever and the lever angle.

1. Select the **Interference comments** view in the tree to visualize the existing interference between the lever and the lever angle parts, as shown in Figure 6–35. Click anywhere in the background to return to normal view.

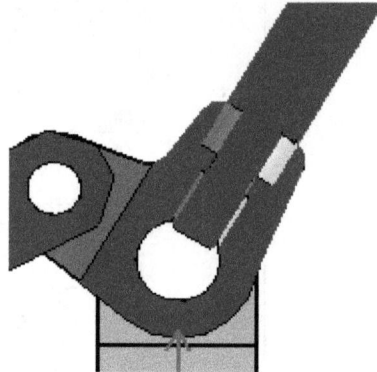

Figure 6–35

2. Click (Text with Leader) and click on the location at the junction between the lever and the lever angle, approximately as shown in Figure 6–36.

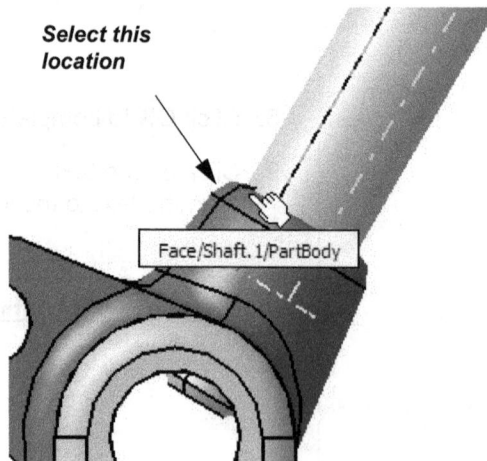

Figure 6–36

3. In the Text Editor, enter **Interference between lever and lever angle**, as shown in Figure 6–37. Click **OK** to complete.

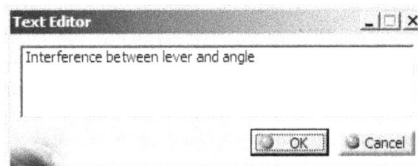

Figure 6–37

4. Modify the text properties (use steps 6 through 8 in Task 3 above as the guideline) as following:

- *Style:* **Bold**
- *Size:* **2.5mm**

5. Drag the text to a new location. The model should display, as shown in Figure 6–38.

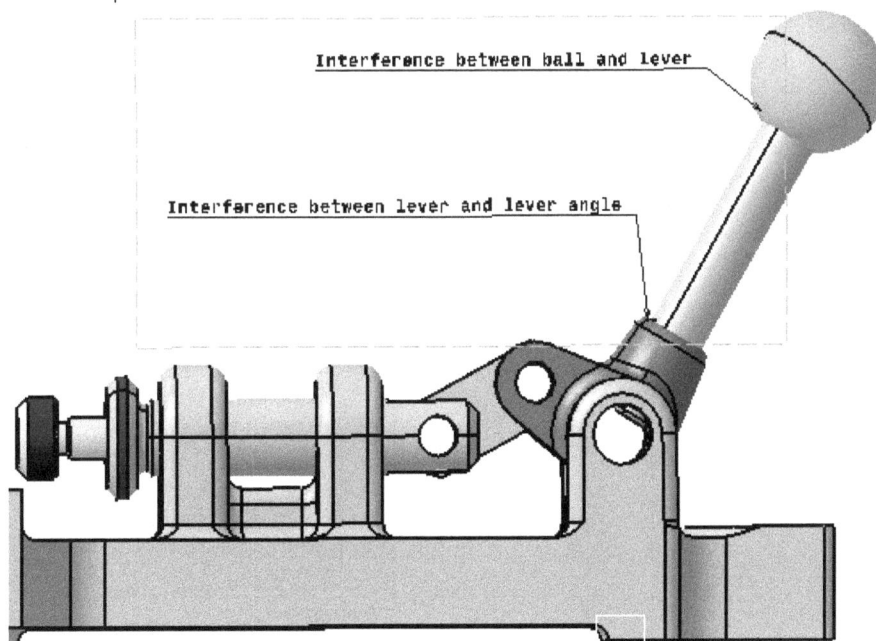

Figure 6–38

Task 5 - Finalize the annotations.

1. Right-click on the **Interference comments** view in the tree and select **Hide/Show**.

2. Change the view to Isometric. The model should display, as shown in Figure 6–39.

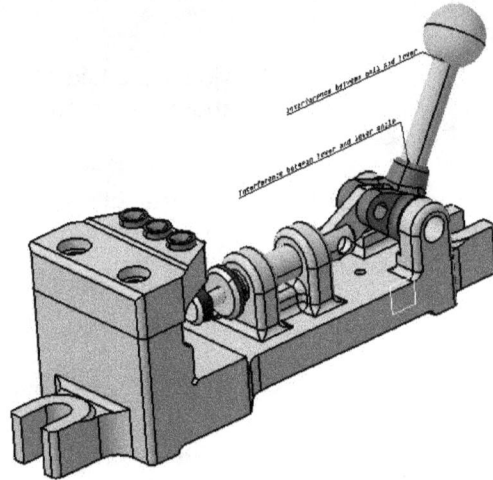

Figure 6–39

3. Right-click on the **Annotation Set.1** in the tree and select **Annotation Set Switch On/Switch Off**, as shown in Figure 6–40.

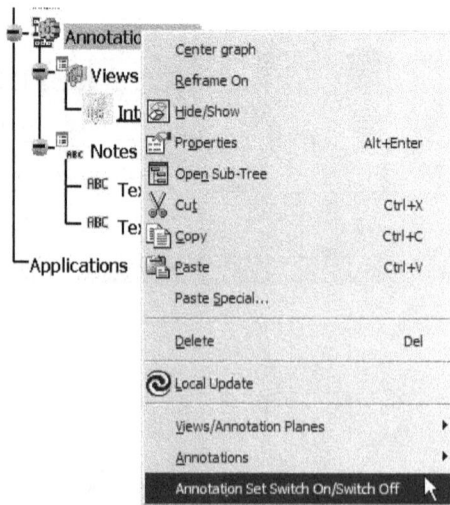

Figure 6–40

4. The annotations are now hidden, and the model displays, as shown in Figure 6–41.

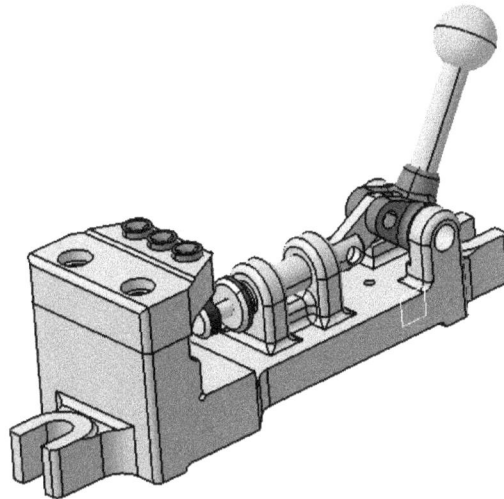

Figure 6–41

5. Save and close the file.

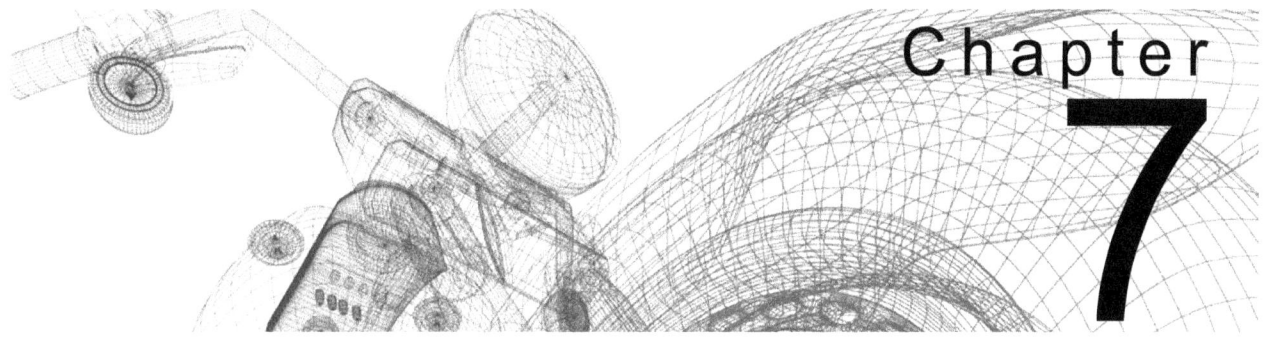

Image Capture

Model images might be required to communicate information about the design to other people. These images can be attached to an e-mail or inserted into product documentation. This chapter also discusses methods of printing images directly from ENOVIA DMU.

Learning Objectives in this Chapter

- Capture model images.
- Learn how to print images.

7.1 Capturing Images

CATIA enables you to capture images from the screen in raster or vector formats. These images can be saved to an album, printed, or copied to a clipboard for use in other applications.

General Steps

Use the following general steps to capture an image:

1. Activate the Capture tool.
2. Define image properties.
3. Capture the image.
4. Define the output of the image.

Step 1 - Activate the Capture tool.

Select **Tools>Image>Capture**. The Capture dialog box opens, as shown in Figure 7–1.

Figure 7–1

Step 2 - Define image properties.

Images can be taken in pixel or vector formats. A pixel image, often called a raster image, consists of squares of color (pixels). When you zoom into a pixel image, you can see each individual pixel. Pixel formats are resolution-dependent; meaning that the higher the resolution of the image, the better the quality when

increasing its size. To create a pixel image, click the ▣ (Pixel Mode) icon in the Capture dialog box.

The next time you open the Capture dialog box, the icon that you had selected last (▣ or ▣) will be selected by default.

Vector images are comprised of mathematical instructions on how to create the image. It is divided into objects, each of which is stored in the file with information about its position in the image, color, size, etc. Vector images are resolution-independent, enabling it to be resized without losing

detail. To create a vector image, click the ▣ (Vector Mode) icon in the Capture dialog box.

Additional options can be set to control the output of the image.

Click the ▣ (Options) icon to open the Capture Options dialog box.

General Tab

The *General* tab shown in Figure 7–2 controls options relevant to both types of image output (pixel and vector).

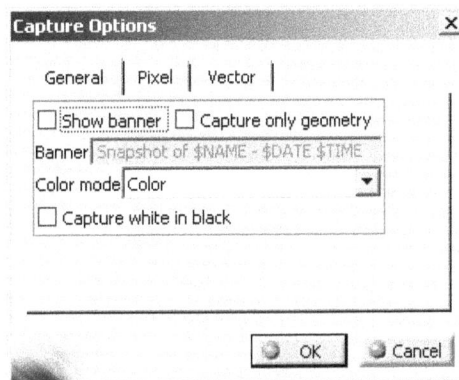

Figure 7–2

Banner

Select the **Show Banner** option to display a banner at the bottom of the image. By default, this banner displays the name of the model and the date and time when the shot was taken, as shown in Figure 7–3. Use the Banner field to modify the information output in the banner.

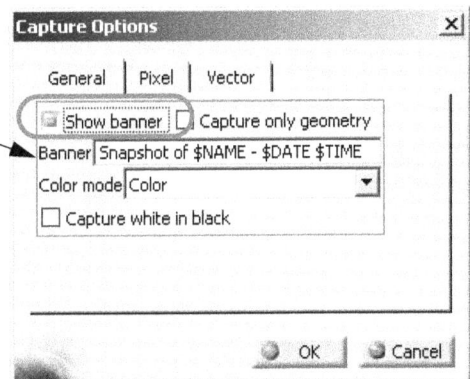

Figure 7–3

Capture Only Geometry

Select the **Capture Only Geometry** option to capture the geometry of the model without the background information, such as the specification tree and compass. For example, the image on the left of Figure 7–4 is taken without having the option selected and the image on the right is taken with the option selected. The **Capture Only Geometry** option cannot be used with vector images.

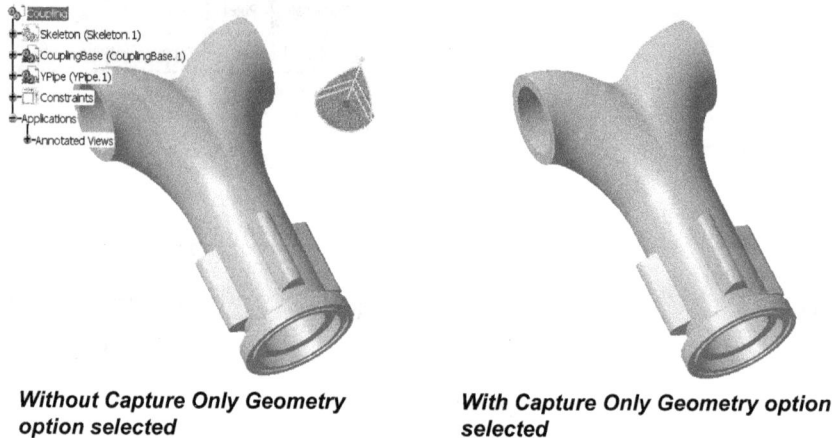

Without Capture Only Geometry option selected

With Capture Only Geometry option selected

Figure 7–4

Color Mode

Use the Color mode drop-down list to select the appropriate output color, as shown in Figure 7–5. By default, images are output in color, but can be changed to Greyscale or Monochrome.

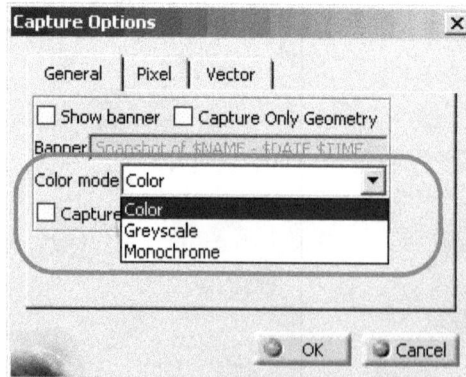

Figure 7–5

Capture White Pixels as Black

Select the **Capture White Pixels as Black** option to change all of the white elements on the screen to black in the image. This is useful if you are creating the image on a white background.

Pixel Tab

Select the *Pixel* tab, as shown in Figure 7–6, to customize options specific to pixel images. The options in this tab are described in the table below.

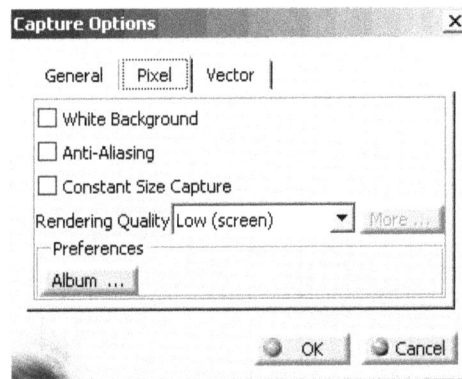

Figure 7–6

Option	Description
White Background	CATIA background color is replaced with white in the image.
Anti-Aliasing	Modifies the appearance of lines to make jagged edges look smoother.
Constant Size Capture	Captures images to a scale of 1:1, no matter the resolution.
Rendering Quality	Sets the quality of the output image. Quality can be set to: • Low (screen) - quality matches the screen resolution. • Medium • Highest • Custom - Image pixel and print size can be customized by clicking **More**.
Album	Defines preferences for storing the images captured to an album.

Vector Tab

Select the *Vector* tab, as shown in Figure 7–7, to customize options specific to vector images. The options in the *Vector* tab are described in the table below.

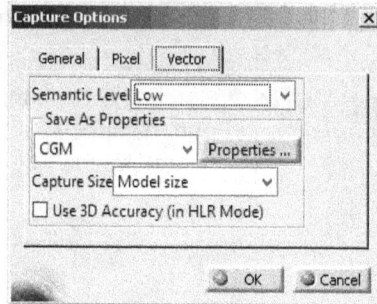

Figure 7–7

Option	Description
Semantic Level	Selects the Rendering mode, which can be: • Discretized • Low • Polyline • Polyline and Conic • Polyline and Spline
Save As Properties	Formats image can be saved as: • CGM • Generic PostScript • Generic HP-GL2 RTL Use **Properties** to customize the format properties.
Capture Size	The image of the model can be saved as: • Model size • Display size
Use 3D Accuracy (in HLR Mode)	Use 3D Accuracy when the display is in HLR Mode.

Step 3 - Capture the image.

You can capture only a selected section of the screen or the entire screen. To capture the entire screen area, click the

(Screen Mode) icon in the Capture dialog box. To capture

only a section of the screen, click the (Select Mode) icon to activate the Selection mode. Click on the screen to open the selection box. While holding the left mouse button, drag the cursor to create the selection area. Release the left mouse button to complete the selection box, as shown in Figure 7–8.

Selection box can be resized by dragging the border of the box.

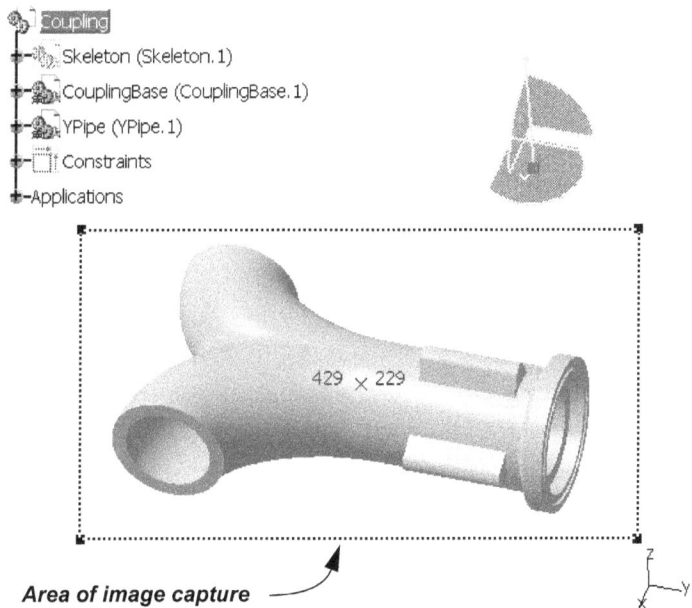

Figure 7–8

To capture the image, click the (Capture) icon. The Capture Preview dialog box opens displaying the captured image, as shown in Figure 7–9.

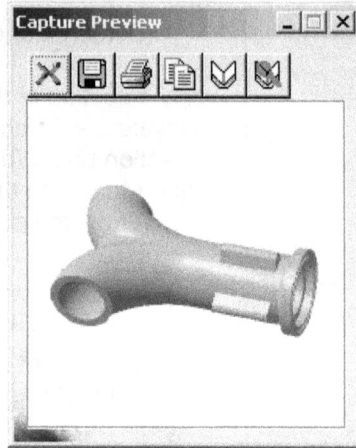

Figure 7–9

Step 4 - Define the output of the image.

You can also open the album by selecting **Tools>Image>Album**.

A number of options are available for the output of the image in the Capture Preview dialog box. These options are described as follows:

Icon	Option	Description
	Cancel	Cancels the capture and closes the preview window.
	Save As	Saves the capture to the hard drive.
	Print	Opens the Print dialog box to print the image.
	Copy	Copies the image to the clipboard where it can be pasted into another Windows application.
	Album	Stores the image in the album.
	Open Album	Opens the album.

Album

The album is used to store images, which are stored on your system in the folder defined by the CATTemp environment variable. You can open the album from the Capture Preview window by clicking the ![icon] (Open Album) icon. The Album dialog box opens, as shown in Figure 7–10. The options that are available in the dialog box and in the shortcut menu are described in the table below.

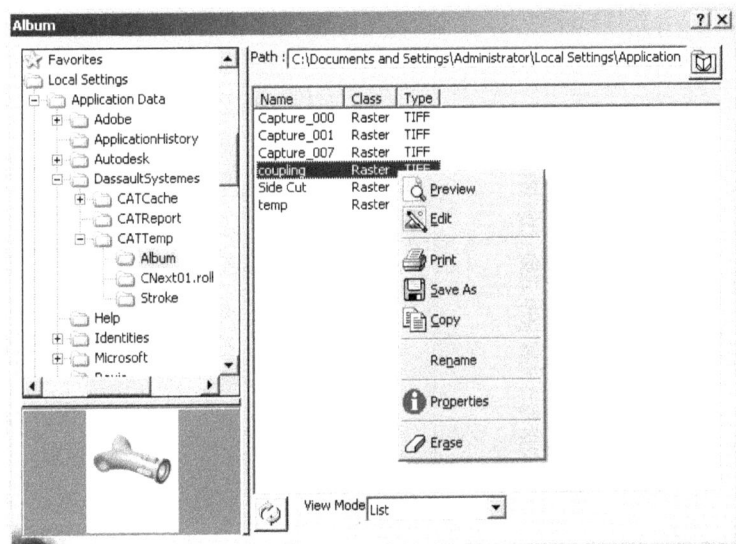

Figure 7–10

Icon	Description
![icon]	Changes the file path to the album folder.
![icon]	Refreshes the list of files stored in the current Album folder.
![icon]	Saves the selected image under another name or in another format.
![icon]	Opens the Print dialog box to print the image.
![icon]	Opens the selected image in the Print Preview dialog box. Use <Ctrl> to select more then one image to print preview at a time. All images are placed on the same sheet for printing.
![icon]	Copies the image to the clipboard where it can be pasted into another windows application.

	Removes the selected image from the album.
	Opens the Image Information Panel for the selected image.
	Opens the Image Editor panel to modify the image. Not available for vector images.
Rename	Enables you to rename the image.

7.2 Printing Images

Once you have completed and saved your image(s), you can print them.

General Steps

Use the following general steps to print a document:

1. Activate the Print tool.
2. Select the printer.
3. Configure the layout.
4. Print the document.

Step 1 - Activate the Print tool.

Select **File>Print** to open the Print dialog box shown in Figure 7–11.

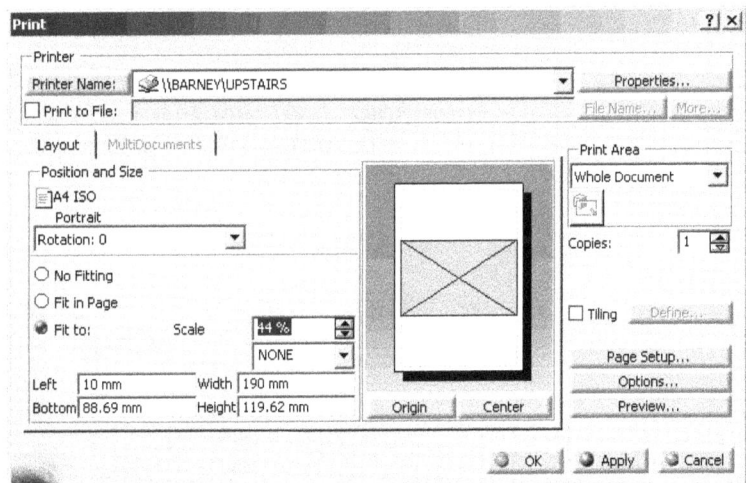

Figure 7–11

Step 2 - Select the printer.

Images can be sent to any printer set up in Windows, or saved to a .PRN file.

Printer

To print to a printer, select it in the Printer drop-down list. If required, the properties of the printer can be modified by clicking **Properties**.

File

Prints can be saved to a .PRN file by selecting the **Print To File** option. Click **File Name** to create a print file to which to save the document. Using the Print to File dialog box, navigate to the directory to which you want to save the print, and enter a name for the print in the *File Name* field, as shown in Figure 7–12.

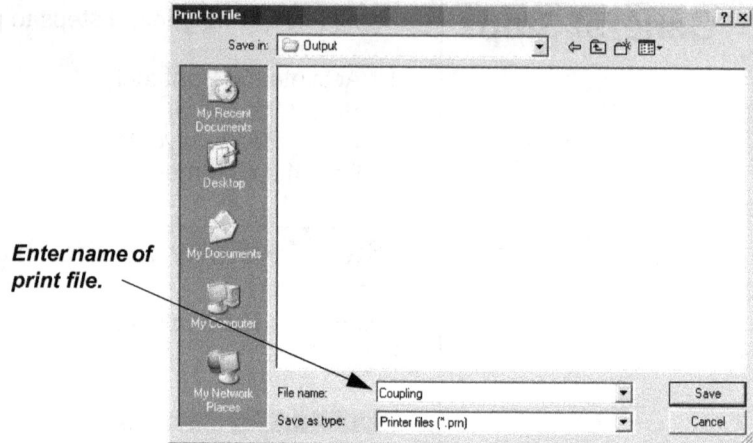

Figure 7–12

Click **Save** to return to the Print dialog box. The Print to File field is populated with the path and filename, as shown in Figure 7–13.

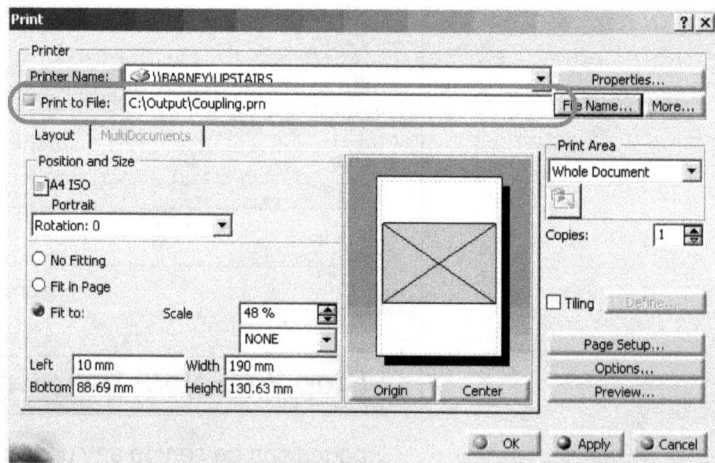

Figure 7–13

Step 3 - Configure the layout.

The layout of the print can be customized to suit your requirements.

Position and Size

The preview window of the Print dialog box indicates how the print displays on the page. If the current position is not correct, you can change it using a number of options.

Documents can be rotated on the sheet using the Rotation drop-down list. To change the scale of the document, use the fitting options **Fit in Page** and **Fit to**.

The **Fit in Page** option scales the document to fit the page based on the selected rotation and also centers the document on the page.

Fitting can be customized by selecting **Fit to**, as shown in Figure 7–14. This option enables you to customize the scale of the document and its location on the page.

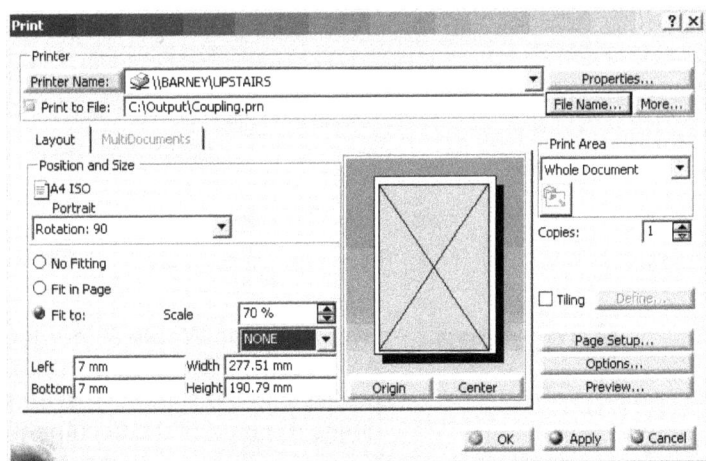

Figure 7–14

The position of the document can also be changed from the center of the page to the origin by clicking **Origin**. An example of both origin and center position is shown in Figure 7–15.

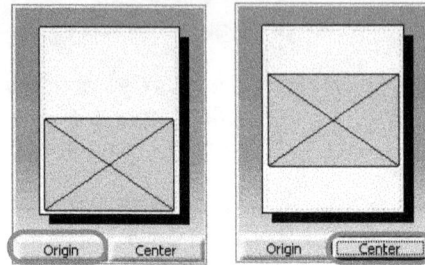

Figure 7–15

You might need to change the paper size to fit the document.

Select the **No Fitting** option to scale the document to a 1:1 scale. Click **Page Setup** to select a new page size, as shown in Figure 7–16.

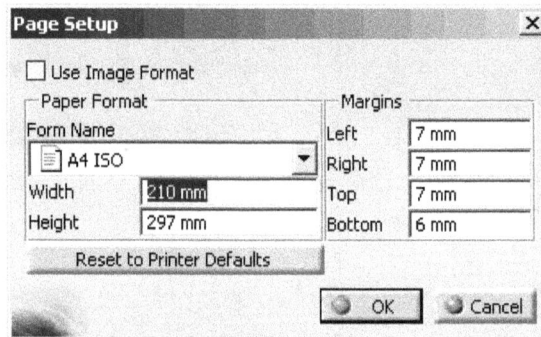

Figure 7–16

Print Area

By default, the **Whole Document** option is selected in the Print Area section. The **Display** option enables you to change what displays on the screen. The **Selection** option enables you to define the area of the document that you want to print. To define the print area, click the 🖼 icon, left-click in the document to start the box and while holding the left mouse button, drag the cursor. Release the left mouse button to finish, as shown in Figure 7–17.

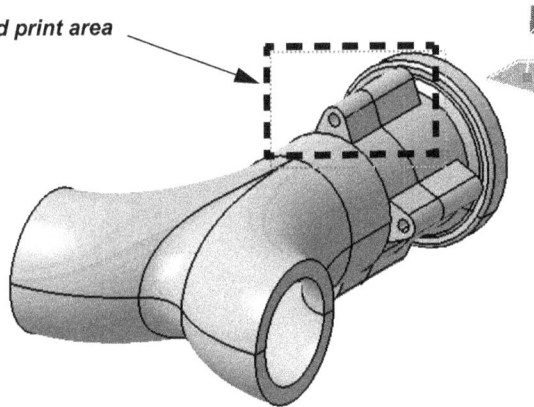

Defined print area

Figure 7–17

Options

Additional options for the print can be configured by clicking **Options** to open the Options dialog box, as shown in Figure 7–18. Using this dialog box, you can adjust the image's color output, add banners and company logos, and customize its quality.

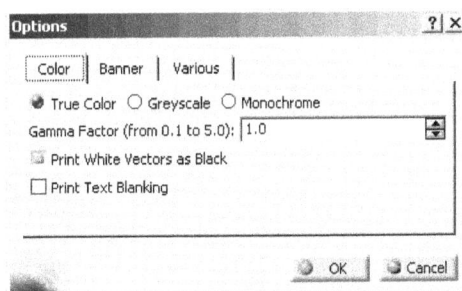

Figure 7–18

Step 4 - Print the document.

Click **OK** to print the image. It is printed to the selected printer with the customized settings.

Quick Print

Documents can also be printed using the **Quick Print** option. With this option, the document is sent to the default printer, using the default settings. To **Quick Print** a document, click the

(Quick Print) icon in the Standard toolbar.

Practice 7a | Capturing Images

Practice Objectives

- Set up an image capture.
- Capture an image.
- Save an image to an album.
- Copy an image to other documents.

In this practice, you will take screen shots of annotation views, which will be used to document your findings. You will save these images to the album and import them into other documents.

Task 1 - Open the assembly.

The files for this practice can be found in the BoreDevice directory.

1. Open **BoreDeviceComplete.CATProduct**. The assembly displays, as shown in Figure 7–19.

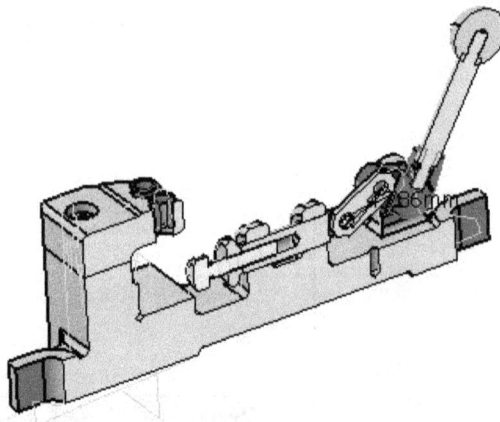

Figure 7–19

2. Ensure that the DMU Navigator workbench is active.

Task 2 - Capture an image.

1. Select **Tools>Image>Capture** to open the Capture dialog box.

2. Click the (Pixel Mode) icon to set the capture to Pixel mode.

3. Click the (Manage Annotated Views) icon in the DMU Review Navigation toolbar, and select the **Interference Comments** view.

4. Click the (Capture) icon to capture the image. A snapshot of the screen is taken and displayed in the Capture Preview window, as shown in Figure 7–20.

Your preview might not look exactly like the preview shown.

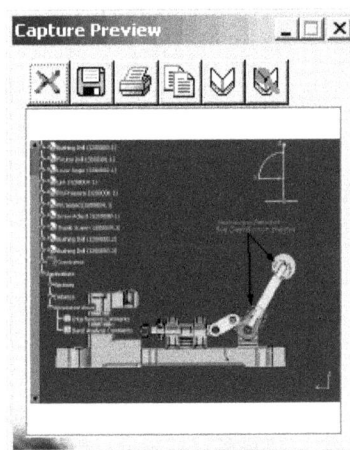

Figure 7–20

This image does not meet the requirements. The background should not have a color, and the compass and specification tree should not be in the view.

5. Click the (Cancel) icon to cancel the image capture.

Task 3 - Change the options for the image.

1. Click the ⬜ (Options) icon to change the configuration of the capture.

2. In the *General* tab, select the **Capture Only Geometry** option to ensure that the specification tree and compass do not appear in the image. Select the **Capture White in black** option to ensure that any white geometry displays when the background is changed to white.

3. Select the **White Background** option in the *Pixel* tab.

4. Click **OK** to return to the Capture dialog box.

5. Click the ⬤ (Capture) icon to recapture the image. The Preview Window displays the new capture, as shown in Figure 7–21.

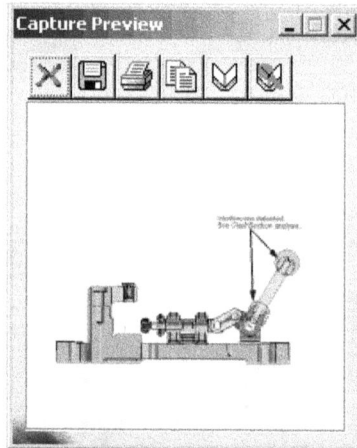

Figure 7–21

Task 4 - Save the image.

1. Click 💾 (Save As) in the Capture Preview window to save the file.

2. Enter **Interference Comments** in the *File Name* field and save the file to the BoreDevice directory. Leave the file format as **Windows Bitmap**.

3. Click **Save** to save the file to the hard drive.

4. In the Capture Preview window, click the ⌄ (Album) icon to save the image to the album.

5. Click the ✕ (Cancel) icon to exit the preview window and return to the Capture dialog box.

Task 5 - Create another image.

1. Click the ⊞ (Manage Annotated Views) icon in the DMU Review Navigation toolbar and select the **Band Analysis Comments** view.

2. Click the ● (Capture) icon to capture the image and the Capture Preview windows displays, as shown in Figure 7–22.

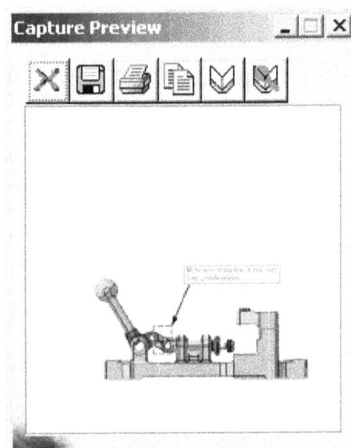

Figure 7–22

In this capture, only the area around the rectangle, including the text, is required.

3. Click the ✕ (Cancel) icon to cancel the capture.

Task 6 - Select the area for capture.

1. In the Capture dialog box, click the ⬚ icon to select the area to be captured.

2. Left-click in the top left corner of the box and drag the cursor to the bottom right of the box. Release the left mouse button to create the selection box, as shown in Figure 7–23.

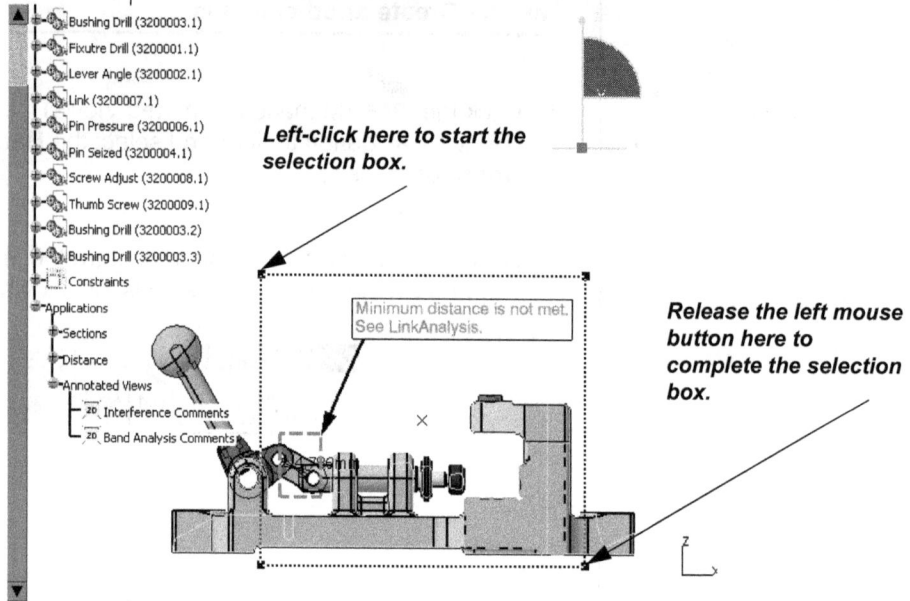

Left-click here to start the selection box.

Release the left mouse button here to complete the selection box.

Bushing Drill (3200003.1)
Fixutre Drill (3200001.1)
Lever Angle (3200002.1)
Link (3200007.1)
Pin Pressure (3200006.1)
Pin Seized (3200004.1)
Screw Adjust (3200008.1)
Thumb Screw (3200009.1)
Bushing Drill (3200003.2)
Bushing Drill (3200003.3)
Constraints
Applications
Sections
Distance
Annotated Views
Interference Comments
Band Analysis Comments

Figure 7–23

3. Click the ● (Capture) icon to capture the image. The Capture Preview window displays the results, as shown in Figure 7–24.

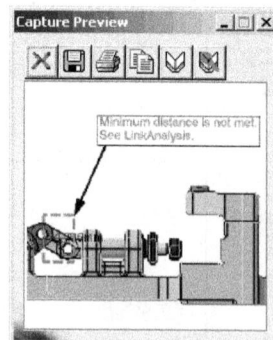

Figure 7–24

Task 7 - Copy an image and save it to an album.

1. Click the (Copy) icon to copy the image to the clipboard.

2. Open Windows Paint by selecting **Start>Run...** in Windows.

3. Enter **mspaint** in the Open field of the Run dialog box, as shown in Figure 7–25.

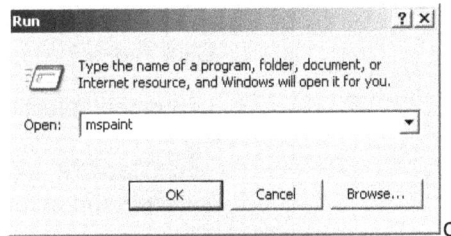

Figure 7–25

4. Click **OK** and the MS Paint application opens.

5. Select **Edit>Paste** in the Paint application. The copied image displays, as shown in Figure 7–26. This technique can be used to copy images to most Windows applications.

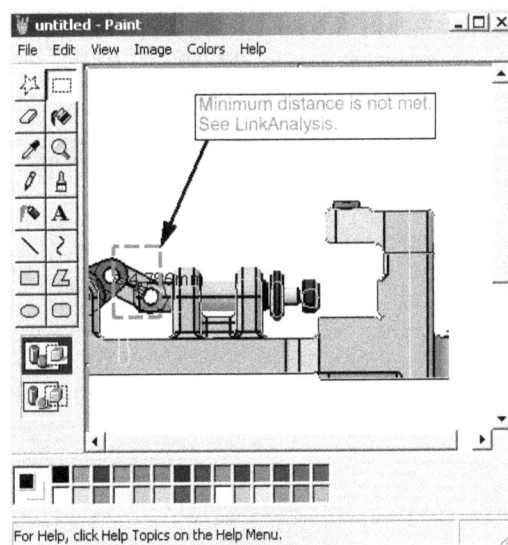

Figure 7–26

6. Close the Paint application. Do not save the image.

7. Click the ⬇ (Album) icon in the Capture Preview Window to save the image to the album.

8. Cancel the Preview to return to the Capture dialog box.

Task 8 - Take a capture in Vector mode.

1. Click the 📐 (Vector Mode) icon to change to Vector mode.

2. Leave the selection area the same and click the

   ● (Capture) icon to capture the image. Note the difference between the outputs of Vector and Pixel modes.

3. Save the Vector image to the album. Do not exit the Capture Preview window.

Task 9 - View the album.

1. Click the ⬇ icon in the Capture Preview dialog box. If you have closed the Capture Preview dialog box, select **Tools> Image>Album**. The Album dialog box opens, as shown in Figure 7–27.

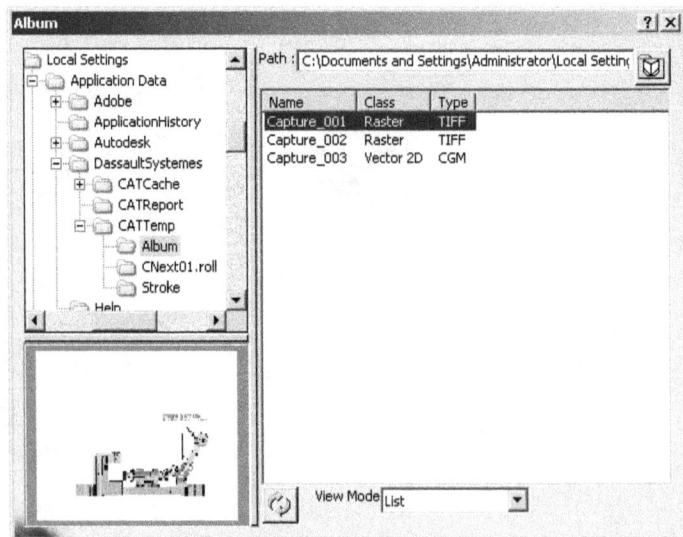

Figure 7–27

2. Right-click on the first image in the album and click the

   (Properties) icon. View the information obtained from the Properties dialog box. It enables you to determine information such as the size, type, and location of the captured files.

3. Click **OK** to close the dialog box.

4. Right-click on the Vector image in the Album. The (Edit) icon is grayed out. Vector images cannot be edited from the Image Editor.

5. Right-click the Vector image and click the (Erase) icon.

6. Click **Yes** to confirm the erase, and the Vector image is removed from the album. Removing an image from the album also removes it from the hard drive.

7. Click to close the Album dialog box.

8. Close the file.

Cache Management

The cache system enables you to load a complete top-level assembly into the viewer using a CGR representation. This management system greatly reduces file retrieval time, view manipulation, and update time.

Learning Objectives in this Chapter

- Learn how to work with the cache system.
- Run in Visualization Mode when working with large product files.

8.1 Working with the Cache System

The cache system enables you to load a complete top-level assembly into the viewer using a CGR representation. This management system greatly reduces file retrieval time, view manipulation, and update time.

When the **Work with the cache system** option is selected, the system converts all of the solid geometry of the assembly into tessellated (or faceted) surfaces, which results in a simplified representation of the geometry.

Design Mode

By default, all parts and products are created and manipulated in Design mode. When working in Design mode, components carry the full geometric weight of the solids they represent. The specification tree of a product in Design mode is shown in Figure 8–1. The specification tree reports the part number and instance number for each part. Each part is expandable and lists the features of that part.

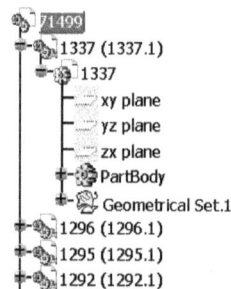

Figure 8–1

Visualization Mode

When a product file is retrieved with the **Work with the cache system** option selected, all components are in Visualization mode. The specification tree of a product in Visualization mode is shown in Figure 8–2. The component instances are listed along with the name of the part or product file and it cannot be expanded to list features.

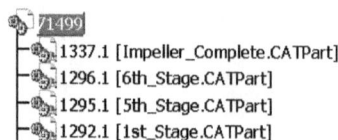

Figure 8–2

CGR File

When working with the cache system, the system displays a representation of the solid geometry. The first time a component is retrieved when working with the cache system, the system writes the geometry representation to a specified directory with a CGR extension.

The Design mode part and product names are shown in Figure 8–3.

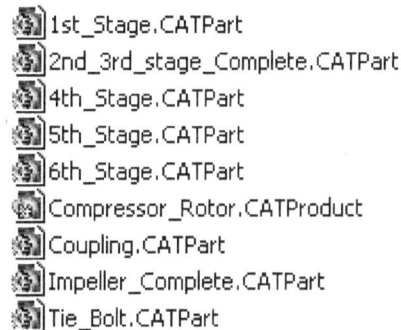

1st_Stage.CATPart
2nd_3rd_stage_Complete.CATPart
4th_Stage.CATPart
5th_Stage.CATPart
6th_Stage.CATPart
Compressor_Rotor.CATProduct
Coupling.CATPart
Impeller_Complete.CATPart
Tie_Bolt.CATPart

Figure 8–3

The same part files that have been written to a.cgr directory as a result of activating and working with the **Cache System** option, are shown in Figure 8–4. The *.cgr file extension and the date code preceding it.

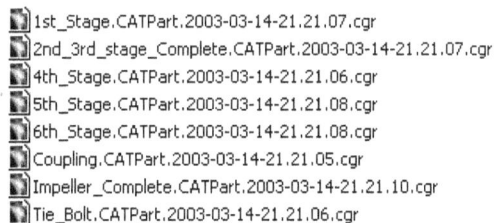

1st_Stage.CATPart.2003-03-14-21.21.07.cgr
2nd_3rd_stage_Complete.CATPart.2003-03-14-21.21.07.cgr
4th_Stage.CATPart.2003-03-14-21.21.06.cgr
5th_Stage.CATPart.2003-03-14-21.21.08.cgr
6th_Stage.CATPart.2003-03-14-21.21.08.cgr
Coupling.CATPart.2003-03-14-21.21.05.cgr
Impeller_Complete.CATPart.2003-03-14-21.21.10.cgr
Tie_Bolt.CATPart.2003-03-14-21.21.06.cgr

Figure 8–4

8.2 Run in Visualization Mode

When working with very large product files it is beneficial to run in Visualization mode. By doing so the time to load, reorient, or make a change to a large product file can be greatly reduced compared to Design mode.

General Steps

Use the following general steps to run in Visualization mode:

1. Activate the cache system.
2. (Optional) Set cache options.
3. Exit and restart ENOVIA.
4. Open a product file for viewing.

Step 1 - Activate the cache system.

Select **Tools>Options>Infrastructure>Product Structure**. Select the *Cache Management* tab and enable the **Work with the cache system** option to activate the cache system, as shown in Figure 8–5.

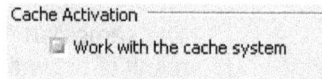

Figure 8–5

A dialog box opens, indicating that the system must be restarted before the cache management setting takes effect, as shown in Figure 8–6.

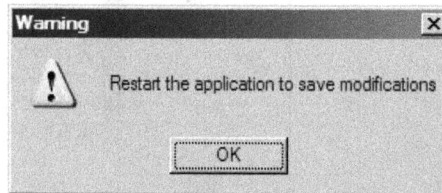

Figure 8–6

| Step 2 - (Optional) Set cache options. |

Local Cache

The local cache directory path specifies the file path to a directory on your system where the *.cgr files are stored. The first time a component is retrieved, it is tessellated, and the corresponding *.cgr file is computed and written to the local cache directory. The next time the component is loaded using cache management, the system searches for the corresponding *.cgr file from the local cache directory and loads it.

For Windows 2000, the system default local cache directory is *C:\Documents and Settings\<user name>\Local Settings\Application Data\DassaultSystemes\CATCache*. (Windows XP).

Click the ⬚ icon beside the Path to the local cache field to browse to the required directory, as shown in Figure 8–7. The file path only needs to be set once; however, it must be set again if the directory changes.

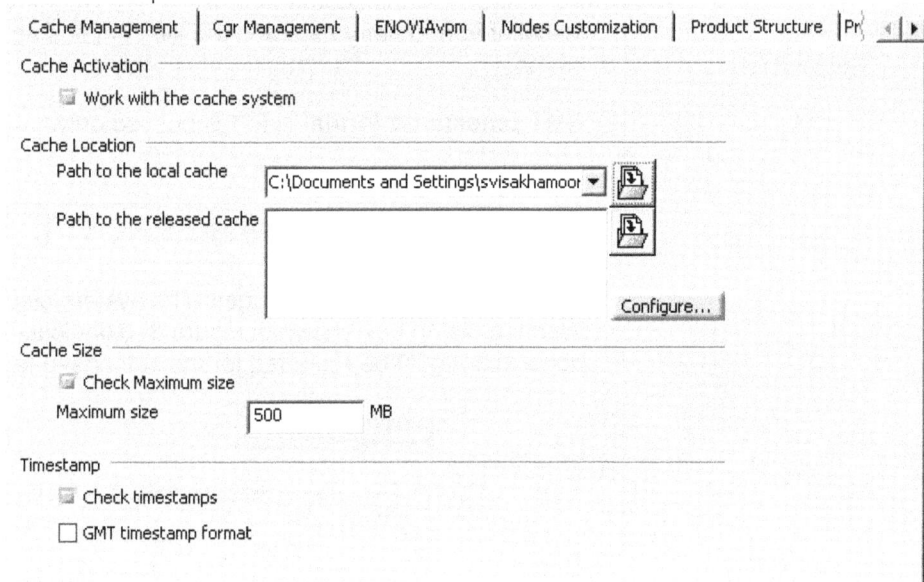

Cache Management | Cgr Management | ENOVIAvpm | Nodes Customization | Product Structure | Pr ◄ ►

Cache Activation
☐ Work with the cache system

Cache Location
Path to the local cache [C:\Documents and Settings\svisakhamoor ▾] ⬚
Path to the released cache [   ] ⬚

Configure...

Cache Size
☐ Check Maximum size
Maximum size [500] MB

Timestamp
☐ Check timestamps
☐ GMT timestamp format

Figure 8–7

Released Cache

A file path and search order can be specified for released cache. Released cache is a read-only cache directory that can be located anywhere on a network. Multiple released cache directories can be specified. Click the icon beside the Path to the released cache field to browse to the required directory.

*Click **Configure** to configure the search order.*

If a *.cgr file is required for loading but cannot be found in the local cache directory, the system searches the released cache directories in the specified search order. If the *.cgr file is not found, the system creates one in the local cache directory. Typically a system administrator manages released cache directories.

Cache Size

The default size of the writable cache is 500 MB. If the value is exceeded the system automatically deletes *.cgr files on a first-in first-out basis.

Time Stamp

If the **Check timestamps** option is enabled, the system saves the *.cgr file with a time stamp. This verifies that no modifications have been made to the model since the creation of the *.cgr file. If a model is modified, the *.cgr file is overwritten with the latest tessellated geometry data and the file contains an updated time stamp.

GMT timestamp format is for global use only.

Step 3 - Exit and restart ENOVIA.

Click **OK** to confirm the changes. The system displays the Warning dialog box shown in Figure 8–8, indicating that the application must be restarted for the settings to take effect.

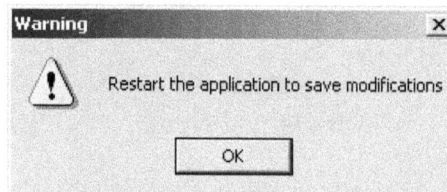

Figure 8–8

Step 4 - Open a product file for viewing.

Restart ENOVIA and open a product file. The system loads all
*.cgr files into the viewer. Selected components can be changed
to Design mode by right-clicking on the component in the
specification tree, and selecting **Representations>Design
mode**, as shown in Figure 8–9.

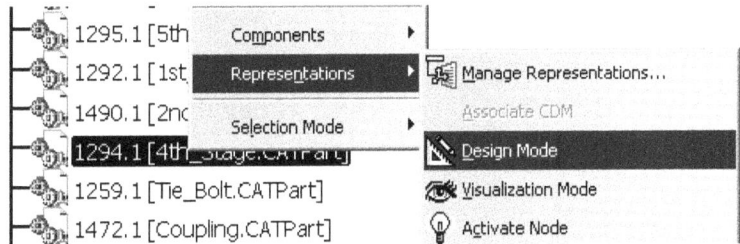

Figure 8–9

Note the following restrictions:

* If the **Work with the cache system** option is selected,
  components can be toggled between Visualization mode and
  Design mode.

* If the **Work with the cache system** option is not selected,
  components cannot be switched from Design mode to
  Visualization mode even if its *.cgr file exists in the local
  cache.

* Mass properties can be calculated from a component that is
  in Visualization mode.

* ENOVIA must be restarted for the **Work with the cache
  system** option to take effect.

Practice 8a

Working with Cache

Practice Objectives

- Work with the cache system.
- Switch between Visualization and Design modes.

In this practice, you will work with the cache system and toggle between the Visualization and Design modes to make changes to a part.

Task 1 - Open the assembly.

The files for this practice can be found in the DriveShaft directory.

1. Open **DriveShaft.CATProduct** from the DriveShaft folder. The assembly displays, as shown in Figure 8–10.

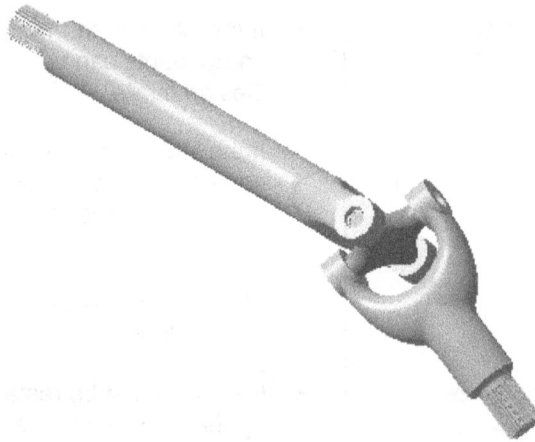

Figure 8–10

2. Spin the model and note the length of time the system requires to process the geometry.

3. Close the model without saving.

Task 2 - Activate the cache system.

1. Select **Tools>Options>Infrastructure>Product Structure** and select the *Cache Management* tab, as shown in Figure 8–11.

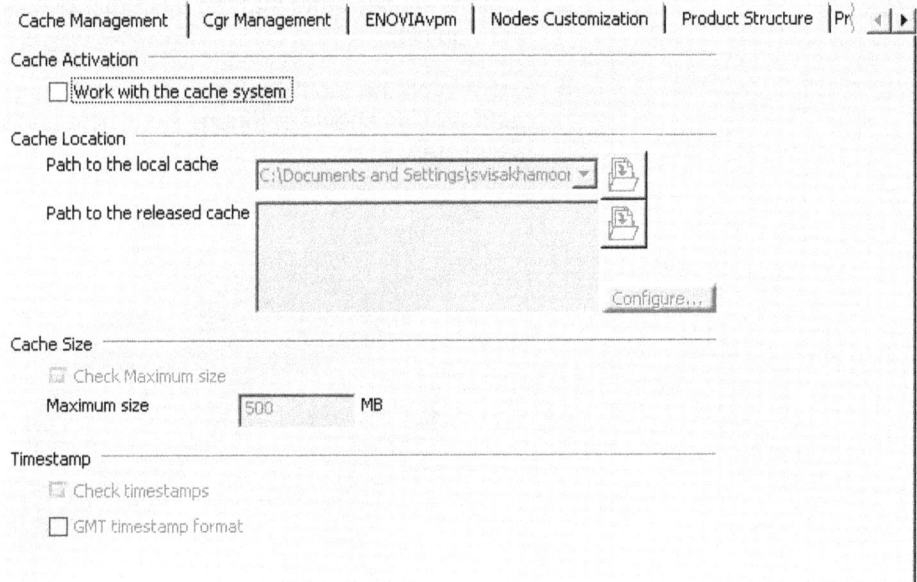

| Cache Management | Cgr Management | ENOVIAvpm | Nodes Customization | Product Structure | Pr ◄ ► |

Cache Activation
☐ Work with the cache system

Cache Location
Path to the local cache   C:\Documents and Settings\svisakhamoor ▼
Path to the released cache

Configure...

Cache Size
☑ Check Maximum size
Maximum size   500   MB

Timestamp
☑ Check timestamps
☐ GMT timestamp format

Figure 8–11

2. Select the **Work with the cache system** option, as shown in Figure 8–12.

Cache Activation
☑ Work with the cache system

Figure 8–12

3. A warning displays indicating that the system must be restarted. Click **OK**.

4. Click **OK**.

5. Exit and restart ENOVIA.

Task 3 - Open another assembly.

1. Open **DriveShaft.CATProduct** from the DriveShaft directory. A Progress window displays indicating that CGR files are being generated.

2. Spin the model. Note that the system processes the display more quickly.

3. Zoom in on the InputShaft part and hold the cursor over the geometry, as shown in Figure 8–13. The surfaces are tessellated.

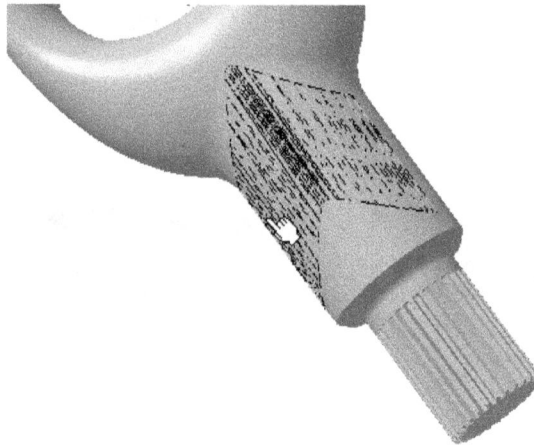

Figure 8–13

4. View the specification tree to see that it is not possible to expand it to the part body level, as shown in Figure 8–14.

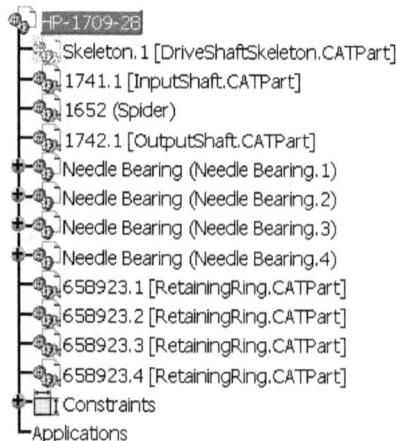

Figure 8–14

Task 4 - Switch component to Design mode.

In this task, you will make changes to a component. Components can only be modified while in Design mode.

1. Right-click on part **1741.1** in the specification tree and select **Representations>Design mode**, as shown in Figure 8–15.

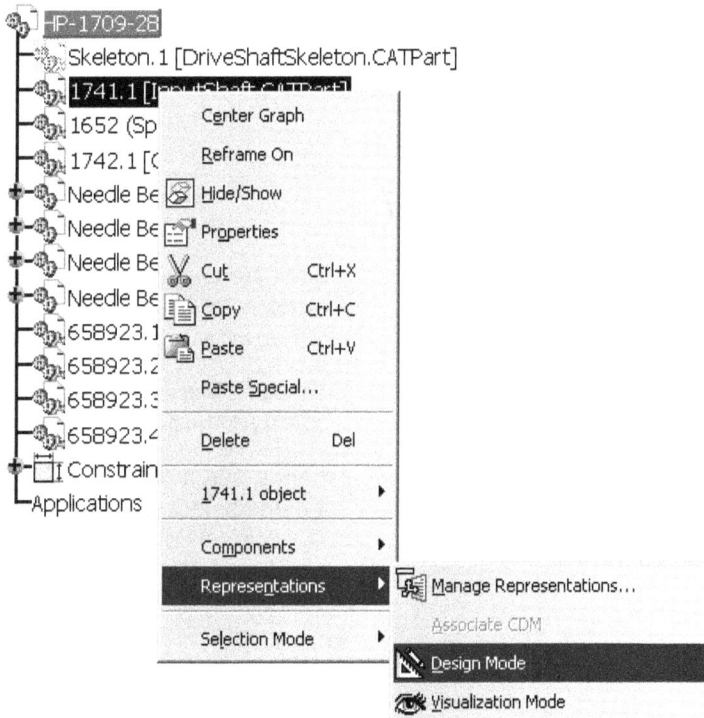

Figure 8–15

2. Part 1741 is now in Design mode, as shown in Figure 8–16.

3. Expand the **1741** node in the specification tree to access and make changes to its features.

4. Right-click on the PartBody for 1741 and select **Properties**, as shown in Figure 8–16.

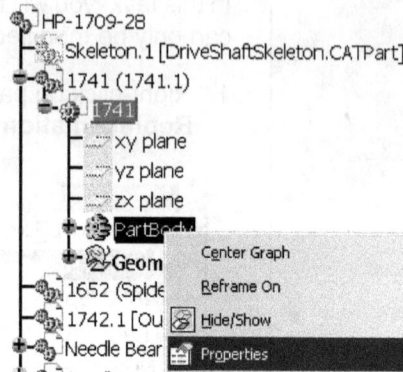

Figure 8–16

5. Select the *Graphics* tab, and change the properties of the PartBody by changing the color to green in the Color drop-down list.

6. Use **Save Management** to save **DriveShaft.CATProduct** and **InputShaft.CATPart**.

7. Change part **1741.1** back to **Visualization** mode. Right-click on it and select **Representations>Visualization Mode**. The **1741** branch collapses and the CGR version of the model is placed back into the assembly, as shown in Figure 8–17.

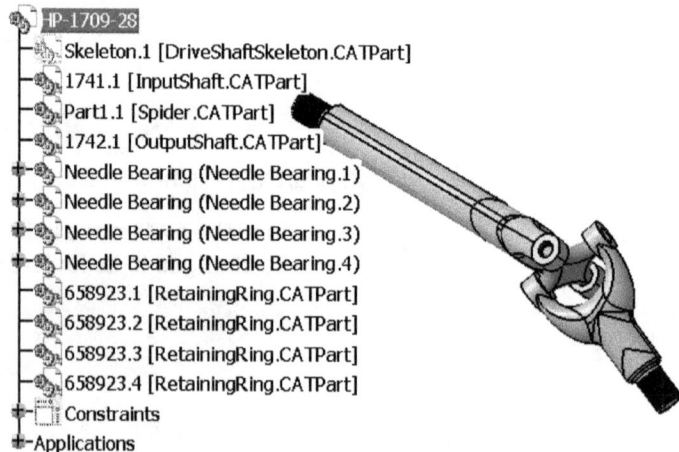

Figure 8–17

8. Select **Tools>Options>Infrastructure>Product Structure** and select the *Cache Management* tab.

9. Clear the **Work with the cache system** option.

10. Close the window without saving.

11. Restart CATIA.

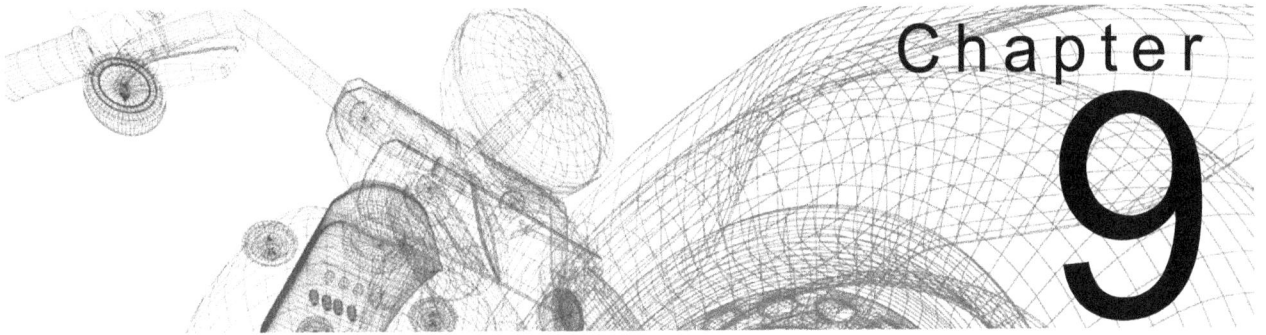

Managing the Assembly

As product models become larger, visualizing and manipulating the model becomes more complex. ENOVIA provides a number of tools that help reduce the complexity of the product model and enable you to work more efficiently with large amounts of data.

Learning Objectives in this Chapter

- Create a group of components for easier selection.
- Use product management techniques to increase your efficiency in working in the DMU Navigator workbench.
- Create Scenes to save the various view setting configurations of your product model for reuse.

9.1 Creating a Group

Several components within a model can be grouped together for easy selection. Grouping enables you to perform operations, such as hide/show or modifying the properties, on several components simultaneously. Groups are saved with the assembly so that they do not need to be recreated each time it is opened.

General Steps

Use the following general steps to create a group:

1. Select components to group.
2. Group components.
3. Select a group.

Step 1 - Select components to group.

Select the components to group in the Main window or specification tree. To select multiple components, press and hold <Ctrl> while making the selection. Selecting components can also be performed using the Search and Spatial Query tools.

Step 2 - Group components.

To group the selected components, click the (Group) icon in the DMU Review Creation toolbar. The Edit Group dialog box opens, as shown in Figure 9–1. A Preview window also opens, showing the selected components.

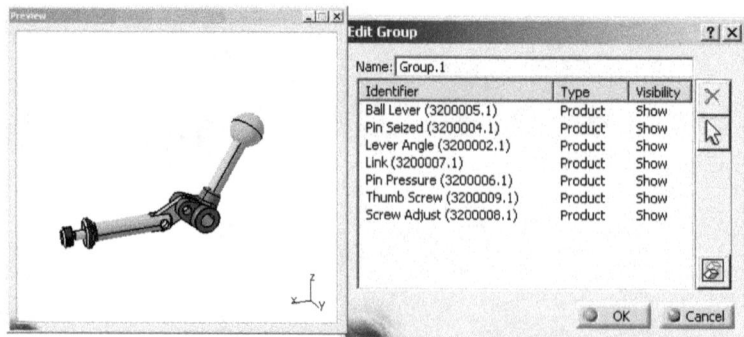

Figure 9–1

Give the group a meaningful name in the Name field. If an undesired component has been included in the group, select it in the specification tree to remove it from the group. To add an additional component to the group, select it from the model or specification tree.

Once you are satisfied with the group of products, click **OK** to finalize the group. A **Group** branch is added under the **Applications** branch of the specification tree, as shown in Figure 9–2.

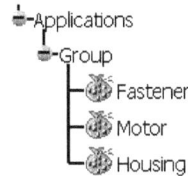

Figure 9–2

Step 3 - Select a group.

To use the group, right-click on it in the specification tree and select **Group.x Object>Select Content**, as shown in Figure 9–3. All components within the group are highlighted. You can then perform operations on the entire group. For example, you can hide the grouped components by clicking the [icon] (Hide/show) icon.

To edit the group, select **Group.x Object>Definition**, as shown in Figure 9–3, to reopen the Edit Group dialog box.

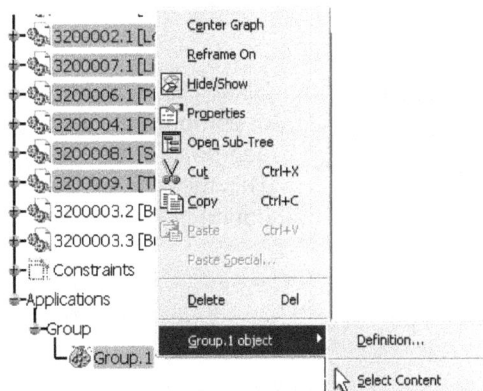

Figure 9–3

9.2 Product Management

Using product management techniques increases your efficiency in working in the DMU Navigator workbench. The techniques enable you to control and simplify your display, which decreases retrieval and refresh times for the product.

Use the following techniques to reduce the update and retrieval times of your assembly and simplify your display:

- Hide/Show

- Activate/Deactivate

- Load/Unload

Hide/Show

The display of components in an assembly can be toggled on and off quickly by right-clicking on the component and selecting **Hide/Show**, or selecting **View>Hide/Show>Hide/Show** in the menu bar.

The Hide/Show operation simplifies your display. The settings for a Hide/Show operation are saved with the product model. The hidden or shown status of a component is indicated by the components symbol in the specification tree, as shown in Figure 9–4.

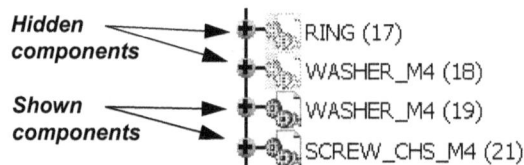

Figure 9–4

Activate/ Deactivate

Similar to Hide/Show, Activate/Deactivate simplifies the display of components in the product. If you deactivate a component, its geometry is also removed from consideration by the assembly. This means that the component is not calculated by the system during update, which decreases update time.

To toggle the activation status, right-click on a component, and select **Representation**. The four options available are described as follows:

Option	Description
Activate Node	Activates the selected part model in the product.
Deactivate Node	Deactivates the selected part model in the product.
Activate Terminal Node	Activates the selected product model (subassembly or top-level assembly).
Deactivate Terminal Node	Deactivates the selected product model (subassembly or top-level assembly).

The settings for an Activate/Deactivate operation are not saved with the product model. Regardless of prior settings, when a product is opened all components are activated. The activated or deactivated status of a node or terminal node is indicated by the components symbol in the specification tree, as shown in Figure 9–5.

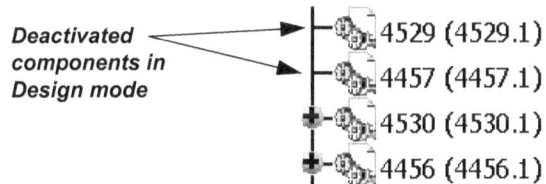

Deactivated components in Design mode → 4529 (4529.1)
4457 (4457.1)
4530 (4530.1)
4456 (4456.1)

Figure 9–5

A method for handling complex assemblies upon loading is by toggling on an option to avoid loading default shapes when opening a product. This enables you to select the components you want to activate from the specification tree after the file has been opened.

To set this option select **Tools>Options>Infrastructure> Product Structure** and select the *Product Visualization* tab. Select the **Do not activate default shapes on open** option, as shown in Figure 9–6.

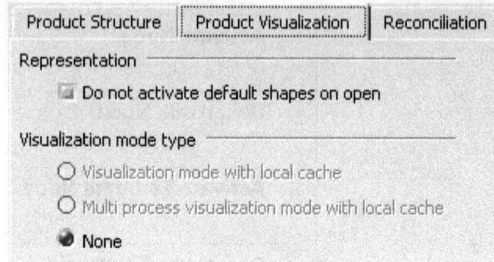

| Product Structure | Product Visualization | Reconciliation |

Representation
  ☑ Do not activate default shapes on open

Visualization mode type
  ○ Visualization mode with local cache
  ○ Multi process visualization mode with local cache
  ● None

Figure 9–6

Load/Unload

Load/Unload enables you to remove or restore components from the product. Right-click on the component and select **Components>Unload** to remove it or select **Load** to restore it.

When unloading a component, it is completely removed from memory. Additionally, if the component is assembled more than once, all instances of it are unloaded from the assembly since the model is removed from memory.

Unloaded components display with a unique symbol in the specification tree, as shown in Figure 9–7.

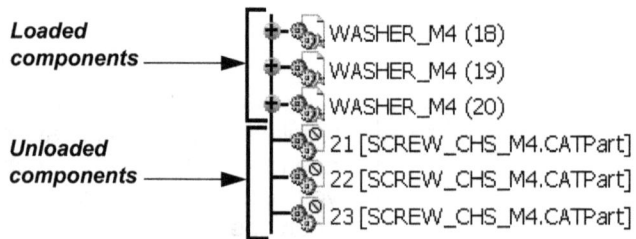

Loaded components → WASHER_M4 (18)
WASHER_M4 (19)
WASHER_M4 (20)

Unloaded components → 21 [SCREW_CHS_M4.CATPart]
22 [SCREW_CHS_M4.CATPart]
23 [SCREW_CHS_M4.CATPart]

Figure 9–7

The settings for a Load/Unload operation are not saved with the product model. By default, all components are loaded when a product is opened. It is possible to configure the system to not load any of the components of an assembly. Select **Tools> Options>General**, and select the *General* tab. Clear the **Load referenced documents** option, as shown in Figure 9–8.

Select this option

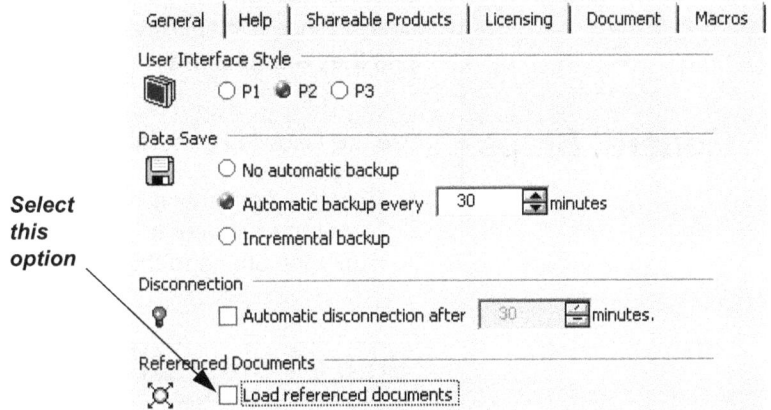

Figure 9–8

With this option disabled, the assembly model loads more quickly. No model geometry displays, but the specification tree lists all of the components of the assembly. You can then individually load only the components of the assembly that you require using the specification tree.

Summary

The Load/Show/Hide operations are summarized in the table below to help you decide which technique best suits your assembly.

Option	Settings saved with model	Removed from memory
Hide/Show	Yes	No
Activate/Deactivate	No	No (visible in drawing)
Load/Unload	No	Yes (not visible in assembly or drawings)

9.3 Creating Scenes

Exploded views and the load/show/hide operations enable you to work with a simplified version of your model. However, the operations must be performed on the fly. Scenes enable you to save the various view setting configurations of your product model for reuse. You can quickly switch between scenes and view settings without having to manually configure them each time they are required.

General Steps

Use the following general steps to configure and save a view:

1. Create a new scene.
2. Configure the scene.
3. Apply the scene to the product.

Step 1 - Create a new scene.

Click the ![icon] (Enhanced Scene) icon in the DMU Review Creation toolbar. The Enhanced Scene dialog box opens, as shown in Figure 9–9.

Enhanced Scene

Definition
Name:

☐ Automatic naming

Overload Mode:
● Partial ○ Full

OK   Cancel

Figure 9–9

Clear the **Automatic naming** option and enter a name for the scene. Click **OK**.

Once the scene is created, the background color changes to indicate that the Scene window is active. The name of the scene is added to the specification tree.

Step 2 - Configure the scene.

You can configure the following settings using scenes:

- Hide/Show components

- Activate/Deactivate components

- Snap two components for placement

- Define explode positions

- Save viewpoints

Hide/Show, Activate/Deactivate, Search, Snap, and Publish are applied to a scene in the same as the Navigator workbench.

The Search and Publish functions available in the Navigator workbench are also available in the Scene workbench.

By default, when the scene is applied, it displays in the orientation that it was first defined in. To define a new viewpoint, orient the model into the required viewpoint and click the

(Save Viewpoint) icon in the Enhanced Scenes toolbar.

Explode

Exploded views enable you to visualize a group of constrained components separately.

To explode an assembly, click the (Explode) icon in the Enhanced Scenes toolbar. The Explode dialog box opens, as shown in Figure 9–10.

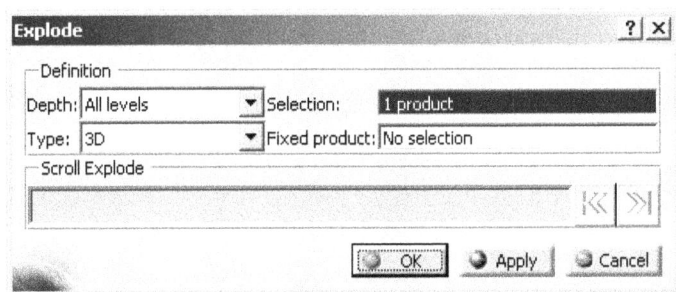

Figure 9–10

The options for the Explode dialog box are described as follows:

Option		Description
Depth		Determines which components in the assembly are exploded.
	All levels	Explodes all levels of the assembly.
	First level	Explodes all first-level components of the assembly. In this case, subassembly components are not exploded.
Type		Determines the exploded placement of the components.
	3D	Places components in a 3D arrangement with respect to the position of the unexploded assembly.
	2D	Explodes components to positions within the 2D plane of the current view. Use named views to determine the 2D explode plane.
	Constrained	Explodes components with respect to the constraints used to contextually place them in the assembly.
Selection		Specifies the product to explode. The active assembly is automatically selected. If multiple levels of the assembly are selected, the assembly explodes in stages.
Fixed Product		Select one component to remain fixed during the explode. If the depth is set to **All levels**, you can select a part. If the depth is set to **First level**, you can select a subassembly.

The components in a 3D explode can be positioned anywhere in 3D space, while the components of the 2D explode can only move within a 2D plane. This plane is always parallel to the screen and is therefore specified by orienting the model. The difference between 3D and 2D explode types is shown in Figure 9–11.

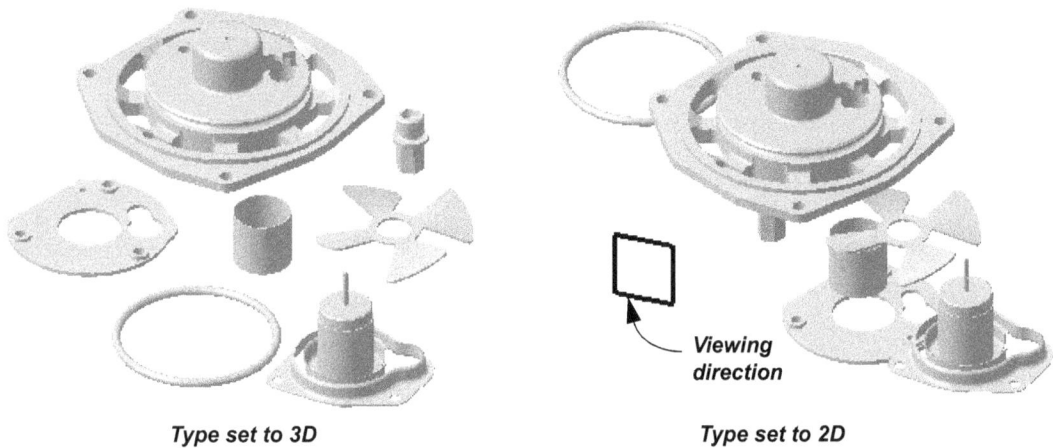

Type set to 3D   Type set to 2D

Figure 9–11

Once the model is exploded, the positions of individual components can be moved using the compass. You can then position the components to display how the assembly is put together. An example is shown in Figure 9–12.

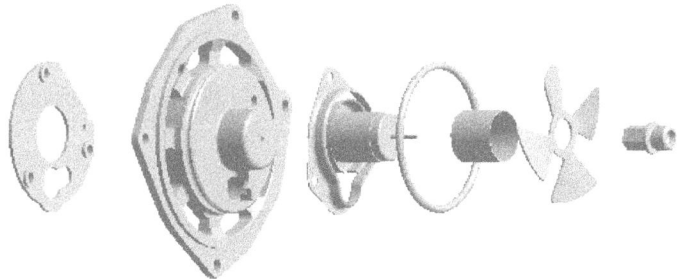

Figure 9–12

To reset the components back to the constraint positions, select the assembly in the specification tree and click to reset the

(Selected Products) icon in the Select toolbar. Individual components can also be reset by selecting them and applying the **Reset** command.

Step 3 - Apply the scene to the product.

There are two ways to work with a scene of a product. You can edit the scene and work with the assembly configuration directly in the scene editor. You can also apply the scene to the product.

To apply the scene to the assembly model, select the scene in Applications in the specification tree. Right-click and select ***object>Apply Scene on Assembly>Apply the Entire Scene**, as shown in Figure 9–13.

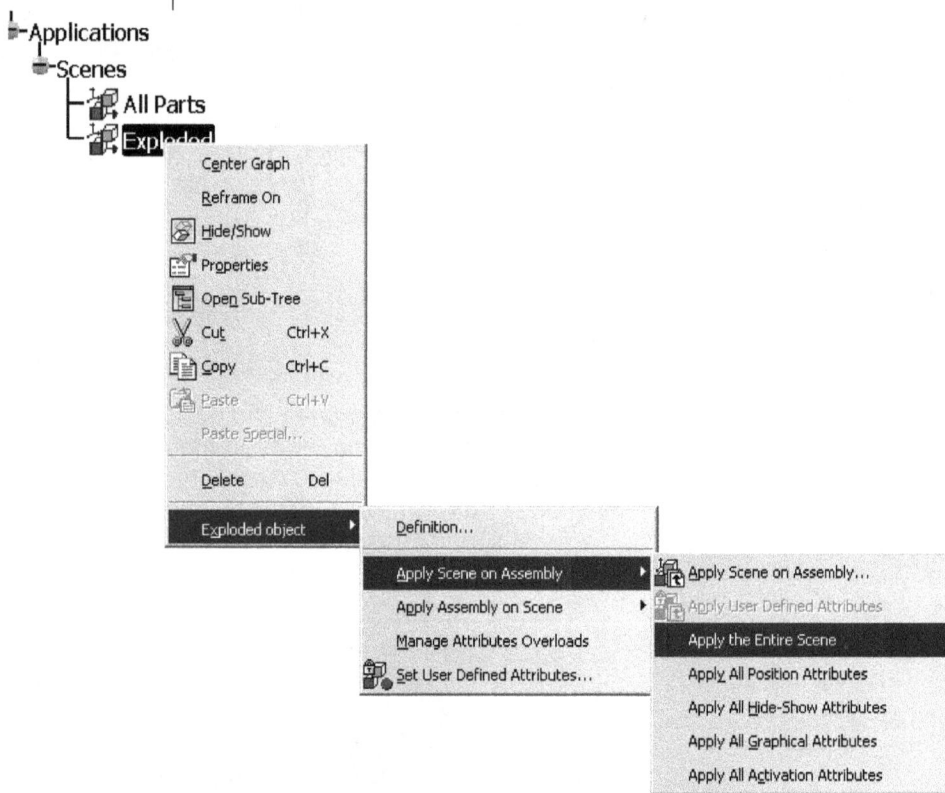

Figure 9–13

No default scene exists for an assembly. Once you have applied a scene with specific view settings, the only way to return to the original settings is to create an additional scene. Therefore, it is recommended that you create a scene with no configurations before creating any additional scenes. This scene can then be used as the default to restore the assembly to its original configuration.

Practice 9a

Creating Groups

Practice Objective

- Create a group.

In this practice, you will create two groups in an assembly model. The groups will facilitate the selection of multiple models when performing operations such as hide/show or changing properties.

Task 1 - Open the assembly.

The files for this practice can be found in the Fan directory.

1. Open **Fan.CATProduct**. The assembly displays, as shown in Figure 9–14.

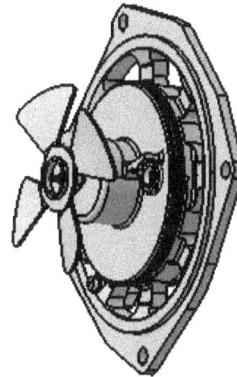

Figure 9–14

2. Investigate the structure of the assembly. The model consists of 17 components, all at the top level. The components can be categorized into three groups: fasteners, fan motor, and housing.

Task 2 - Create a group for the housing components.

During the use of this model, you will need to view the internal components of the fan assembly. In this task, you will create a group that contains the housing components. This will enable you to change the properties and hide/show these components quickly.

1. Click the (Group) icon in the DMU Review Creation toolbar. The Edit Group dialog box opens, as shown in Figure 9–15. A Preview window also displays displaying the components that have been added to the group.

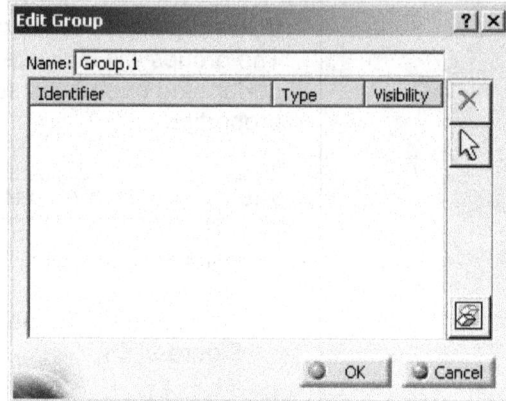

Figure 9–15

2. Enter **Housing** in the Name field.

3. Select the following four components in the specification tree:

   - **yoke**
   - **fan_contact_cylinder**
   - **plunger_contact**
   - **ring**

   The Edit Group dialog box and Preview window appear, as shown in Figure 9–16.

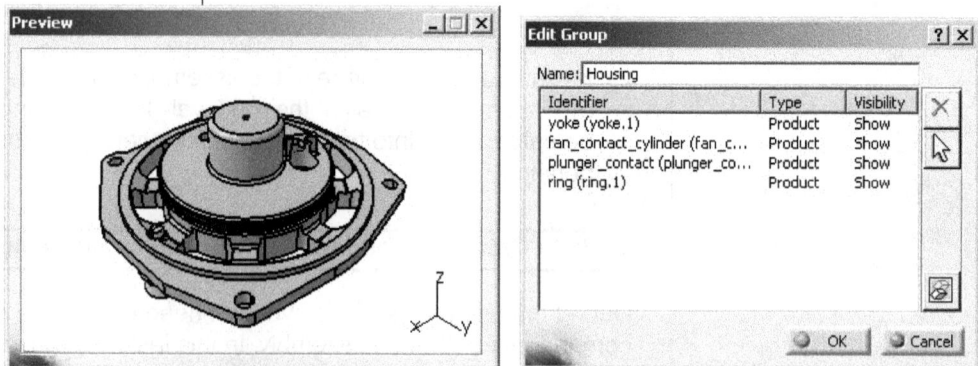

Figure 9–16

4. Click **OK** to complete the creation of the group.

5. Expand the **Applications** and **Group** branches of the specification tree. A new Housing group has been added, as shown in Figure 9–17.

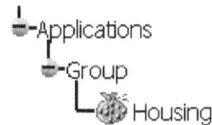

Figure 9–17

Task 3 - Hide the housing group.

1. Select the Housing entry in the **Applications** branch of the specification tree. When selected, the four models belonging to the group are highlighted automatically.

2. Click the [icon] (Hide/Show) icon to hide the group. The model displays, as shown in Figure 9–18.

Figure 9–18

Task 4 - Create a fastener group using a search.

Small components, such as screws and washers, increase the visual complexity and update times of a large product. In this task, you will create a group to facilitate the selection of the fasteners in the fan product. The components to be added to the group are selected using the Search tool.

1. Select **Edit>Search**. The Search dialog box opens.

2. Enter **screw*** in the Name field and click the [icon] icon. The system locates three components.

3. Click **Select** and **OK**.

4. To add these components to a group, click the ⬚ icon. The Edit Group dialog box and Preview window appear, as shown in Figure 9–19.

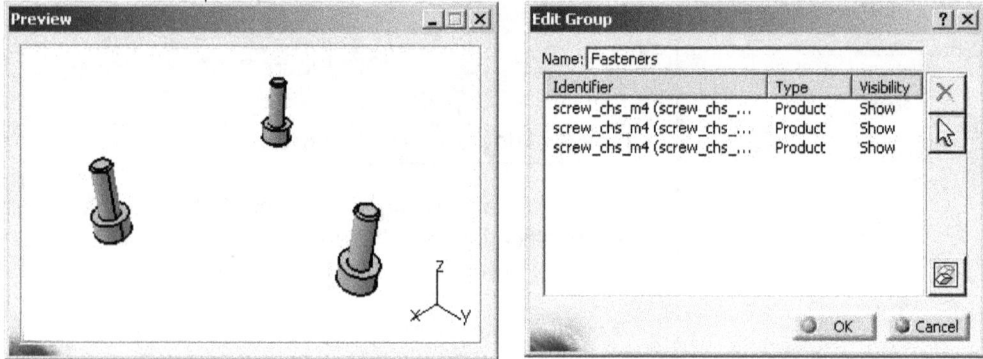

Figure 9–19

5. Name the group **Fasteners** and click **OK**. The group is added to the **Applications** branch of the specification tree.

Task 5 - Edit the group and add additional components.

A group can also be edited by double-clicking on it in the specification tree.

1. Right-click on the **Fasteners** group in the specification tree and select **Fasteners object>Definition**. The Edit Group dialog box opens.

2. Another search is performed to locate the additional components. Leave the Edit Group dialog box open and select **Edit>Search**.

3. Perform a search that locates all of the models that start with the word washer. The search results appear, as shown in Figure 9–20.

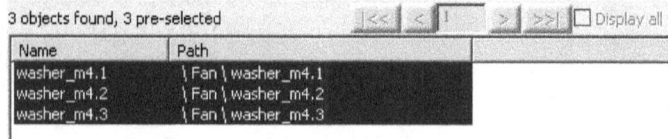

Figure 9–20

4. Click **Select**. The components are automatically added to the Edit Group dialog box. Do not close the Search dialog box until you have completed the Group.

5. The Edit Group dialog box and Preview window appear, as shown in Figure 9–21. Click **OK** to close the Edit Group dialog box.

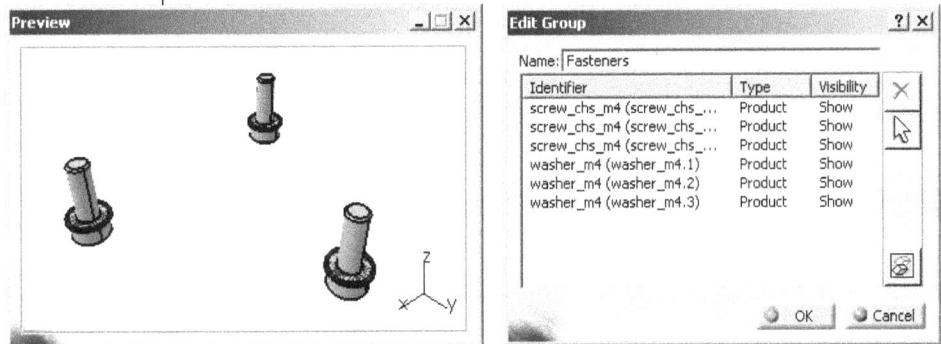

Figure 9–21

6. Click **OK** to close the Search dialog box.

7. Using the Fasteners group, hide the screw and washer components. The model displays, as shown in Figure 9–22.

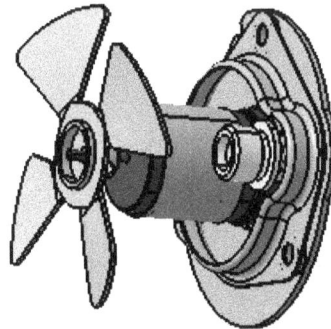

Figure 9–22

Task 6 - Show the housing group and change the properties.

In this task, you will show the housing group and then modify its properties to visualize the assembly more clearly.

1. Show the Housing group.

2. Right-click on **Housing** in the specification tree and select **Properties**.

3. Select the *Graphic* tab and set the following properties:

   - *Color:* **Cyan**
   - *Linetype:* **6**
   - *Thickness*: **1**
   - *Transparency:* **80**

   The assembly displays, as shown in Figure 9–23.

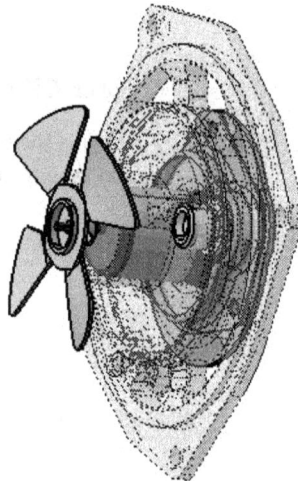

Figure 9–23

4. Show the Fasteners group.

5. Save the assembly and close the window.

Practice 9b

Creating Scenes

Practice Objectives

- Create a scene.
- Apply a scene to an assembly.

In this practice, you will create various scenes and apply them to the assembly to facilitate assembly of additional components.

Task 1 - Create a scene.

If you completed the last practice, you can also continue using the same model.

1. Open **Fan_b.CATProduct** from the Fan directory. The assembly displays, as shown in Figure 9–24.

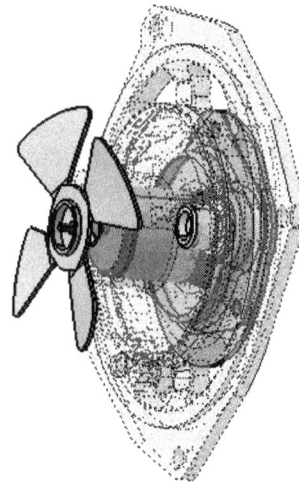

Figure 9–24

2. Click the (Enhanced Scene) icon.

3. Clear the **Automatic naming** option.

4. Enter **All Parts** as the name, as shown in Figure 9–25.

Figure 9–25

5. Click **OK**.

6. The system activates the Scene window. Select **Do not display this message again** in the Warning dialog box and close it.

7. Since this is a scene of all parts, no changes are required. Click the (Exit Scene) icon to exit the Scene window. The scene name is added to the **Scenes** node under **Applications** in the specification tree, as shown in Figure 9–26.

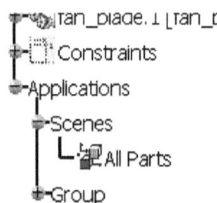

Figure 9–26

8. Create a scene named **Exploded**, as shown in Figure 9–27.

Figure 9–27

9. In the Scene window, click the [icon] (Explode) icon.

10. Select **First level** from the Depth drop-down list, as shown in Figure 9–28.

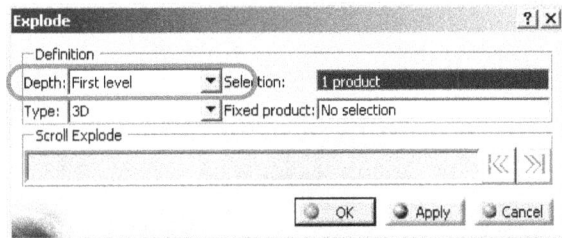

Figure 9–28

11. Click **OK** in the Explode dialog box. The updated scene displays, as shown in Figure 9–29.

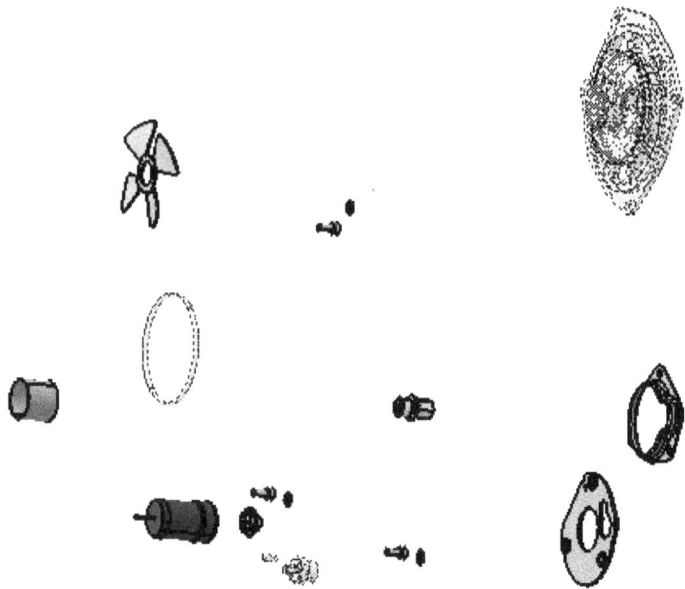

Figure 9–29

12. Click the [icon] (Exit Scene) icon to exit the Scene window.

Task 2 - Apply a scene to the assembly.

1. Right-click on the **Exploded** scene and select **Exploded object>Apply Scene on Assembly>Apply the Entire Scene**, as shown in Figure 9–30.

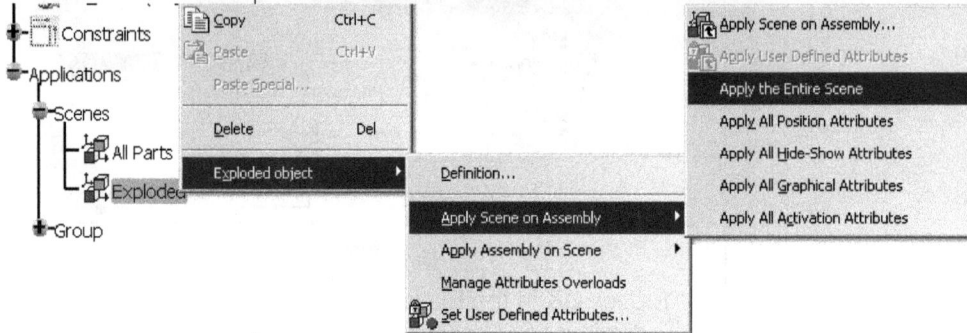

Figure 9–30

2. Click ![icon](Reset Positions) (Reset Positions) to unexplode the assembly. You might need to click the ![icon] icon twice to get all of the components to return to their original positions.

Task 3 - Create a scene.

1. Create a scene named **Yoke Removed**, as shown in Figure 9–31.

Figure 9–31

2. Once in the Scene window, right-click on the yoke component and select **Representations>Deactivate Node**, as shown in Figure 9–32.

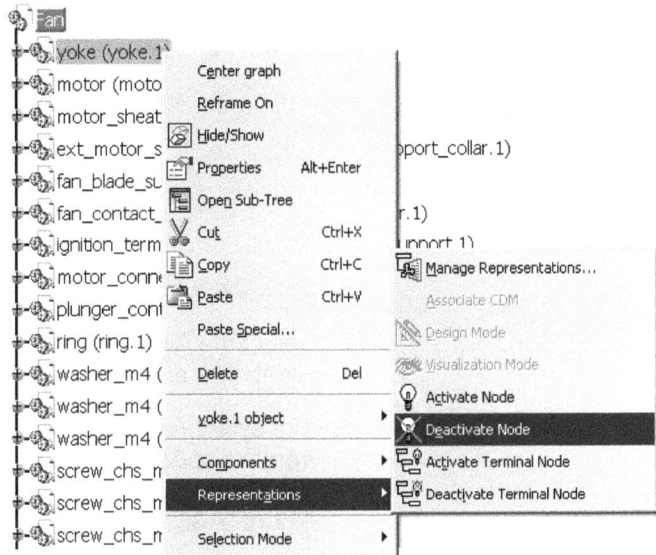

Figure 9–32

3. Click the (Exit Scene) icon to exit the Scene window.

4. Apply the **Yoke Removed** scene to the assembly. The assembly displays, as shown in Figure 9–33.

Figure 9–33

5. Apply the All Parts scene to the assembly. The system gives an error shown in Figure 9–34. Since there is no difference between this scene and the main assembly, it cannot be applied this way.

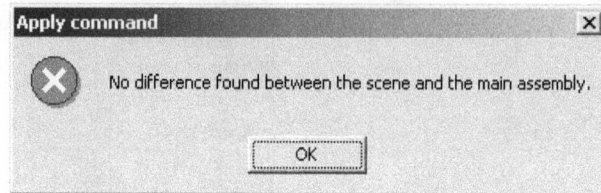

Apply command ✕

No difference found between the scene and the main assembly.

OK

Figure 9–34

6. Click **OK** to close the Apply command window.

7. Select the All Parts scene from the specification tree. Right-click and select **All Parts.object>Definition**.

8. The system activates the scene window. Right-click on **Fan** from the specification tree select **Representations>Activate Terminal Node**. The assembly displays, as shown in Figure 9–35.

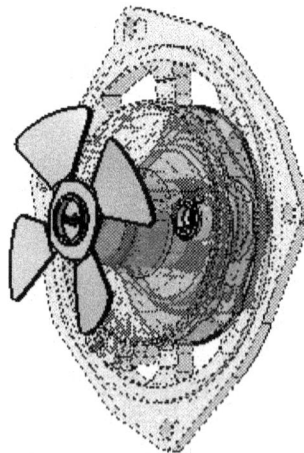

Figure 9–35

9. Click the ⬆ (Exit Scene) icon to exit the Scene window.

10. Apply the All Parts scene to the assembly.

11. Close the file without saving.

Chapter
10

Generative Drafting

This chapter introduces the Generative Drafting workbench by outlining the drawing creation process. You learn how to create, modify, and manipulate drawing views. Once drawing views are placed on a drawing sheet, you must add dimensions and notes to communicate manufacturing information.

Learning Objectives in this Chapter

- Understand the steps required to create a drawing.
- Review the Drafting workbench interface.
- Add views and create a drawing frame and title block.
- Understand the view orientation compass.
- Review the available view properties.
- Learn how to manipulate views.
- Manually create dimensions and move dimensions.
- Learn how to update a drawing when geometry changes.

10.1 Creating a New Drawing

All view geometry and dimension information comes from the 3D model. The 3D model must be open to create a drawing.

How To: Create a New Drawing

1. Open the model that is included in the new drawing as shown in Figure 10–1.

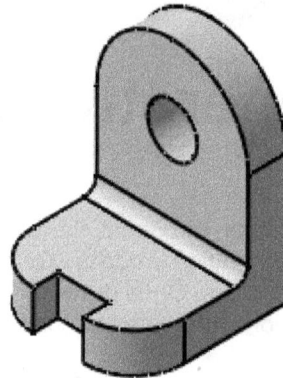

Figure 10–1

2. With the model active, enter the Drafting workbench by selecting **Start>Mechanical Design>Drafting**. The New Drawing Creation dialog box opens, as shown in Figure 10–2.

Begin with a blank sheet.

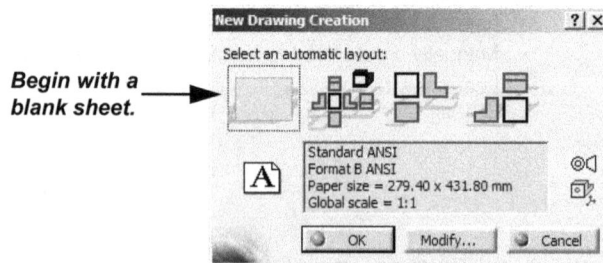

Figure 10–2

3. Click the **Blank Sheet** icon to begin with an empty drawing.
4. Click **Modify** to change the settings. The New Drawing dialog box opens, as shown in Figure 10–3.

Figure 10–3

5. Select the drawing standard (e.g., ANSI, ISO, JIS, etc.). Then select the drawing format and orientation, as required.
6. Click **OK** in the New Drawing dialog box and **OK** in the New Drawing Creation dialog box. A new drawing file opens in the Drafting workbench. Views can now be added to the drawing.

10.2 Drafting Workbench

The user interface of the Drafting workbench displays as shown in Figure 10–4.

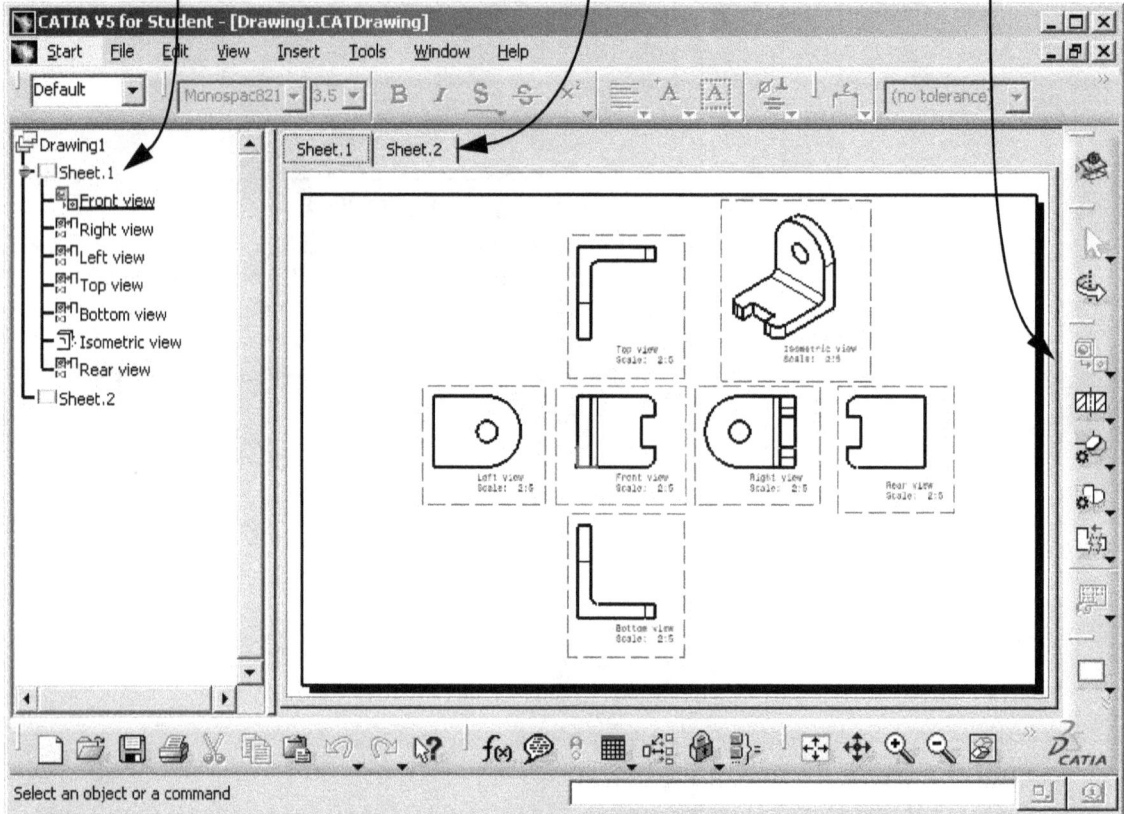

Figure 10–4

10.3 Creating Drawing Frame and Title Block

Title Block

You can assign titles to identify the drawings.

How To: Insert a Title Block

1. Select **Edit>Sheet Background** to set the Drawing mode to Background mode. Note that the background of the drawing changes to blue to indicate that you are in the background.
2. Select **Insert>Drawing>Frame and Title Block**, or click

   ⬜ (Frame Creation). The Insert Frame and Title Block dialog box opens as shown in Figure 10–5, where you can select the required title block.

*You can also use this process to delete, resize, and update a title block, as well as to add **CheckedBy** and revision information.*

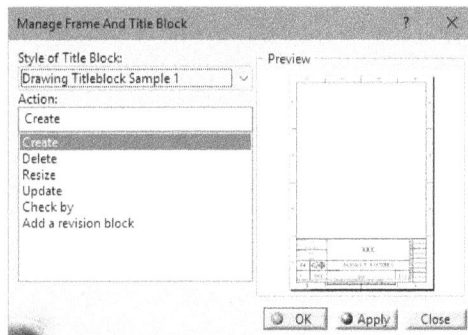

Figure 10–5

3. Select **Edit>Working views** to exit Background mode.

10.4 Adding Views

Generative views are added to the drawing using the icons in the Views toolbar, as shown in Figure 10–6.

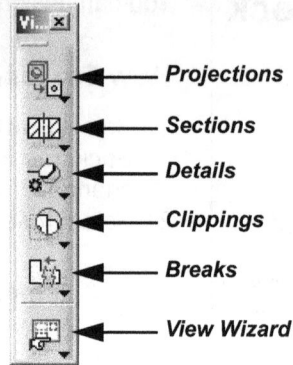

Figure 10–6

General Steps

Use the following general steps to add views to a drawing:

1. Arrange the model and drawing windows (optional).
2. Initiate view creation.
3. Select an orientation reference.
4. Place the view.
5. Add additional views, as required.

Step 1 - Arrange the model and drawing windows (optional).

The placement and orientation of the first drawing view requires the selection of a reference from the 3D model. To facilitate this selection, tile the two windows (recommended) so that you can access them simultaneously.

Select **Window>Tile Horizontally**. The drawing and model windows display as shown in Figure 10–7.

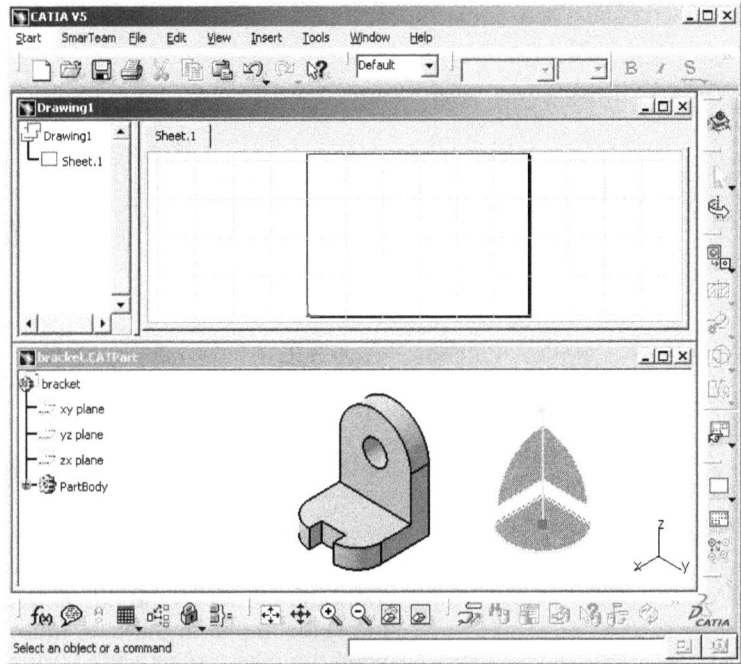

Figure 10–7

Step 2 - Initiate view creation.

The first drawing view can be one of the view types listed below. Select the appropriate icon in the Projections toolbar to initiate the creation of the first view.

View Type	Description
(Front View)	The front view is also known as the main view. You can use the view compass to orient it. Front view Scale: 1:2

(Isometric View)

An isometric view is used as a reference view, and is typically set at a smaller scale. A reference surface must be selected from the 3D model. You can use the view compass to orient this view.

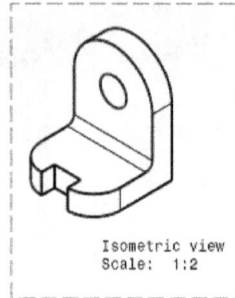

Isometric view
Scale: 1:2

Step 3 - Select an orientation reference.

Once a view icon has been clicked, the software prompts you to select a reference plane on the 3D geometry so that you can orient the model on the drawing. Switch to the model window and select a planar surface, face, or reference plane. As you move the cursor over each surface, a preview displays to help you select the correct surface, as shown in Figure 10–8.

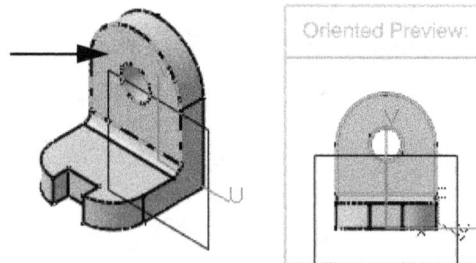

Oriented Preview:

Figure 10–8

Step 4 - Place the view.

Once a reference surface is selected on the 3D model, the view orientation compass displays in the top right corner of the interface, as shown in Figure 10–9.

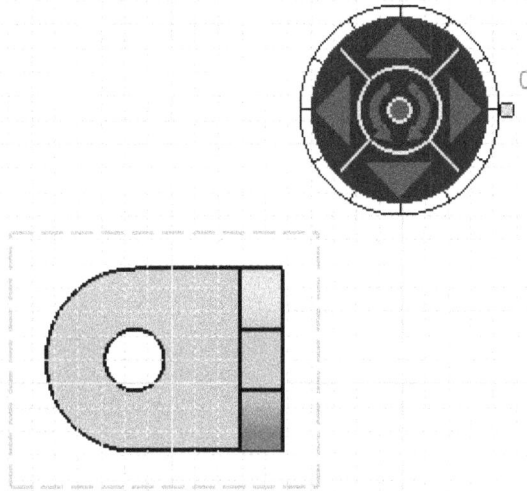

0

Figure 10–9

View Orientation Compass

The view orientation compass enables you to rotate and flip the front view until you achieve the required orientation. The view compass functionality is shown in Figure 10–10.

Use the shortcut menu to change the compass properties, as shown in Figure 10–11 (right-click over the green rotate handle).

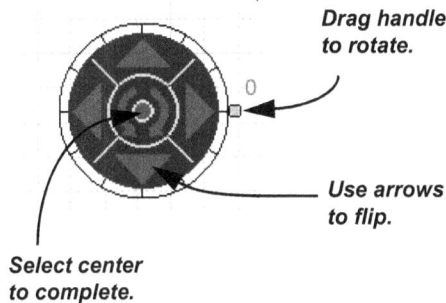

Drag handle to rotate.

0

Use arrows to flip.

Select center to complete.

Figure 10–10

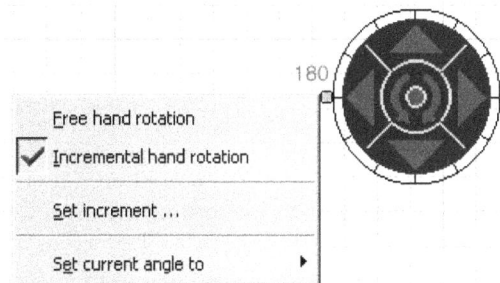

180

Free hand rotation

✓ Incremental hand rotation

Set increment ...

Set current angle to   ▶

Figure 10–11

When you reach the required view orientation, select the center of the compass or select the active view to complete the view definition. The completed view definition is shown in Figure 10–12.

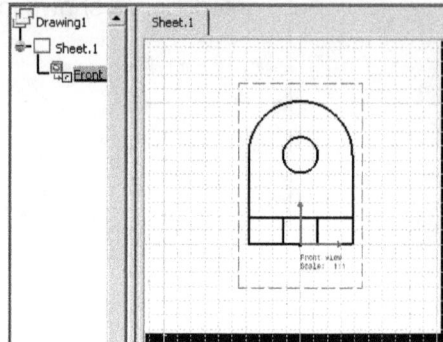

Figure 10–12

The view is added to the sheet in the drawing specification tree. The view displays on the drawing with a red border, indicating that it is the active view. When more than one view is present, a view can be activated by double-clicking on its border.

Step 5 - Add additional views, as required.

A variety of view types can be added to complete the drawing. Three of these view types are as follows:

View Type	Description
 (Projection View)	The projection view projects a view from the front view. This creates views such as top, right, left, and bottom. It is placed by selecting a location on the screen. The software applies the correct label (name) based on its position relative to the front view. A projection view maintains the same scale value as its parent view.

(Detail View)	The detail view creates a scaled view focusing on a specific area of an existing view. The detailed view is created by sketching a circle on an existing, active view that encloses the geometry to be represented. To complete the view, assign a name, boundary type, and note location. The software automatically assigns a label identifying the scale value and view name of the detailed view. Orientation of this view corresponds to its parent view.

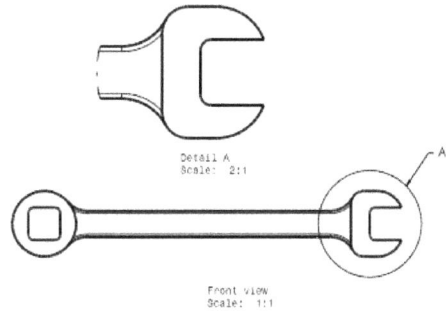

Detail A
Scale: 2:1

A

Front view
Scale: 1:1

(Offset Section View)	The offset section view creates a section that displays all edges that are behind the cutting plane. You can create this view as planar, or as a sketched cutting plane.

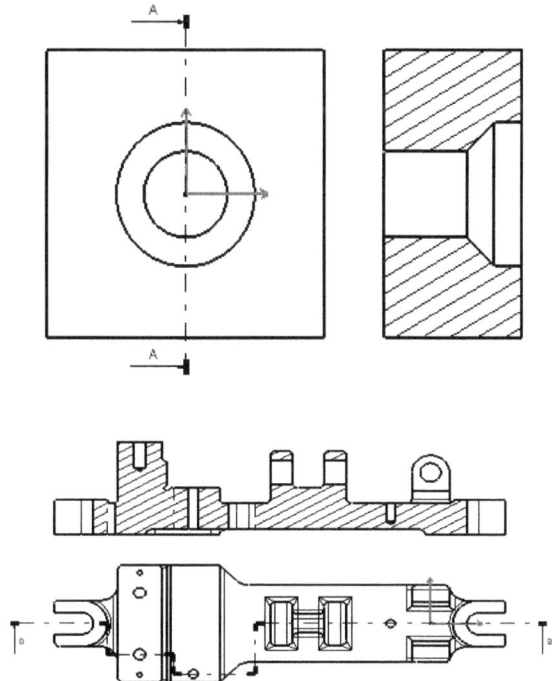

A

A

10.5 View Properties

View properties include scale and orientation, view name, frame display, hidden line display, and fillet display. The Properties dialog box is shown in Figure 10–13.

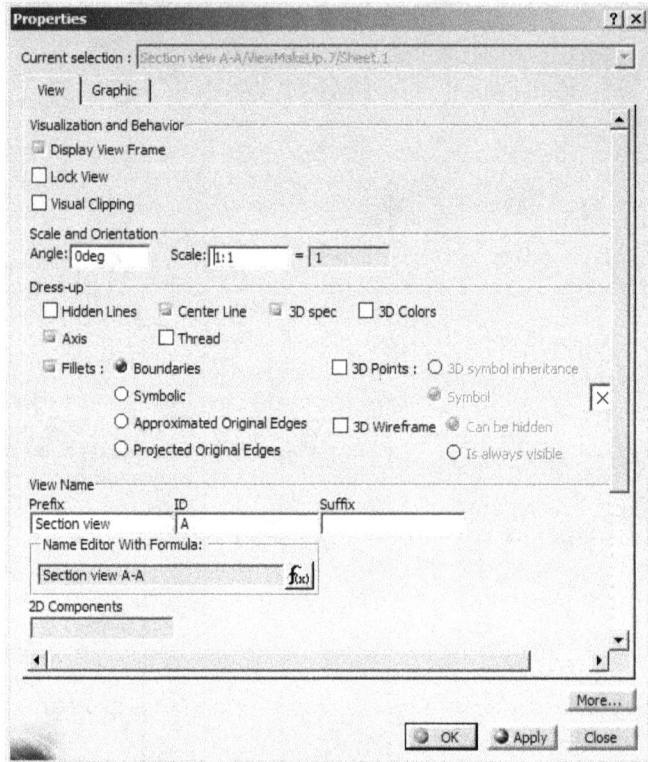

Figure 10–13

You can select to display your views in various ways, as shown in Figure 10–14.

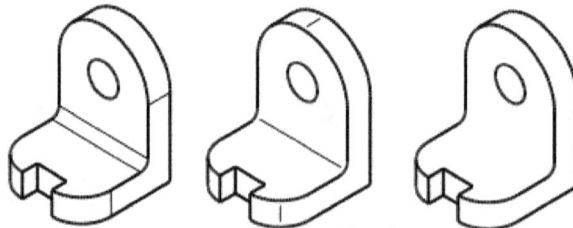

Figure 10–14

Moving Views	You can move a view to another sheet or in the same sheet by selecting the dashed line frame of the view and draging it to the required location.
	• Standard windows shortcut keys can also be used: Cut (<Ctrl>+<X>) and Paste (<Ctrl>+<V>)
	To move a view to another sheet, cut and paste it from the display or in the specification tree.
Delete View	To delete a view, select the view from the display or in the specification tree, right-click and select **Delete**.
Hide/Show	You can hide a view to simplify the sheet. To hide a view, select the view from the display or specification tree, right-click and select **Hide/Show**.
Section Arrow Properties	To modify section arrows, select the arrows, right-click and select **Properties**.
Hatching	To modify section hatching, select the section view from the display, right-click and select **Properties**.

10.6 Manually Creating Dimensions

Use the Dimensions flyout in the Dimensioning toolbar, as shown in Figure 10–15, to manually create dimensions.

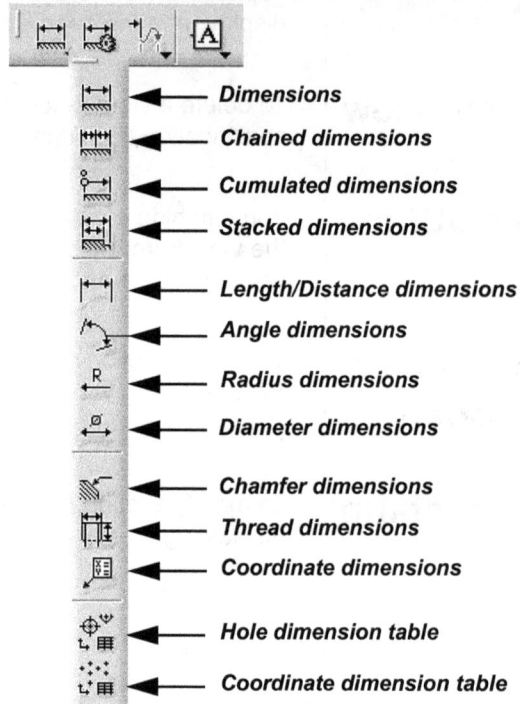

Dimensions

Chained dimensions

Cumulated dimensions

Stacked dimensions

Length/Distance dimensions

Angle dimensions

Radius dimensions

Diameter dimensions

Chamfer dimensions

Thread dimensions

Coordinate dimensions

Hole dimension table

Coordinate dimension table

Figure 10–15

How To: Manually Create a Dimension

1. Click the icon that resembles the required dimension type.
2. Select entities as dimension references, as shown in Figure 10–16.

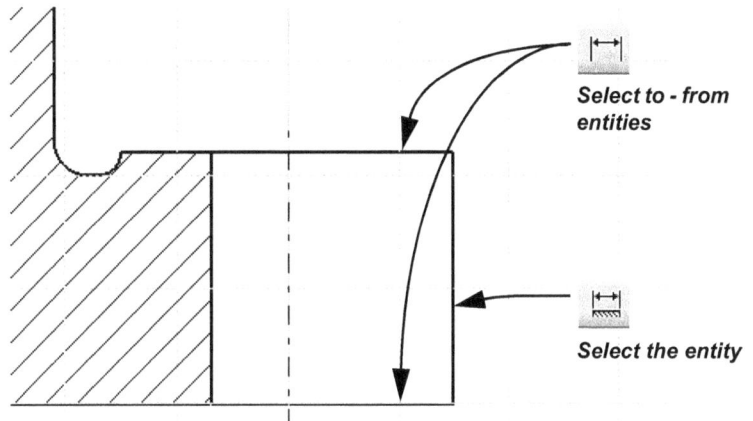

Select to - from entities

Select the entity

Figure 10–16

3. Place the dimension, as shown in Figure 10–17.

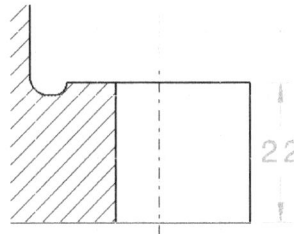

Figure 10–17

Moving Dimensions

To clean up the display move dimensions using one of the following methods:

- Click and drag on a handle to move both witness lines.

- Click and drag on a dimension to move it left, right, up, or down.

- Click on an arrow head to *flip* it.

These methods are shown in Figure 10–18.

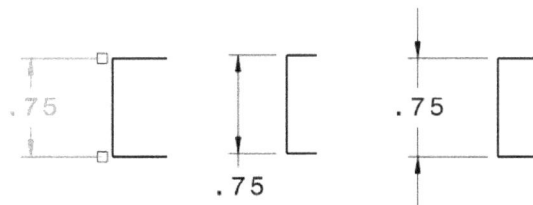

Figure 10–18

10.7 Changed Geometry

Updating a Drawing

If a drawing has been created from a 3D model and the model geometry has changed, the drawing must be updated to reflect the changes.

- To update the drawing, click (Update current sheet) or press <Ctrl>+<U>.

- A grayed out indicates that the 3D model has not changed, and that the model does not need to be updated.

Links to 3D Models

The drawing cannot update if a drawing is open but the 3D model it references is not. To open the referenced model, select **Edit>Links>**_Pointed Documents_ tab.

The software displays the file path to the referenced 3D model. Click **Open** to bring the model in session.

Practice 10a | Create a Drawing

Practice Objectives

- Create a new drawing.
- Place views using the View Wizard.
- Manipulate the views in various ways.

In this practice, you will use a part to create a new drawing. The drawing will consist of two sheets and multiple views. One of the sheets displays as shown in Figure 10–19. You will use the View Wizard to place and modify the views.

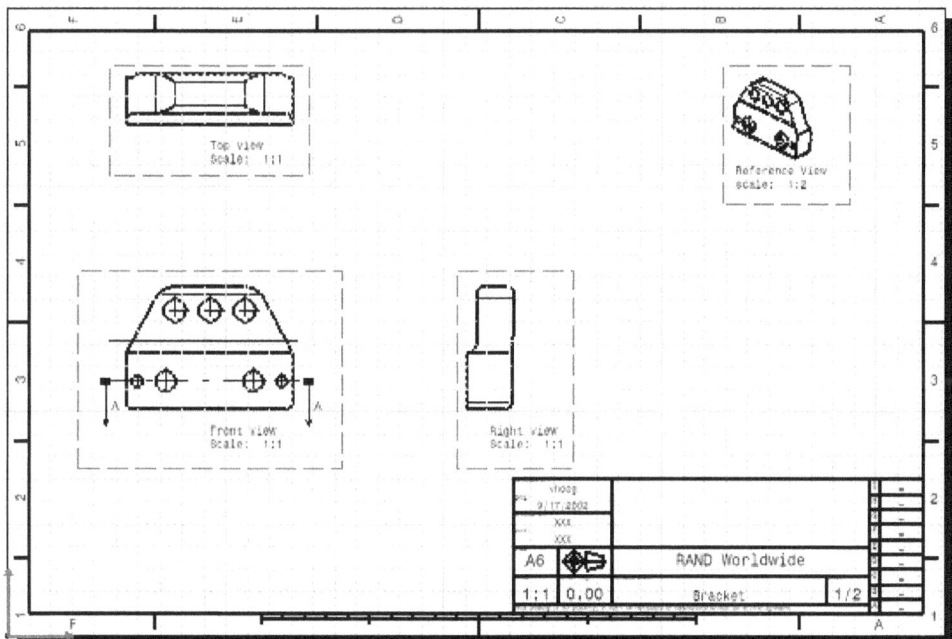

Figure 10–19

Task 1 - Create a blank drawing.

1. Select **File>Open** and select **Bracket.CATPart**.

2. Select **Start>Mechanical Design>Drafting**. The New Drawing Creation dialog box opens.

3. Click the **Blank Sheet** icon, as shown in Figure 10–20.

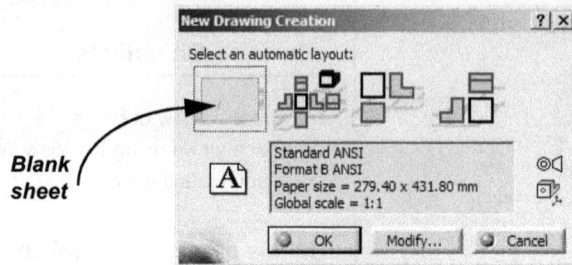

Figure 10–20

4. Click **Modify**. In the New Drawing dialog box that opens, select the following options, as shown in Figure 10–21:

- *Standard:* **ANSI**
- *Format:* **B ANSI**
- *Orientation:* **Landscape**

Figure 10–21

5. Click **OK** twice to create an empty drawing.

Task 2 - Create a front view.

---

1. Arrange the windows by selecting **Window>Tile Horizontally**. This enables you to select from the drawing or model without having to switch windows.

2. Click ⬚ (Front View) in the Views toolbar.

3. You must now orient the view by selecting a face from the model. Select anywhere in the **Bracket.CATPart** window and hover over the faces of the model. An Orientation Preview window displays the resulting view orientation.

4. Select the face shown in Figure 10–22. This surface is selected to face the front of the screen in the front view.

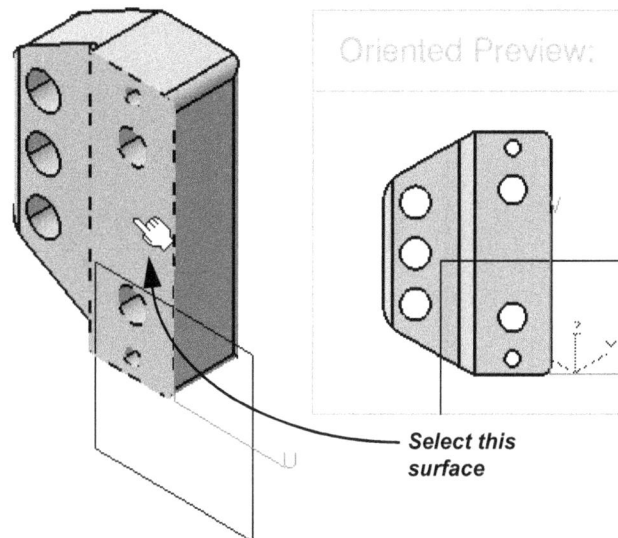

Oriented Preview:

Select this surface

Figure 10–22

The grid is displayed in the following images. To enable it, click

(Sketcher Grid).

5. The display automatically toggles back to the drawing sheet. A compass displays in the top right corner of the interface. Use the cursor to drag the green handle to the 270° location. The front view is oriented as shown in Figure 10–23.

Set required orientation of the Front view by dragging the green handle.

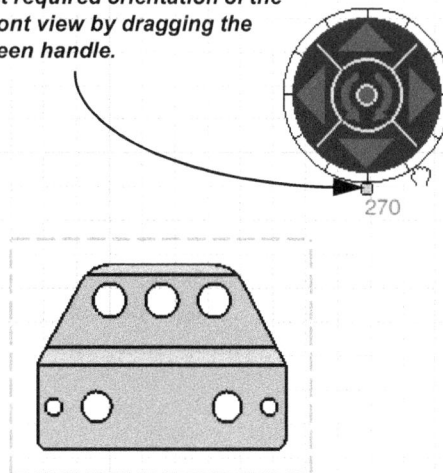

270

Figure 10–23

6. Select the center of the compass to complete the orientation. The drawing sheet is shown in Figure 10–24.

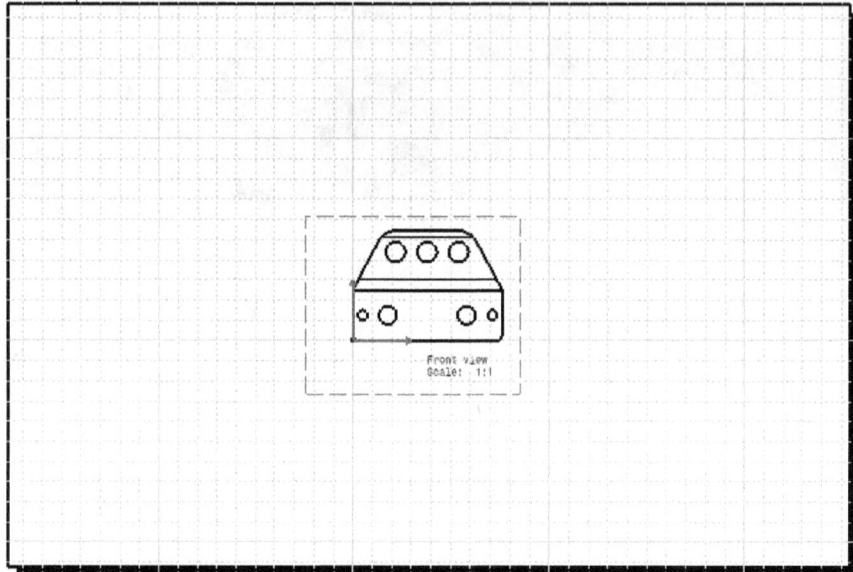

Figure 10–24

Task 3 - Create an isometric view.

1. Click ⬚ (Isometric View) in the Projections flyout in the Views toolbar.

2. Activate the **Bracket.CATPart** window and select a face on the model. The software orients the isometric view using the current model orientation. Therefore, the face selected is not important. The software places the view on the drawing and the orientation compass displays.

3. Select the dashed green border of the view and drag it to the top right corner of the drawing, as shown in Figure 10–25.

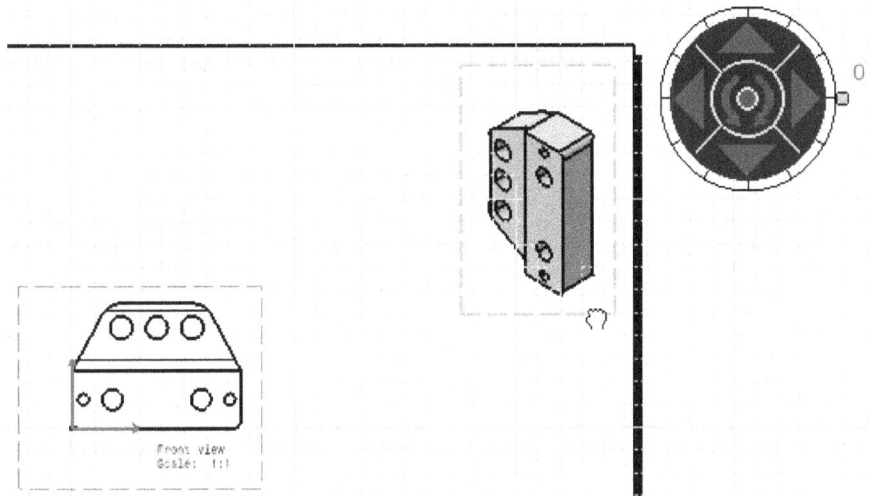

Figure 10–25

4. Select anywhere on the drawing to complete the creation of the view.

Design Considerations

The border of the front view is currently red, while the border of the isometric view is blue. The red border indicates that this is the active view. Any view operations are always performed on the active view. As well, the creation of a section or projection view will reference the active view. Double-click on the view border to activate a view.

Task 4 - Create a projection view.

In this task, you will project a view from the front view. The front view must be active.

1. Ensure that the front view is active.

2. Click ⬚ (Projection View).

3. Position the cursor around the front view. Four possible projections can be created, as shown in Figure 10–26.

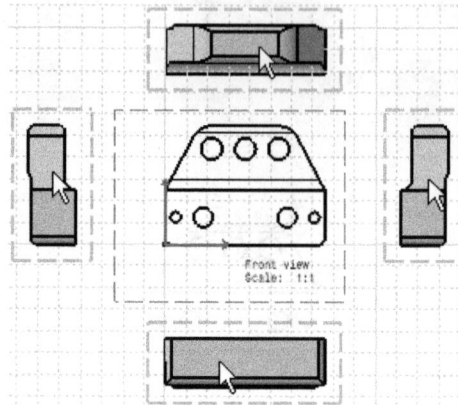

Figure 10–26

4. Create the projection to the right of the front view. The drawing displays as shown in Figure 10–27.

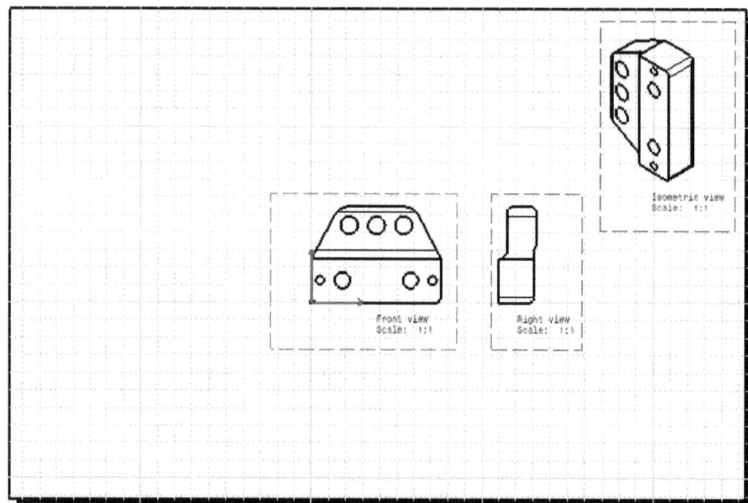

Figure 10–27

Task 5 - Move the views.

1. Select the dashed view frame of the front view and drag it to the bottom left corner of the sheet.

2. Experiment by moving the right view. Move the isometric view as well and note the differences between the linked and unlinked views.

Design Considerations

The projected right view is a child of the front view, so it maintains an aligned position with it. The isometric view can be moved independent of the front view.

Task 6 - Change the properties of a view

1. Right-click on the Front view in the specification tree and select **Properties**.

2. Select **Center Line** and **Axis** in the *Dress-up* area in the *View* tab of the Properties dialog box, as shown in Figure 10–28.

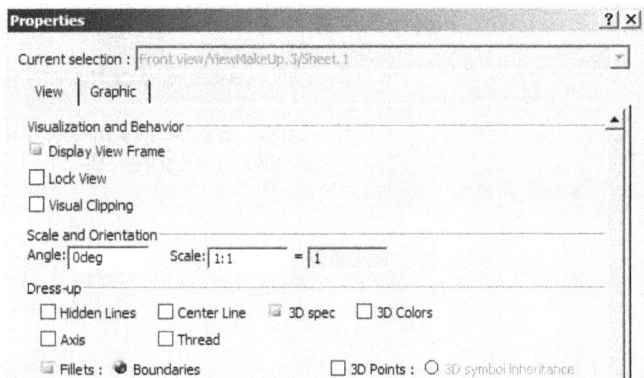

Figure 10–28

3. Click **OK**.

Task 7 - Create a section view.

1. Zoom in on the front view.

2. Click (Offset Section View) in the Views toolbar.

To align the start of the section line with the hole, try positioning the cursor over the hole to create a coincidence constraint before starting the creation of the line.

3. Sketch a line that starts approximately one grid square space to the left of the view, as shown in Figure 10–29. Enable the system to assume an alignment with the axis of the Hole feature.

4. Drag the line across the front view and select a location approximately one grid square space to the right of the view, as shown in Figure 10–30.

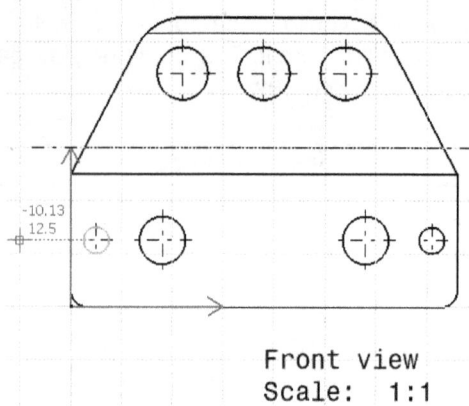

Front view
Scale: 1:1

Figure 10–29

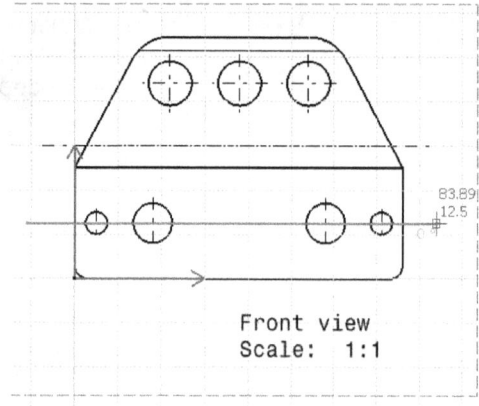

Front view
Scale: 1:1

Figure 10–30

5. Double-click to complete the x-section definition.

6. Select a location above the front view. The view displays as shown in Figure 10–31.

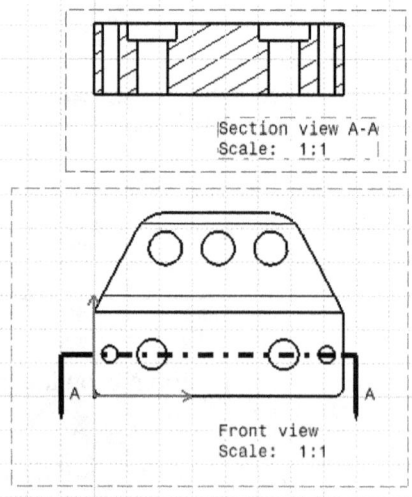

Section view A-A
Scale: 1:1

Front view
Scale: 1:1

Figure 10–31

7. **ONLY IF** the section view call out arrows are pointing in the wrong direction, complete the following steps:

   1. Right-click on the arrow. From the shortcut menu, select **Callout (Section View).x object>Definition** as shown in Figure 10–32.

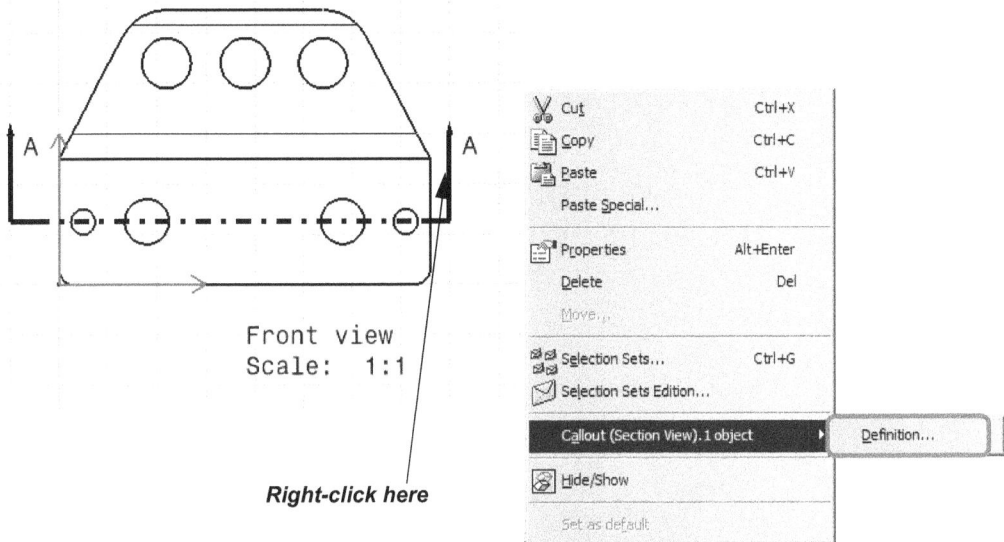

Front view
Scale: 1:1

Right-click here

✂ Cut	Ctrl+X	
📋 Copy	Ctrl+C	
📋 Paste	Ctrl+V	
Paste Special...		
📋 Properties	Alt+Enter	
Delete	Del	
Move...		
📇 Selection Sets...	Ctrl+G	
📇 Selection Sets Edition...		
Callout (Section View).1 object	▶	Definition...
📇 Hide/Show		
Set as default		

Figure 10–32

   2. The Profile Edition mode displays. From the Edit/Replace toolbar, click ⬚ (Invert Profile Direction).

   3. Click ⬚ (End Profile Edition) to complete the action.

Task 8 - Add a detail view.

---

1. Zoom in on the section view.

2. Double-click on the dashed frame of the section view to make it active. The border turns red and the name of the view in the view tree is underlined, indicating that this view is the active view.

3. Click ⬚ (Quick Detail View) in the Views toolbar.

---

4. Select the right edge of the counterbored hole feature, and then drag the cursor to create a circle callout, as shown in Figure 10–33.

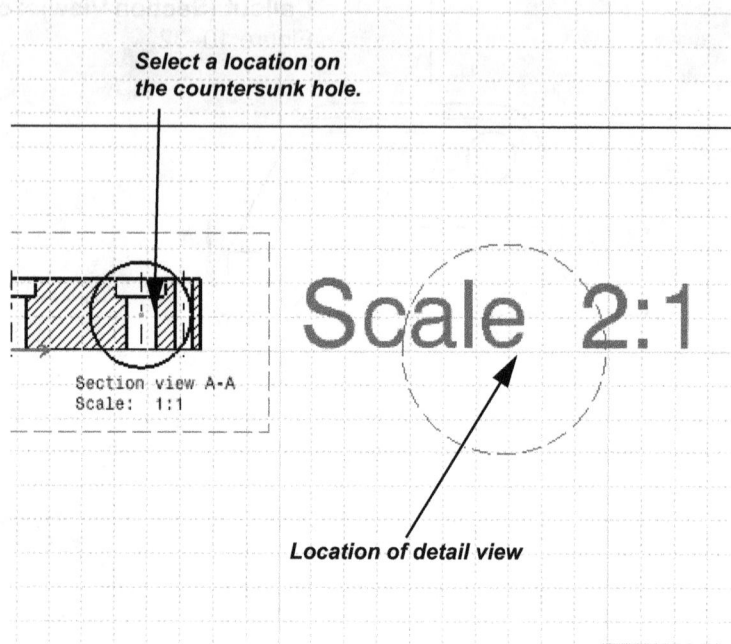

Select a location on the countersunk hole.

Scale 2:1

Section view A-A
Scale: 1:1

Location of detail view

Figure 10–33

*If the axis is not visible, right-click and select **Properties>Axis** in the View tab, in the Properties dialog box.*

5. Select a point to the right of the section view to define a location for the detail view. The complete detail view containing the callout is shown in Figure 10–34.

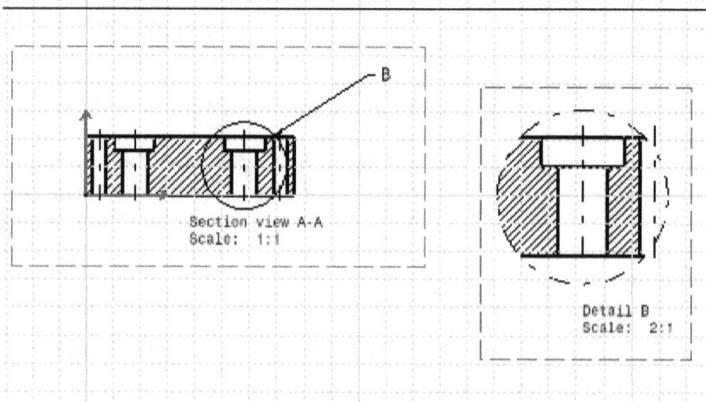

B

Section view A-A
Scale: 1:1

Detail B
Scale: 2:1

Figure 10–34

Task 9 - Insert a frame and title block.

1. You must change the mode for the drawing to enable editing of the background. Select **Edit>Sheet Background** to set the Drawing mode to Background mode.

2. Select **Insert>Drawing>Frame and Title Block**. The Insert Frame and Title Block dialog box opens.

3. Set *Style of Titleblock* to **Drawing_Titleblock_RAND**, as shown in Figure 10–35.

*If Drawing_Titleblock_ RAND is not available, select **Drawing Titleblock Sample 1**.*

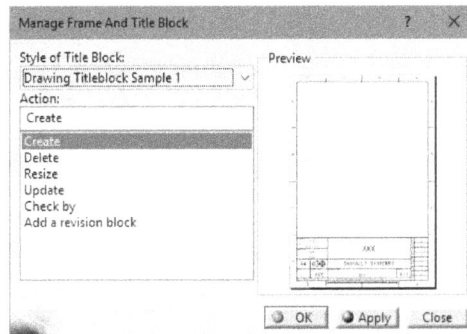

Figure 10–35

4. Click **Apply**. The frame and title block display. Close the Insert Frame and Title Block dialog box.

5. Select **Edit>Working Views** and reposition the drawing views as required.

6. Save the drawing as **Bracket.CATDrawing**.

7. Do not close the file. It is used in the next practice.

Practice 10b | Annotate a Drawing

Practice Objective

- Create and manipulate dimensions.

In this practice, you will add dimensions to a drawing. You will modify these dimensions and explore their various properties. The end result is shown in Figure 10–36.

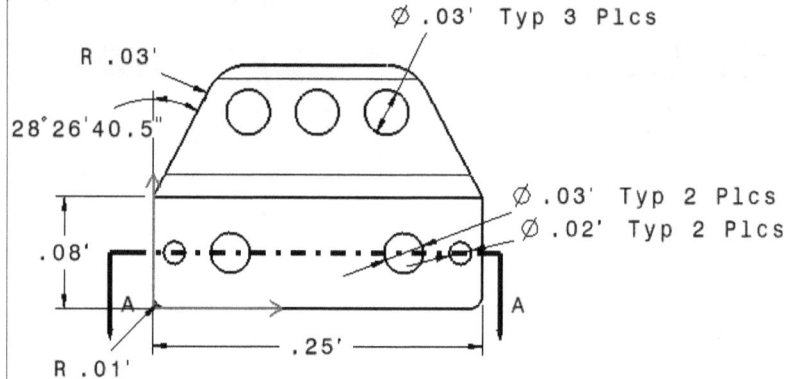

Front view
Scale: 1:1

Figure 10–36

Task 1 - Generate manual dimensions.

1. Open **Bracket_Views.CATDrawing**.

2. Activate the front view.

3. Hide all views except the front view.

*If you completed the last practice you can continue to use **Bracket.CATDrawing** instead.*

4. Zoom in on the front view and click ⊞ (Dimensions).

5. Select the edge shown in Figure 10–37. The software creates a linear dimension for the edge.

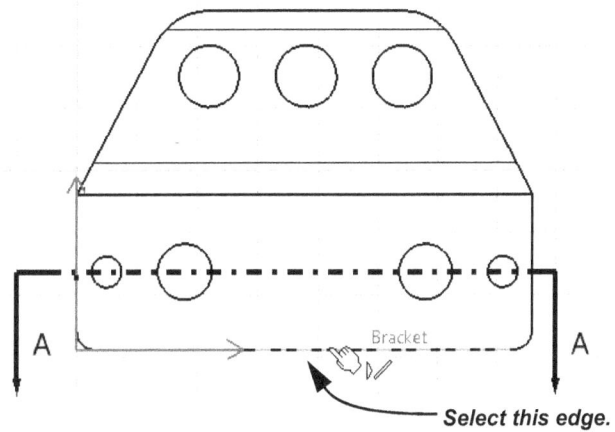

Figure 10–37

6. Select a second reference for the dimension, as shown in Figure 10–38. The software displays a length dimension between the two references.

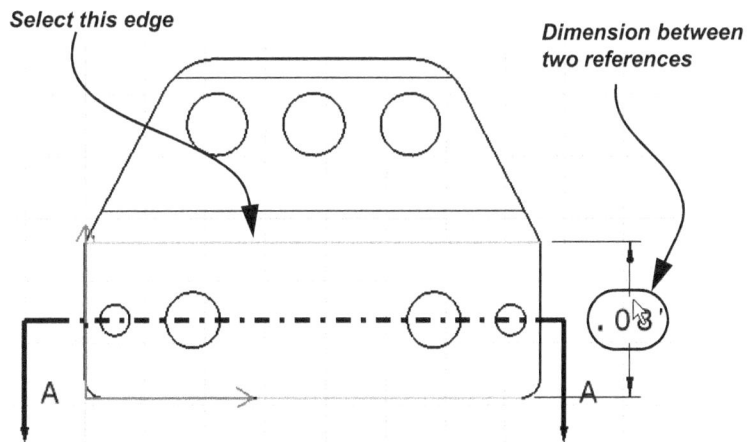

Front view
Scale: 1:1

Figure 10–38

7. Press the left mouse button to complete the reference selection and place the dimension. The dimension highlights in orange and can now be moved.

8. Move the dimension to the side, as shown in Figure 10–39.

9. Create the horizontal dimension shown in Figure 10–40.

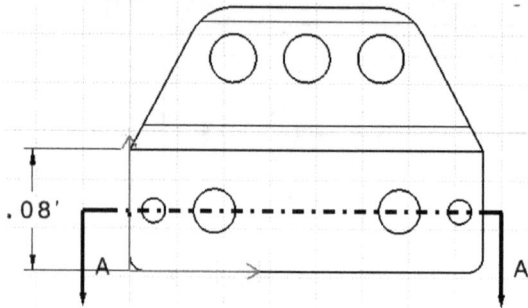

Figure 10–39

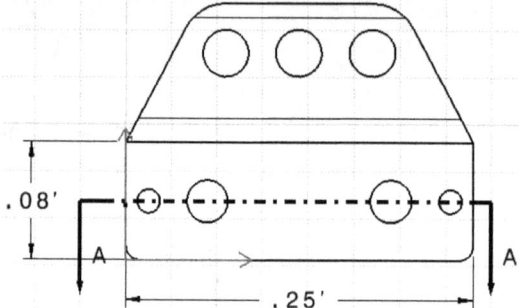

Figure 10–40

10. Click [⌀] (Diameter Dimensions) in the Dimensions toolbar.

11. Select the circle as shown in Figure 10–41, and place the diameter dimension.

Create a diameter dimension for this circle

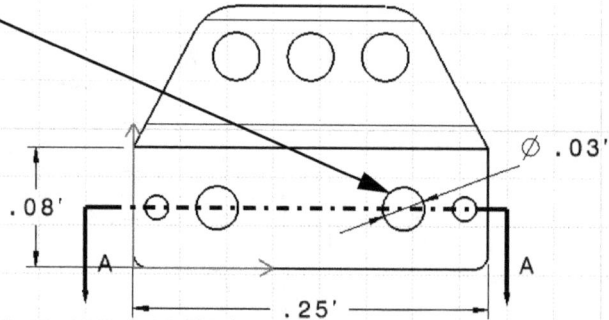

Figure 10–41

12. Use ⬚ (Diameter Dimensions) and ⬚ (Radius Dimensions) to create the four other dimensions as shown in Figure 10–42.

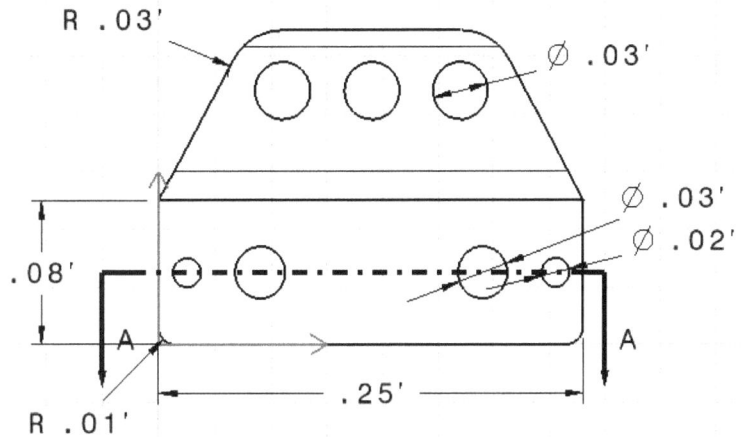

Figure 10–42

Task 2 - Manipulate dimensions.

1. Select the **.03'** diameter dimension on the right Hole feature, as shown in Figure 10–43.

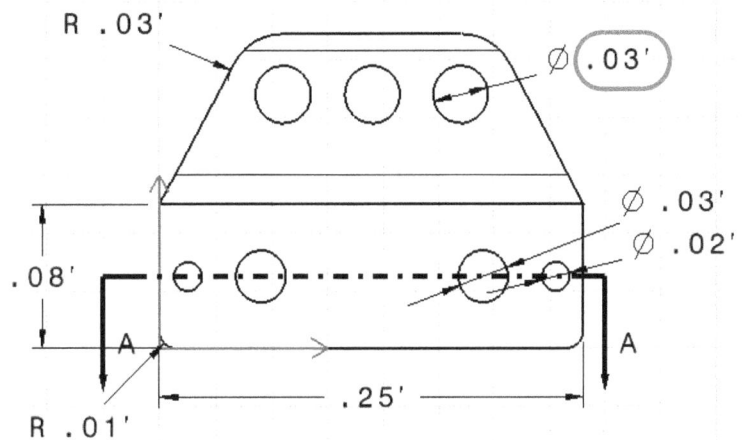

Figure 10–43

2. Right-click and select **Properties**.

3. Select the *Dimension Texts* tab in the Properties dialog box.

4. Enter **Typ 3 Plcs** in the suffix text field, as shown in Figure 10–44.

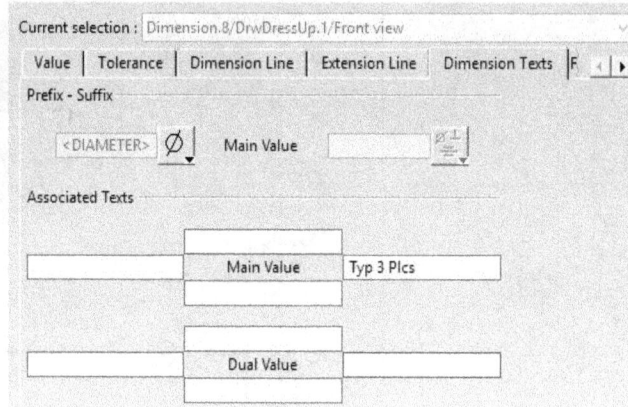

Figure 10–44

5. Click **Apply** and **OK**. The dimension updates with the changes, as shown in Figure 10–45.

6. Select the **.03'** and **.02'** diameter dimensions (hold <Ctrl> to select both) and add the suffix dimension text, as shown in Figure 10–46.

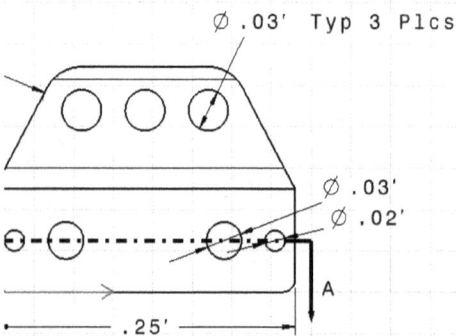

Figure 10–45

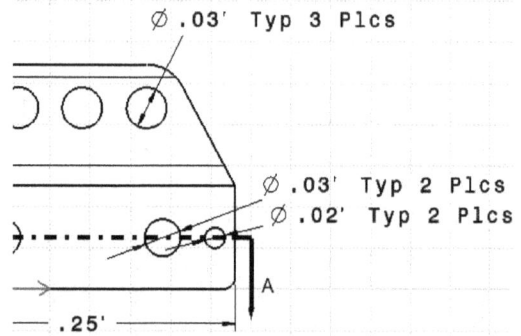

Figure 10–46

Task 3 - Create an angle dimension on the Front view.

1. Click ![Angle Dimensions icon] (Angle Dimensions) (click the flyout arrow if not visible) and select the two entities shown in Figure 10–47.

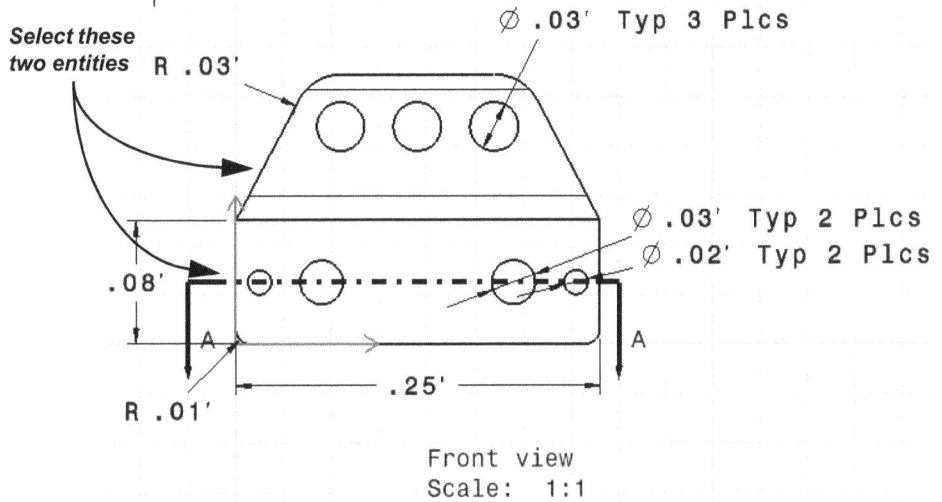

Select these two entities

∅ .03' Typ 3 Plcs
R .03'
∅ .03' Typ 2 Plcs
∅ .02' Typ 2 Plcs
.08'
A
A
R .01'
.25'

Front view
Scale: 1:1

Figure 10–47

2. Define how the angled dimension is generated. While moving the dimension into position, right-click and select **Angle Sector>Sector 2**, as shown in Figure 10–48.

Depending on where the cursor is located, you might need to select a different angle sector to get the result shown in Figure 10–49.

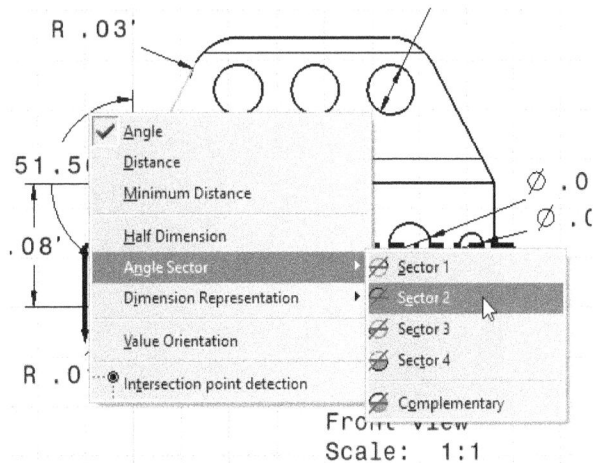

R .03'

51.5(

.08'

R .0

✓ Angle
Distance
Minimum Distance
Half Dimension
Angle Sector ▸
Dimension Representation ▸
Value Orientation
● Intersection point detection

∅ .0
∅ .(

Sector 1
Sector 2
Sector 3
Sector 4
Complementary

Front view
Scale: 1:1

Figure 10–48

3. Place the dimension with the left mouse button. The dimension displays as shown in Figure 10–49.

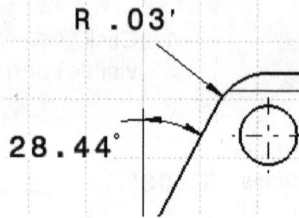

Figure 10–49

4. Modify the format of the angle dimension by right-clicking it and selecting **Properties**.

5. Select the *Value* tab in the Properties dialog box. Modify the value in the *Display* field to **3 factors** and the value in the *Precision* field to **0.1** as shown in Figure 10–50.

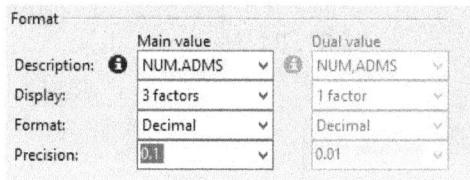

Figure 10–50

6. Apply the changes and close the Properties dialog box. The dimension displays as shown in Figure 10–51.

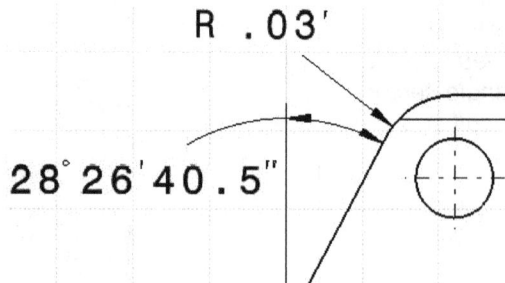

Figure 10–51

7. The completed drawing is shown in Figure 10–52. Save the drawing and close the window.

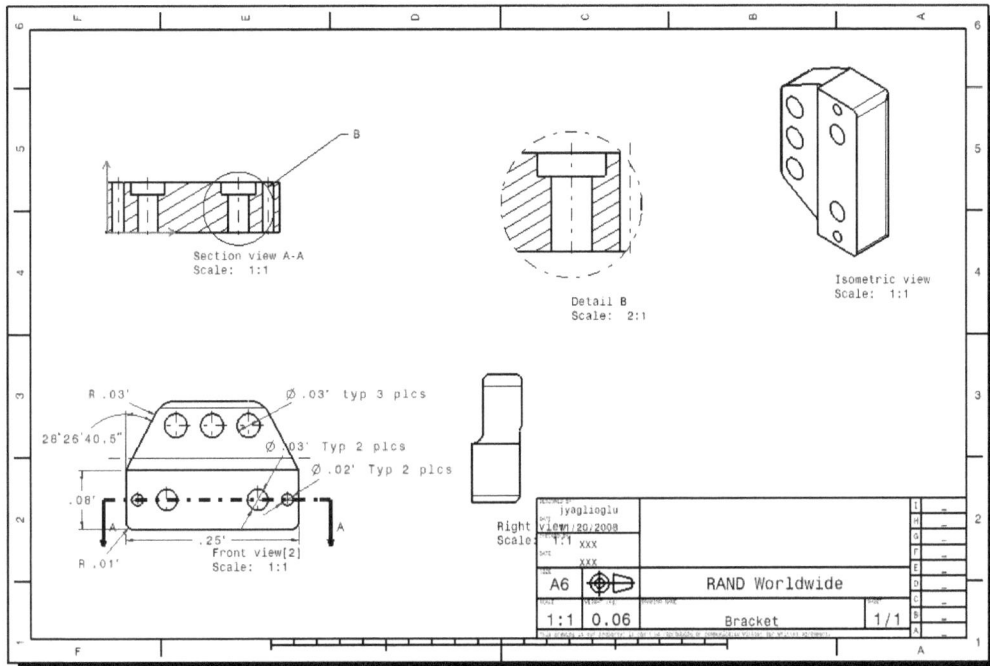

Figure 10–52

Practice 10c | (Optional) Piston Drawing

Practice Objective

* Create a drawing without instruction.

1. Finish the **Piston.CATPart** model if it has not been completed.

2. Create a new drawing called **Piston**. Add views and detailing, as shown in Figure 10–53.

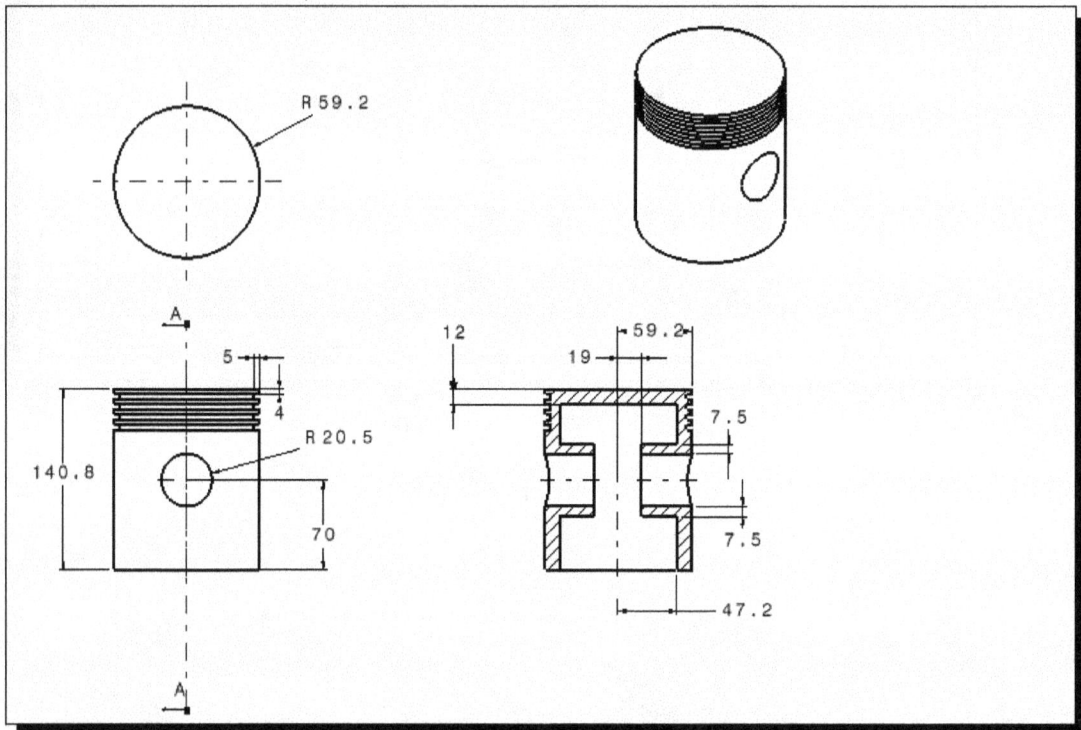

Figure 10–53

Practice 10d | (Optional) Flange Drawing

Practice Objective

- Create a drawing without instruction.

1. Finish the **Flange.CATPart** model if it has not been completed.

2. Create a new drawing called **Flange**. Add views and detailing, as shown in Figure 10–54.

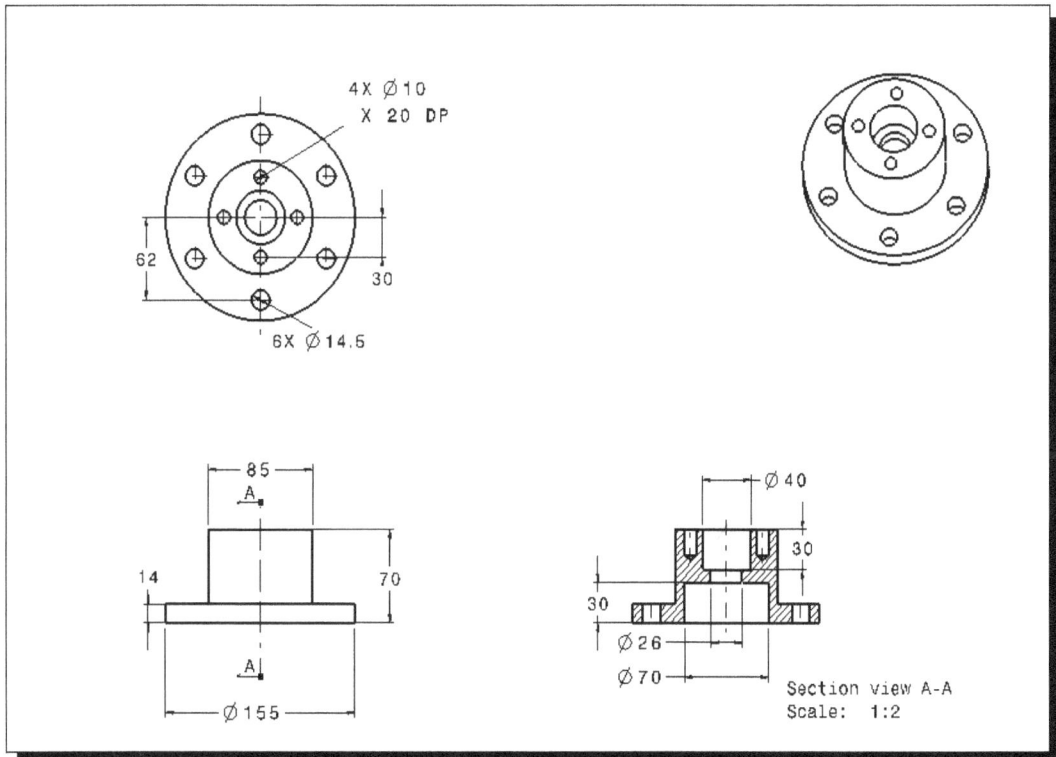

Figure 10–54

Creating Sketches

In this chapter, you will learn how sketches are used to create features. You will learn some of the basic capabilities of the Sketcher Workbench, which enables you to create sketch-based features. You will use reference planes and surfaces to orient and sketch the profile of your first feature.

Learning Objectives in this Chapter

- Understand the basics of sketched features.
- Review the general steps for creating a new part.
- Understand the use of default and reference planes for sketching.
- Review the basic tools that you can use to create entities in sketches.
- Create a sketch for the model profile.
- Understand several operations for editing sketches.
- Learn various tips and techniques for working with sketches.
- Understand how features and sketches display in the specification tree.

11.1 Getting Started on Sketching Features

2D sketches are used to create 3D features. A sketching plane is selected and used to create a sketched feature, as shown in Figure 11–1.

Sketching plane

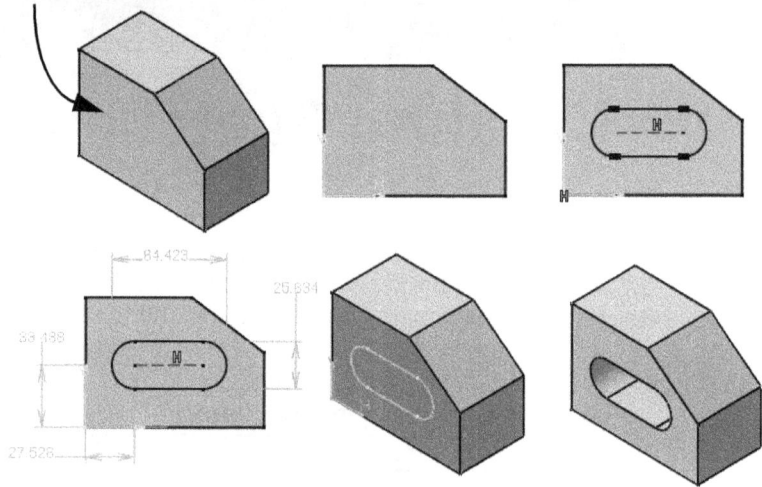

Figure 11–1

How To: Create a Sketched Feature

1. Select a sketching plane and enter the Sketcher workbench. The plane you select is initially oriented parallel to the screen. The Y-axis faces the top of the screen and the X-axis faces the right side of the screen.
2. Sketch the required profile or cross-section.
3. Create constraints/dimensions to define the size and location of the sketch.
4. Exit the Sketcher workbench.
5. Use the sketch to create a solid feature, such as a Pad or Pocket.

11.2 Creating a New Part

Sketches are an integral part of creating solid features in a CATPart file. To create a sketch, open an existing model (**File>Open**), or create a new part file.

How To: Create a New Part

1. Select **File>New**. The New dialog box opens, which enables you to define the type of file that is created.

*All part models created and opened have been created with the **Enable Hybrid Design** option cleared.*

2. Select **Part** in the List of Types drop-down list (shown in Figure 11–2), and then click **OK**. The New Part dialog box opens as shown in Figure 11–3.

| Figure 11–2 | Figure 11–3 |

The following parameters can be configured for the new part:

Parameter	Description
Enter part name field	Enter a name for the part model. This name is automatically assigned to the Part Number of the new file.
Enable hybrid design option	Hybrid design uses a special type of body, called a hybrid body. It can contain both wireframe/surface and solid features. This enables direct integration of the surface and part design environments into a single body. For current purposes, the hybrid design environment is disabled.
Create a geometrical set option	When the hybrid design environment is disabled, a geometrical set is used to store wireframe and surface elements, as well as sketched elements. A geometrical set is automatically added to the new part file when this option is selected.

Create an ordered geometrical set option	When the hybrid design environment is enabled, an ordered geometrical set can be used to group together wireframe or surface geometry with order preserved.
Do not show this dialog box at startup option	The software does not open the dialog box when creating a new part file when this option is selected. Instead, the software automatically names the new part *Part#*, where # increments to the next available number, starting at 1.
	If this option is selected, the Part name dialog box can be restored by selecting **Tools>Options> Infrastructure>Part Infrastructure**, selecting the *Part Document* tab, and selecting the **'Display the New Part' dialog box** option.

3. Click **OK** when the part parameters have been specified. The model is created with three default reference planes that can be used as sketching planes, as shown in Figure 11–4.

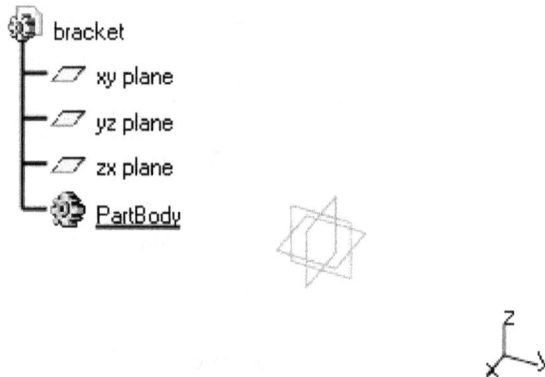

Figure 11–4

11.3 Sketching Planes

A new part always starts with three default reference planes. The model and specification tree display is shown in Figure 11–5. The planes are automatically named to match the directions of the coordinate system that they are parallel to, such as the XY plane.

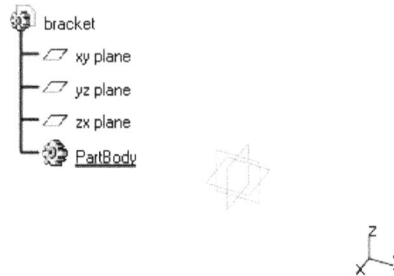

Figure 11–5

When you create a new part, the software uses the part name as the part number. To modify a part number, select the part name in the specification tree, right-click and select **Properties**. Enter the required part number in the *Part Number* field of the Properties dialog box, shown in Figure 11–6.

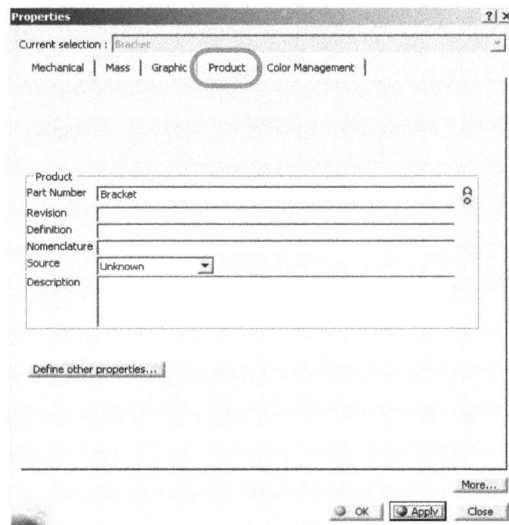

Figure 11–6

The part number is not the name of the CATPart file. When you first save the model, you are prompted for a filename and location. You can use different values for the part number and filename.

Reference Planes

All CATParts contain default reference planes as the first three features. The default reference planes remain the same size relative to screen, regardless of model size or zoom level, as shown in Figure 11–7.

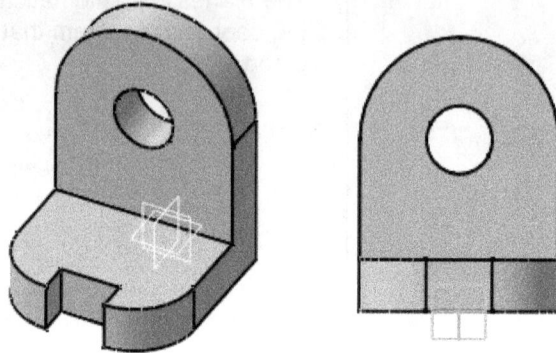

Figure 11–7

Planes cannot be displayed as shaded. This is for illustration only.

For better visualization, highlight each plane by placing the cursor over a reference plane in the specification tree or on the screen.

Default reference planes are useful for creating a new model because they provide a planar reference to place the first sketch. Figure 11–8 shows three shaded rectangular surfaces to help visualize the reference planes orientation.

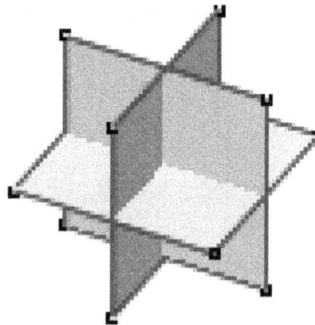

Figure 11–8

Selecting a Plane for Sketching

Selecting one plane over another impacts the Quick Views and the default orientation of the model. The YZ plane is considered the front of the part, as shown in Figure 11–9. However, this does not mean that you always sketch on the YZ plane.

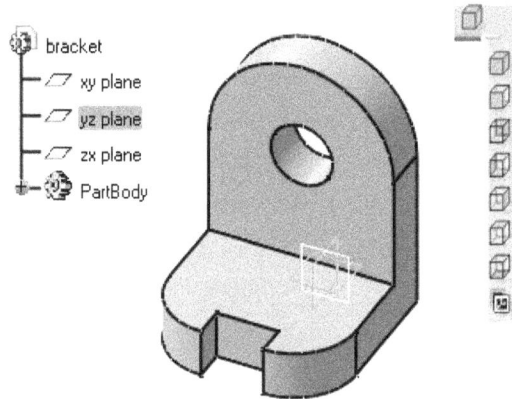

Figure 11–9

Sketch a front profile on the YZ plane, a side profile on the ZX plane, and a top profile on the XY plane.

The L-shape profile of a part is also a side profile. Therefore, the L-shape sketch of the bracket part is sketched on the ZX plane. The possible default orientations of a cylinder are shown in Figure 11–10 when a particular sketching plane is selected for sketching.

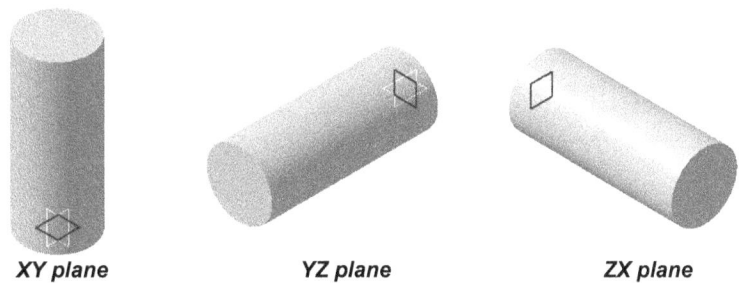

XY plane   YZ plane   ZX plane

Figure 11–10

11.4 Sketcher Workbench

How To: Create a Sketch

1. Select an appropriate sketching plane and click

   ▢ (Sketch).

2. Create your sketch.

3. Click ▢ (Exit workbench) to complete the sketch.

Sketcher Grid

When you first enter the Sketcher workbench, the following objects display, as shown in Figure 11–11:

- Sketcher grid over your sketch plane

- Three default reference planes

- Horizontal and Vertical axes

- Compass

- Specification tree

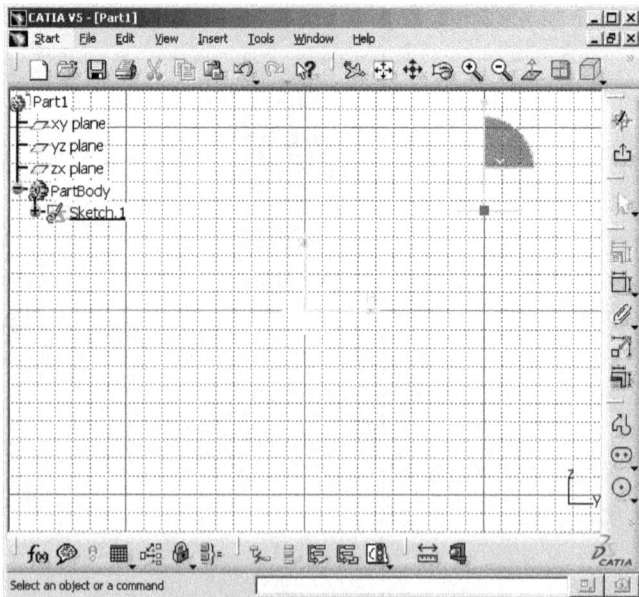

Figure 11–11

To modify the sketcher grid, select **Tools>Options**, and then select **Mechanical Design>Sketcher** in the Options dialog box that opens, as shown in Figure 11–12. You can define the following information on the sketcher display:

- Primary spacing

- Number of graduations

- Enable/disable the snap function

- Enable/disable the grid

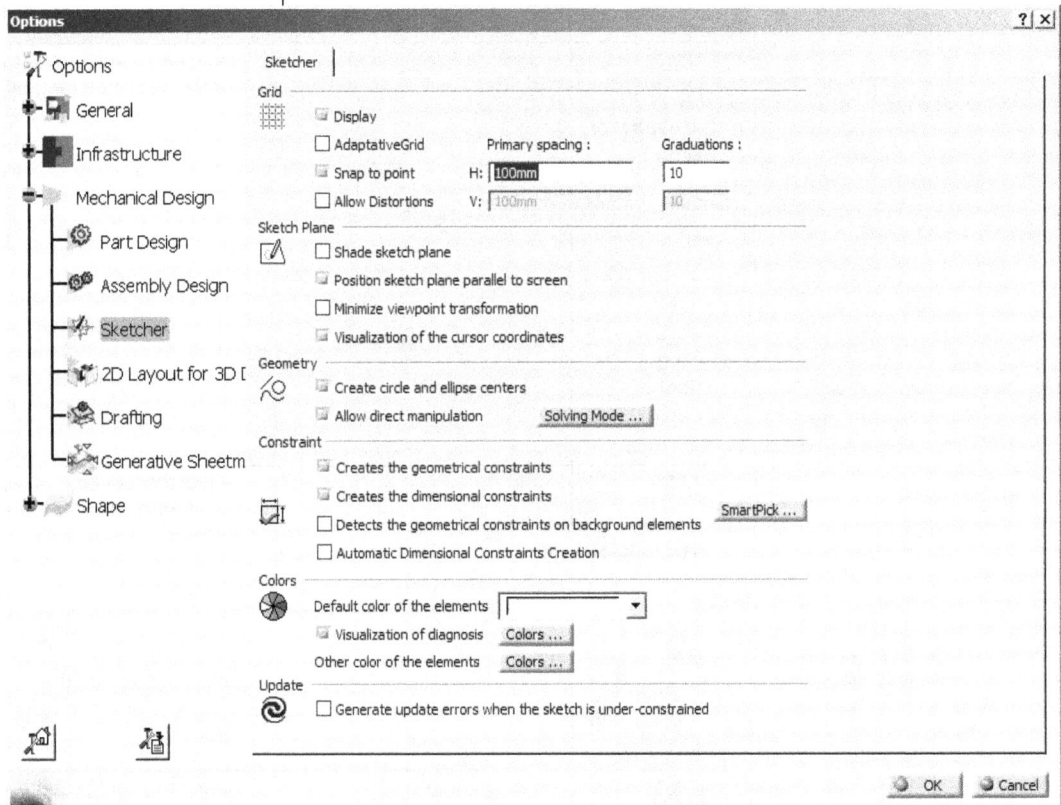

Figure 11–12

11.5 Basic Shapes

Other sketch tools are available. These are covered in a different chapter.

Once inside the Sketcher workbench, the feature's profile (or cross-section) must be sketched. The most commonly used tools for sketching are described as follows:

Icon	Sequence	Description
(Line)		Select the start and end points of the line.
(Bi-Tangent Line)		Select two arcs or circles for the line to be tangent to.
(Line Normal To Curve)		Select a location on a curve, or a point on a curve. Then select the end point of the line.
(Rectangle)		Select the location for two diagonal corners of the rectangle.
(3-Point Arc starting with limits)		Select the start point of the arc, end point of the arc, and then another point for the arc to pass through.
(Circle)		Select the center of the circle and a point on its perimeter to define the diameter.

(Elongated Hole)		Select the center of each arc, and then select a location on the profile to define the diameter.
(Corner)		Select the two lines the corner is tangent to, and then drag the corner out to the required size.
(Chamfer)		Select the two lines the chamfer contacts, and then drag the chamfer out to the required size.
(Axis)		Select the start and end points of the axis.

Manual Definition

With many sketch tools, you can use another toolbar that contains additional functions for that specific type of geometry. Some of these options are described as follows:

Option	Description
Lines	Manually enter the coordinates of the start point, end point, line length, and angle into the Sketch Tools toolbar.

Start Point: H: 20mm   V: 20mm   L: 0mm   A: 0deg

Option	Description
Rectangle	Manually enter the coordinates of the first point, the coordinates of the second point, and the height and width of the rectangle.
Circle	Manually enter the coordinates for the circle's center and specify its radius.
Corner	Specify how to trim the existing lines when the corner is completed.

11.6 Profile Sketching

To create a connected series of lines and arcs, use

[icon] (Profile). Sketch a series of connected lines, then when you have formed a closed loop, the profile automatically terminates, as shown in Figure 11–13. You can also terminate the profile with an open loop by double-clicking the left mouse button at the end of the last line, as shown in Figure 11–14.

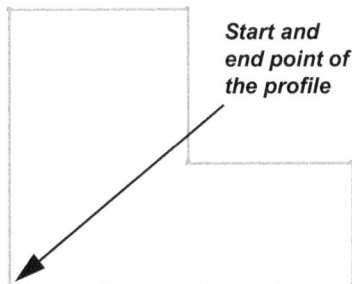

Start and end point of the profile

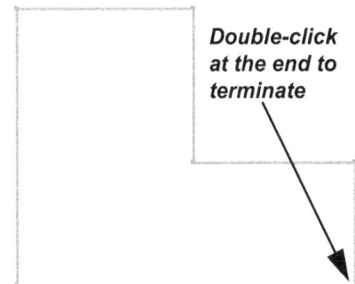

Double-click at the end to terminate

Figure 11–13   **Figure 11–14**

You can toggle from sketching a line to sketching a tangent arc (as shown in Figure 11–15) or three-point arc (as shown in Figure 11–16), by using the temporary icons in the Sketch tools toolbar. You return to sketching a line after you finish the arc.

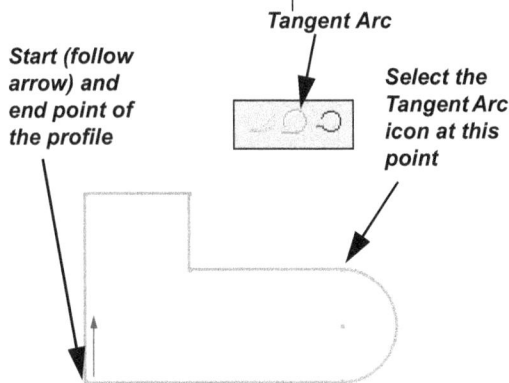

Tangent Arc

Start (follow arrow) and end point of the profile

Select the Tangent Arc icon at this point

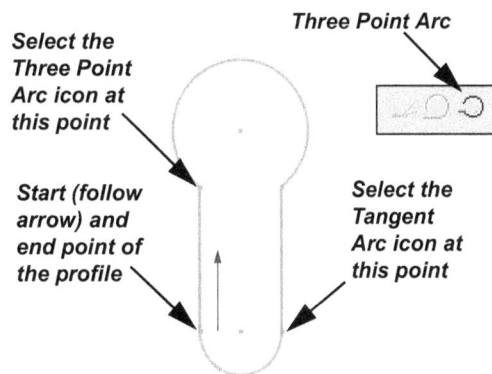

Select the Three Point Arc icon at this point

Three Point Arc

Start (follow arrow) and end point of the profile

Select the Tangent Arc icon at this point

Figure 11–15   **Figure 11–16**

11.7 Sketcher Editing Operations

Trimming

(Trim) extends or trims sketched entities to form a closed corner. Select each entity on the side of the intersection that you want to keep. Figure 11–17 shows three examples of trimming and extending line segments.

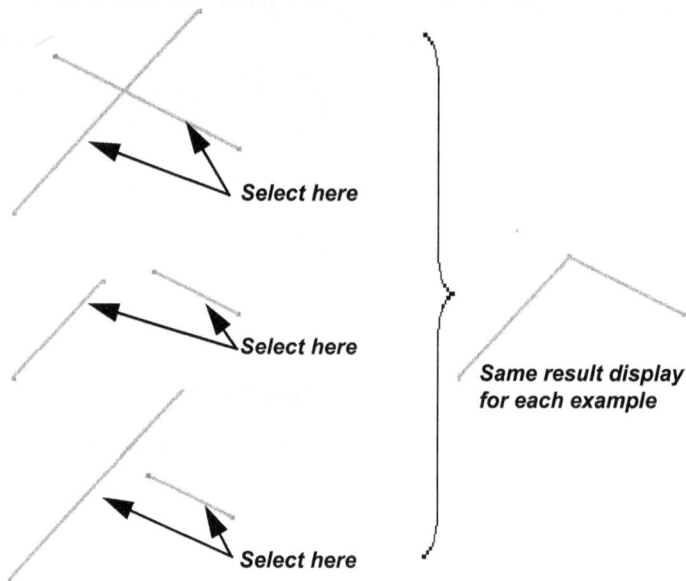

Select here

Select here

Select here

Same result display for each example

Figure 11–17

You can also choose to trim only the first selected entity by clicking (Trim First Element) in the Sketch tools toolbar, and selecting the entity to which the first element should be trimmed, as shown in Figure 11–18.

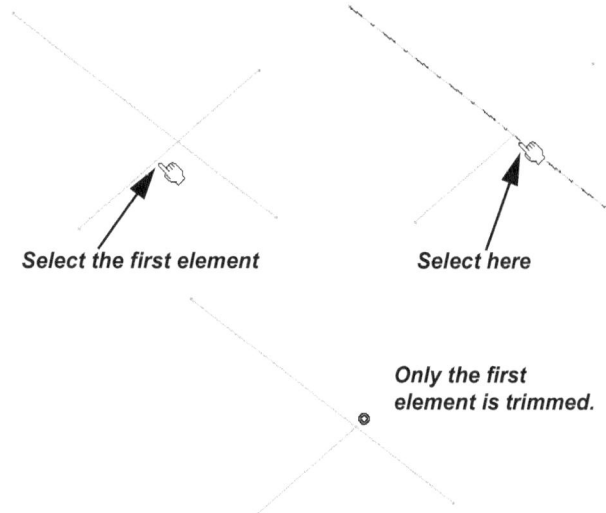

Select the first element

Select here

Only the first
element is trimmed.

Figure 11–18

Break

⬜ (Break) divides a sketched entity at its intersection with another sketched entity. To use the **Break** tool, select the feature you want to divide and select the intersecting feature. The intersection point is projected if the feature does not intersect the first entity.

- The **Break** tool is used to break circles into arcs using an intersecting line, as shown in Figure 11–19. Note that a closed entity, such as the circle, is also divided by an implicit 360° mark.

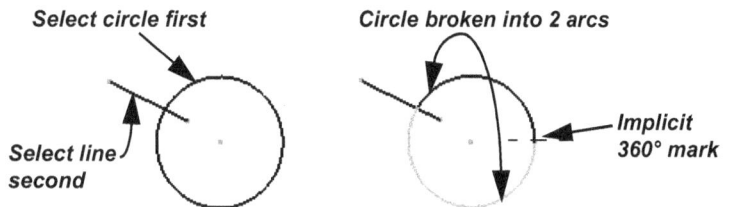

Select circle first

Circle broken into 2 arcs

Select line second

Implicit 360° mark

Figure 11–19

Quick Trim

(Quick Trim) deletes the selected portion of a feature. The software automatically breaks the element at its intersections with other sketched elements.

- The **Quick Trim** method is used to remove the arc segment between two vertical lines, as shown in Figure 11–20.

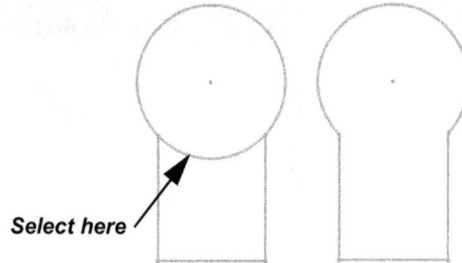

Select here

Figure 11–20

Delete and Undo

Pressing <Delete> enables you to remove portions (one or more lines) of a model or the entire sketch (rectangle).

- To completely eliminate a feature you just sketched, you can press <Ctrl>+<Z> or click (Undo). The keyboard shortcut executes the **Undo** command. CATIA records your previous actions, enabling you to undo multiple times.

11.8 Tips and Techniques

Repeating a Command

When you use any of the geometry creation icons, the command is automatically deactivated once you perform the action. However, by double-clicking on the icon, you can perform that command multiple times.

An active icon displays in an orange color.

•   Click [icon] to deactivate it. This technique is more efficient than repeatedly selecting the same icon.

Sketching in 3D

Sketching in a 3D orientation can be useful when solid geometry exists and you are sketching on the face of a previously defined feature.

•   To return to the planar sketch view, click [icon] (Normal View).

Construction Geometry

You can use construction geometry to help create lines, shapes, and points for your standard geometry. Construction geometry is useful when working with more complex sketches, as shown in Figure 11–21.

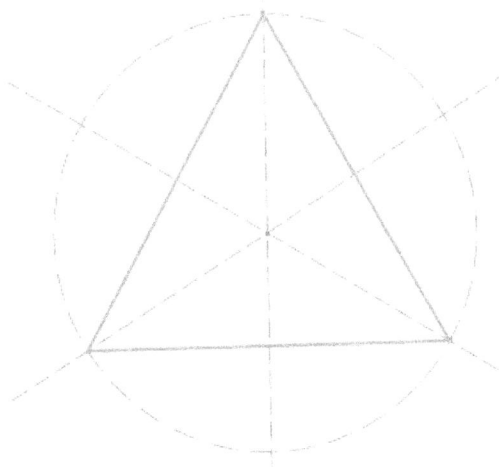

Figure 11–21

You can create construction geometry using one of the following methods:

Do not forget to return to Standard elements when you are done.

- Click ⬡ (Construction/Standard Element) in the Tools toolbar, as shown in Figure 11–22. Any geometry you sketch displays as construction geometry.

Construction/Standard Element

Figure 11–22

- Select the existing standard geometry and click

  ⬡ (Construction/Standard Element) to convert it to construction geometry.

Auto Search

Use the **Auto Search** tool to automatically select all entities that are connected to the selected entity.

- To use the **Auto Search** tool, select a sketched entity that belongs to the profile you want to select, then right-click and select * **object>Auto Search**, as shown in Figure 11–23. The continuous chain of entities is highlighted for the next operation.

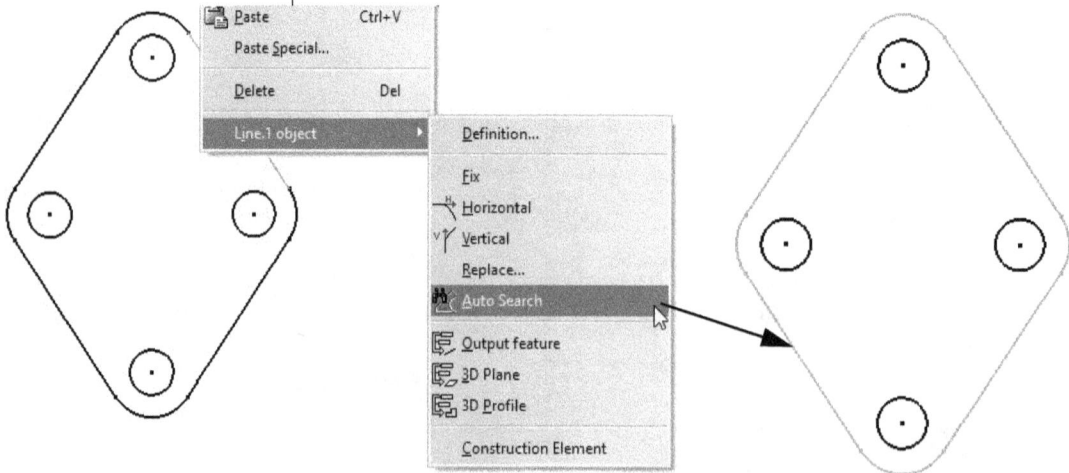

Figure 11–23

Sketching at Origin

If you select the origin of the sketch during the creation of a profile, CATIA automatically creates an implicit constraint between the vertex of the sketch and the origin. This constraint restricts the vertex of the profile from being moved at a later time, but can be broken by selecting the profile, selecting **Edit>Cut** and **Edit>Paste**. This pastes the profile on its original position without the constraint, so you can move it. This only works if the sketched entity has not been referenced by any other features. Any features that reference the entity being cut and pasted fail because the pasted item is considered a new sketched entity and does not maintain the references.

- This type of constraint can be used for a base feature since it is unlikely to move later. However, for other features that should be constrained to the origin, it is recommended to sketch offset from the origin and manually constrain the sketch to it. Figure 11–24 shows a circle that can be manually constrained to the origin using a **Coincident** constraint.

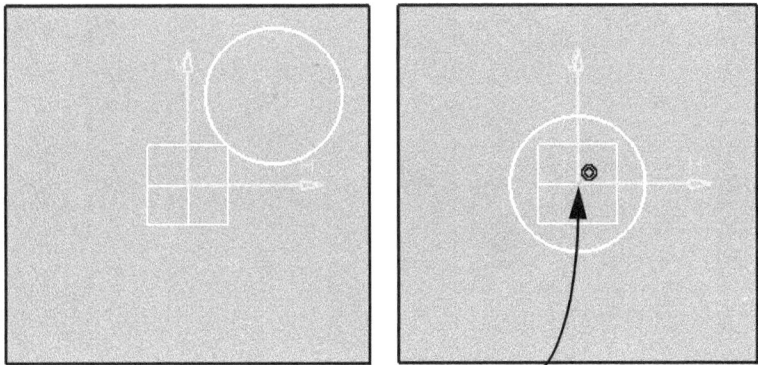

Coincident constraint
Figure 11–24

11.9 Specification Tree

The features you create are listed in the specification tree in the order in which you create them. Solid geometry features are listed under PartBody, as shown in Figure 11–25.

Sketches are automatically listed under the feature branch that uses them.

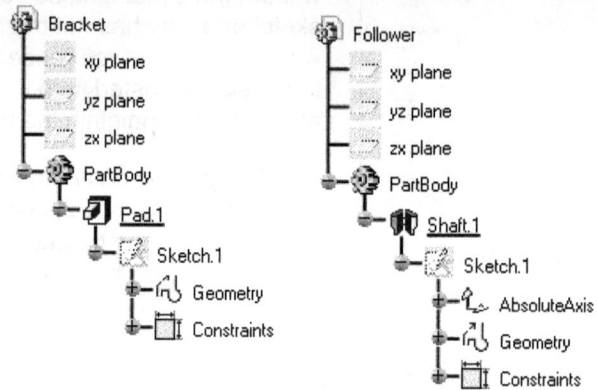

Figure 11–25

- A sketch is automatically hidden once referenced by a solid feature. Right-click on the sketch and select **Hide/Show** to toggle on its display.

Practice 11a

Sketching Basic Shapes

Practice Objectives

- Sketch a line, arc, rectangle, circle, and elongated hole.
- Trim overlapping shapes.

In this practice, you will create a sketch as shown in Figure 11–26. You will use various constraints to help constrain the sketch.

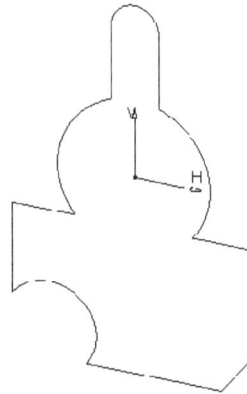

Figure 11–26

Task 1 - Create a new part and set the length units to millimeter.

1. Click (New) to create a new part.

2. In the New dialog box, select the **Part** option and click **OK**, as shown in Figure 11–27.

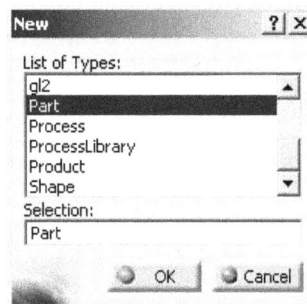

Figure 11–27

3. The New Part dialog box opens, as shown in Figure 11–28. Enter **Sketch_1** as the part name. If required, deactivate **Enable hybrid Design**.

Figure 11–28

4. Click **OK** to create the new part model.

Task 2 - Select the sketching plane and enter the Sketcher workbench.

---

1. In the specification tree, select the YZ plane. Note which plane highlights on the screen.

2. Click [icon] (Sketch) to enter the Sketcher workbench. The selected reference plane displays parallel to the screen, as shown in Figure 11–29.

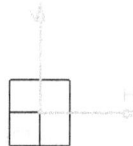

Figure 11–29

Task 3 - Sketch a circle.

Automatic Dimensional Constraints are discussed in more detail in a later chapter.

1. In the Sketch tools toolbar, ensure that [icon] (Automatic Dimensional Constraints) is toggled off.

2. Click [icon] (Circle) to sketch a circle.

*Read the message area
for your next selection.*

3. Place the cursor over the intersection of the horizontal and vertical axes. Select the **0.0**, **0.0** location of the XY axis to define the circle's center point.

4. Drag the cursor and select a location to define the radius of the circle. The sketch displays as shown in Figure 11–30.

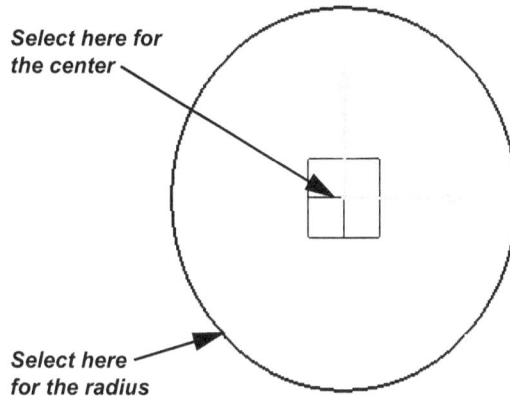

Select here for the center

Select here for the radius

Figure 11–30

Task 4 - Sketch a rectangle that overlaps the circle.

---

1. Click [ ] (Rectangle) to sketch a rectangle.

2. Select the first point of the rectangle and the second point of the rectangle, as shown in Figure 11–31.

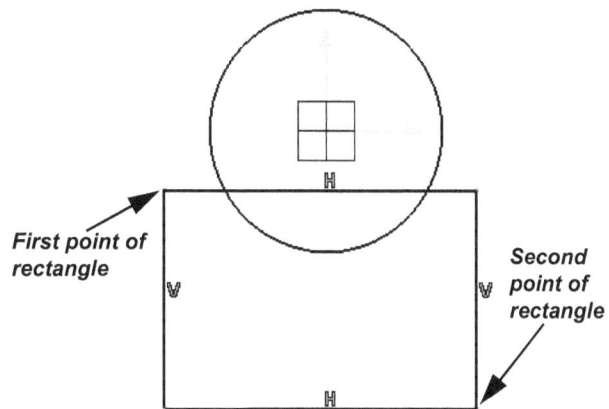

First point of rectangle

Second point of rectangle

Figure 11–31

Task 5 - Sketch a line.

1. Click [Line icon] (Line) to sketch a line.

2. Select the locations for the start and end points of the line, as shown in Figure 11–32.

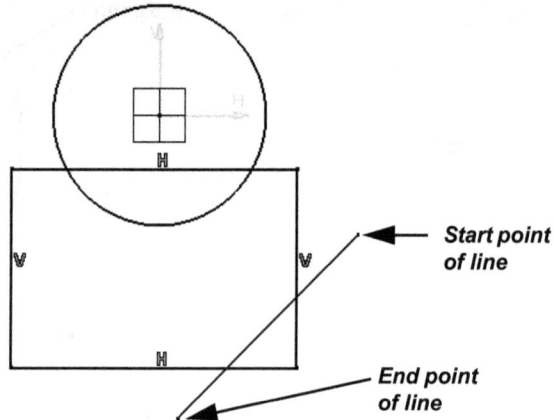

Start point of line

End point of line

Figure 11–32

Task 6 - Sketch an arc.

1. Expand the [Circle icon] (Circle) flyout and click [Three Point Arc icon] (Three Point Arc) to sketch an arc.

2. Select the second point that the arc passes through and select the end point of the arc, as shown in Figure 11–33.

Select the start point of the arc. Note that the lines of the rectangle highlight in orange when the cursor is over them. This color change indicates that the ends of the arc are aligned with that feature.

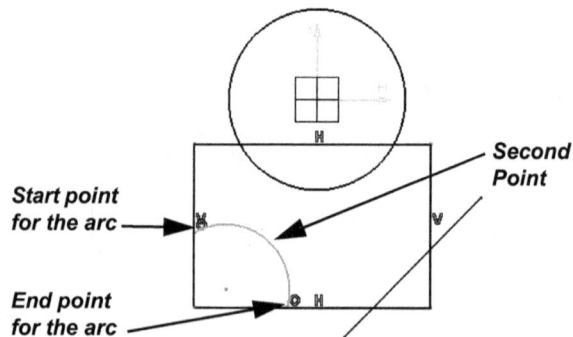

Start point for the arc

Second Point

End point for the arc

Figure 11–33

Task 7 - Sketch an elongated hole.

1. Expand the ⬜ (Rectangle) flyout and click 🔳 (Elongated Hole) to sketch an elongated hole.

2. Select the locations for the two arc centers, and a location to define the width of the elongated hole, as shown in Figure 11–34.

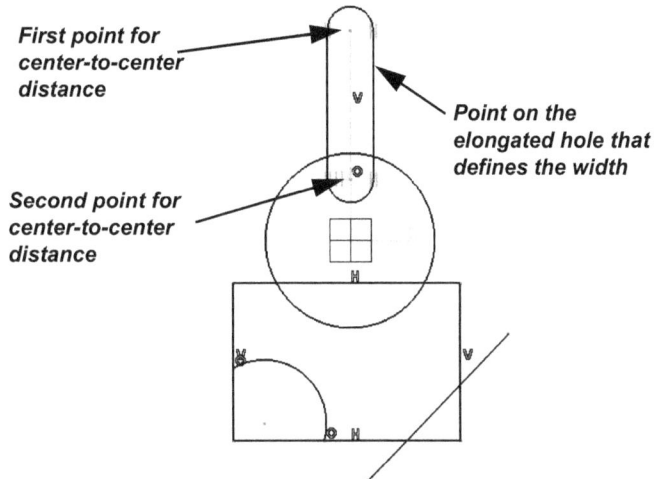

First point for center-to-center distance

Point on the elongated hole that defines the width

Second point for center-to-center distance

Figure 11–34

Task 8 - Trim the rectangle to the line and the circle.

Read Message area for your next selection.

1. Click ✂ (Trim) to trim the rectangle.

2. Select the line and the bottom of the rectangle, as shown in Figure 11–35.

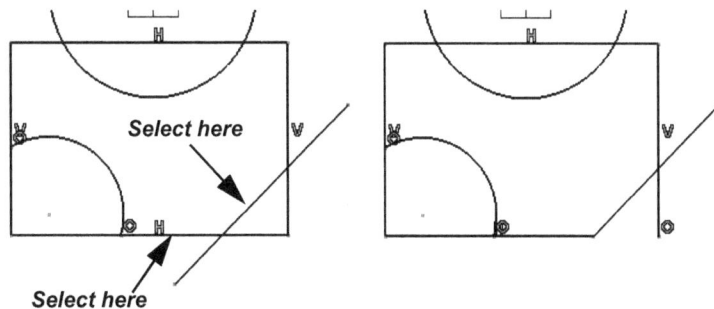

Select here

Select here

Figure 11–35

3. Note that ⊠ (Trim) is no longer highlighted. This means you have to click the icon again to perform another trim.

Double-click on ⊠ (Trim) so you can trim multiple times.

4. Trim the other side of the rectangle and the line using the same technique. The elements to select are labeled **Trim #2** in Figure 11–36.

5. Trim two more times to trim the arc to the box. The elements to select are labeled **Trim #3** and **Trim #4** in Figure 11–36.

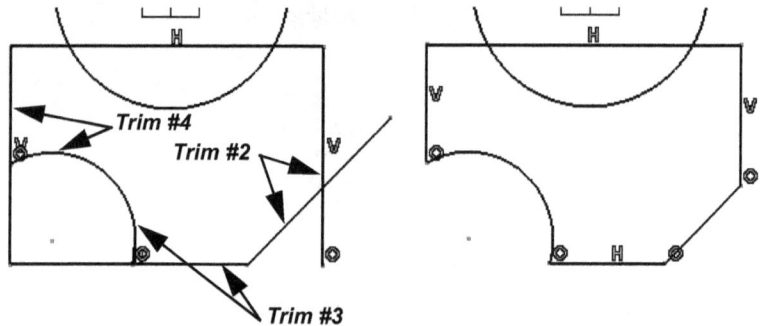

Figure 11–36

Task 9 - Trim the rectangle to the circle and the circle to the elongated hole using the Quick Trim method.

1. Expand the ⊠ (Trim) flyout menu and click ⬭ (Quick Trim) to perform a **Quick Trim**.

2. Select the bottom of the circle to delete that segment, as shown in Figure 11–37.

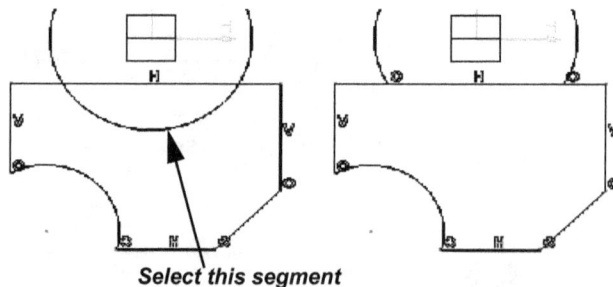

Figure 11–37

3. Double-click on ⬭ (Quick Trim) so you can trim multiple times.

4. Select the remaining intersecting segments to clean up the sketch, as shown in Figure 11–38.

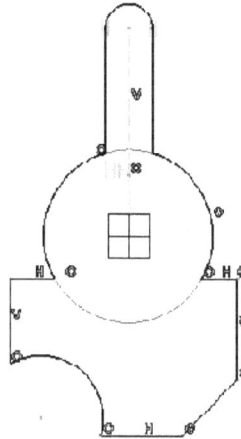

Figure 11–38

Task 10 - Save the part and exit the Sketcher workbench.

1. Click ⬆ (Exit workbench) to exit the Sketcher workbench. The sketch displays as shown in Figure 11–39.

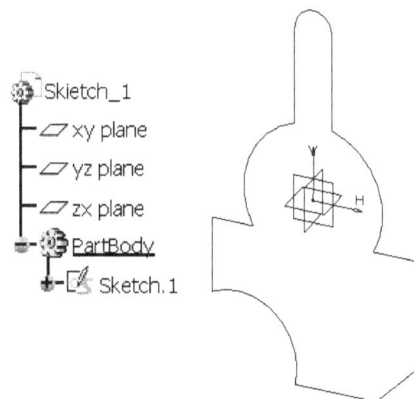

Figure 11–39

2. Click (Save) to save the part.

3. Accept the default part name of **Sketch_1.CATPart**.

4. Click **Save**.

5. Select **File>Close** to close the part window.

Practice 11b | Profile Sketching

Practice Objective

- Use Profile Sketching to create lines and arcs.

In this practice, you will use the profile sketcher to create the sketch shown in Figure 11–40.

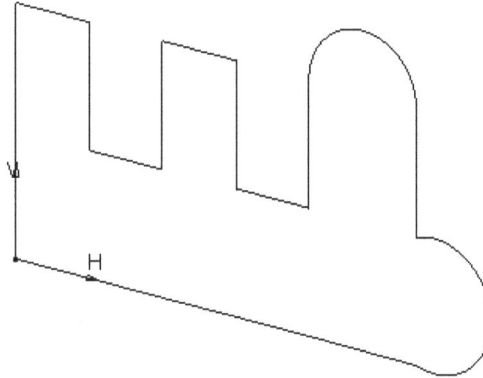

Figure 11–40

Task 1 - Create a new part and begin creating a sketch.

1. Click [ ] (New).

2. In the New dialog box, select **Part** and click **OK**.

3. Enter **Sketch_2** as the part name and click **OK**.

4. In the specification tree, select the YZ plane.

5. Click [ ] (Sketch).

Task 2 - Begin sketching a profile.

1. Ensure that the Sketch Tools toolbar displays and that [ ] (Automatic Dimensional Constraints) is toggled off.

2. Click [ ] (Profile).

3. Place the cursor at the intersection of the horizontal and vertical axes, as shown in Figure 11–41. Press the left mouse button to begin sketching.

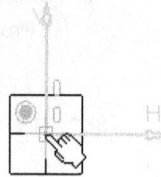

Figure 11–41

4. Sketch the series of connected vertical and horizontal lines, as shown in Figure 11–42. Note that the line turns blue when it is vertical or horizontal. Also note that the software displays a line to indicate when the cursor is coincident with other sketched elements.

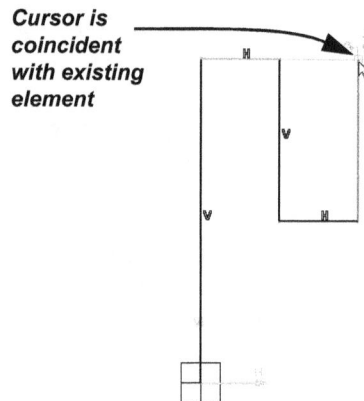

Cursor is coincident with existing element

Figure 11–42

5. Continue sketching the profile until the section displays as shown in Figure 11–43. DO NOT end the profile yet.

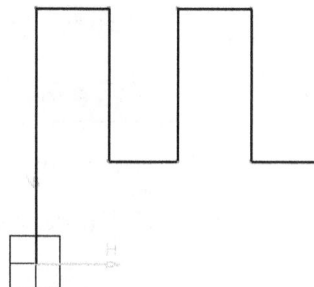

Figure 11–43

6. After selecting the end point of the last vertical line segment, click ⌓ (Tangent Arc) in the Sketch tools toolbar, as shown in Figure 11–44.

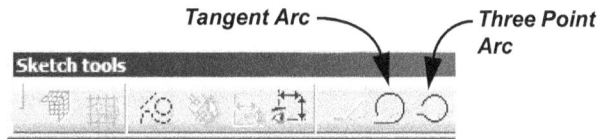

*The **Profile** tool needs to be active to display the **Tangent Arc** icon in the Sketch tools toolbar.*

Tangent Arc ——— ———— Three Point Arc

Sketch tools

Figure 11–44

7. Drag the arc to **180°**, as shown in Figure 11–45. The arc highlights in blue once you reach 180°.

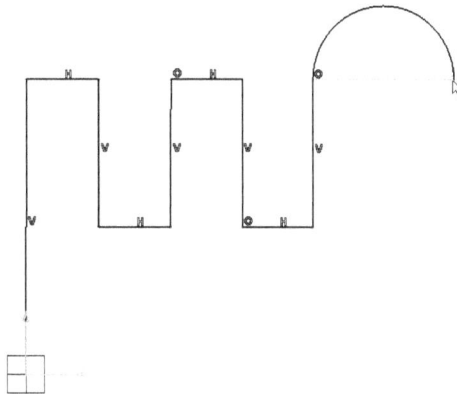

Figure 11–45

8. Draw a vertical line that is coincident with the intermediate horizontal lines, as shown in Figure 11–46.

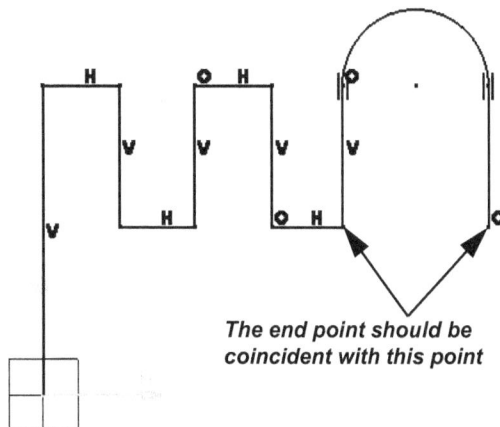

The end point should be coincident with this point

Figure 11–46

9. In the Tools toolbar, click [icon] (Three Point Arc).

10. Sketch the three point arc shown in Figure 11–47. Try to make the end of the arc coincident with the horizontal axis and your last vertical line.

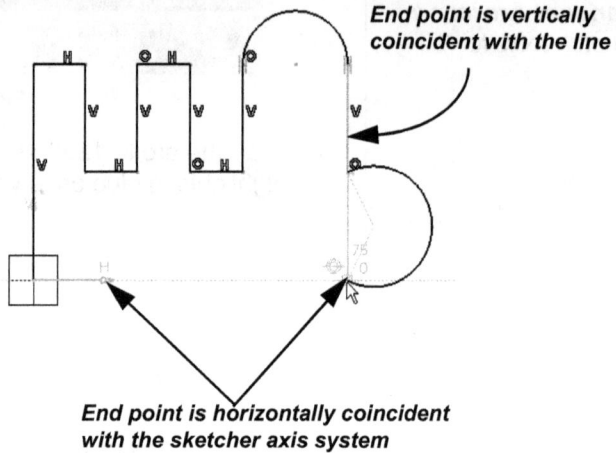

End point is vertically coincident with the line

End point is horizontally coincident with the sketcher axis system

Figure 11–47

11. Drag the last horizontal line and connect it to the start point to close the sketch as shown in Figure 11–48.

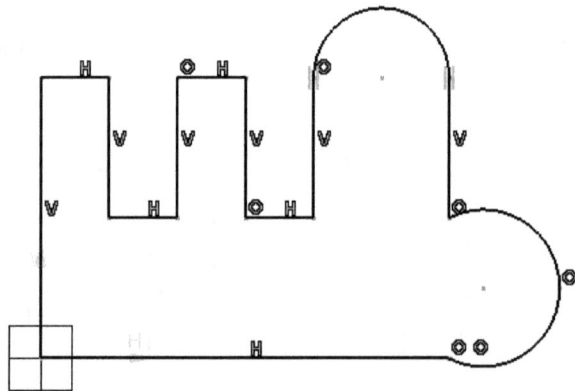

Figure 11–48

Task 3 - Select the profile.

In this task you will demonstrate the use of the **Auto Search** option by selecting the 13 entities of the sketch.

1. Select any entity in the sketch.

2. Right-click and select *** object>Auto Search**. The software highlights the entire profile.

3. Select anywhere on the background to clear the profile.

Task 4 - Exit the Sketcher workbench and save the part.

1. Click ⬆️ (Exit workbench) to exit the Sketcher workbench.

2. Click 💾 (Save).

3. Accept the default name of **Sketch_2.CATPart**.

4. Click **Save**.

5. Select **File>Close** to close the part window.

Practice 11c | (Optional) Sketch Practice I

Practice Objective

- Create a sketch without instructions.

Create a new part called **SketchProfile** and sketch the profile shown in Figure 11–49. Use the YZ plane as the support for the sketch. Do not be concerned with the size of the profile; just ensure that the same shape is developed.

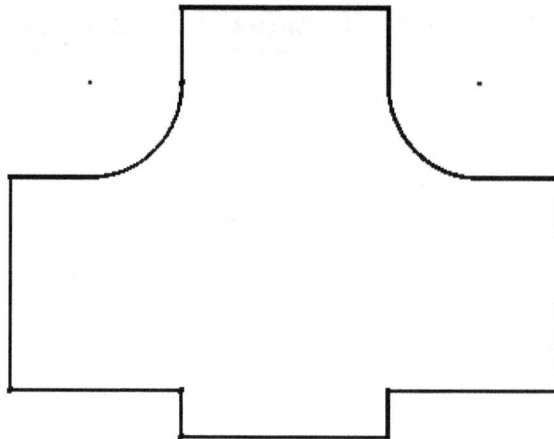

Figure 11–49

Practice 11d | (Optional) Sketch Practice II

Practice Objective

*   Create a sketch without instructions.

Create a new part called **OutletProfile** and sketch the profile shown in Figure 11–50. Use the YZ plane as the support for the sketch. Do not be concerned with the size of the profile; just ensure that the same shape is developed.

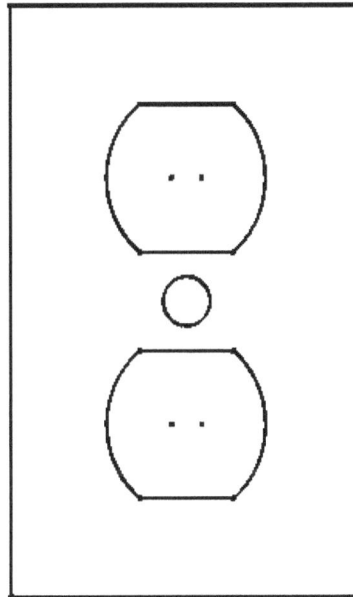

Figure 11–50

Constraining Sketches

Constraints can be either geometric or dimensional. Geometric Constraints assess a relationship between geometric elements that forces a limitation, whereas dimensional constraints define the size and location of an element. In addition, the Auto Constraint feature creates the missing constraints to make the profile fully constrained.

Learning Objectives in this Chapter

- Understand the difference between Geometric, Dimensional, and Automatic Dimensional Constraints.
- Understand the advantages of using constraints to control sketches.
- Understand the various geometric constraints.
- Work with constraints and learn how to automatically constrain a sketch.
- Use the Edit Multi-Constraint dialog box to edit multiple dimensions before the section updates.
- Understand the system-defined constraint colors for the sketch status.
- Understand the Sketch Analysis dialog box and how to use its various tabs to analyze a sketch.

12.1 Constraints

Constraints define the size and location of a sketch. You can use two types of constraints, as shown in Figure 12–1.

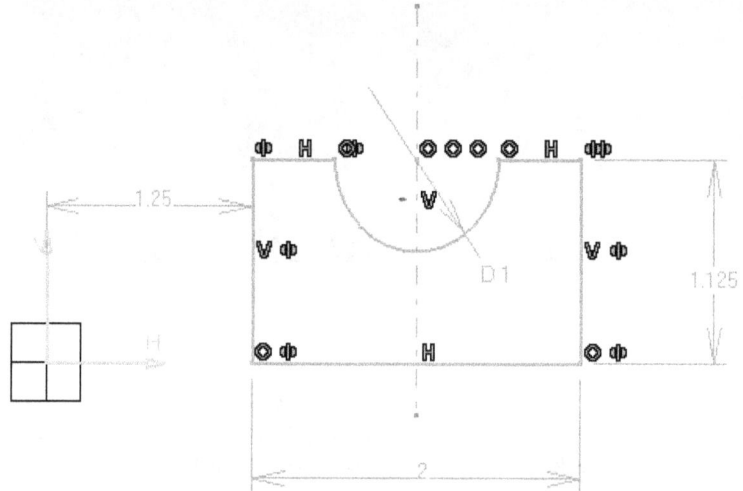

Figure 12–1

The constraints available, along with their icons in the Sketch Tools toolbar, are used to control their display. They are described as follows:

Icon	Constraint	Description
	Geometrical Constraints	Relationships between geometric elements that describe how they are oriented.
	Dimensional Constraints	Values used to define the size, distance, or angle of an element.
	Automatic Dimensional Constraints	Automatically apply the values used to define the size or angle of elements as you sketch.

You can develop sketches that are completely unconstrained or partially unconstrained. Thus, you do not need to place any unnecessary dimensions on a sketch. However, it is recommended that you fully constrain your sketches.

Figure 12–2 shows an example of a partially constrained sketch. Initially, the box is 50 wide. When this dimensional constraint is changed to 100, the software updates one side of the box and leaves the other side in its original state. If the design intent of this sketch is to create a rectangle, the current design of this part requires additional constraints to maintain the geometry over time.

Vertical

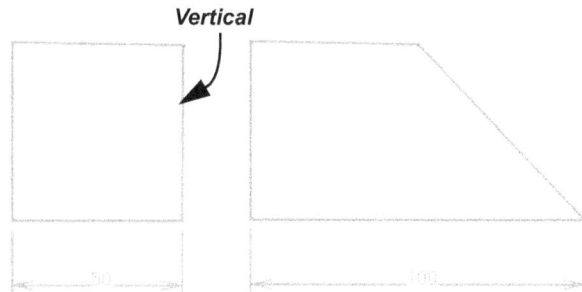

Figure 12–2

If you start constructing 3D solid models with features that are unconstrained, the models is more complex. Figure 12–3 shows an example of an unconstrained Pocket. If the block is made wider or taller, what happens to the Pocket? Should it remain centered on the block or should it remain the same distance from the right or left side? This unpredictable nature means that the designs must be thoroughly checked each time a change is made.

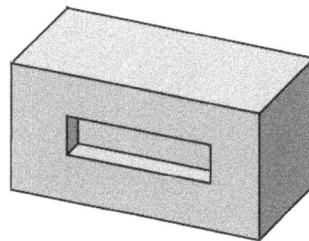

Figure 12–3

Advantages of Using Constraints

Using constraints has the following advantages:

- Dimensional constraints enable you to precisely define the size of your sketch and to quickly and accurately change its size.

- Geometric constraints enable you to incorporate design intent into your sketches, which automates the geometry update process.

12.2 Geometric Constraints

Geometric constraints are accessed using (Constraints Defined in Dialog Box). Geometric constraints consist of a relationship between geometric elements that forces a limitation of some type. For example, you can constrain a line in a sketch to be vertical. With the vertical constraint in place, the line is limited and cannot be at an angle.

The most commonly-used geometric constraints are described as follows:

Constraint	Example	Description
Horizontal		Use <Ctrl> to preselect the lines that are to be horizontal.
Vertical		Use <Ctrl> to preselect the lines that are to be vertical.

Parallelism	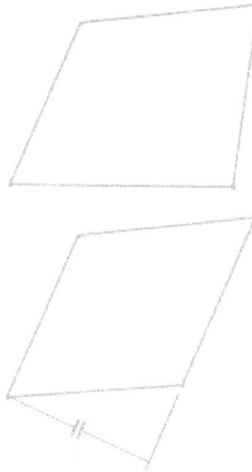	Select the first line to remain fixed, and select the second line to make parallel to the first.
Perpendicular	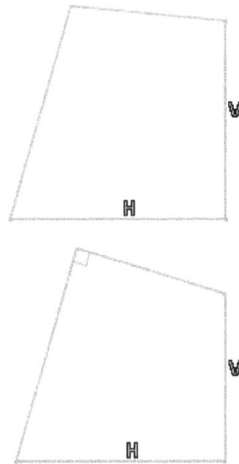	Use <Ctrl> to preselect lines to be perpendicular.
Concentricity	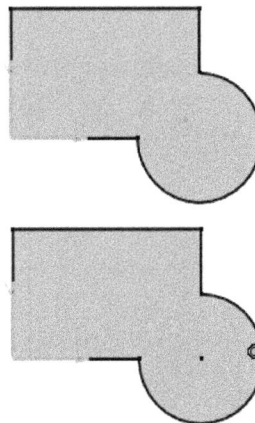	Select a curved edge of a Pad feature and the sketched circle. Concentricity only works with existing geometry.

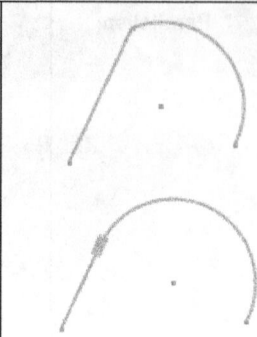

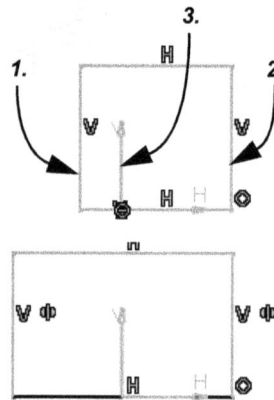

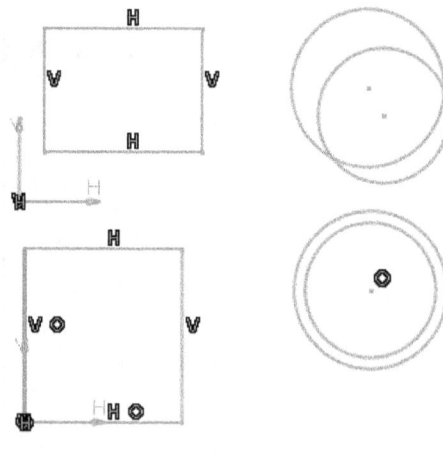

Tangency		Use <Ctrl> to preselect the entities to be tangent.
Symmetry		Press and hold <Ctrl> while selecting references in the following order: first symmetric element, second symmetric element, and symmetry reference.
Coincidence		Select end points of entities to be coincident with one another and/or to another point. For circles, you must select the circle centers.

How To: Apply a Constraint

1. Use <Ctrl> to preselect the elements in the correct sequence.

2. Click ▣ (Constraints Defined in Dialog Box).
3. Select the required constraint in the Constraint Definition dialog box shown in Figure 12–4.

Only the constraints that are valid for the elements you selected are available.

Figure 12–4

4. Click **OK**.

Note that you can apply constraints between entities using the **Create Multiple Constraints** option. In the Constraint Definition dialog box, enable **Target Element**, click in the *Target Element* field and select an element from the sketch. The selected element will drive the resulting constraints.

Three lines were selected in Figure 12–5, and the top line, **Line.3**, is used as the Target Element. When the **Distance** constraint is selected, the dimensions for the distance between the lines, are added, using **Line.3** as the baseline.

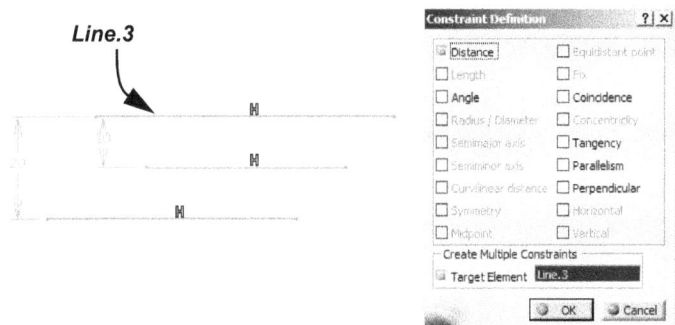

Figure 12–5

Deleting Constraints

Use one of the following methods to remove a constraint:

- Select the constraint symbol on the screen to highlight it, and press <Delete>.

- Select the constraint in the specification tree and press <Delete>.

Shortcut Menu

The shortcut menu provides access to frequently used geometric constraints and operations such as **Horizontal** or **Vertical** constraints for linear elements and **Close** or **Complement** operations for arcs. For example, a slanted line can be vertically constrained by right-clicking and selecting **Line.# object> Vertical**, as shown in Figure 12–6.

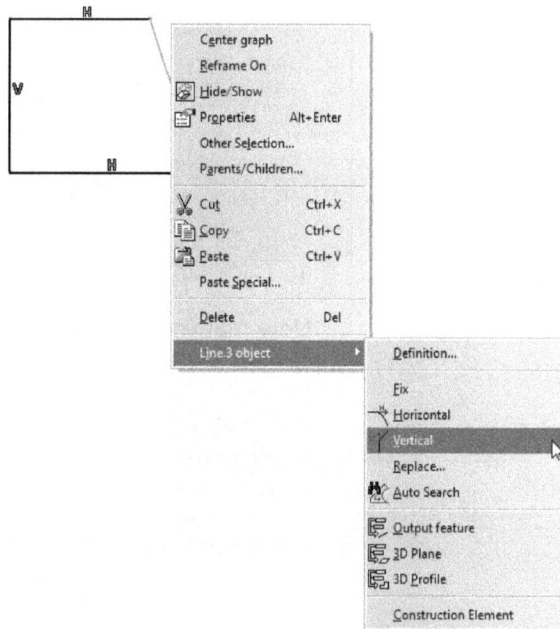

Figure 12–6

Centering a Sketch

To center a sketch on a part, sketch an axis and use the **Symmetry** constraint to constrain the axis to the middle of the part. Use <Ctrl> to multi-select the two edges of the part, and then the axis. Click (Constraints Defined in Dialog Box) and select **Symmetry**. When the **Symmetry** constraint is applied, the axis becomes centered, as shown in Figure 12–7.

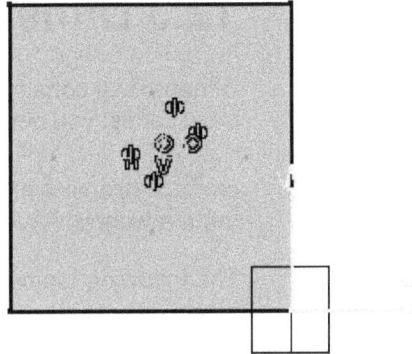

Figure 12–7

Fix Together Constraint

The **Fix Together** constraint constrains selected sketched elements together so that they can be moved as one entity.

How To: Fix Sketched Elements Together

1. Select the entities to add by drawing a selection box around them, or by multi-selecting with <Ctrl>.

2. Click [icon] (Fix Together). The Fix Together Definition dialog box opens as shown in Figure 12–8.

3. Click **OK**. The sketch elements can be dynamically moved using the cursor, as shown in Figure 12–9.

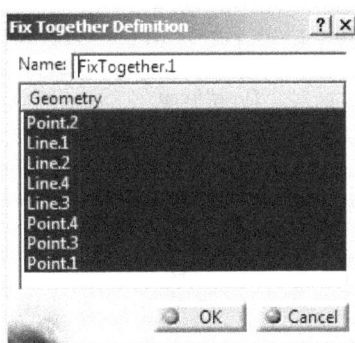

Figure 12–8

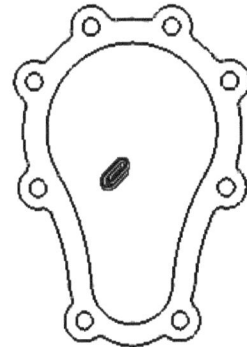

Figure 12–9

12.3 Dimensional Constraints

Dimensional constraints define an element's size and location. In most cases, you need to create several dimensions. Double-click

on ⬚ (Constraint) to create as many dimensions as you require without having to click the icon every time.

The following topics describe how to create various dimension types.

Line Length Dimension

To dimension a line, select the line to be dimensioned and drag the dimension to the required location, as shown in Figure 12–10.

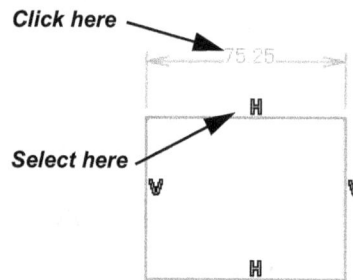

Figure 12–10

Distance between Parallel Lines

To dimension the distance between parallel lines, select the first line. A length dimension displays. Select the second line. The distance between the two lines displays. Click to place the dimension. An example is shown in Figure 12–11.

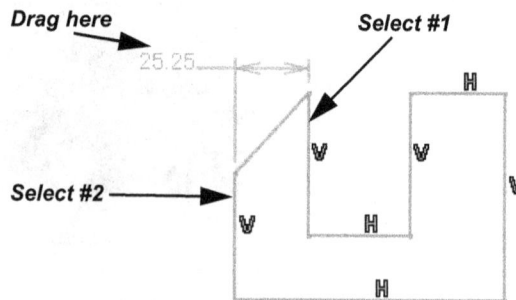

Figure 12–11

Arc Radius

To create an arc radius dimension, sketch a corner and the dimension is automatically created. To manually create an arc radius dimension, select the arc and click a location on the screen to place the dimension, as shown in Figure 12–12.

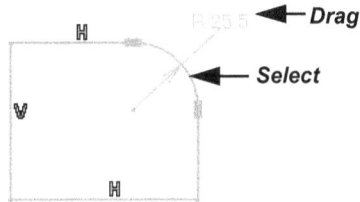

Figure 12–12

Arc Diameter

To dimension an arc as a diameter, you can use one of the following methods:

- A radius dimension displays by default when you select the arc. Before placing the dimension, right-click and select **Diameter**, as shown in Figure 12–13.

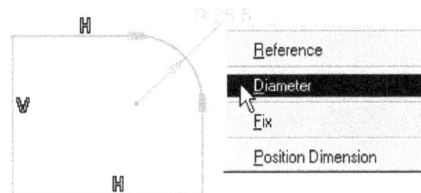

Figure 12–13

- Convert an existing arc radius dimension into a diameter dimension by double-clicking on the radius dimension. The Constraint Definition dialog box opens. Select **Diameter** in the drop-down list and click **OK** to complete the change, as shown in Figure 12–14.

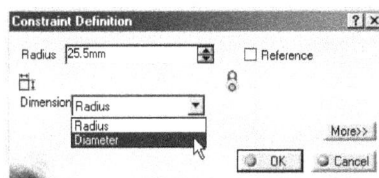

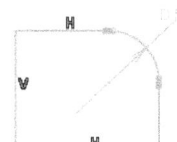

Figure 12–14

Revolved Diameter

When creating sketches for revolved features, only half of the profile is sketched. It is then revolved about the centerline. To create this dimension, select a line element and an axis. By default, a dimension representing the distance between the two parallel elements displays. Before placing the dimension, right-click and select **Diameter**, as shown in Figure 12–15.

The revolved diameter can only be created using an axis and not a construction line.

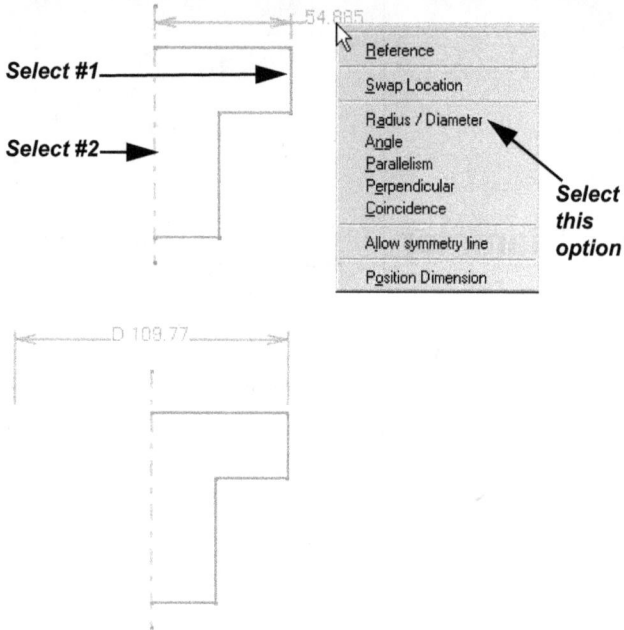

Figure 12–15

Angle Dimension

To create an angle dimension, select two non-parallel lines and an angle dimension displays. The dimension location determines how the angle dimension displays. The result of placing an angle dimension in four different locations is shown in Figure 12–16.

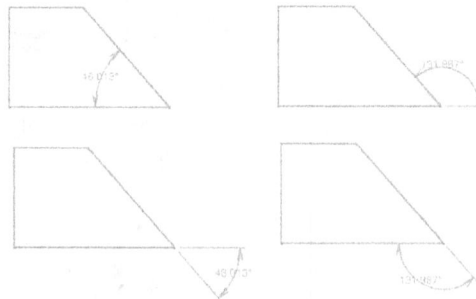

Figure 12–16

Point-to-Point Dimension

Point-to-point dimensions can be created between any two of the following elements:

- Center of an arc or circle

- End of a straight line

- Construction point

By default, the dimension displays as the absolute distance between the points. Before placing the dimension, use the shortcut menu to display the dimension as the horizontal or vertical distance between the points. These dimension options are shown in Figure 12–17.

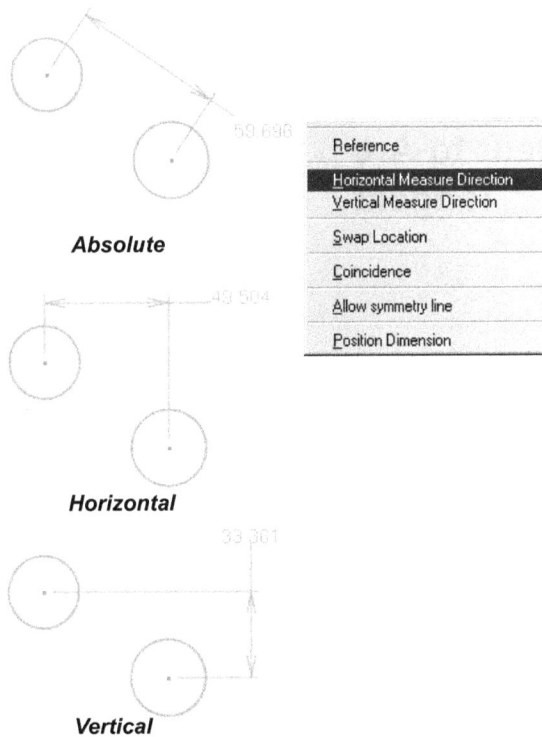

Absolute

Horizontal

Vertical

Figure 12–17

Line-to-Arc Tangent

You can also dimension to the arc center by selecting on the point.

To create a line-to-arc tangent dimension, select the line as the first element to dimension from. The line length dimension displays. Ignore this dimension and select the arc. The arc tangent dimension displays as shown in Figure 12–18.

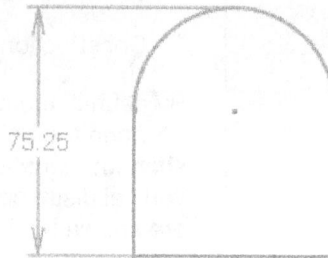

75.25

Figure 12–18

Arc Tangent-to-Arc Tangent

Select each of the arcs and drag the dimension to the required location. By default, the dimension displays as the absolute distance between the arc tangents, as shown in Figure 12–19.

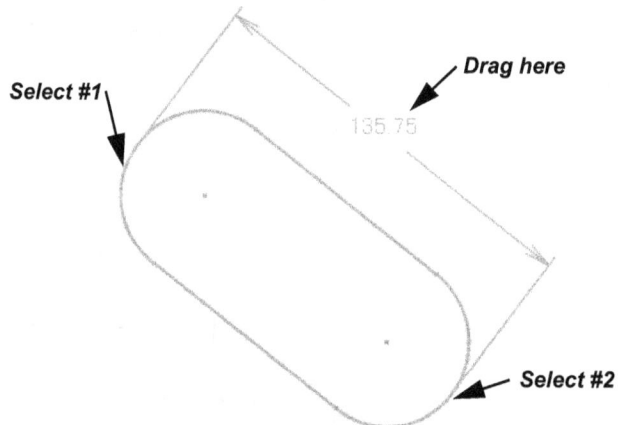

Drag here

Select #1

135.75

Select #2

Figure 12–19

Before placing the dimension, you can use the shortcut menu to display the dimension as the horizontal or vertical distance between the arcs.

Shortcut Menu

Geometric Constraints can also be generated using

 (Constraint) in conjunction with the shortcut menu. This enables you to double-click on the **Constraints** icon and create nearly all of the geometric and dimensional constraints for a profile with a single tool.

How To: Place Geometric Constraints Using the Shortcut Menu

1. Double-click on [icon] (Constraint).
2. Select one or more geometric entities in your sketch.
3. Instead of clicking to place the dimension that displays, right-click to display the shortcut menu shown in Figure 12–20.

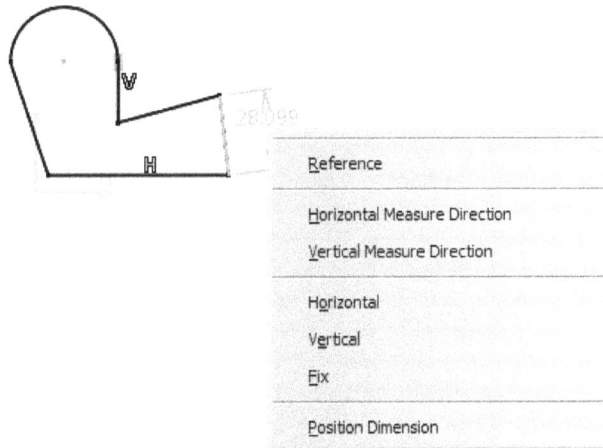

| Reference |
| Horizontal Measure Direction |
| Vertical Measure Direction |
| Horizontal |
| Vertical |
| Fix |
| Position Dimension |

Figure 12–20

4. Select the geometric constraint you want to apply to the selected geometry from the shortcut menu. The geometric constraint is now applied as shown in Figure 12–21.

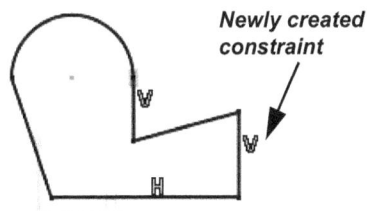

Newly created constraint

Figure 12–21

5. Repeat Steps 2 to 4 to place more geometric constraints.

6. Click [icon] (Constraint) to deactivate the **Constraint** tool.

12.4 Automatic Dimensional Constraints

In the Sketch Tools toolbar, you can use [icon] (Automatic Dimensional Constraints), as shown in Figure 12–22, to automatically add dimensional constraints as you sketch geometry.

Figure 12–22

In Figure 12–23, as soon as the rectangle is sketched, the system automatically determined the required dimensions to constrain it and applied them accordingly.

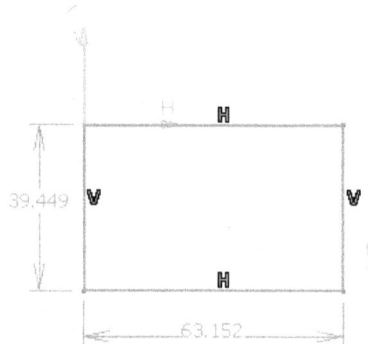

Figure 12–23

You can edit the dimensions to finalize them, as required. Automatic dimensional constraints are only applied to rectangles, circles, arcs and ellipses, and will only be added to define the size of an element, not its location relative to other elements.

12.5 Edit Multi-Constraint Dialog Box

The Edit Multi-Constraint dialog box enables you to modify the value of more than one dimension before updating the section. This is useful when modifying all dimensions of an oversized section. Typically, you would have to select the order of modification carefully to ensure that the modified dimension does not cause the section to fail. Using the **Edit Multi-Constraint** tool, you can modify all dimension values, and then preview and accept the changes.

The **Multi-Constraint** tool is found in the Constraint toolbar shown in Figure 12–24.

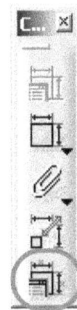

Figure 12–24

How To: Modify Dimensions Using the Edit Multi-Constraint tool

1. Click ⬚ (Edit Multi-Constraint) in the Constraint toolbar.
2. The Edit Multi-Constraint dialog box opens. The software displays the constraint name, initial value, current value, and the maximum and minimum tolerances for each dimension in the section as shown in Figure 12–25.

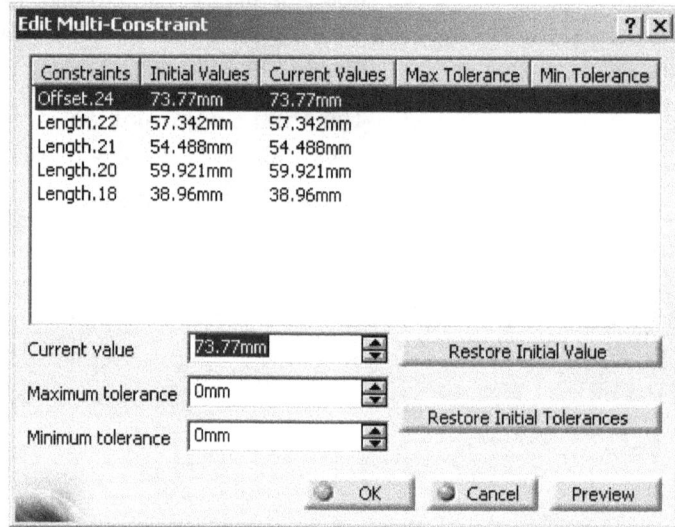

Constraints	Initial Values	Current Values	Max Tolerance	Min Tolerance
Offset.24	73.77mm	73.77mm		
Length.22	57.342mm	57.342mm		
Length.21	54.488mm	54.488mm		
Length.20	59.921mm	59.921mm		
Length.18	38.96mm	38.96mm		

Current value   73.77mm   Restore Initial Value

Maximum tolerance   0mm

Minimum tolerance   0mm   Restore Initial Tolerances

OK   Cancel   Preview

Figure 12–25

3. Select the dimension from the list or directly from the model. The corresponding dimension highlights in orange on the section.
4. In the *Current value* field, enter a new value. The dimension highlights in cyan to indicate that the initial value has been modified.
5. Once all dimensions have been modified, click **Preview** to preview the changes to the section.

6. Click **OK** to complete the changes. If an error occurs, click **Restore Initial Value** to undo the modification to the selected dimension.

Tips and techniques

- You can modify or restore multiple dimensions by using <Ctrl> to select them.

- Maximum and minimum tolerances can be added to any dimension by selecting it and entering the tolerance in the appropriate field.

- You can right-click in the *Current value* field in the Edit Multi-Constraint dialog box to access standard constraint editing options, as shown in Figure 12–26.

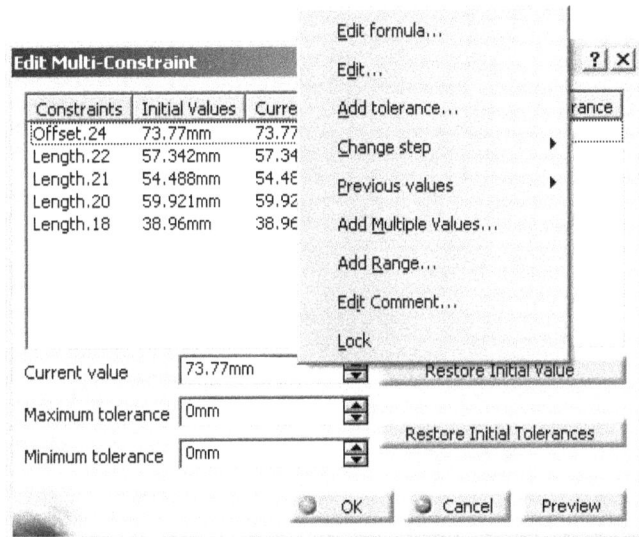

Figure 12–26

- For large, complex sections, click **Preview** frequently to update and test the section. If an error occurs, it is likely a dimension that was modified after the last preview.

- Selecting dimensions before clicking (Edit Multi-Constraint) only adds those dimensions to the Edit Multi-Constraint dialog box.

12.6 Constraint Colors

To fully constrain your sketches, you must define the size and location of the sketch. For the first sketch on a new part, you must constrain the sketch to the horizontal and vertical axes, as shown in Figure 12–27.

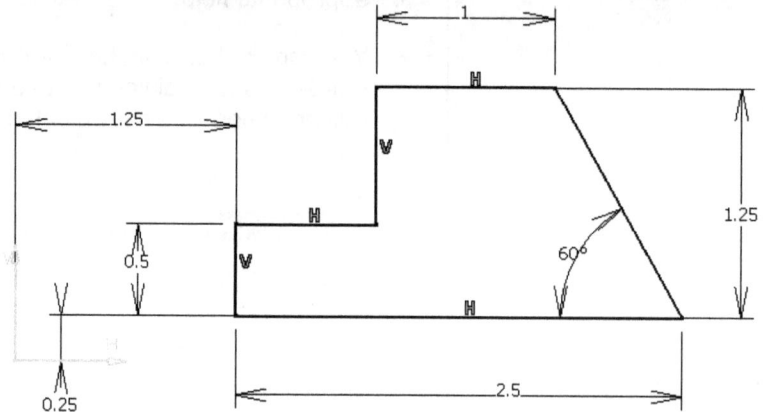

Figure 12–27

The software uses colors on the elements of your sketch to visually indicate the constraint status. These colors are described as follows:

Color	Definition	Description
White	Under constrained	Some degrees of freedom still remain for the element.
Green	Constrained	The geometry is completely fixed and cannot be moved without altering a dimensional value.
Purple	Over constrained	Too many dimensions or geometric constraints are on the element.
Red	Inconsistent	The sketch cannot be solved with the current combination of constraints and values.
Brown	Not changed	Geometry that is dependent on over-defined or inconsistent elements and is not up to date.

12.7 Sketch Analysis

Once the sketch is created and constrained, you can analyze the sketch by clicking ⬚ (Sketch Analysis) or selecting **Tools> Sketch Analysis**. The Sketch Analysis dialog box opens as shown in Figure 12–28.

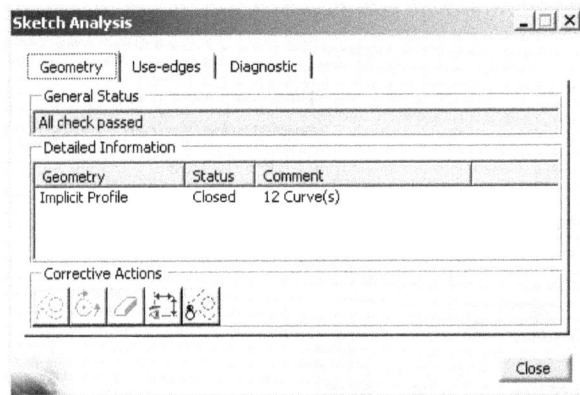

Figure 12–28

The following are examples of the types of analyses that can be performed:

* Ensure that the section meets the design intent.

* Ensure that the section is fully constrained.

* Check the status of projections and intersections.

* Perform corrective actions, as required.

Geometry Tab

The *Geometry* tab is used to analyze individual elements of the sketch. It displays the general status of the elements being analyzed. It is used to analyze the sketched elements and determine the status of each element in the model. The different values available in the *Status* column are described as follows:

Status	Description
Opened	A collection of sketched entities that form an open loop. Open loops can occur when the start and end points of a loop appear to be touching, but actually have a gap between them.

Closed	A collection of sketched entities that form a closed loop.
Isolated	A single sketched entity that is not touching or connected to any other geometry in the section. This could indicate a line which should be converted to a construction line, or a line which should belong to a loop of entities, but has gaps at either end.
Wrong Point	A sketched point is connected to existing geometry. This indicates that the point should be converted to a construction point to be a valid section to create 3D geometry.

The *Geometry* tab also displays detailed information about each selected element type and general comments, as shown in Figure 12–29.

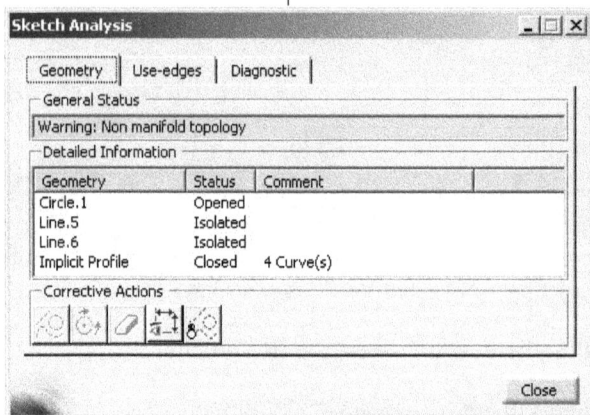

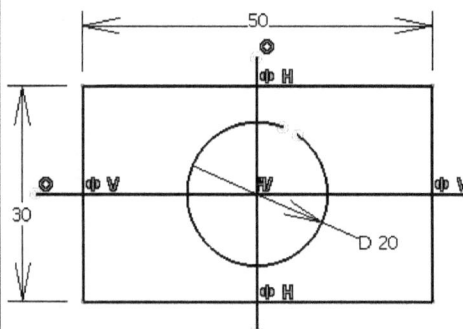

Figure 12–29

If you select an item in the Detailed Information area, the entity highlights on the screen, making it easier to find.

The sketch shown in Figure 12–29 has several problems. The detailed information displays that the circle is not closed (which is not the design intent) and that two line entities in the profile should be construction lines. The icons in the *Corrective Actions* area of the dialog box enable you to correct the problems in your sketch.

These icons are described as follows:

Icon	Description
	Changes the selected entity to a construction entity.
	Closes the open profile.
	Deletes the selected entity from the sketch.
	Toggles the display of constraints on and off in the sketch.
	Toggles the display of construction geometry on and off in the sketch.

The icons in the *Corrective Actions* area correct the problem, as shown in Figure 12–30. **Line.5** and **Line.6** were converted to construction entities using . **Circle.1** was closed using .

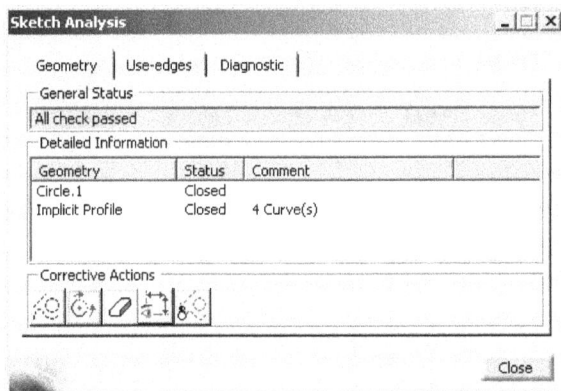

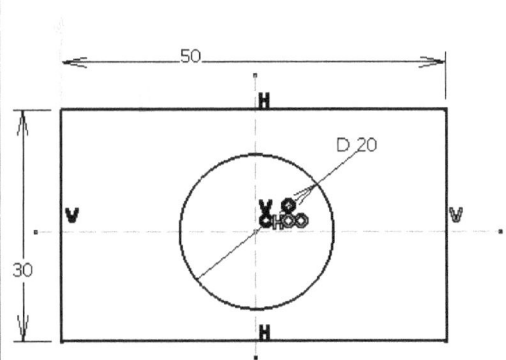

Figure 12–30

Use-edges

The *Use-edges* tab displays the status of all entities that are projected from existing geometry. The contents of this tab are discussed in detail once the concept of projecting 3D geometry has been introduced.

Diagnostic Tab

The *Diagnostic* tab provides a detailed summary of each sketched entity and the solving status of the sketch. A sketched entity can have one of the following three status values:

- **Under-Constrained:** Additional dimensions or constraints must be applied to the sketched entity.

- **Over-Constrained:** Too many dimensions or constraints have been applied to the element.

- **ISO-Constrained:** The entity is fully constrained.

The *Detailed Information* area lists all sketched entities, their current constraint status, and the type of entity (i.e., geometry, constraint, construction geometry, etc.), as shown in Figure 12–31.

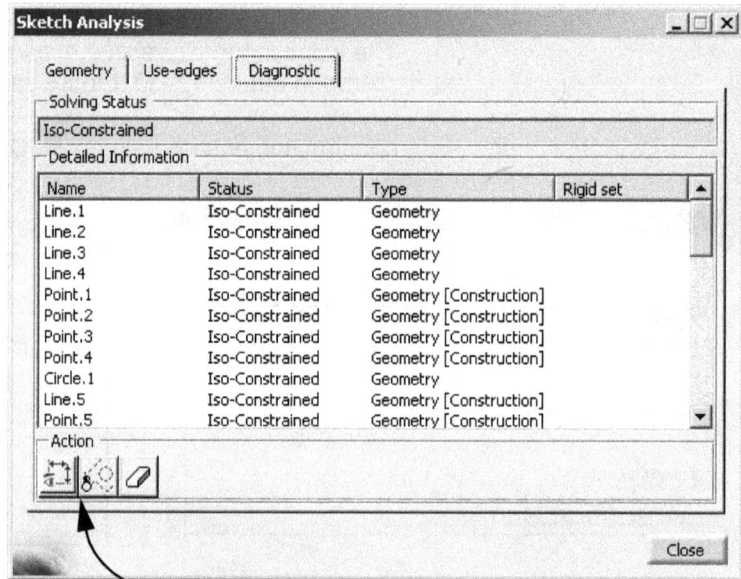

Hide/Show icons

Figure 12–31

You cannot edit the sketch while the tab is open. You must first exit the Sketch Analysis dialog box, solve any constraint issues, and re-open the dialog box to verify.

The **Hide/Show** icons in the *Action* area can be used to simplify the screen. Select an entity in the *Detailed Information* area and select the appropriate icon to hide or show the entity.

Sketch Solving Status

The Sketch Solving Status dialog box is used to determine the constraint status of the sketch. A sketch can either be under-constrained, over-constrained, or fully constrained (ISO-constrained). If the section is over-constrained or under-constrained, the software highlights the affected entities on the sketch.

Click (Sketch Solving Status) in the Tools toolbar to open the Sketch Solving Status dialog box, as shown in Figure 12–32.

Figure 12–32

You can open the **Sketch Analysis** tool from this dialog box by clicking (Sketch Analysis).

12.8 Auto Constraint

If you are having trouble eliminating all degrees of freedom, you can use ▢ (Auto Constraint) to fully constrain your sketch. The **Auto Constraint** tool is found in the Constraint toolbar, as shown in Figure 12–33.

Figure 12–33

The Auto Constraint dialog box requires up to three sets of information. These are described as follows:

Information	Description
Elements to be constrained	These elements of your sketch display in white. When in doubt, select your entire sketch.
Reference elements	These elements are what your sketch is located to. For new sketches, select the horizontal and vertical axes.
Symmetry lines	If you want your sketch to be symmetrical, select the horizontal axis, the vertical axis, or a sketched axis.

The Auto Constraint dialog box opens as shown in Figure 12–34.

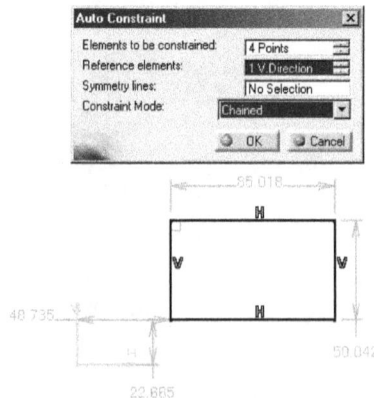

Figure 12–34

Practice 12a | Dimensions

Practice Objectives

- Create a sketched profile.
- Create the dimensions required to fully define a sketch.
- Recognize when a sketch is under-constrained or constrained.

In this practice, you will create the sketch shown in Figure 12–35. You will constrain the sketch using geometrical and dimensional constraints. You will also be able recognize whether a sketch is under-constrained or over-constrained.

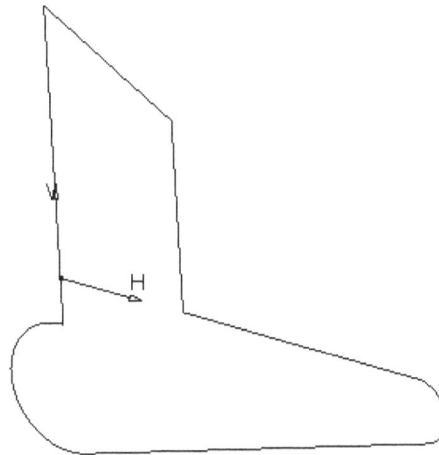

Figure 12–35

Task 1 - Create a new part and begin creating a sketch.

1. Click ⬜ (New).

2. In the New dialog box, select **Part**, enter **Constraints_1** as the part name, and click **OK**.

3. In the specification tree, select the YZ plane.

4. Click ✏️ (Sketch).

Task 2 - Begin sketching the profile.

1. Verify that the Sketch Tools toolbar is available.

The activated icon displays in orange.

2. Verify ![icon] (Geometrical Constraints) is selected to enable automatic geometric constraints.

3. Sketch the part profile shown in Figure 12–36 using

   ![icon] (Profile). Verify that the arcs are tangent in the locations shown.

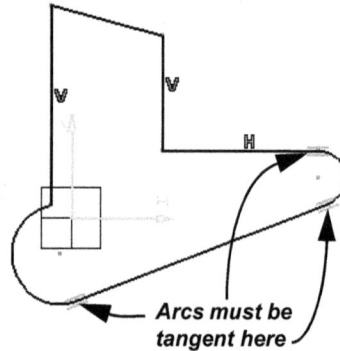

Arcs must be tangent here

Figure 12–36

Task 3 - Perform a sketch analysis.

1. In the Tools toolbar, click ![icon] (Sketch Solving Status). The Sketch Solving Status dialog box opens as shown in Figure 12–37.

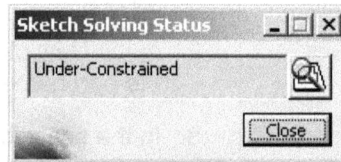

Figure 12–37

Design Considerations

The software reports that the section is under-constrained. Since no dimensions have been applied to the section, all entities are highlighted to indicate that they are under-constrained. You will apply dimensions to the section to constrain it in the part.

2. In the Sketch Solving Status dialog box, click ▣ (Sketch Analysis). The Sketch Analysis dialog box opens as shown in Figure 12–38.

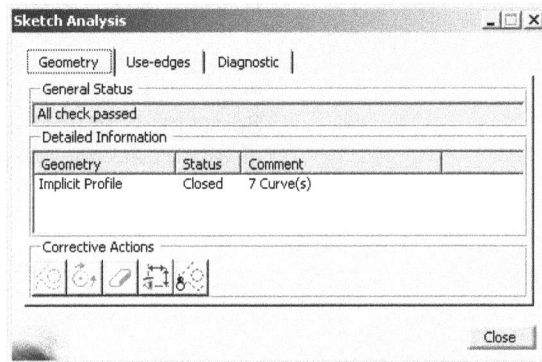

Figure 12–38

3. Verify that the software reports a closed status for the sketch and that only seven curves exist. If you receive a different result, verify that your section has been created correctly.

4. Close the Sketch Analysis dialog box.

Task 4 - Dimension the length of a straight line.

1. Click ▣ (Constraint) to start constraining. The icon turns orange to indicate that it is active.

2. Select the vertical line shown in Figure 12–39. Click the dimension to the left side of the line. Do not modify the default values of your sketch. You will adjust them later.

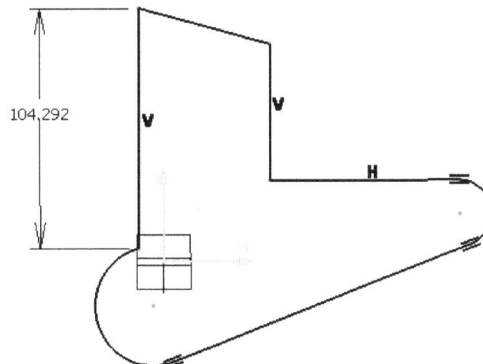

Figure 12–39

Task 5 - Dimension between parallel lines.

1. Note that ⬚ (Constraint) is no longer active. Select it again to create another dimension.

2. Select the short vertical line, as shown in Figure 12–40. A length dimension displays. You do not want this dimension. Select the long vertical line, and a dimension displays for the distance between the two lines.

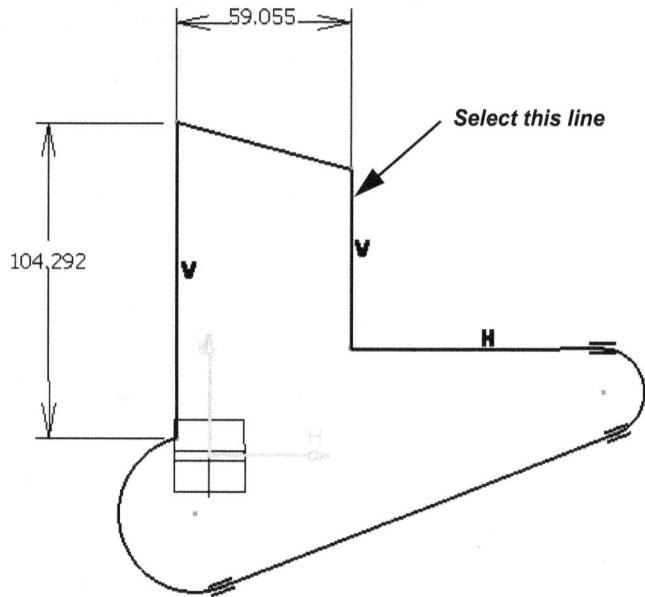

Figure 12–40

Task 6 - Enable continuous dimensioning and dimension the two arcs, one as a radius and one as a diameter.

1. Double-click on ⊡ (Constraint) to enable continuous dimensioning. The icon remains orange until you select another action.

2. Select the arc on the left side and click the radius dimension outside the sketch, as shown in Figure 12–41.

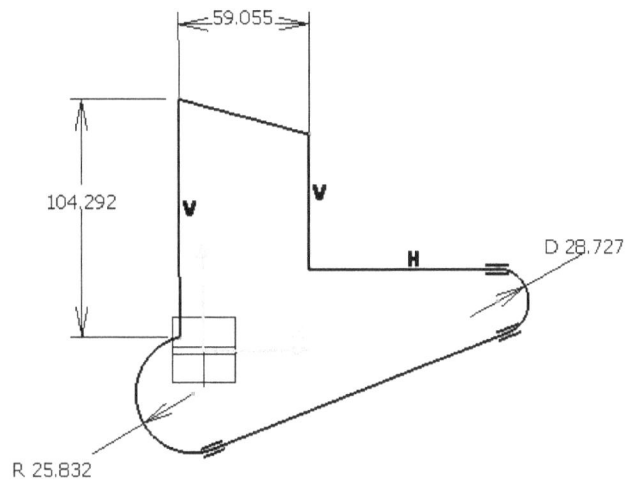

Figure 12–41

3. Select the arc on the right side, right-click and select **Diameter**.

Task 7 - Change the radius dimension to a diameter dimension.

1. Click ⌖ to terminate dimension creation.

2. Double-click on the radius dimension.

3. In the Constraint Definition dialog box, in the Dimension drop-down list, select **Diameter**.

4. Click **OK** to complete the change.

Task 8 - Create an angle dimension.

1. Double-click on ⬚ (Constraint).

2. Select the slanted line as the first element and the long vertical line as the second element, as shown in Figure 12–42. Before you place the dimension in its final location, move the cursor to other positions to preview the possible angle dimensions.

3. Place the angle dimension as shown in Figure 12–42.

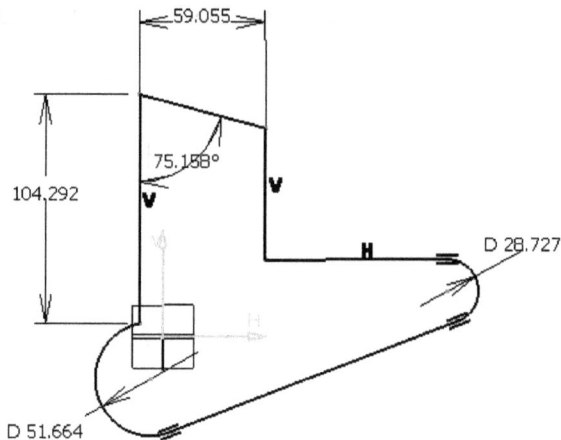

Figure 12–42

Task 9 - Create a horizontal dimension between the two arcs.

1. With ⬚ (Constraint) still be active, select each arc to initially create an absolute arc tangent dimension, but do not place the dimension.

2. Right-click and select **Horizontal Measure Direction**. The sketch displays as shown in Figure 12–43.

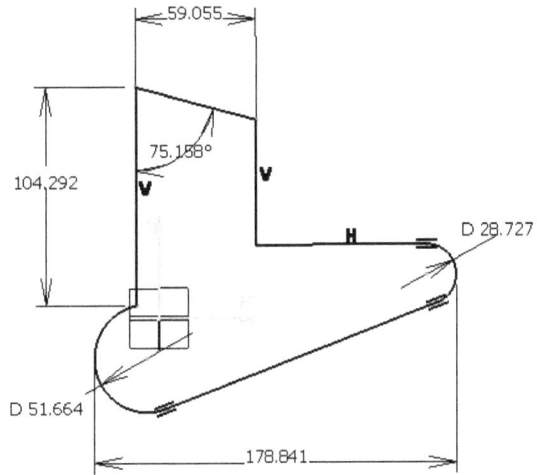

Figure 12–43

Task 10 - Create dimensions to fully constrain the sketch.

1. To finish constraining the shape of the sketch, create the two dimensions circled in Figure 12–44.

The 5.08 dimension is created by selecting the center point of the D51.664 arc and the 104.292 vertical line.

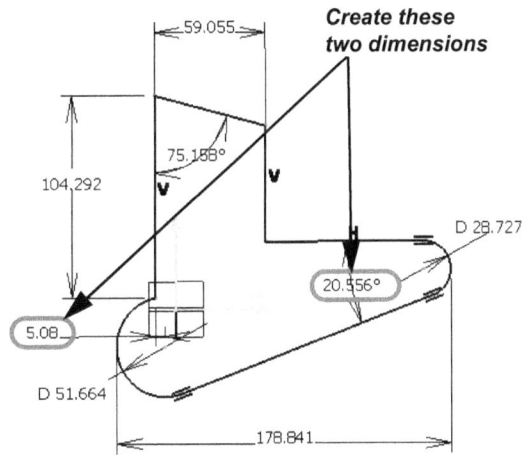

Figure 12–44

2. To constrain the location of the sketch relative to the datum planes, create the two dimensions circled in Figure 12–45. Create each dimension from the line to the horizontal or vertical axis.

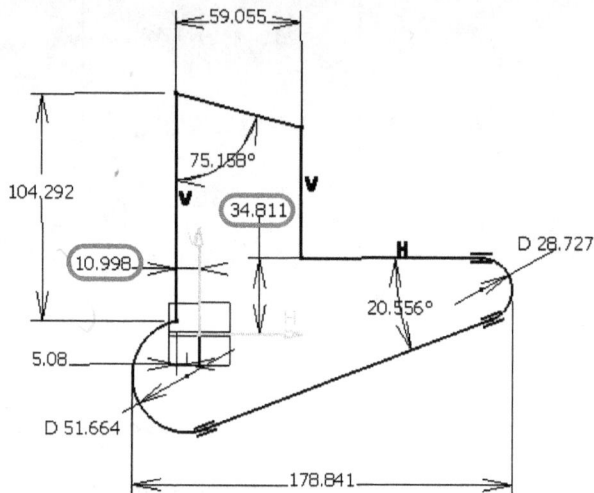

Figure 12–45

3. Click (Sketch Solving Status) to open the Sketch Solving Status dialog box, and verify that the software reports that the section is fully constrained, as shown in Figure 12–46.

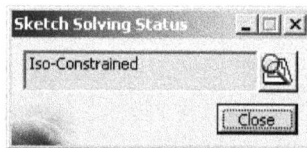

Figure 12–46

Task 11 - Over-constrain the sketch.

1. Create a dimension for the length of the angled line, as shown in Figure 12–47.

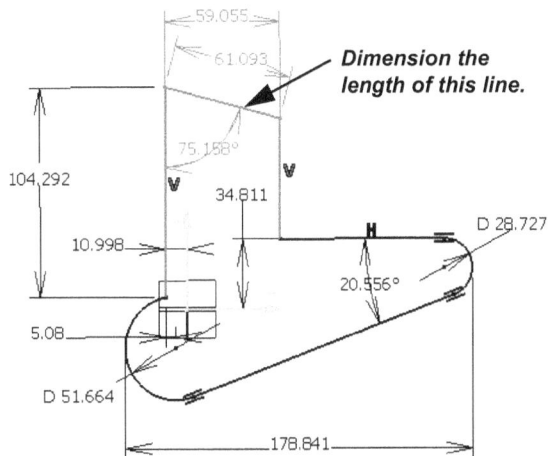

Figure 12–47

The sketch is now over-constrained, as indicated by the purple color of the affected sketch entities.

2. Click [icon] (Sketch Solving Status). The software now reports that the sketch is over-constrained and highlights the three impacted sketch entities in orange.

3. Close the Sketch Solving Status dialog box.

Task 12 - Manipulate the dimensions.

1. Select the **59.055** dimension and press <Delete>. The sketch is once again correctly constrained.

2. Practice moving dimensions, as shown in Figure 12–48. Select the dimension number to move the dimension along the arrow. Select the arrow to move the dimension closer or farther from the sketch.

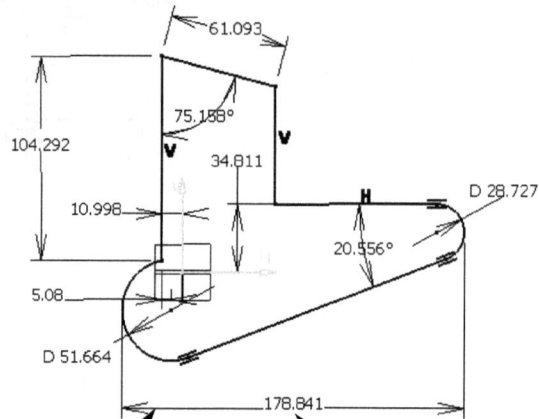

Click and drag here to move the dimension up and down.   *Click and drag here to move the dimension left and right.*

Figure 12–48

Task 13 - Modify the size of the dimensions.

1. Double-click on the **75.158** angle dimension.

2. In the *Value* field, enter **60.00** and click **OK**.

3. Click (Edit Multi-Constraint). The Edit Multi-Constraint dialog box opens as shown in Figure 12–49. It contains all constraints in the sketch and their values.

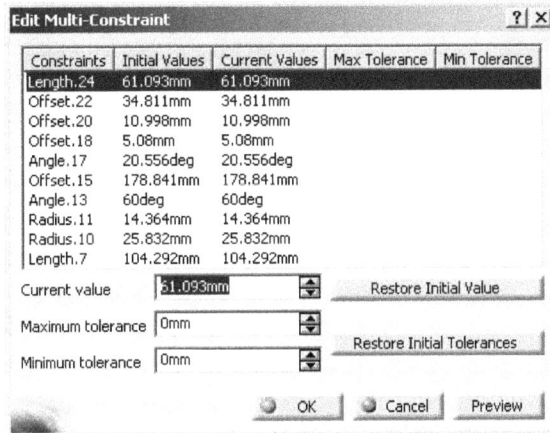

Figure 12–49

The constraint is highlighted in the sketch when you select it in the list.

Design Considerations

Be sure to enter half the diameter for the radius constraints, since both radius and diameter dimensions are represented using a radius.

4. In the Edit Multi-Constraint dialog box, select each dimension and modify its value in the field below the list to the value shown in Figure 12–50.

Note that all entities are green, indicating that the sketch is fully constrained.

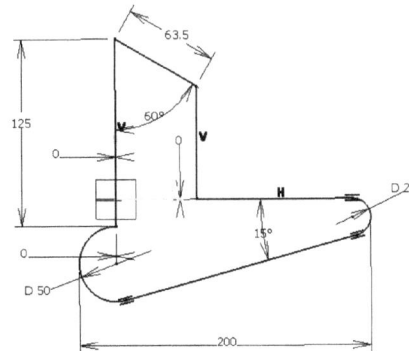

Figure 12–50

5. Click **Preview** to display the changes and then click **OK**.

Task 14 - Exit Sketcher and close the window.

1. Click ⬆ (Exit workbench). The sketch displays as shown in Figure 12–51.

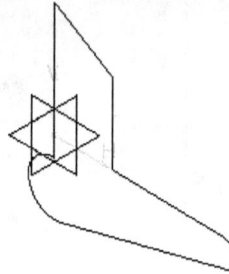

Figure 12–51

2. Click 💾 (Save) and save the part model.

3. Select **File>Close** to close the window.

Practice 12b | Constraints

Practice Objective

- Apply a variety of constraints to document the design intent of the sketch.

In this practice, you will create the sketch shown in Figure 12–52. You will gain an understanding of how geometrical constraints interact with one another. This practice will focus on driving the geometry through the use of constraints.

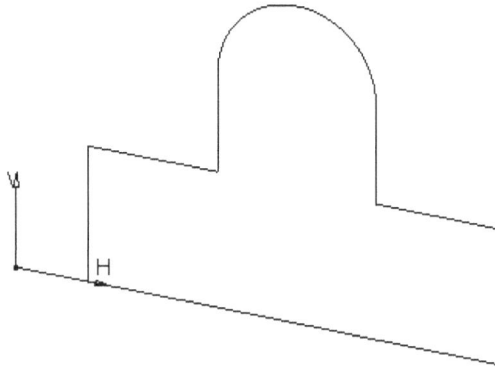

Figure 12–52

Task 1 - Create a new part and begin creating a sketch.

1. Click [ ] (New).

2. In the New dialog box, select **Part**, enter **Constraints_2** as the part name, and click **OK**.

3. In the specification tree, select the YZ plane.

4. Click [ ] (Sketch).

Task 2 - Begin sketching the profile.

1. Ensure that the Sketch Tools toolbar is available.

2. Ensure that ⬛ (Geometrical Constraints) is selected, to enable automatic geometric constraints.

3. Sketch the profile and the axis, as shown in Figure 12–53.

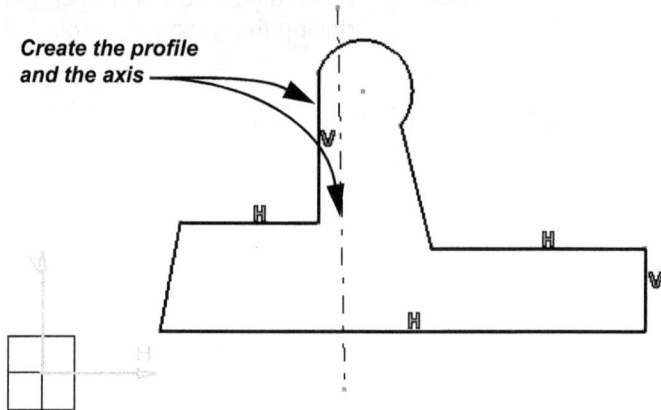

Create the profile and the axis

Figure 12–53

4. Use the Sketch Analysis to confirm that the section consists of one close profile that is constructed using 8 curves.

Task 3 - Make a slanted line vertical.

1. Select the slanted line shown in Figure 12–54.

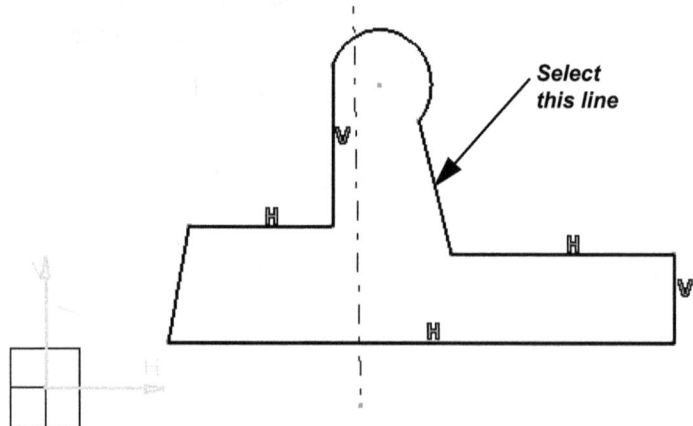

Select this line

Figure 12–54

2. Right-click and select **Line.# object>Vertical**, as shown in Figure 12–55.

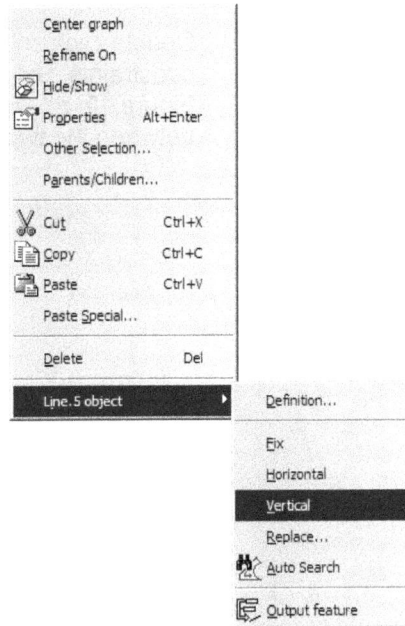

Figure 12–55

Design Considerations

This practice demonstrates the most efficient method of creating a geometric constraint in a sketch. Depending on the scenario, this might involve using a combination of icons and shortcut menu options. In each case, ⬚ (Constraints Definition) can be used instead. The corresponding option in the dialog box will be indicated in the margin. For example, the option for the **Horizontal** constraint displays as shown in Figure 12–56.

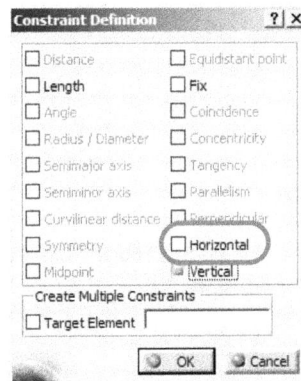

Figure 12–56

Task 4 - Make two lines coincident.

1. Double-click on ▣⌶ (Constraint) to define a series of constraints. Select the horizontal lines shown in Figure 12–57. This will begin the creation of a dimension between the two entities. Do not place the dimension.

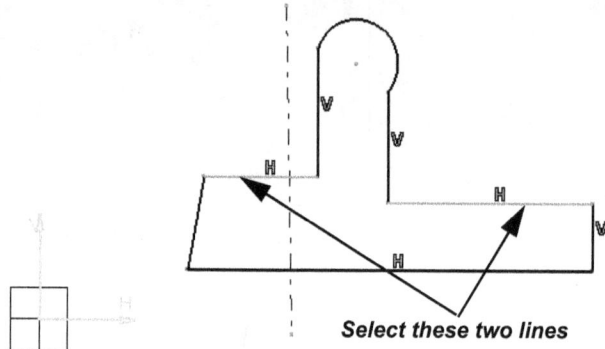

Select these two lines

Figure 12–57

2. Right-click and select **Coincidence**.

Task 5 - Make two lines parallel.

1. Select the vertical lines shown in Figure 12–58.

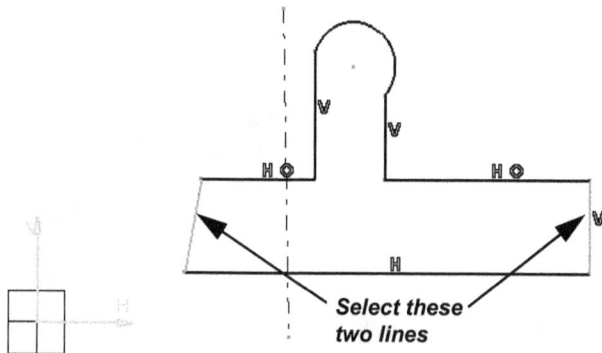

Select these two lines

Figure 12–58

2. Right-click and select **Parallelism**.

3. Place the parallel constraint using the left mouse button.

Task 6 - Make the arc tangent to the adjacent lines.

1. Select the arc and one of the adjacent straight lines as shown in Figure 12–59.

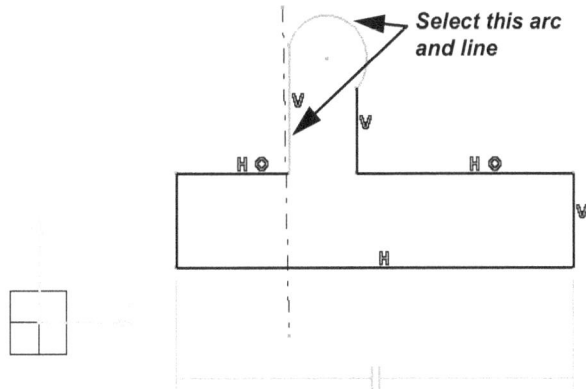

Figure 12–59

2. Right-click and select **Tangency**.

3. Repeat this task for the arc and for the line on the other side.

Task 7 - Make arc center coincident with a sketched axis.

1. Select the sketched axis and the center of the arc shown in Figure 12–60.

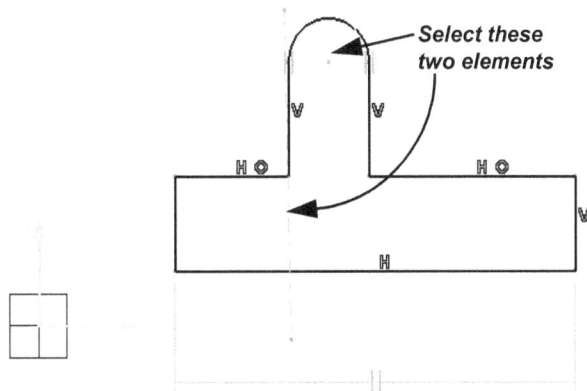

Figure 12–60

2. Right-click and select **Coincidence**.

Task 8 - Make the sketch symmetrical about the sketched axis.

To make two elements symmetrical about an axis, start by selecting the elements to be made symmetrical (in this case, two vertical lines). Once you have identified the symmetry constraint, select the symmetry element (in this case, the vertical axis).

1. Select the two vertical lines shown in Figure 12–61.

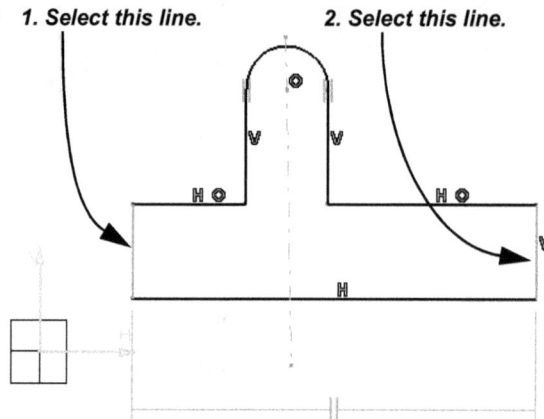

1. Select this line.   **2. Select this line.**

Figure 12–61

2. Right-click and select **Allow Symmetry Line**, as shown in Figure 12–62.

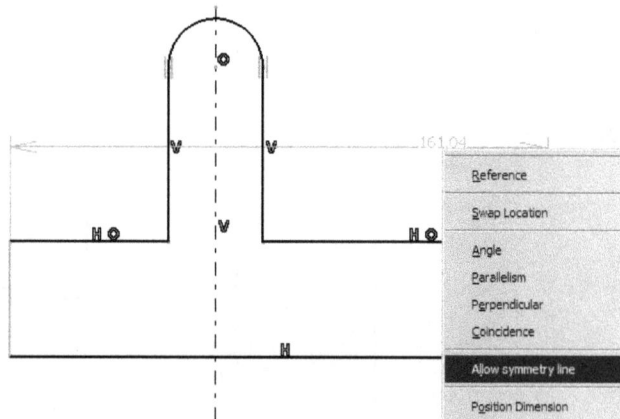

Figure 12–62

3. Select the axis shown in Figure 12–63 to complete the **Symmetry** constraint.

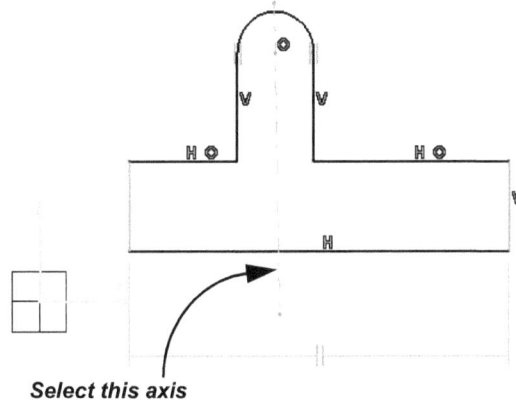

Select this axis

Figure 12–63

Task 9 - Constrain the sketch to the datum planes.

1. Create a **Coincidence** constraint between the bottom horizontal line and the horizontal axis, as shown in Figure 12–64.

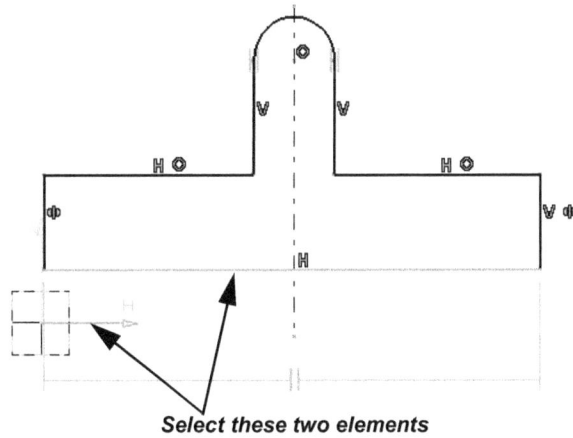

Select these two elements

Figure 12–64

2. Click to clear ⬜ (Constraint) and to stop creating constraints.

Task 10 - Drag the sketch to test your constraints.

1. Select the vertical line on the far right side of the sketch and drag it left and right. The sketch updates to remain symmetrical.

2. Drag other elements to test your constraints, as shown in Figure 12–65.

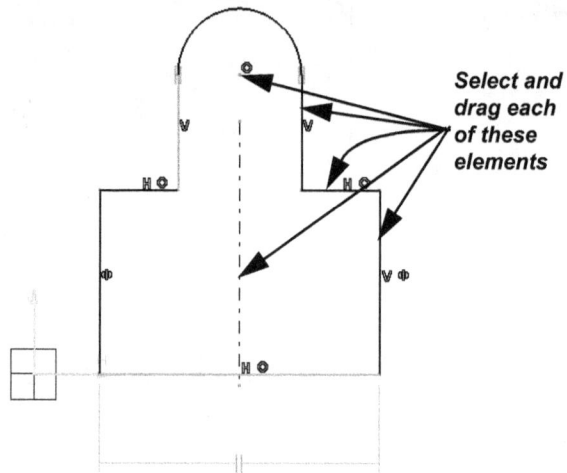

Figure 12–65

Task 11 - Dimension the section.

1. Add the dimensions and constraints shown in Figure 12–66. Adjust the dimension values accordingly.

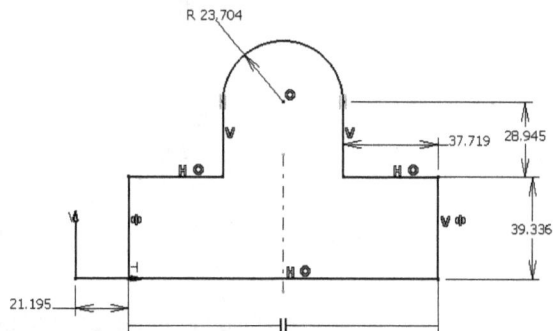

Figure 12–66

Task 12 - Exit the sketch and close the window.

1. Click ⬆ (Exit workbench) to exit the sketch.

2. Click 💾 (Save) and save the part.

3. Select **File>Close** to close the window.

Pad and Pocket Features

This chapter introduces the creation and modification of Pad and Pocket features, which serve as the foundation of your model. Understanding the various base features and the process of creating them will help you develop robust and flexible models. You will learn how to create pads to add material and pockets to remove material. When creating sketches for features, you can have sketches that form a closed loop, or sketches that are open, depending on the existing geometry. You will learn how to make changes to sketches.

Learning Objectives in this Chapter

- Use the various base features available.
- Use opened and closed sketches.
- Understand the basic process of creating a pad feature.
- Understand the restrictions on sketches used for pad features.
- Use the various options available for creating pad features.
- Understand the difference between a Pad and a Pocket.
- Understand the Limit options for the depth of Pad features.
- Learn how to use Open profiles.
- Learn about the types of changes that can be made to sketches, and the restrictions on those changes.

13.1 Base Features

When designing a new part, one of your first modeling decisions is to select which feature form to use as the Base feature. The Base feature is the first solid feature created in the model and it provides the foundation on which the entire model is constructed.

You can use one of the following features for your Base feature geometry:

- Pad
- Shaft
- Multi-sections Solid
- Rib

Figure 13–1 shows an example of a Pad feature.

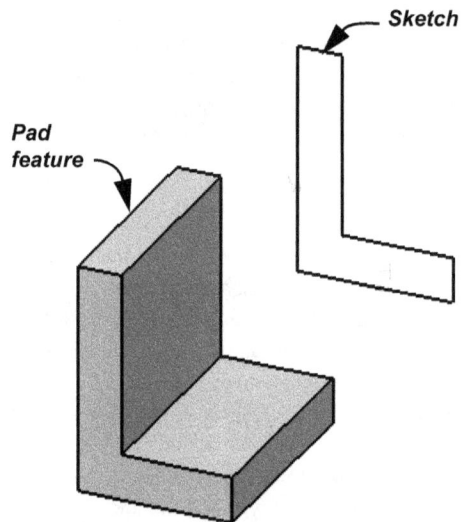

Figure 13–1

13.2 Creating a Pad Feature

With a Pad feature, an existing sketch is extruded a specified distance to define the solid geometry.

How To: Create a Pad Feature

1. Select a profile or surface. The shape of a Pad is determined by the profile that is used to create the feature. Select the sketch. Selected items display in orange by default, as shown in Figure 13–2.

Figure 13–2

2. Click (Pad). The software initially constructs the Pad feature using the default values, as shown in Figure 13–3. The Pad Definition dialog box opens.

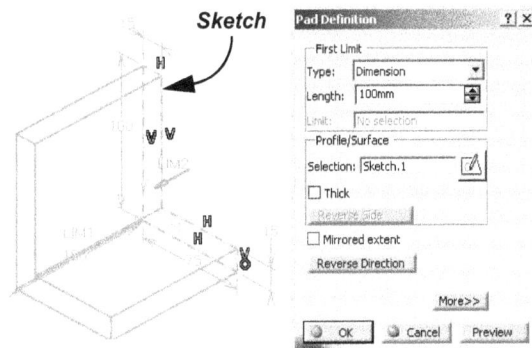

Sketch

Figure 13–3

Additional limit types for Pad features are discussed later.

3. Specify Pad limit options.

   The distance that the sketch is extruded is known as the limit. The default limit type is dimension, which enables you to manually specify the extrusion distance. To specify the length of the feature, simply enter the distance in the *Length* field.

4. Click **Preview** to examine the geometry before completing the feature.

5. Click **OK** to complete the feature.

Mirrored Extent

The total depth of a Mirrored extent Pad feature is twice the length value entered in the Pad Definition dialog box.

You can select the **Mirrored extent** option in the Pad Definition dialog box to create geometry on both sides of the sketch, as shown in Figure 13–4.

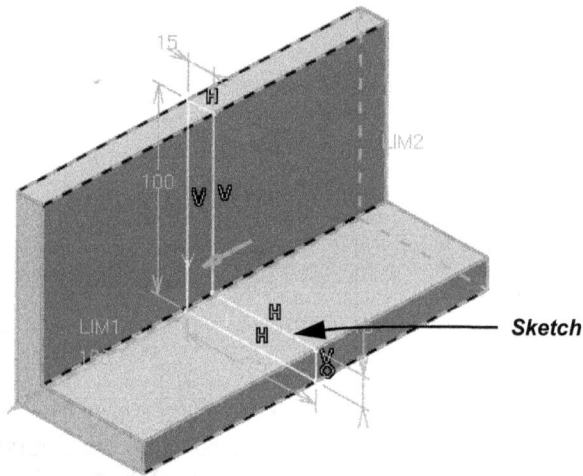

Figure 13–4

It is common practice to start a model with symmetrical geometry. This enables you to capture the design intent from the very beginning. Using this technique, additional features can be easily located relative to the center of the part and automatically remain centered, even when the size of the Base feature is changed.

Second Limit

As a reference, the software displays an arrow to indicate the direction of the First Limit.

Click **More** to fully expand the Pad Definition dialog box, as shown in Figure 13–5. By expanding the dialog box, you have access to a set of advanced feature options, such as the **Second Limit** distance. By changing the value from the default *zero* to a new value, you can create asymmetrical geometry about the sketch.

*   You can enter a negative value for the First or Second Limit.

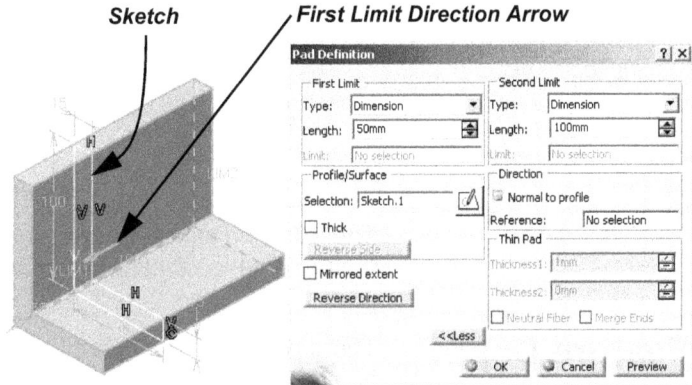

Figure 13–5

Sketch Restrictions for Pad Features

Not every sketch is valid for use with a Pad feature. Comparisons of valid and invalid sketches are described as follows:

Valid Sketch	Invalid Sketch	Description
		Multiple sections are acceptable, but they cannot intersect each other. You can use the trim function to eliminate the overlap condition.
		Open sections are not permitted for the first solid feature on the part unless the **Thick** option is used to create the Pad.

*   If you try to create a Pad feature with an invalid section, an error message displays and you are not able to create the feature.

13.3 Pad Feature Options

As features are added to a model, planar surfaces of existing geometry can be selected as sketching planes, as shown in Figure 13–6.

To facilitate sketched feature creation, additional reference planes can be created at specific locations.

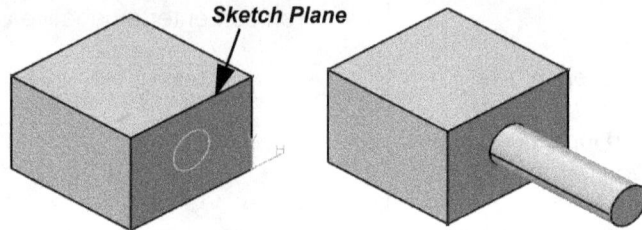

Figure 13–6

The following topics discuss several options available during Pad feature creation that help capture design intent.

Feature Depth Options

There are a number of methods that can be used to define the depth of a Pad feature. These options are shown in Figure 13–7.

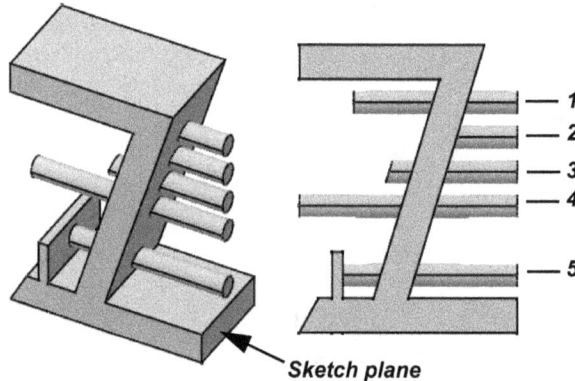

Figure 13–7

The depth options, set in the *Type* drop-down list of the Pad Dialog box, are described as follows:

Example	Option	Description
1	**Dimension**	Manually enter length of feature.
2	**Up to next, with Offset**	Feature extruded to next solid surface that completely intersects sketch. Offset enables you to specify a positive or negative distance from that terminating plane.

3	Up to last, with Offset	Feature terminates at last solid surface that sketch completely intersects. Offset enables you to specify a positive or negative distance from that terminating plane.
4	Up to plane	Feature can be terminated at selected planar surface or reference plane.
5	Up to surface	Feature can be terminated at selected planar or non-planar surface that completely intersects sketch.

Second Limit Option

With Pad features, you can extrude the sketch on either side or both sides of the sketching plane. To access this functionality, click **More** in the Pad Definition dialog box.

For example, a circle is sketched on the planar surface of the Pad feature, as shown in Figure 13–8 and Figure 13–9.

- First limit type is **Dimension** with a length value of **20**.

- Second limit type is **Up to surface** and the cylindrical surface is selected.

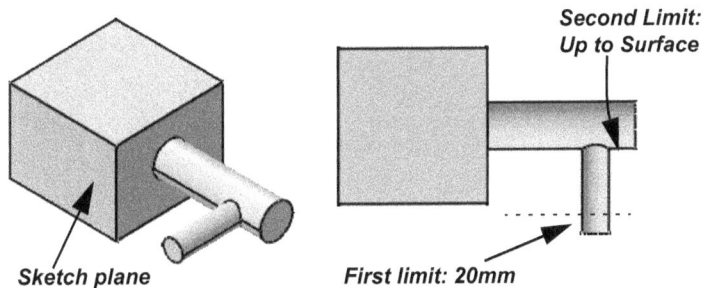

Figure 13–8

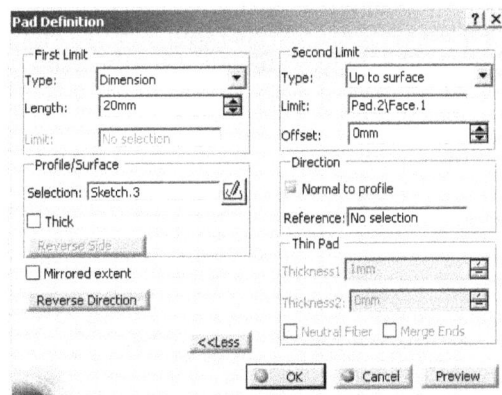

Figure 13–9

Non-Normal Direction

By default, Pads are extruded perpendicular (normal) to the sketch plane. You can disable this action by clearing the **Normal to Profile** option and selecting a straight line or edge to define the feature direction.

In the example shown in Figure 13–10, note that the sketch does not extend the entire length of the Pad feature. This sketch is used to define the direction only; the length of the line is not important.

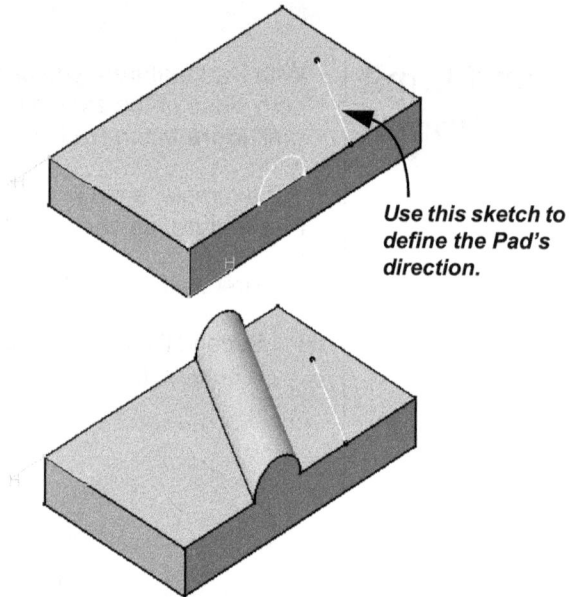

Use this sketch to define the Pad's direction.

Figure 13–10

Open and Closed Sketches

Your profile sketches do not have to form a closed loop. An open profile is acceptable under certain circumstances. However, the open end of the sketch must be bounded by existing geometry. This means the existing geometry must touch the open ends of the sketch at all times. If the Pad shown in Figure 13–11 is lengthened so that it extends off the part, the feature fails.

Using open profiles for feature creation increases update time and introduces instability into the model. A closed profile should be developed whenever possible.

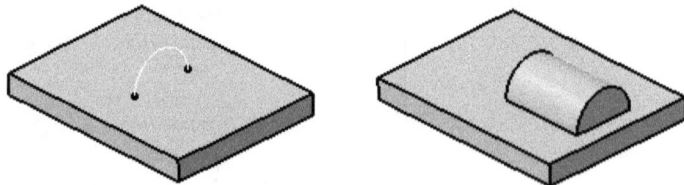

Figure 13–11

13.4 Pocket

A Pocket feature removes material by extruding a profile. It is similar to a Pad feature, except that a Pad adds material and a Pocket removes material, as shown in Figure 13–12.

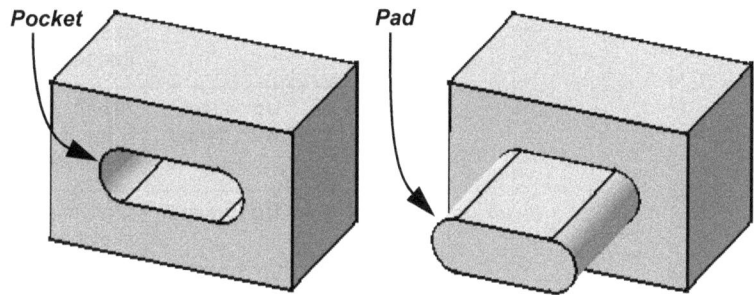

Figure 13–12

Limit Options

Several options are available to control the limits of a Pocket feature. These options are similar to those for the Pad feature, as shown in Figure 13–13.

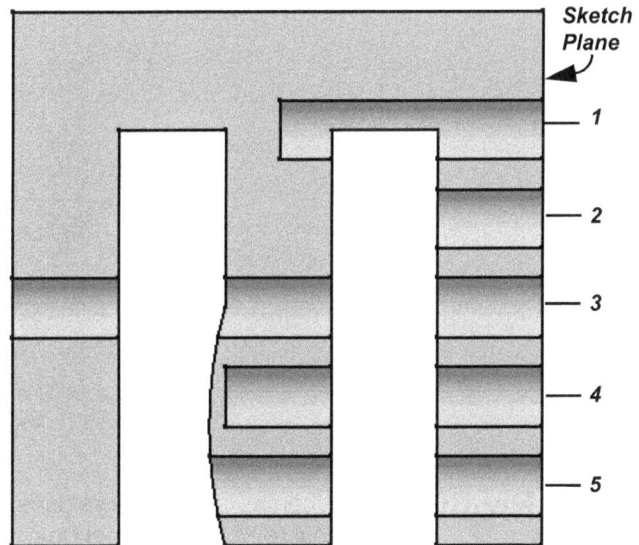

Figure 13–13

The limit options are described as follows:

Example	Option	Description
1	**Dimension**	Manually enter the depth of the Pocket.
2	**Up to next, with Offset**	Sketch is extruded to the next surface that intersects the entire sketch. Offset enables you to specify a positive or negative distance from that terminating plane.
3	**Up to last, with Offset**	Sketch is extruded through the entire model. Offset enables you to specify a positive or negative distance from that terminating plane.
4	**Up to plane**	Sketch is extruded to a specified plane. The sketch does not need to reside on the plane.
5	**Up to surface**	Sketch is extruded to a specified surface. The surface can be planar or non-planar. The surface must intersect the entire sketch.

All of the limit options, except for **Dimension**, have a default offset value of 0. You can change it to a positive value to extend the Pocket beyond the reference or change it to a negative value to pull it back from the reference, as shown in Figure 13–14.

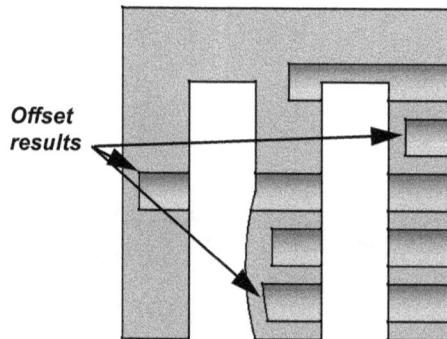

Offset results

Figure 13–14

Open Profiles

When a Pocket feature uses an open profile sketch, the software only removes material from one side of the sketch to the boundaries of the model. Clicking **Reverse Side** in the dialog box enables you to remove material on the other side, as shown in Figure 13–15.

If the open ends of the sketch are not coincident with the sides of the part, the software automatically extends them, as shown in Figure 13–16.

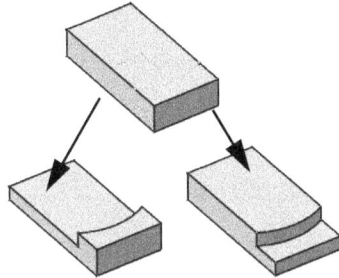

Figure 13–15

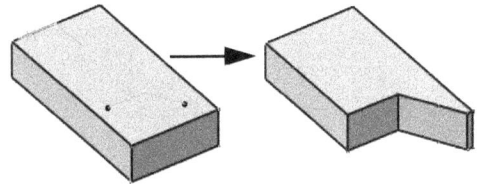

Figure 13–16

- Open profiles are subject to increased update time and introduce instability in the model. Avoid them whenever possible.

Other Feature Options

As is the case with Pads, Pocket features can have a unique second limit; they can be mirrored about the sketch and can be extruded in various ways, as shown in Figure 13–17.

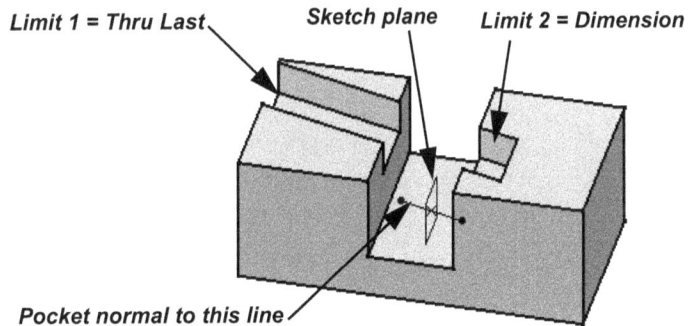

Figure 13–17

The Pocket Definition dialog box is shown in Figure 13–18.

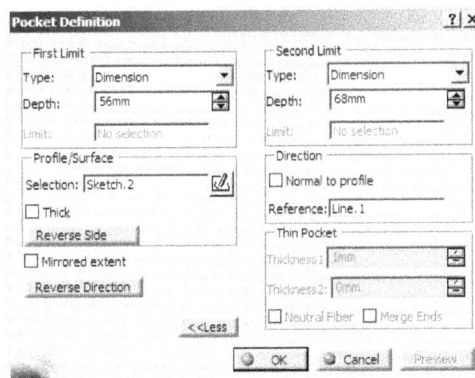

Figure 13–18

13.5 Making Changes to a Sketch

You can easily change the information of a feature, such as the length, sketch dimensions, shape of the sketch, and attributes of the feature (e.g., Mirrored extent).

The following topics discuss these changes in more detail.

Dimensional Changes

How To: Change Dimensions

1. Double-click on a feature on the model to open its dialog box. The software also displays all dimensions of the feature, including the sketch dimensions.
2. Double-click on dimension to open the Constraint Definition dialog box.
3. Enter a new value and click **OK** to complete the change. The software automatically updates the geometry, as shown in Figure 13–19.

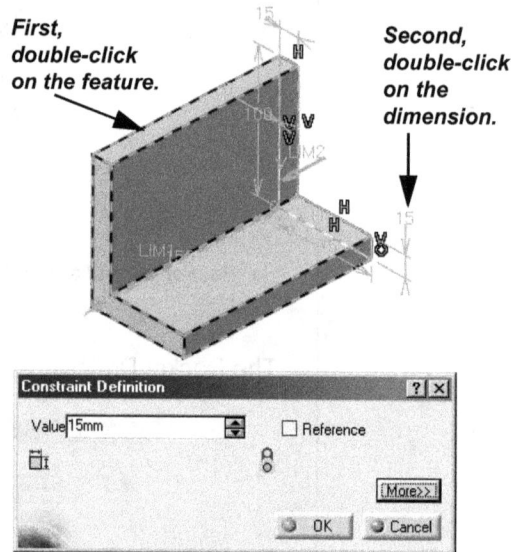

Figure 13–19

Changing the Sketch

The software automatically hides the sketch once you have used it for a Solid feature. To modify the sketch in the Sketcher workbench, you can use one of the following methods:

- Double-click on the sketch in the specification tree. Even if the sketch is hidden from the display, it displays in the Sketcher workbench.

- Click ◪ (Sketcher Workbench) in the dialog box for the feature, as shown in Figure 13–20. You enter the Sketcher workbench, where you can modify the sketch. When you exit Sketcher, you return to editing the feature in the Part Design workbench.

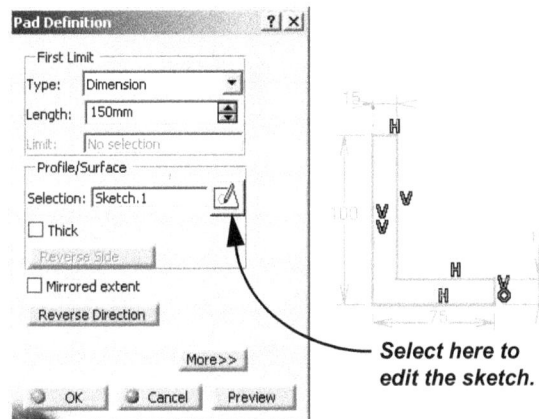

Figure 13–20

Deleting the Feature

Deleting a feature removes the geometry from the model. When a feature is deleted, the sketch remains. This enables you to use the sketch again, as required. Remember that you can use the **Undo** and **Redo** commands to restore features that are accidentally deleted or changed.

You can delete a Pad or a Pocket feature in one of the following ways:

- Select the feature in the specification tree and press <Delete>.

- Select the feature in the specification tree and select **Edit>Delete**.

- Select the feature in the specification tree, right-click and select **Delete**, as shown in Figure 13–21.

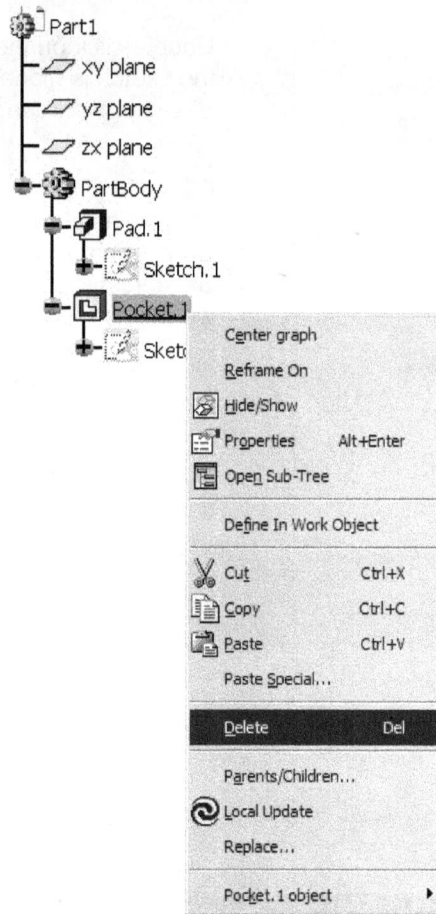

Figure 13–21

Change Restrictions

The only restriction to feature changes is on the feature form. You cannot change a Pad feature into a Pocket feature. You must delete the Pad feature, select the sketch, and then create a Pocket feature.

Practice 13a

Creating and Modifying Pad Features

Practice Objectives

- Create a sketch to create a Pad feature.
- Modify a Pad feature.

In this practice, you will create Pad features and modify them using the Pad Definition dialog box. You will create the part shown in Figure 13–22.

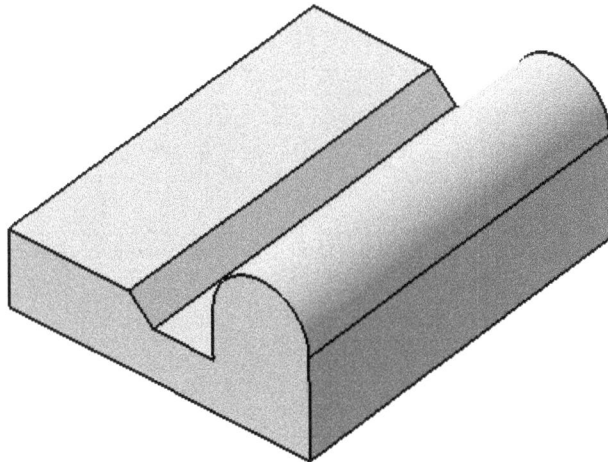

Figure 13–22

Task 1 - Create a new part.

1. Click ⬚ (New).

2. In the New dialog box, select the **Part** option and click **OK**.

3. Enter **Pad_Sketch** as the part name, and click **OK**.

4. In the specification tree, select the YZ plane.

5. Click ⬚ (Sketch).

Task 2 - Sketch the profile.

1. Sketch and constrain the part profile, as shown in Figure 13–23.

    - 50 (1.969 in)
    - 60 (2.362 in)
    - 25 (4.921 in)
    - 125 (4.921 in)
    - 20 (0.787 in)
    - 45 (1.772 in)

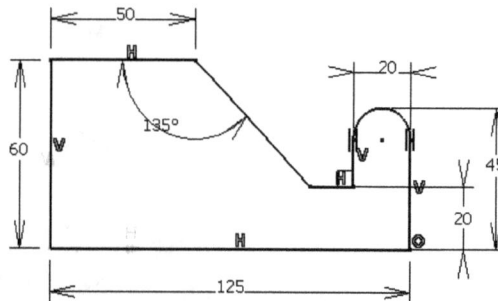

Figure 13–23

2. Click ⬆ (Exit workbench) to exit the Sketcher workbench.

Task 3 - Create a Pad feature from the sketch.

1. With the sketch highlighted, click 🗗 (Pad). The Pad Definition dialog box opens.

2. In the *Length* field, enter **75 (2.953 in)**. Click **OK** to complete the feature. The resulting geometry displays as shown in Figure 13–24.

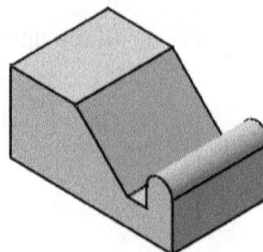

Figure 13–24

Task 4 - Make dimensional changes to the Pad feature.

1. Double-click on any face of the Pad feature. All of the dimensions of the feature display in green. The Pad Definition dialog box also opens.

2. Double-click on the *60* (2.362 in) dimension and change it to **30 (1.181 in)**, as shown in Figure 13–25.

You can press <Enter> instead of clicking OK.

3. In the Constraint Definition dialog box, click **OK**.

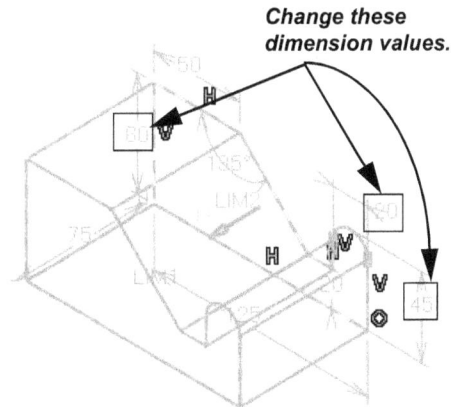

Figure 13–25

4. Repeat this process to change the *20* (0.787 in) dimension to **40 (1.575 in)** and the *45* (1.772 in) dimension to **60 (2.362 in)**.

5. Click **OK** in the Pad Definition dialog box to complete the dimensional changes and update the geometry. The resulting geometry displays as shown in Figure 13–26.

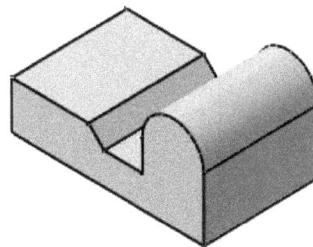

Figure 13–26

Task 5 - Change the attributes of the feature.

1. Double-click on the Pad feature again to open the Pad Definition dialog box.

2. Select the **Mirrored extent** option. The software previews the geometry in wireframe, as shown in Figure 13–27. The geometry is symmetrical about the sketch and has a total length of 150 (5.906 in).

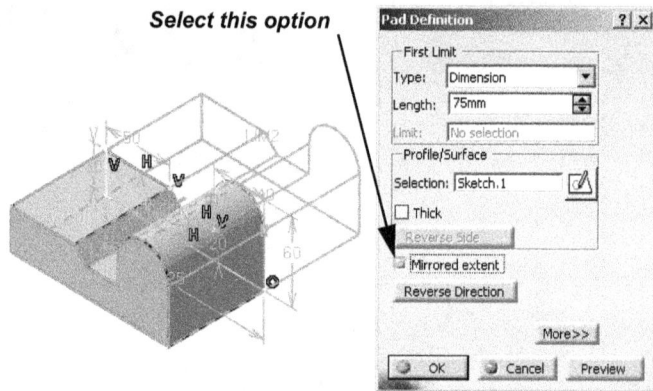

Figure 13–27

3. Clear the **Mirrored extent** option.

4. Click **More**. In the *First Limit* area, enter **50 (1.969 in)** for the length.

5. In the *Second Limit* area, enter **100 (3.937 in)** for the length. Click **Preview** and the resulting geometry displays as shown in Figure 13–28.

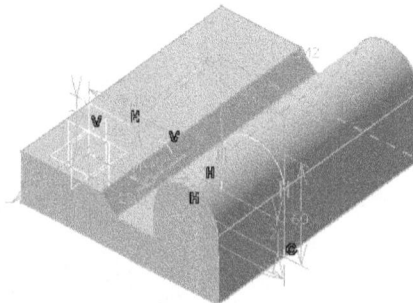

Figure 13–28

6. Click **OK** in the Pad Definition dialog box to complete the change and update the geometry.

Task 6 - Save the part and close the window.

1. Click [save icon] (Save) and save the part.

2. Select **File>Close** to close the window.

Practice 13b | Creating Pocket Features

Practice Objectives

- Create a sketch to create a Pocket feature.
- Modify a Pocket feature.

In this practice, you will create and modify three Pocket features. The first feature will represent a hole with a keyway Groove to accept a Shaft. The second feature will create a cylindrical elongated hole cutout on the flange of the part. The completed model displays as shown in Figure 13-29.

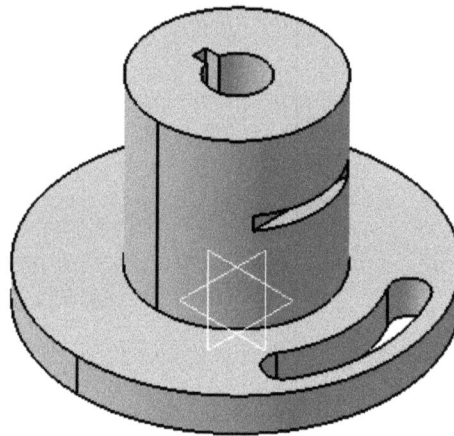

Figure 13-29

Task 1 - Open a model and create a profile on the top of it.

1. Click ⬜ (Open).

2. Select **Pockets.CATPart** and click **Open**.

3. Select the top cylindrical face of the model and click ⬜ (Sketch).

4. Sketch the profile as shown in Figure 13–30. Note that the arc is concentric with the cylindrical face and the keyway geometry is symmetrical about the vertical axis.

- 4 (0.157 in)
- 8 (0.315 in)
- 12 (0.472 in)

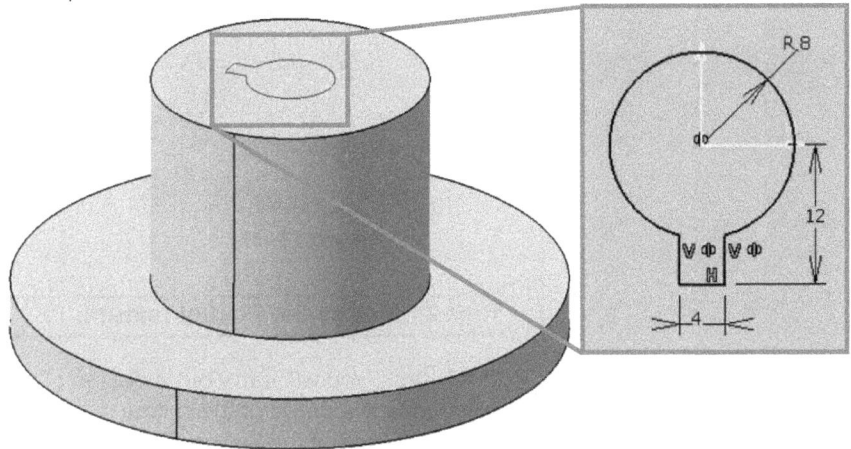

Figure 13–30

5. Exit the Sketcher workbench to complete the sketch.

6. With the sketch selected, click ▣ (Pocket). The Pocket Definition dialog box opens as shown in Figure 13–31, indicating a *Depth* of **33 (1.299 in)**.

Figure 13–31

7. Verify that the arrow indicating direction points down into the part. Also confirm that the arrow indicating the material side, points toward the inside of the profile, as shown in Figure 13–32.

8. Enter a depth of **40 (1.575 in)** and click **OK**. The completed Pocket feature displays as shown in Figure 13–33.

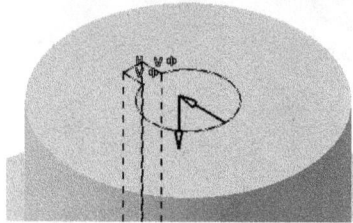

Figure 13–32

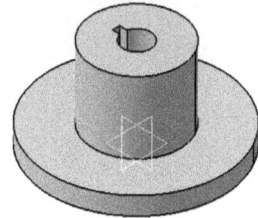

Figure 13–33

Task 2 - Modify the Pocket feature.

In this task, you will carry out a design change on the model. You will modify the depth of the cutout so that it will always extend up to the top face of the flange. This is done by modifying the depth options for the Pocket feature.

1. Locate the Pocket feature in the specification tree and double-click on it to open the Pocket Definition dialog box.

2. In the *First Limit* area, set *Type* to **Up to plane** and select the face as shown in Figure 13–34.

*Since the section does not entirely intersect the selected face, the **Up to surface** option cannot be used.*

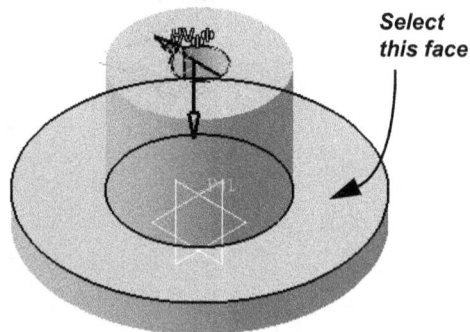

Select this face

Figure 13–34

3. Click **OK** to complete the modification.

4. Use (Shading with Edges and Hidden Edges) View mode to review the depth of the feature.

5. Modify the depth of Pad.1 from *40* (1.575 in) to **50 (1.969 in)**. Review the model to verify that the Pocket feature is behaving correctly.

6. Once complete, return the model to the **Shading with Edges** display.

Task 3 - Create a second Pocket feature.

1. Select the face of the model as shown in Figure 13–35 and click [✎] (Sketch).

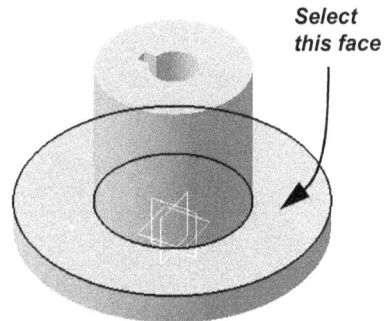

Select this face

Figure 13–35

2. Sketch the profile as shown in Figure 13–36, using Cylindrical Elongated Hole. To create the angle dimension, create two construction lines that are symmetrical about the vertical axis and pass through the center of each arc.

- 5 (0.197 in)
- 40 (1.575 in)

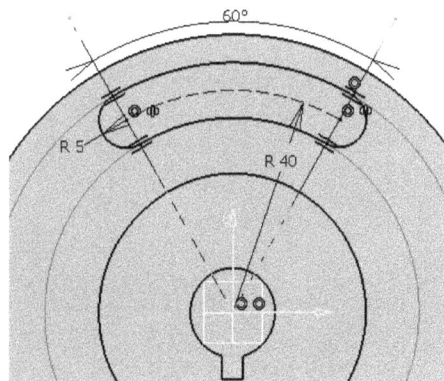

Figure 13–36

3. Exit the Sketcher workbench to complete the sketch.

4. Create a Pocket feature using the sketch just created. Define the depth using the **Up to last** option. The completed feature displays as shown in Figure 13–37.

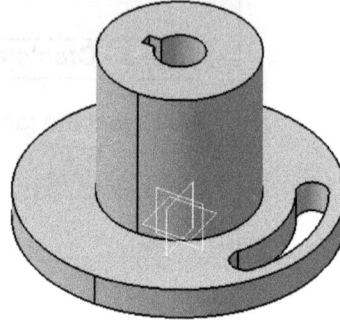

Figure 13–37

Task 4 - Create a Pocket using two limits.

In this task, you will sketch a profile for a Pocket feature on the YZ plane. Then you will create a Pocket feature that cuts material from both sides of the sketch plane.

1. Create a sketch on the YZ plane. Sketch the profile as shown in Figure 13–38.

   • 4 (0.157 in)
   • 10 (0.394 in)
   • 20 (0.787 in
   • 40 (1.575 in)

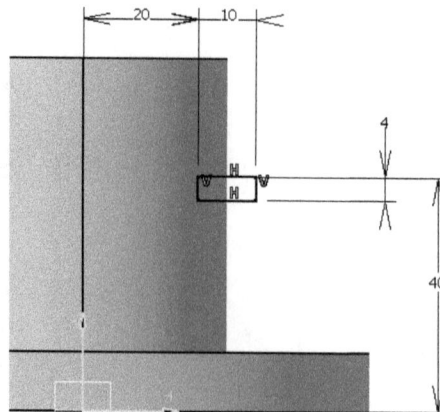

Figure 13–38

2. Exit the Sketcher workbench to complete the sketch.

3. Create a Pocket feature using the sketch just created.

4. Set the *First Limit* type as **Up to last**.

5. Click **More**. The Pocket Definition dialog box opens as shown in Figure 13–39.

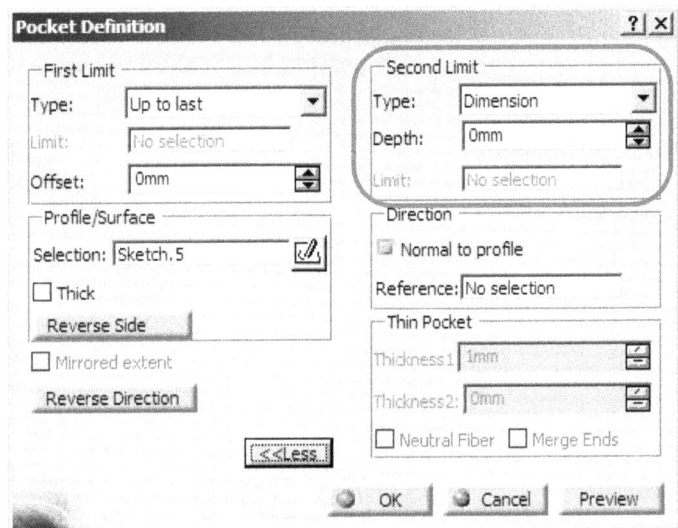

Figure 13–39

6. In the *Second Limit* area, set *Type* to **Up to last**.

7. Complete the feature. The model displays as shown in Figure 13–40.

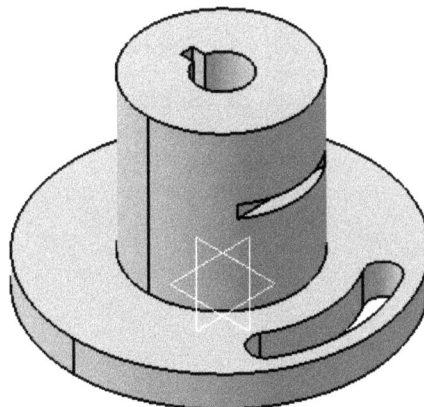

Figure 13–40

8. Save the model and close the window.

Practice 13c

Working with Open Sketches

Practice Objectives

- Correctly sketch and constrain an open profile.
- Use an open sketch to create a Pad feature.

In this practice you will add a Rib to a part, as shown in Figure 13–41. You will need to create an open profile sketch and use the Pad feature to create the Rib.

You can also use a stiffener to create the Rib geometry. Stiffeners are described later.

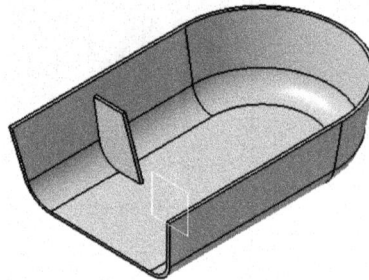

Figure 13–41

Task 1 - Create an open profile on the YZ plane.

1. Click (Open).

2. Select **Open_Sketch.CATPart** and click **Open**.

3. Set the model part length units to **millimeters** (mm).

4. Select the YZ plane and click (Sketch).

5. Sketch a horizontal and angled line as shown in Figure 13–42.

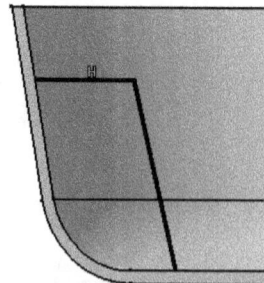

Figure 13–42

Design Considerations

To successfully use an open sketch as a Pad feature, the sketch must be fully constrained to other geometry. This way, CATIA knows how to extrude the open sections of the profile.

6. To constrain the open ends of the profile to existing geometry, click ⬚ (Constraints).

7. Select one of the open end points and the adjacent edge of the part, as shown in Figure 13–43.

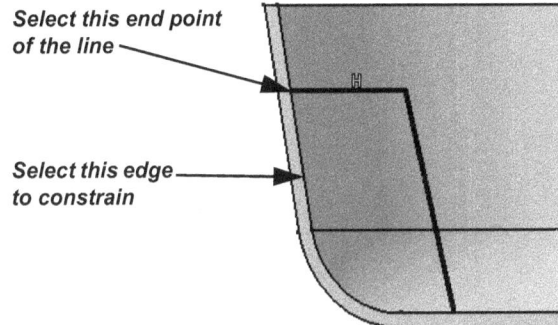

Select this end point of the line

Select this edge to constrain

Figure 13–43

8. Right-click and select **Coincidence**.

9. Repeat Steps 1 to 5 for the other open end.

10. Create the **12.5 (0.492 in)** and **32 (1.260 in)** dimensions as shown in Figure 13–44.

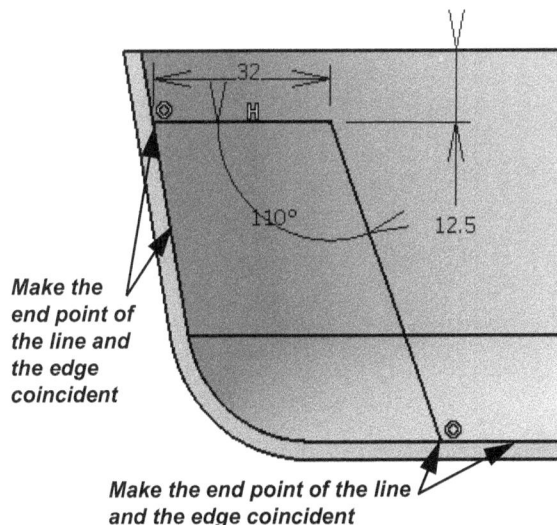

Make the end point of the line and the edge coincident

Make the end point of the line and the edge coincident

Figure 13–44

11. Exit the Sketcher workbench to complete the sketch. The part displays as shown in Figure 13–45.

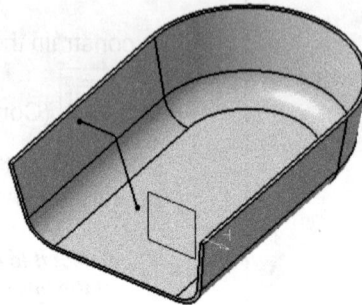

Figure 13–45

Task 2 - Create a Pad feature that represents the Rib's geometry.

1. Select the sketch and click ![Pad icon] (Pad).

2. Enter **1.60 (0.063 in)** for the length.

3. Select the **Mirrored extent** option to add material on both sides of the sketch plane.

4. Click **OK** to complete the feature. The part displays as shown in Figure 13–46.

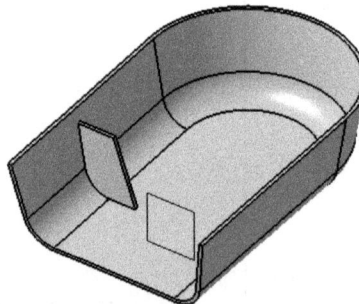

Figure 13–46

5. Click ![Save icon] (Save).

6. Select **File>Close**.

Practice 13d | Pad and Pocket

Practice Objective

- Create a Pad feature and a Pocket feature.

In this practice, you will create the model shown in Figure 13–47 using Pad and Pocket features.

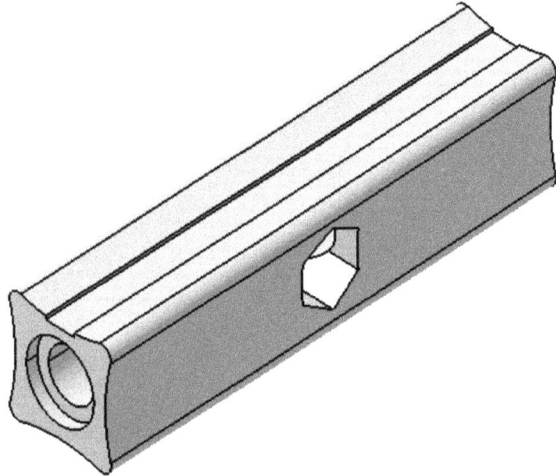

Figure 13–47

Task 1 - Create a Pad feature.

In this task, you will create a Pad feature to define the base feature for the model.

1. Create a new part called **Pad_Pocket.CATPart**.

2. Access the Sketcher workbench using the YZ plane as the sketch support.

3. To create the required profile, start by creating two centered rectangle construction squares, using dimensions of **80 (3.150 in)** and **100 (3.937 in)**, as shown in Figure 13–48.

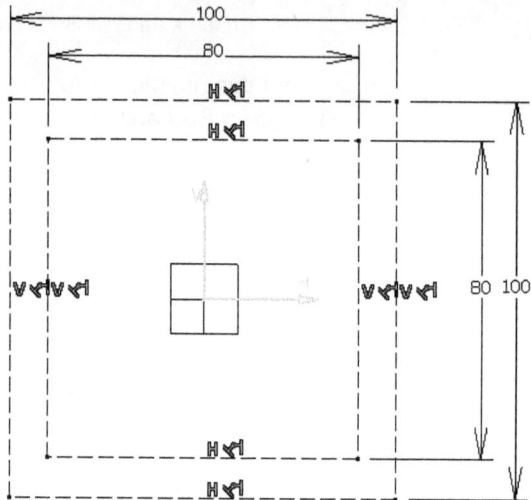

Figure 13–48

4. Click ⟳ (Three Point Arc).

5. Select the three points as shown in Figure 13–49 to create the arc.

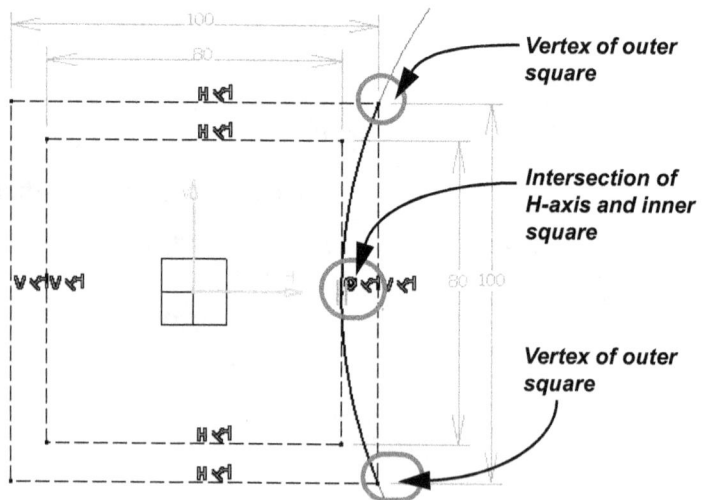

Figure 13–49

6. Create three more arcs using the method described in the previous step. The completed arcs display as shown in Figure 13–50.

7. Select one of the arcs. Right-click and select * **object>Auto Search**.

8. Click $\curvearrowleft$ (Corner).

9. Locate the Sketch Tools toolbar. With the **Corner** tool activated, the toolbar will update, enabling you to enter a radius. Enter **8 (0.315 in)**. The completed profile displays as shown in Figure 13–51.

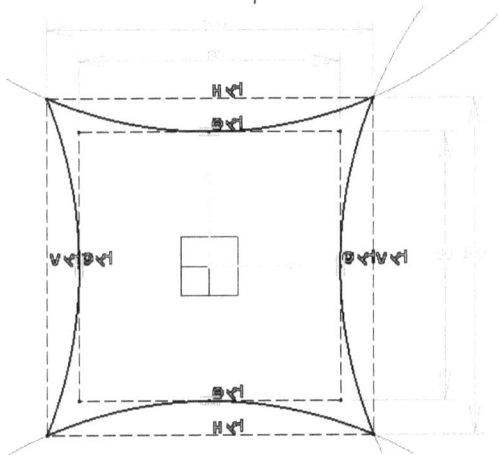

Figure 13–50

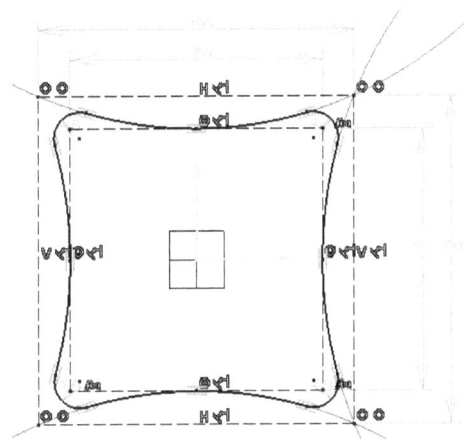

Figure 13–51

10. Exit the Sketcher workbench to complete the sketch.

Task 2 - Create a Pad feature.

1. Click $\boxed{\square}$ (Pad) and enter the following properties:

   - *Profile:* **Sketch.1**
   - *Length:* **400mm (15.748 in)**

2. Click **OK**.

Task 3 - Create a Pocket profile.

1. Create a sketch on the face as shown in Figure 13–52.

2. Sketch the **60 (2.362 in)** diameter circular profile as shown in Figure 13–53.

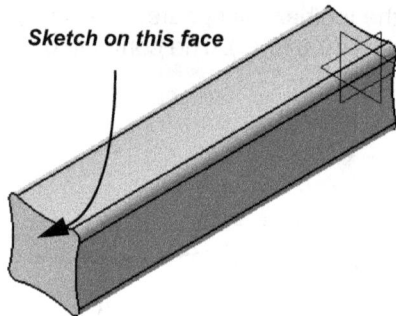

Figure 13–52

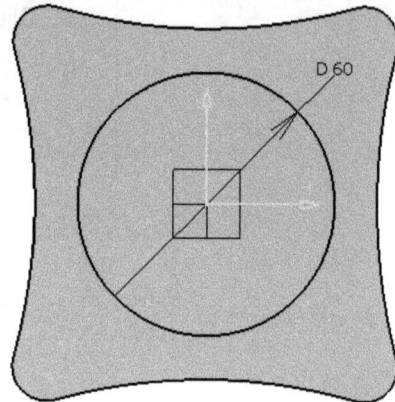

Figure 13–53

3. Exit Sketcher.

Task 4 - Create a Pocket.

1. Create a Pocket feature using the profile just created. Enter a depth of **10 (0.394 in)**. The completed feature displays as shown in Figure 13–54.

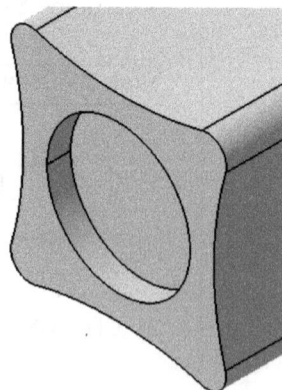

Figure 13–54

Task 5 - Create a through Pocket.

To create this Pocket, you will copy and paste a Sketch. This Sketch will act independently of the original profile.

1. In the specification tree, locate and select **Sketch.2**. This is the 60mm diameter profile used to create the previous Pocket feature.

2. Select **Edit>Copy**.

3. Select the face as shown in Figure 13–55.

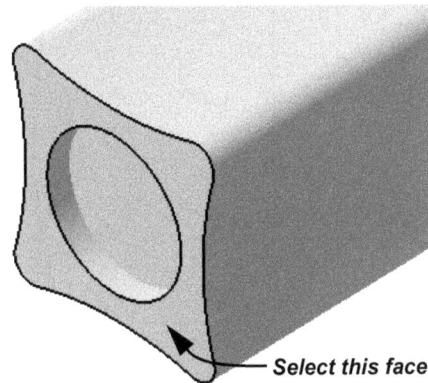

Figure 13–55

4. Select **Edit>Paste**. The profile is pasted onto the part as **Sketch.3**, as shown in Figure 13–56.

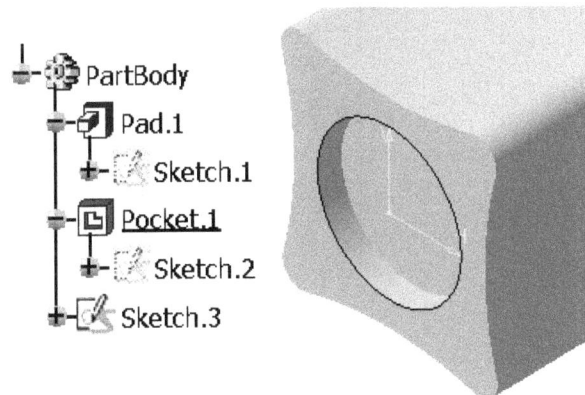

Figure 13–56

5. Edit **Sketch.3** and change the diameter from *60* (2.362 in) to **40 (1.575 in)**. Do not exit Sketcher.

6. Sketch and dimension a rectangular profile, as shown in Figure 13–57. Verify that the rectangle is symmetrical about the vertical axis.

- 10 (0.394 in)
- 20 (0.787 in)
- 38 (1.496 in)
- 40 (1.575 in)

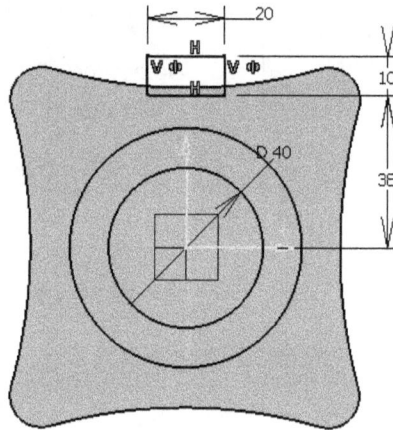

Figure 13–57

Design Considerations

Creating a profile that has more than one closed section has advantages and disadvantages. One advantage is that fewer sketched based features need to be created (in this case, one less sketch and Pocket will be created). However, the disadvantage is that the rectangular Pocket cannot be deactivated without deactivating the circular Pocket. Verify that you structure your model according to your design intent.

7. Create a Pocket feature using **Sketch.3**. Set the *First Limit Type* to **Up to last**. The model displays as shown in Figure 13–58.

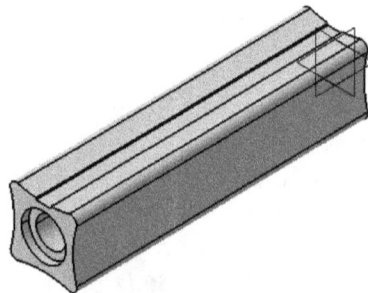

Figure 13–58

Task 6 - Create a Pocket.

1. Create a sketch on the ZX plane. Sketch the hexagonal profile using a dimension of **50 (1.969 in)**, as shown in Figure 13–59.

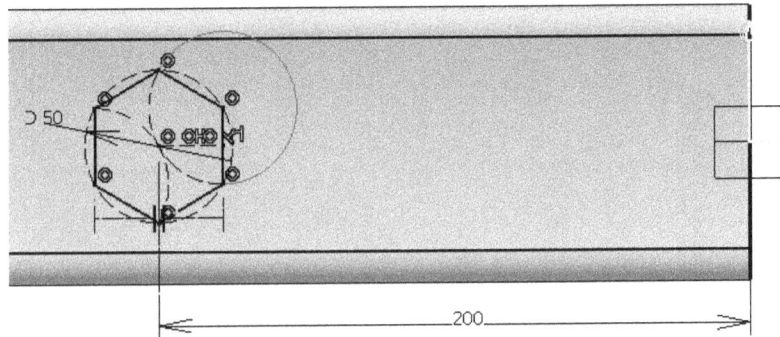

Figure 13–59

2. Create a Pocket feature that removes the hexagonal section from both sides of the sketch plane, using the **Up to last** option.

3. Hide the default reference planes. The completed model displays as shown in Figure 13–60.

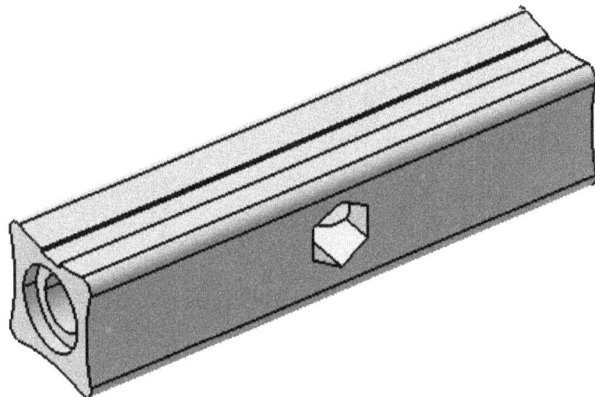

Figure 13–60

4. Save the model and close the window.

Practice 13e

(Optional) Additional Pockets

Practice Objective

- Create a Pocket feature.

In this practice, you will create the part shown in Figure 13–61. You will open an existing part and add two Pocket features.

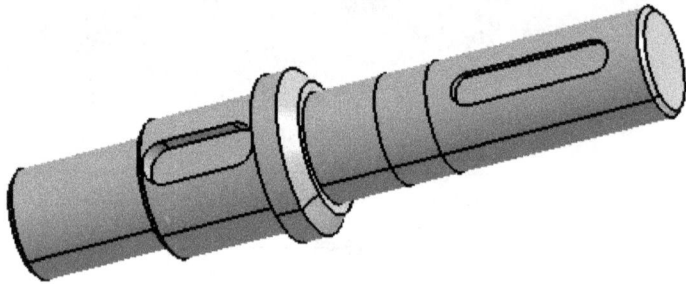

Figure 13–61

1. Open **Shaft.CATPart**.

2. Create the two Pocket features as shown in Figure 13–62. Place them in the approximate locations as shown with appropriate dimensioning schemes.

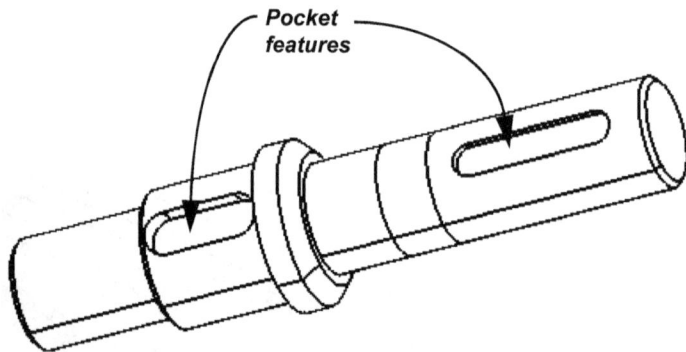

Figure 13–62

3. Click ⊞ (Save).

4. Select **File>Close**.

Practice 13f | (Optional) Crank

Practice Objective

- Create a part using pads without any instructions.

Create the **Crank.CATPart** shown in Figure 13–63.

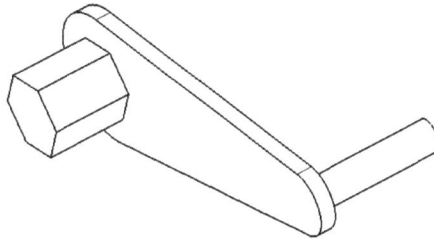

Isometric view
Scale: 1:1

Figure 13–63

Drawing views are shown in Figure 13–63 and Figure 13–64.

- 10 (0.394 in)
- 20 (0.787 in)
- 25 (0.984 in)
- 40 (1.575 in)

- 50 (1.969 in)
- 80 (3.150 in)
- 200 (7.874 in)

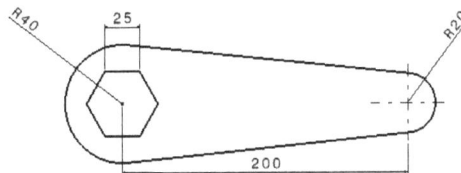

Front view
Scale: 1:1

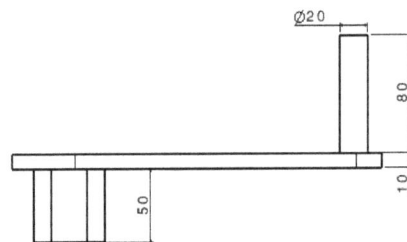

Top view
Scale: 1:1

Figure 13–64

Practice 13g | (Optional) Cylinder Block

Practice Objective

- Create a base feature and Pocket features without instruction.

Create the **CylinderBlock.CATPart** model shown in Figure 13–65.

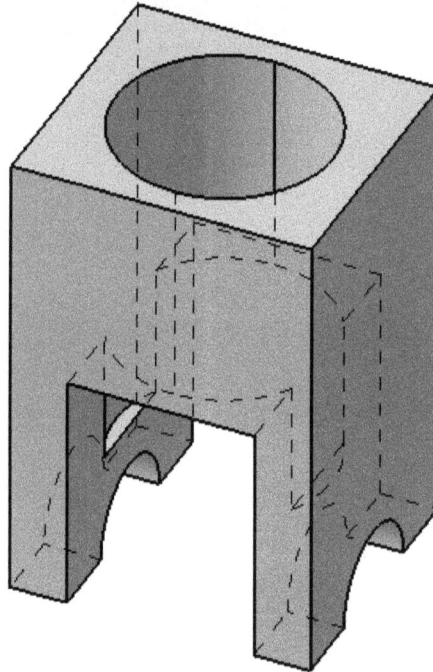

Figure 13–65

Drawing views are shown in Figure 13–66 and Figure 13–67.

- 31 (1.220 in)
- 35 (1.378 in)
- 103 (4.055 in)
- 120 (4.724 in)
- 130 (5.118 in)

- 150 (5.906 in)
- 165 (6.496 in)
- 192 (7.559 in)
- 250 (9.843 in)

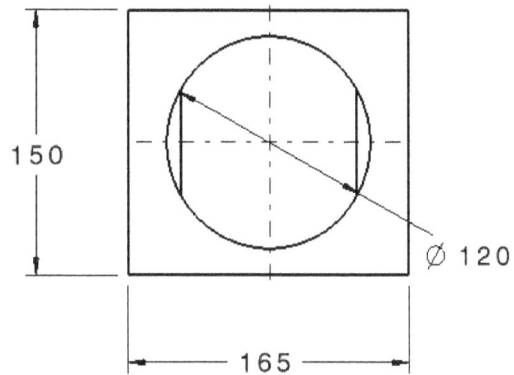

Figure 13–66

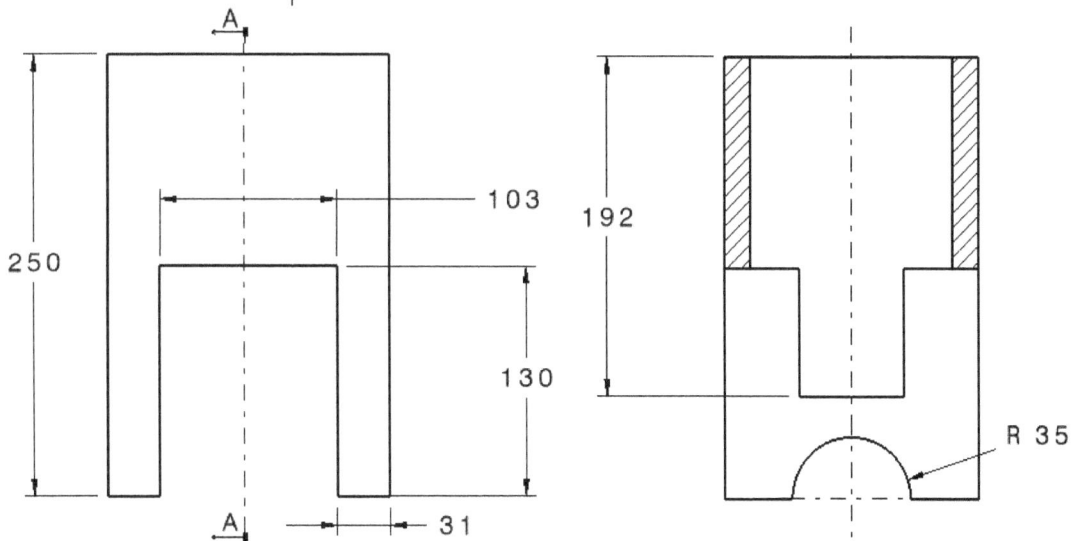

Figure 13–67

Shaft and Groove Features

The Shaft and Groove features are used in a similar way to the Pad and Pocket features, except that their sketches rotate about an axis. This chapter covers the requirements for sketches used in Shaft features. Additionally, you will learn how to create grooves to remove material from the model and how you can create grooves on both planar and cylindrical surfaces.

Learning Objectives in this Chapter

- Learn the steps required to create a shaft feature.
- Understand the restrictions on sketches used for shaft features.
- Learn the steps required to create a groove feature.
- Create grooves on cylinders.

14.1 Shaft Feature

A Shaft feature consists of an existing sketch rotated about an axis. Figure 14–1 shows an example of a section rotated 360° about a sketched axis.

You can also use the vertical axis of the sketch.

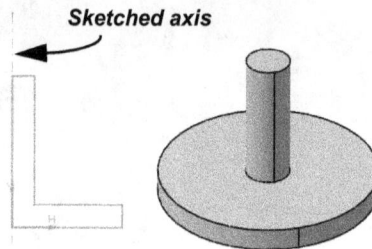

Figure 14–1

General Steps

Use the following general steps to create a Shaft feature:

1. Select a profile.
2. Initiate the creation of a Shaft.
3. Select a rotational axis.
4. Specify **Shaft limit** options.
5. Complete the Shaft feature.

Step 1 - Select a profile.

The shape of a Shaft is determined by the profile that is used to create the feature.

• By default, selected items display in orange, as shown in Figure 14–2.

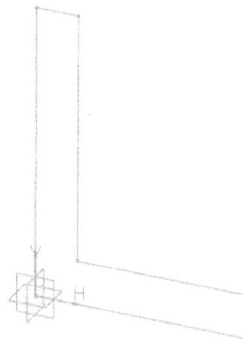

Figure 14–2

Sketch Restrictions

The sketch you select for a Shaft feature requires valid sketch geometry and an axis. The valid and invalid combinations of geometry and axis are described as follows:

Sketch	Shaft Geometry	Description
		This is a closed sketch with the axis on the edge of the profile.
		This is a closed sketch with the axis offset from the profile. The result is a hole in the Shaft.
	Invalid	This is a closed sketch with the axis inside the profile. A Shaft feature cannot sketch geometry on both sides of the axis of rotation, since the geometry would overlap.
		This is an open sketch with the axis coincident with the open ends of the profile. This sketch is valid, because the axis closes the sketch.
	Invalid	This is an open sketch with the axis offset from the profile. This sketch is invalid, because no sketched geometry exists that generates a surface on the inside of the hole in the Shaft.

Step 2 - Initiate the creation of a Shaft.

To create a shaft, click ![Shaft icon] (Shaft). The software initially creates the feature using the default values shown in the Shaft Definition dialog box in Figure 14–3

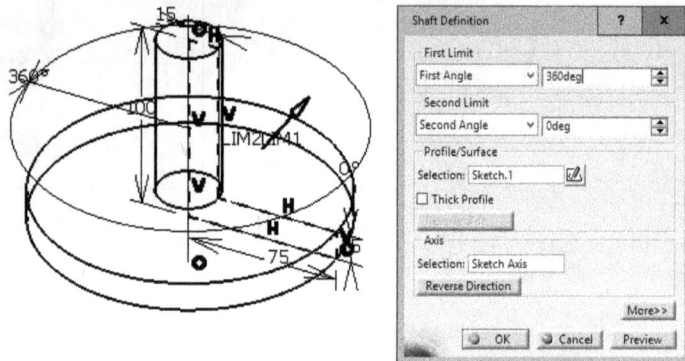

Figure 14–3

Step 3 - Select a rotational axis.

To create the Shaft feature, the rotational axis about which the profile is going to be revolved is required. By default, the software uses the first sketched axis created in the profile. If the sketch does not contain an axis, click ![icon] in the Shaft Definition dialog box to alter the sketch without leaving the definition of this feature.

* While in the Sketcher workbench, click ![Axis icon] (Axis) to sketch an axis, as shown in Figure 14–4.

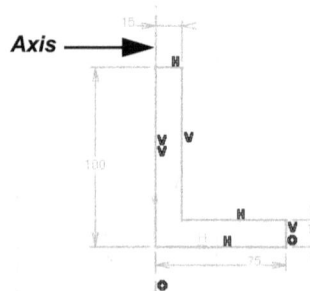

Figure 14–4

- Alternatively, you can select an existing edge, line, or axis. Figure 14–5 shows the selected vertical absolute axis of the sketch.

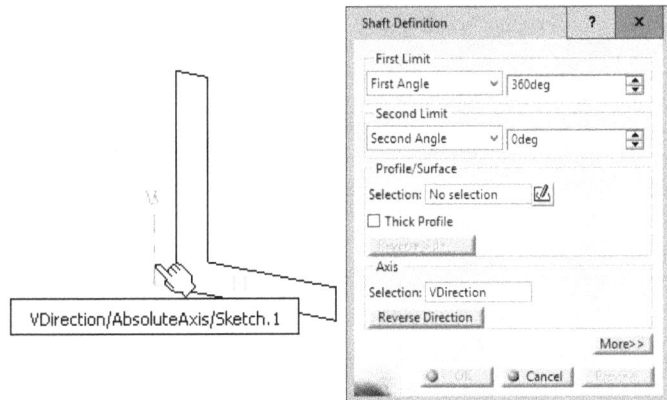

VDirection/AbsoluteAxis/Sketch.1

Figure 14–5

Step 4 - Specify Shaft limit options.

The angle that the sketch is rotated through is known as the limit. By default, the sketch is rotated 360° about the axis.
This value can be changed, as required.

Rotation Angle

The default rotation angle is 360°. If you enter a smaller angle, the sketch is rotated in the direction indicated by the first angle direction arrow, as shown in Figure 14–6.

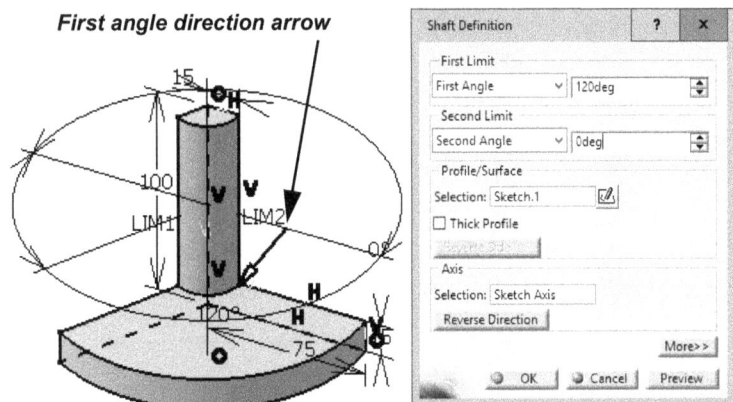

First angle direction arrow

Figure 14–6

Entering a negative first angle value enables you to specify the angle of material to be removed from a 360° Shaft, as shown in Figure 14–7.

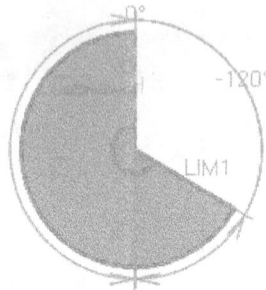

Figure 14–7

You can also change the default zero value of the second angle to rotate the sketch to the opposite side, as shown in Figure 14–8.

The sum of the first and second angles must be greater than zero and no more than 360°.

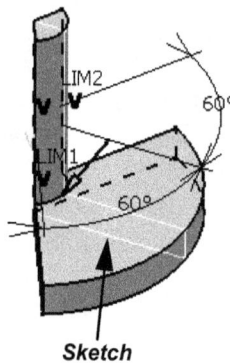

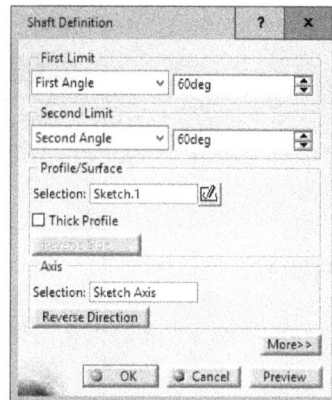

Figure 14–8

- Entering **0** for *First angle* and a value for the *Second angle* enables you to reverse the direction of the Shaft feature.

- Ensure that the sum of the two angles is 360 degrees or less.

- To examine the geometry before you complete the feature, click **Preview**.

In addition to entering the *First Angle* and *Second Angle* limits, you can apply any of the following limiting types, which are similar to those used for Pad and Pocket features:

- **First Angle or Second Angle**: Creates a feature up to the defined angle value.

- **Up to next**: Creates a feature up to the next intersecting feature.

- **Up to last**: Creates a feature up to the last intersecting feature.

- **Up to plane**: Creates a feature up to the defined plane.

- **Up to surface**: Creates a feature up to the defined surface.

Step 5 - Complete the Shaft feature.

Click **OK** to complete the feature.

14.2 Groove Feature

A Groove feature removes material by rotating a sketch about an axis, as shown in Figure 14–9. It is similar to the Shaft feature, except that material is removed, instead of being added.

- As with the Shaft feature, you can accept the default value of 360° for the first limit and 0 for the second limit value. Figure 14–10 shows a model where the first limit value is changed to 90° and the second limit value is changed to 45°.

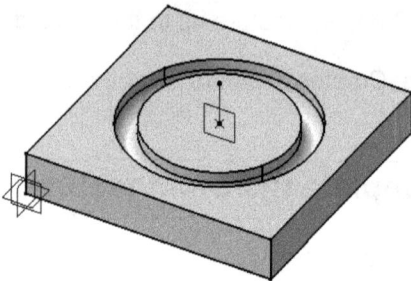

Figure 14–9

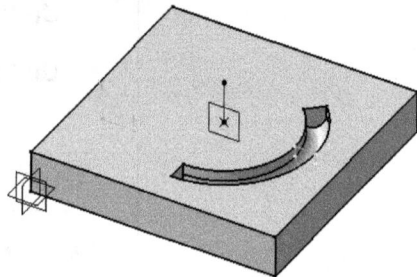

Figure 14–10

In addition to entering the *First Angle* and *Second Angle* limits, you can apply any of the following limiting types:

- **First Angle or Second Angle**: Creates a feature up to the defined angle value.

- **Up to next**: Creates a feature up to the next intersecting feature.

- **Up to last**: Creates a feature up to the last intersecting feature.

- **Up to plane**: Creates a feature up to the defined plane.

- **Up to surface**: Creates a feature up to the defined surface.

Requirements

To create a Groove feature, you must meet the following requirements:

- You must provide a rotation axis for the sketch. It can be a line, a sketched axis in the profile, or the implicit axis.

- Your profile must only be on one side of the axis.

- The section must be closed.

Grooves on Cylinders

To create a Groove feature on a cylindrical feature, a sketch plane must pass through the center of the cylindrical feature. If a suitable plane does not exist, you can use the **Angle/Normal to Plane** option when creating the reference plane. An axis must be selected as a placement reference.

- To select an implicit axis, hold <Shift> and place the cursor over the cylinder to highlight it, as shown in Figure 14–11. You can then select this axis as the rotation axis for the new plane.

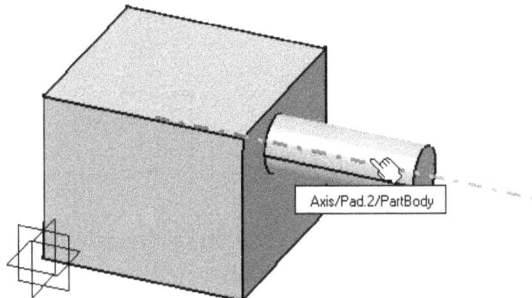

Axis/Pad.2/PartBody

Figure 14–11

Rotation Axis

The implicit axis can be used to define the rotation axis for the Groove feature. This reduces the need to create additional line or sketched axis features.

Silhouette Edges

In some cases, you might need to constrain the sketch so that one or more sketched entities are coincident with the silhouette edge of the cylinder, as shown in Figure 14–12.

This horizontal line of the sketch must be coincident with the silhouette edge of the cylinder.

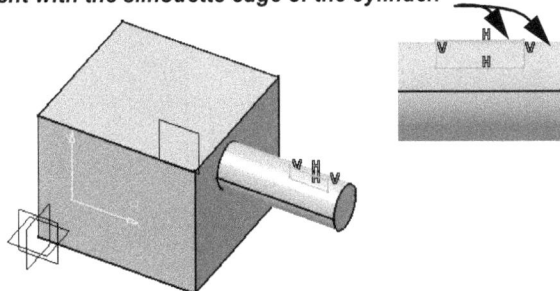

Figure 14–12

You cannot apply a coincidence constraint between the line and the silhouette edge. Therefore, click ![icon] (Project 3D Canonical Silhouette Edge) and select the cylinder. This copies the top and bottom edges into the sketch, as shown in Figure 14–13.

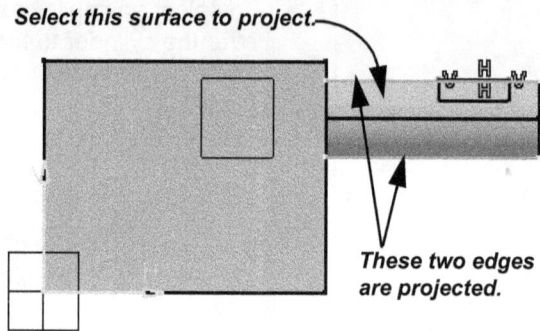

Figure 14–13

Once the silhouette edges are copied into your sketch, they display in yellow, which indicates projected geometry. To complete your sketch, use one or a combination of the following methods:

- Delete the top or bottom silhouette edge that is not required.

- Convert the silhouette edge to construction geometry, and constrain your sketch to it.

- Leave the silhouette edge as a geometry element.

Dimension the Remaining Material Diameter

If the design intent is to control the diameter of a Groove feature, create a diameter dimension between the bottom of the sketch and the sketched axis, as shown in Figure 14–14.

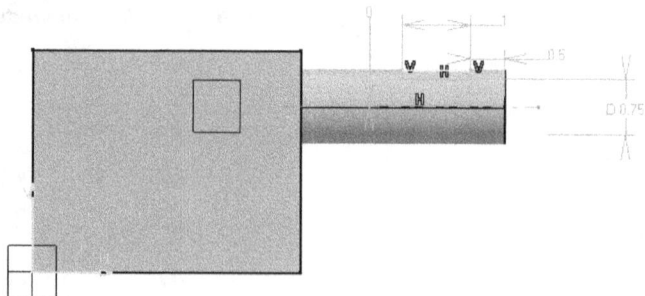

Figure 14–14

Practice 14a | Shaft and Groove Features

Practice Objective

- Create a Shaft feature and a Groove feature.

In this practice, you will create the part shown in Figure 14–15. The base feature for the model is created using a Shaft feature by revolving a profile about the Y-axis. A Groove feature is then used to develop the lubrication grooves.

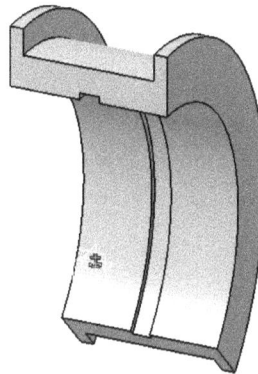

Figure 14–15

Task 1 - Create a new part.

1. Click (New).

2. In the New dialog box, select the **Part** option and click **OK**.

3. Name the part **Bearing** and click **OK**.

Task 2 - Create a sketch.

1. Create a sketch on the YZ plane.

2. Sketch the horizontal axis, as shown in Figure 14–16. This will define the rotational axis of the Shaft feature.

Figure 14–16

3. Sketch the profile as shown in Figure 14–17. Verify that the vertical elements are symmetrical about the vertical axis, and that the top horizontal elements are coincident.

- 2 (0.079 in)
- 5 (0.197 in)
- 9 (0.354 in)
- 24 (0.945 in)
- 60 (2.362 in)

*To create the diameter dimension, right-click and select **Radius/Diameter**.*

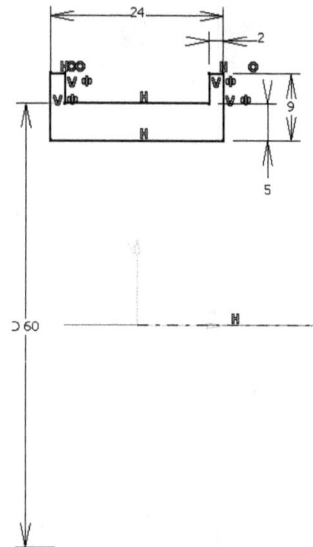

Figure 14–17

4. Click ![Exit workbench icon] (Exit workbench) to exit the Sketcher workbench.

Task 3 - Create a datum plane for use later in this practice.

---

1. In the Reference Elements toolbar, click ![Plane icon] (Plane).

2. In the Plane Definition dialog box, in the Plane type drop-down list, select **Angle/Normal to plane**.

3. Right-click in the *Rotation axis* field and select **Y Axis**, as shown in Figure 14–18.

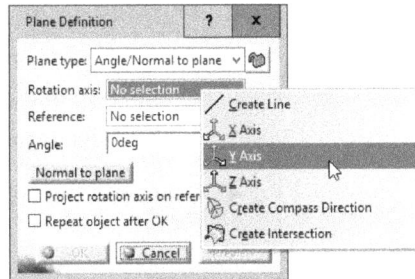

Figure 14–18

4. For the *Reference*, select **yz plane** in the Specification Tree.

5. Edit the angle to **100**, as shown in Figure 14–19.

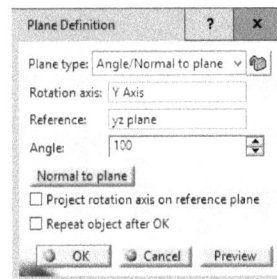

Figure 14–19

6. Click **OK** in the Plane Definition dialog box.

Task 4 - Create a Shaft feature.

---

1. Select **Sketch.1**.

2. Click ⬚ (Shaft). The Shaft Definition dialog box opens as shown in Figure 14–20.

Figure 14–20

---

3. Enter the following parameters to define the Shaft feature:

- *First angle:* **180deg**
- *Second angle:* **0deg**
- Click **Reverse Direction**.

4. Complete the feature. The model displays as shown in Figure 14–21.

Figure 14–21

Task 5 - Create a Groove feature.

In this task, you will create a feature to represent the lubrication Groove on the inside diameter of the bearing. The completed feature displays as shown in Figure 14–22.

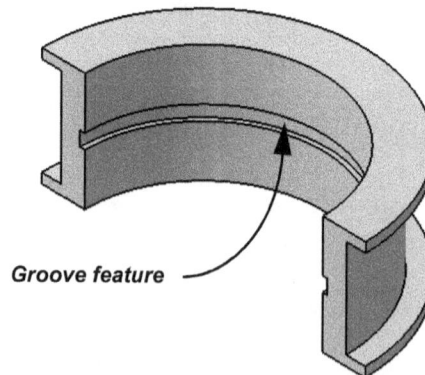

Groove feature

Figure 14–22

1. Create a positioned sketch on the YZ plane. To define the origin, use the **Middle Point** type and select the edge shown in Figure 14–23.

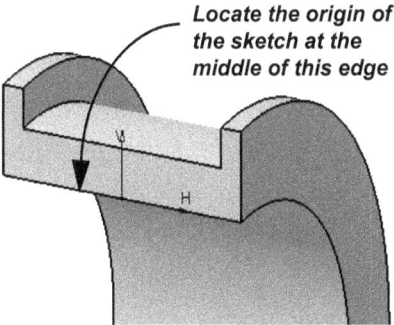

Locate the origin of the sketch at the middle of this edge

Figure 14–23

2. Sketch the profile shown in Figure 14–24, using the dimensions of **1 (0.039 in)** and **3 (0.118 in)**. Verify that the profile is symmetrical about the vertical sketch axis.

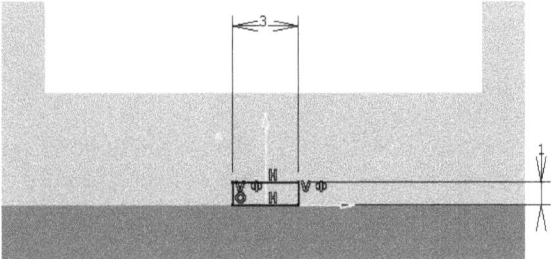

Figure 14–24

3. Exit Sketcher.

4. With the sketch preselected, click (Groove). The Groove Definition dialog box opens as shown in Figure 14–25.

Figure 14–25

Design Considerations

Note ⚠ next to the *Selection* field in the *Axis* area. An axis was not sketched into the profile used for the Groove, so a rotation axis for the feature is not automatically defined.

5. Select the **Shaft.1** feature to select its axis. The Groove Definition dialog box updates as shown in Figure 14–26.

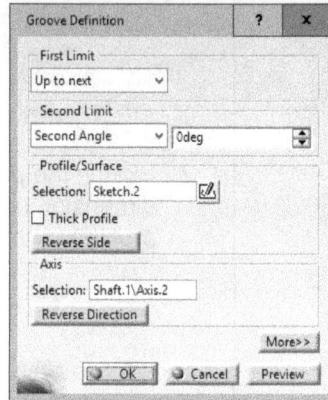

Figure 14–26

You might need to click **Reverse Direction** *to get the required result.*

6. Modify the options in the Groove Definition dialog box so that the resulting feature displays as shown in Figure 14–27.

Figure 14–27

Task 6 - Change the shaft to reference the datum plane.

1. In the Specification Tree, double-click on **Shaft.1**.

2. In the Shaft Definition dialog box, select **Up to plane** from the First Limit drop-down list.

3. Select **Plane.1** in the Specification Tree.

4. Click **OK**.

5. In the Update Diagnosis Shaft.1 dialog box, click **Sub Elements**.

6. In the Sub Elements in Error dialog box, click **OK**. The model updates as shown in Figure 14–28.

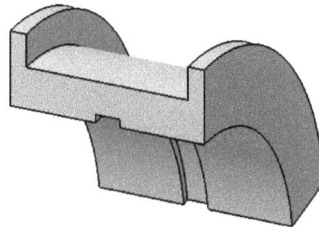

Figure 14–28

Task 7 - Edit the angle of the plane.

1. In the Specification Tree, right-click on **Plane.1** and select **Plane.1 object>Edit Parameters**.

2. Edit the *100* angle dimension to **45** and click **OK**.

3. In the Tools toolbar, click [icon] (Update All). The model updates as shown in Figure 14–29.

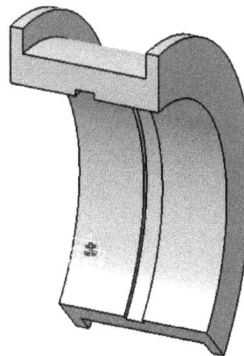

Figure 14–29

4. Save the model and close the window.

Practice 14b	Groove Features

Practice Objectives

- Create a Groove feature.
- Locate revolved sketches to cylindrical geometry.

In this practice, you will create the part shown in Figure 14–30. The part will consist of two Groove features. You will also use silhouette projections to locate a sketch onto cylindrical geometry.

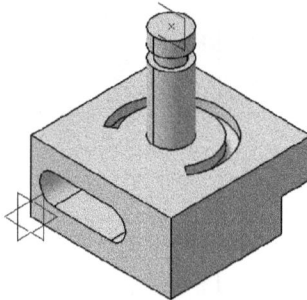

Figure 14–30

Task 1 - Create a point.

Design Considerations

This point will mark the center of the cylinder. It will be used as a reference for a plane, which will be used to create the two profiles in this task.

1. Click [⌷] (Open).

2. Select **Groove.CATPart** and click **Open**.

3. Click [▪] (Point) in the Reference Elements toolbar.

4. Select **Circle/Sphere/Ellipse center** as the point type.

5. Select the circular edge on the top of the cylinder, as shown in Figure 14–31.

6. Click **OK** to complete the feature.

7. Click [▱] (Plane) and select **Parallel through point** as the plane type.

8. Select the YZ plane as the parallel reference for the new plane, and select the point to locate the plane.

9. Click **OK** to complete the feature. The new point and plane display as shown in Figure 14–31.

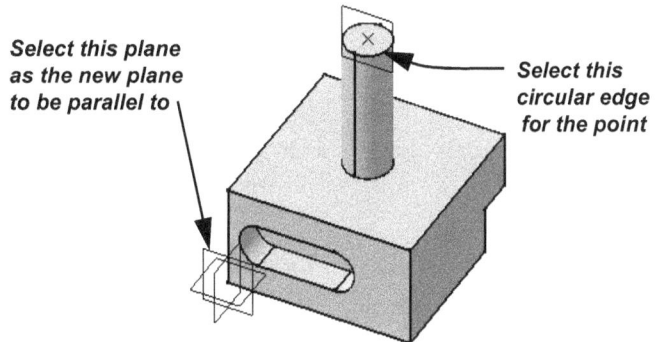

Select this plane as the new plane to be parallel to

Select this circular edge for the point

Figure 14–31

Task 2 - Create a sketch to be used for a Groove feature.

---

1. Create a positioned sketch on the newly created reference plane, using **Point.1** as the origin.

2. Click (Profile) to sketch the shape. Dimension the width and height of the shape, as shown in Figure 14–32.

   - 22.5 (0.886 in)
   - 32 (1.260 in)
   - 95 (3.740 in)

This sketched profile should be closed to avoid feature failure.

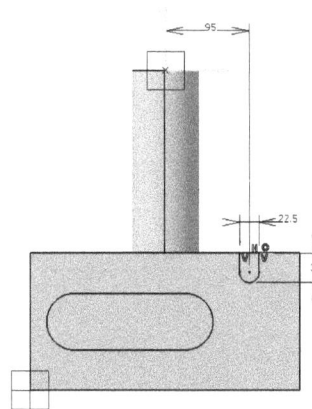

Figure 14–32

---

3. Constrain the horizontal line of the sketch with the horizontal edge of the part.

4. Dimension the center of the arc to the vertical sketcher axis.

5. When the sketch is fully constrained, click ⬆ (Exit workbench).

6. With the sketch still highlighted, click 🅱 (Groove) to create a Groove feature. The software does not automatically build a preview of the Groove because the sketch does not have an axis. Note that the axis selection box is active.

7. Place the cursor over the cylinder. The implicit axis displays. Select this axis and click **Preview**. The feature displays as shown in Figure 14–33.

8. Set the *First Angle* as **90** and click **Preview**. Set the *Second Angle* as **150** and click **Preview**. The part displays as shown in Figure 14–33.

9. Select and drag the **LIM1** and **LIM2** tags of the Groove to dynamically modify the rotation angles.

10. When you have set the limits to an angle similar to that shown in Figure 14–33. Click **OK**.

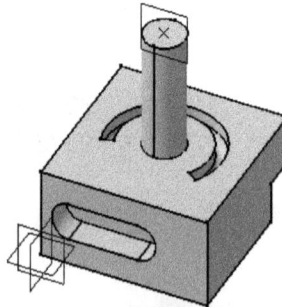

Figure 14–33

Task 3 - Create a sketch for a Groove feature on the cylinder.

1. Create a positioned sketch on the newly created reference plane using **Point.1** as the origin.

2. Select **View>Zoom Area** and zoom into the top of the cylinder by dragging a box around it.

---

3. Click ![icon] (Project 3D Elements) and select the cylinder then click **OK**. This creates an axis that is automatically constrained to the center of the cylinder, as shown in Figure 14–34.

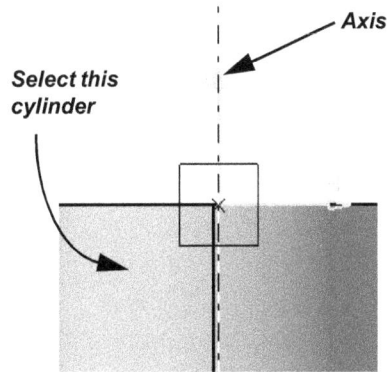

Axis

Select this cylinder

Figure 14–34

4. Click ![icon] (Project 3D Canonical Silhouette Edges).

5. Select the cylinder. Two vertical lines display. The warning message box opens, as shown in Figure 14–35.

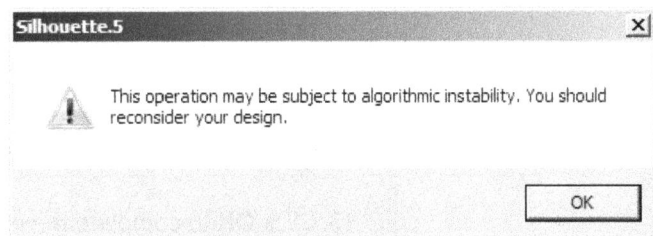

Silhouette.5

This operation may be subject to algorithmic instability. You should reconsider your design.

OK

Figure 14–35

Design Considerations

The warning message displays to make you aware that features using silhouette edge projections in a sketch might become unstable. CATIA occasionally loses references to silhouetted edges. Use caution when using this type of projection in your models.

6. Click **OK**.

7. With the two silhouette projections selected, click

![icon] (Construction/Standard Element). The silhouette edges are now changed to construction lines.

8. Select the background area of the display to clear the geometry and click ___ (Construction/Standard Element) to return to Standard Element creation.

9. Sketch and dimension the rectangle as shown in Figure 14–36. Verify that the right vertical edge of the rectangle is coincident with the construction line.

   - 25 (0.984 in)
   - 27 (1.063 in)
   - 32 (1.260 in)

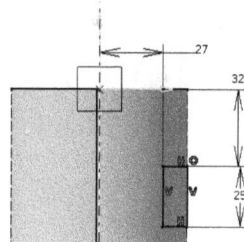

Figure 14–36

10. Exit the Sketcher workbench.

11. With the sketch highlighted, click (Groove). Note that the sketch axis is automatically selected as the rotational axis for the Groove feature.

12. The software has maintained your previous values for the first and second angles. Reset these values to rotate the sketch 360°.

13. Click **OK** to complete the feature. The part displays as shown in Figure 14–37.

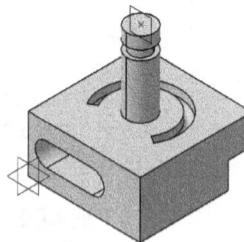

Figure 14–37

14. Click (Save).

15. Select **File>Close**.

Practice 14c | (Optional) King Chess Piece

Practice Objective

- Create Pad and Shaft features without instructions.

Create a new part called **King_Piece** with a part number of **03051976**, as shown in Figure 14–38. Exact dimensions are not required.

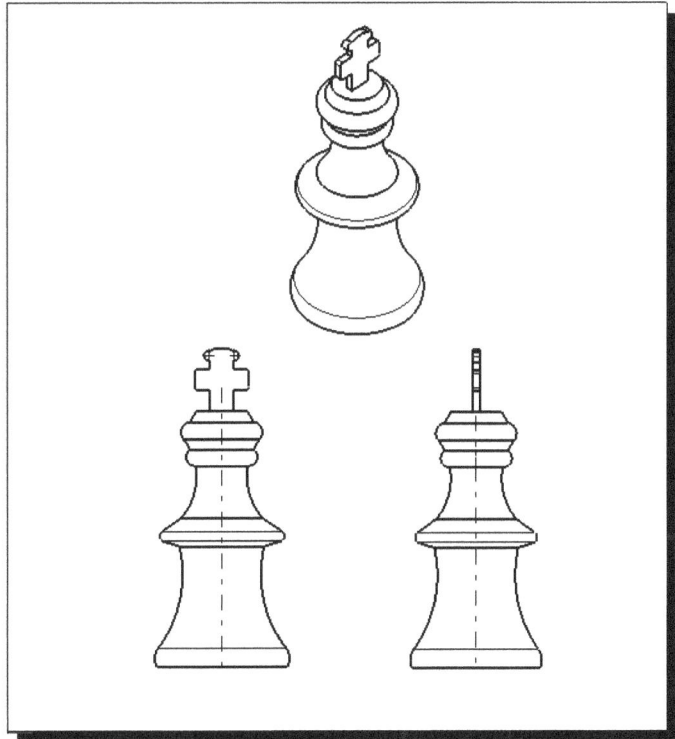

Figure 14–38

Practice 14d | (Optional) Creating Shafts and Grooves

Practice Objective

- Create Shaft and Groove features with minimal instruction.

In this practice, you will create a model of a spinning top using Shaft and Groove features. The completed model is shown in Figure 14–39. As a good practice, create an axis system in the drawing as a foundation for building features.

Figure 14–39

Task 1 - Create a new model.

1. Create a new part called **SpinningTop.CATPart**.

2. Use the dimensioned drawings in Figure 14–40,
    Figure 14–41, Figure 14–42, Figure 14–43, and
    Figure 14–44 to create the required geometry.

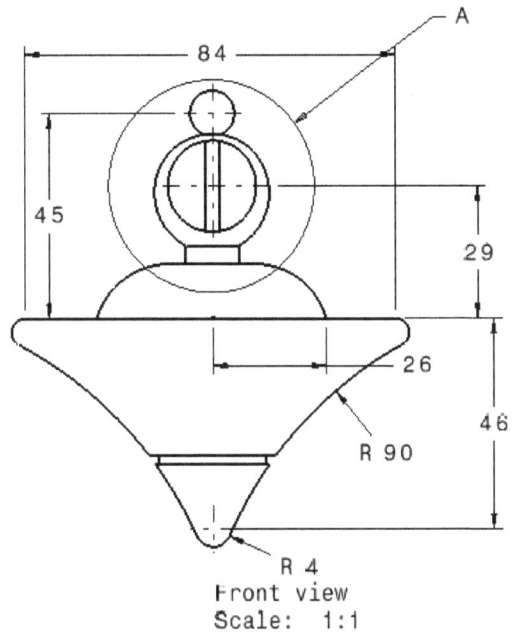

Front view
Scale: 1:1

Figure 14–40

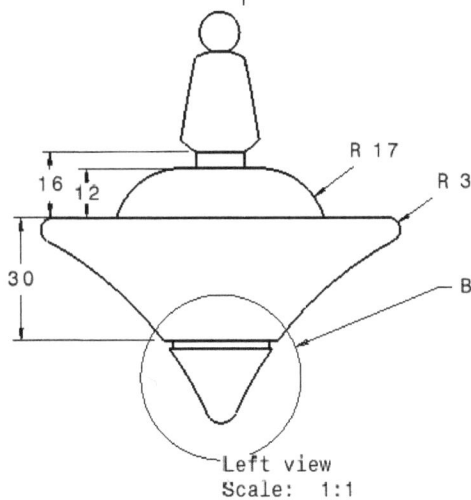

Left view
Scale: 1:1

Figure 14–41

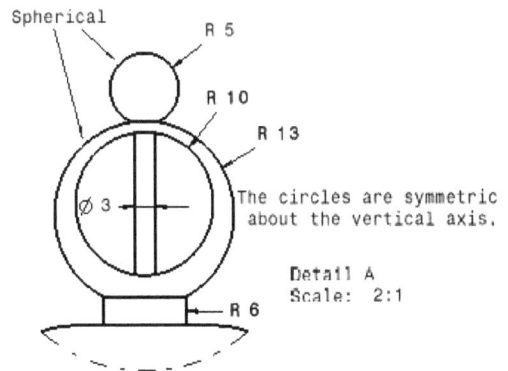

The circles are symmetric
about the vertical axis.

Detail A
Scale: 2:1

Figure 14–42

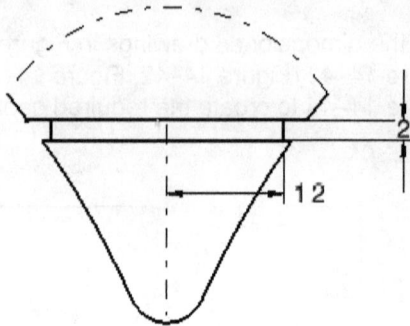

Detail B
Scale: 2:1
Figure 14–43

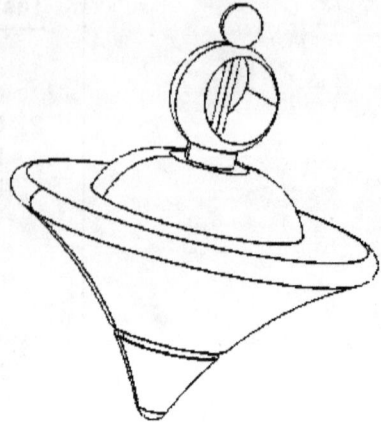

Isometric view
Scale: 1:1
Figure 14–44